William De Maria is in the Centre for Public Administration at the University of Queensland. He has had a long and controversial career as a public policy activist and outspoken academic. He has established many innovative programs, including the Brisbane Welfare Rights Centre, and more recently the Queensland Whistleblower Action Group. Highly regarded as a provocative teacher, he is widely published in Australia and overseas on issues such as official secrecy and government corruption. Dr De Maria conducted the first systematic analysis of public interest disclosures when he led the trailblazing Queensland Whistleblower Study. He continues to act as a consultant to government and the private sector on ethical conduct, and is in demand as a public speaker.

DEADLY DISCLOSURES

WHISTLEBLOWING AND THE ETHICAL MELTDOWN OF AUSTRALIA

WILLIAM DE MARIA

Wakefield Press

Wakefield Press
17 Rundle Street
Kent Town
South Australia 5071

First published 1999

Copyright © William De Maria, 1999

All rights reserved. This book is copyright. Apart from any fair dealing for
the purposes of private study, research, criticism or review, as permitted
under the Copyright Act, no part may be reproduced without written
permission. Enquiries should be addressed to the publisher.

Cover design by Dean Lahn, Lahn Stafford Design, Adelaide
Designed and typeset by Clinton Ellicott, Adelaide
Printed and bound by Hyde Park Press, Adelaide

National Library of Australia
Cataloguing-in-publication entry

De Maria, William.
Deadly disclosures: whistleblowing and the ethical meltdown of Australia.

Bibliography.
Includes index.
ISBN 1 86254 457 3.

1. Whistleblowing – Australia. 2. Leaks (Disclosure of information) –
Australia. I. Title.

331.25980994

 This project has been assisted by the Commonwealth
Government through the Australia Council, its arts
funding and advisory body.

Contents

Foreword by Evan Whitton — ix

Preface — xii

Part 1 Whistleblowing The Big Picture — 1

   1 **Ethical Australia? A Guided Tour** — 4

   2 **Disclosure The Inside Story** — 12

Part 2 Whistleblowing The Lived Experience — 37

   3 **Radioactive Whistleblowing** Philip Nitschke — 40

   4 **Vetting the Vet** The David Obendorf Case — 60

   5 **Religious Dissenter** Peter Cameron and the Heresy Trial — 74

   6 **Academic Dissenters** On Being Unfree in Free Spaces — 88

   7 **Whistleblowing on Eight Cents a Day**
      Disclosure at the ABC — 119

   8 **'Shreddergate'** The Battles of Kevin Lindeberg — 134

   9 **Up Against the NCA** The Mick Skrijel Affair — 160

  10 **The Dark Side of Whistleblowing** War at the Memorial — 176

Part 3	**The State Control of Dissent**	193
11	**The Shut-eyed Sentries** Notes on Incompetence and Unlawfulness	196
12	**Whistleblowing Laws** The State Responds	210
13	**Codes of Conduct** Moral Bondage in the Age of Anything Goes	234

Appendix Whistleblower Laws ... 243

Notes ... 253

Selected Readings ... 281

Index ... 297

*To my wonderful family, Janine my wife and our three boys,
Nigal, Adrian and Julian.*

They were there.

Sometimes the only alternative to cringing before a parched collective is to commit an act drenched in courage.

Clarissa Pinola-Estes
Women Who Run With the Wolves

Foreword

Evan Whitton

Flatteringly accused by a whistleblowers' organ of being one of them, I had to admit I never had the courage or the talent for that sort of thing. But in some vague way I may be qualified to offer a few thoughts on the phenomenon. Thirty years ago I observed at first hand three of the first and greatest whistleblowers: Dr Bertram Wainer, concerned medico; Peggy Berman, paymistress for police extortions from doctors; and Charlie Wyatt, policeman turned backyard aborter and extortee.

I'm not sure where all three fit into the Queensland research definition noted in *Deadly Disclosures*: 'The whistleblower is a concerned citizen, totally or predominantly motivated by notions of public interest, who initiates of her or his own free will an open disclosure about significant wrongdoing in a particular occupational role to a person or agency capable of investigating the complaint and facilitating the correction of wrongdoing, and who suffers accordingly.'

They certainly faced most of the fearful odds detailed in Bill De Maria's brilliant analysis: the expert cover-up, the cobber-dobber syndrome, reprisals, vilification, getting ratbagged by the media, libel law, etcetera, etcetera. Those who would name the guilty thus need to be pretty fly and to understand that the crucial element of strategy is to identify (and stick to) the aim; as Marshal Ferdinand Foch put it: *De quoi s'agit-il*? What's it all about?

Dr Wainer was thus in some ways the model of the successful whistleblower. He was a sharply intelligent man and he had studied *On War*, Karl Marie von Clausewitz's treatise on strategy. When the sodden and sinister Sir Arthur Rylah refused to reform abortion law, Bert's aim was to demonstrate that bad laws make bad cops. Rylah resisted, but Bert and Peggy and Charlie mounted a series of spectacular manoeuvres which forced Rylah to hold an inquiry into corruption in the Homicide Squad, and three bent cops went to prison.

As well as courage and a sense of strategy, stamina must be a key requirement. Wainer's campaign was a relatively brief 18 months; most of the principals in these absorbing case studies would confirm that there may well be a God, but it often takes her or him five or ten years, if ever, to move off inertia.

Soi-disant whistleblowers must thus be prepared to keep chipping away, usually against a mulishly intransigent authority, and seemingly without end, but they can take heart from the Cameron Effect. That is, the process of making an impression on public opinion (and hence of striking fear into the heart of the trade of authority) is rather like making an atom bomb: the public is bombarded with particles (facts) until critical mass is reached; one more substantial fact and action is suddenly and surprisingly taken.

The bombardment needs two arms: disclosure of new fact, which is what the whistleblower basically does, and disclosure of a new pattern, which is what *Deadly Disclosures* compellingly does. The astute thus do not fire all their bullets at once, and seek to engage the interest of first rate reporters with stamina similar to their own, as Kevin Lindeberg famously did with my distinguished colleague, Bruce Grundy, in the wretched shreddergate affair.

Laurie Oakes once rightly told public servants they have an obligation to break the local equivalent of the Official Secrets Act, on a daily basis if necessary. But, as Bill De Maria notes, reporters and media organisations fear committing libel. With good reason; defending a case can cripple all but the wealthiest. When a former employer of Sir Les Thiess blew the whistle on what a jury later found was Thiess's bribery of Sir Johannes Bjelke-Petersen 'on a large scale and on many occasions', Channel 9 won the subsequent libel case, but did not get back anything like the $5 million it cost to defend it.

Whistleblowers' organisations thus help their cause by agitating against the libel laws, and it is useful to remind judges and politicians of their origins: eighteenth-century judges concocted them to prevent whistleblowers in the press from exposing corrupt politicians in the Whig oligarchy, eg Sir Robert Walpole and his great bagman, the Duke of Newcastle.

However, not even the NSW Defamation Act, thoughtfully produced in 1974 by Bob Askin's attorney-general, Ken McCaw, can fully protect the corrupt when public servants drop documents over the transom to a trustworthy and capable reporter. That steady ululation you hear in the newsroom is of reporters wailing into telephones: 'That's all very well, but where are the doccoes?'

Bob Bottom, perhaps the greatest of all disclosure reporters, was thus armour-plated to the waterline: whistleblowers in the NSW force gave him transcripts and tapes from telephone taps on the corrupt and their corrupters. The Queensland definition may disqualify such police as pure whistleblowers: they did not do it openly and did not suffer. But the aim is surely to maximise the chance of exposure and correction in the public interest, and to minimise suffering. *Deadly Disclosures* notes that Acts purporting to protect whistleblowers exist only in SA, the ACT, NSW and Queensland, and that all are ineffectual.

Gary Sturgess's observation that Sydney has no memory applies throughout Australia. Bill De Maria has written an important and fascinating book which reminds us how corruption protects itself and how it can be exposed by honest and brave soldiers for truth.

Evan Whitton's books include *Can of Worms: A Citizen's Reference Book to Crime and the Administration of Justice*, *Trial by Voodoo: How the Law Defeats Justice and Democracy*, and *The Cartel: Lawyers and Their Nine Magic Tricks*.

Preface

9.00 am: I take a call from a former shire clerk who was sacked after reporting wrongdoing to the government. She is trying to reconstruct her life, but it is not easy. Bitter and depressed, she feels herself unravelling. She is becoming house-bound – sleeping when she should be awake and awake when she should be sleeping. She was once a senior executive making big decisions. Now compiling the shopping list is a major task.

Midday: a former university student counsellor calls. Same story, different details. She took an enormous pride in her work, and from all accounts was very good at it. Then it started – bullying, official denials in the face of her complaints, more bullying, and finally, out. She is depressed and thinks of suicide, though she says she would never go through with it because she wouldn't want to hurt her loving family.

My day is not yet over. At 9.00 pm comes the third call. It's from a whistleblower in the prison system. We had planned to address a community meeting together. He was going to talk about his experiences, and I was to give an overview. He can't do it. The thought of retelling his story of being savaged by management makes him panic. He is back on medication.

When he hangs up, I can't help feeling depressed myself. Three lives now on the brink of despair, and why? Because these people stood up to wrongdoing. I feel for these people. But more than that I feel anguish about what is happening in Australia. I recall Xavier Herbert's sigh: 'Poor fellow my country'.

This book is about whistleblowers and the carnivorous structures that process them. But in a sense it's about us all. In many ways, whistleblowers and dissenters are very ordinary Australians who become caught up in a cycle of retribution that is beyond their control. It's partly this ordinariness that makes their story our story. In other words, this book is about us. More than that, it is an elegy to Australia at the start of a new millennium.

A gentle warning. This book is best read on a sunny day. Do not expect a comfortable read. There is nothing to celebrate on this tour through the entrails of our society, except perhaps the valour of the whistleblowers who guide us into the netherworld of corruption, incompetence, cover-ups and organisational vendettas.

Be warned, too, that this is not a dispassionate analysis. I am a whistleblower myself, with sharp experiences of the wrath of organised power hell-bent on reprisal. Even while I was writing this book I was experiencing the same processes that I have attempted to analyse – a bit like Jenner testing smallpox on himself. Let the lawyers, senior bureaucrats, academic researchers and politicians who dabble in this area (but who would never disclose or dissent themselves) provide the 'even-handed' analysis. Whistleblowing and dissent are passionate topics, and deserve a passionate analysis.

At the same time, while I identify strongly with people who dissent and disclose in the public interest, I have no desire to bend the truth. The subject matter of *Deadly Disclosures* is a stirred-up wasp-nest of competing claims, interpretations, and conclusions. In tackling it, I have tried hard to be scrupulous, if not downright tedious, in making visible how I identified the relevant facts, how I chose from competing interpretations, and how I built up my conclusions. I have made extensive use of documents in the public domain in the hope that this will facilitate independent verification. All source material is clearly identified in the end notes.

I hope I have avoided writing with the hagiographer's pen. My sympathetic view of people who disclose and dissent in the public interest does not mean that I wish to canonise them. While their pain rudely beckons us, I hope I have avoided being captured in their victimhood. This book is not just a collection of war stories and tortured biographies. If that was the case I could write such a book every fortnight. Australian whistleblowers, like miners with lights on their hats, take us into a world of wrongdoing that few of us know or want to believe exists. The light that whistleblowers and dissenters throw on this netherworld is a social legacy to us all, and lasts long after the pain of their narratives has dulled. The case studies that form the central section of this book are like postcards from this netherworld. Whistleblowers will get us to these places, and a deeper understanding of the forces at work to bring down women and men of conscience will get us out.

Achieving this deeper understanding is the great challenge. While whistleblower narratives offer a grim audit on the human price of justice-seeking, the social analysis must go beyond this, to an examination of the modern Australian workplace, where authoritarianism and fear weave in and out of production and marketing processes. As any whistleblower experience will tell us, these economic processes are so in control that workplace justice often remains exiled in its waiting room, uninvited, unwelcome and unnecessary. Under the rigid economic protocols, dissent and disclosure are anathematised. How this happens is of vital interest in this book.

As I was piecing together the account of whistleblowers' experiences, there were times when I almost wished that our society frogmarched these people into the town square and garrotted them for their sins, or shut them up in prison and threw away the key. It would have been all so simple to document! Instead, the researcher into whistleblowing and dissent must document a *subtle* play of force and abuse. Most strikes against whistleblowers are wrapped in the beguiling garb of 'due process', 'fairness', and 'thorough investigation', making it difficult to record the secret deals, document the ostracism and chronicle the intimidation. These days whistleblowers are not hanged in the public square, but swing from the clean ropes of due process and natural justice.[1]

Part 1
Whistleblowing
The Big Picture

I confess that I do not know what a shucked oyster is, but I would soon have found out had I been invited to mingle with the glitterati at the Victorian government's Grand Prix party in March 1997. I also would have had a chance to taste 'whole sides of smoked Atlantic salmon, drizzled with extra virgin olive oil and cracked pepper garnished with bunches of citrus leaves'. In the Premier's suite alone, I would have seen food and drink being consumed at the rate of $6000 per hour. At the end of the party I would have had a full belly, and a soul with the needle heading towards empty.

Across town around the same time, Mai was not having nearly as much fun. Mai is one of an estimated 300,000 migrant outworkers in Australia.[1] She is paid 77 cents an hour to make clothes for Australian fashion labels, some of which were probably being worn by people at the Grand Prix party.[2] Even though she works 112 hours per week, it would take Mai sixteen months to earn the cost of an hour's munching by the company in the Premier's suite.

This stark juxtaposition of want and plenty is a sign of what I call ethical meltdown in Australia. To say that is not to indulge in nostalgia for some past era of righteousness, but merely to say that Australia is rapidly entering a red zone of danger because of the collapse of three ethical standards that we once believed we had to meet if we wanted to build humane societies.

The first of these is the deteriorating standard of ethical behaviour of people who control economic and political power, whether they be politicians, bureaucrats or company directors. The second is the erosion of our collective sense of responsibility to speak out against wrongdoing and injustice. The third is the impoverishment and collapse of the public sphere – public welfare, public ownership (both actual and moral) and public service. In accord with the harsh rules of economic rationalism, the elite dogma of the late twentieth century, we are ransacking the moral core of our society and converting everything to cash equivalents.

Whistleblowing and its related phenomenon, public interest dissenting, are best understood in this context of ethical degeneration. What is remarkable about whistleblowers and dissenters is their resistance to ethical decline. I am not saying that people of conscience maintain a thin white line of integrity between us and despotism. If only they had the power! In fact, wrongdoing gets through without much trouble. Against this, whistleblowers make their desperately outnumbered stand. Like the hard rocks that form mesas and buttes in the Utah badlands, defying the forces of nature, whistleblowers are there, stark and persistent, islands of resistance to the assault on democracy. They are also there for us as a vision of a re-ethicalised Australia.

Chapter one, *Ethical Australia? A Guided Tour*, elaborates the hard-to-hear message about ethical meltdown. This piece reads like a charge sheet on contemporary government and corporate wrongdoing. While it is short (for who amongst us needs further proof of official wrongdoing?), the chapter poses an essential question: is it right to depict wrongdoing as an epochal phenomenon? Do we splash and flounder in a sea of reform-speak which tells us to believe that the 'bad old days' are just that, 'old'? Is it accurate to see the 1980s as the decade of corporate greed and official corruption, and the 1990s and beyond as eras of goodness? Or is there some systemically ingrained continuity to corruption? These questions are posed at the outset because the issue of time-framed wrongdoing lies at the nerve centre of my analysis.

If there is no such thing as the bad *old* days, then how do we explain corruption's continuous existence? This is the job of chapter two, *Disclosure: The Inside Story*. The chapter explains why whistleblowers and dissenters are so vilified in Australia. The chapter then develops the notion that despite our failure to recognise true heroes in our midst, whistleblowers continue to raise, on our account, shocking cases of wrongdoing in a disturbingly wide range of areas. Let's be frank: people die from wrongdoing and more people die when it is not disclosed. A little Queensland boy ('the boy in the box'), brutalised and tortured in 1998, would be dead today if not for the actions of a whistleblower. The Mistral fan disaster is another example. In that case people on the manufacturing-line knew that the fans they made could become fire balls. A few whistleblowers on that line could have prevented the deaths of children.

The chapter then goes on to distinguish between a history of informing, which starts (as far as Australia is concerned) in the asymmetrical relationships between convicts and guards, and the more recent phenomenon of whistleblowing. Separate as informing and whistleblowing are, the latter continues to carry the mark of Cain of the former.

1 | Ethical Australia?

A Guided Tour

In December 1997 I found the following questions side-by-side in a national newspaper quiz:

Q1. *What were the scores of the respective Australian Rugby League and Super League grand finals in 1997?*
Q2. *As at the end of 1997 how many Federal MPs are before the courts?*[1]

I was struck by the matter-of-fact way the quiz master had placed a piece of sporting trivia next to a question of public ethics. Does this represent a new and dangerous familiarity with official wrongdoing? A series of travel rort scandals had claimed the scalps of seven senior Coalition parliamentarians and resulted in a spate of prosecutions, a casualty rate unparalleled in Australia's political history.[2] Yet the topic was raised with breezy informality in a newspaper quiz. What's next – Fantale wrappers with humorous vignettes of corrupt political and corporate figures?

Why start a book on whistleblowing with a discussion about falling ethical standards when most people know that to be the case? Precisely for that reason. Whistleblowing only makes sense in a context of ethical degeneration. Our familiarity with wrongdoing threatens a clear view of this highly complex issue of public interest disclosure. As a community we may have a superficial view of both.

Many of the sites on this tour are well known, but taken together they highlight some of the basic questions central to any analysis of public interest disclosures. For a start: is corporate and official wrongdoing endemic to our society? If this is the case is a whistleblower's disclosure tantamount to the toils of Sisyphus, who was forever condemned to roll a rock up a hill only for it to roll down again?

What is it in the value makeup of our society that makes it so difficult for us to accept that whole institutions can be corrupt? We watch as authorities cart off the odd copper caught on the take. We observe isolated cases of paedophile teachers being eliminated from the education system, and we note the fraudster company manager being hustled into a paddy wagon on his way to a stretch in prison. We note all this in individual terms, never quite getting to the idea of whole-of-system corruption.

On 4 December 1996, hunched over a microphone in the Western Australian Supreme Court, Alan Bond, in a weak, hoarse voice, pleaded guilty to two counts of failing to act honestly in his duties as a company director.[3] These blandly stated charges camouflage the biggest fraud (one billion dollars) in Australia's corporate history.[4] The face that smiled from the prison vehicle returning Bond to Karnet Prison Farm became the logo of private sector greed and corruption in the 1980s[5].

Bond may have been a symbol of what happens when rapacious capitalism is let off the chain, but he was in crowded company. Trevor Sykes's book *Bold Riders* identifies a sardine-packed rogues' gallery. In his final analysis Sykes captures the minority moral view:

Give or take a billion dollars the [men] mentioned in [my] book lost around $16 billion ... the biggest string of corporate disasters in Australian history ... The men who ran these companies were widely admired ... They built some new assets such as the Port Douglas Mirage, but more often they re-organised assets which had been created by others ... Anything bought by Alan Bond or Abe Goldberg was quickly loaded with debt to the Plimsoll Line and sometimes beyond. In a sense, they were parasites of Australian society and finance. The savings of ordinary Australians ... were splurged on spending sprees for their companies and themselves. They lived lavish lifestyles on other people's money and never repaid it. Their companies paid little or nothing in taxes, yet they assiduously sought favours and subsidies from governments ...[6]

That was the 1980s. Bad old days? Yes in one sense, as long as we don't fool ourselves that we as a community are now getting into some serious ethical renewal. Let us have a quick look at the 'bad old' 1990s.

In 1995 and 1996 alone, the government's corporate watchdog, the Australian Securities Commission (ASC)[7] opened 155 new investigations of corporate wrongdoing. This led to the gaoling, in the same period, of nineteen corporate offenders, including Garry Allan Carter, sentenced to four years imprisonment for diverting up to $37m of public funds from Equity Group Ltd.[8] In December 1995 ASC also laid the first insider-trading charges against four directors of Australian Coachline.[9]

Can we ever forget the corruption of former Coles Myer chief, Brian Quinn, home renovator of the decade, sent down for four years for defrauding the retail giant of $4.8m? In sentencing Quinn on 7 May 1997, Mr Justice Wood referred to him as a 'vain, greedy thief'.[10] While Quinn can be described as one of the last of the 1980s corporate crooks to be brought to justice, there was nothing 'yesterday' about one of the most telling aspects of his trial. On the day of sentencing, a parade of character witnesses attempted damage-control on Quinn's behalf. The most prominent was the Premier of Victoria, Jeff Kennett. If Alan Bond's smile as he was carted off to prison is a symbol of the 1980s, is the intercession of a senior politician on behalf of a white-collar crook the sight and sound of the nineties? Maybe not. Perhaps it was the emphysemic grin of Christopher Skase in his resort on Majorca.

When Mr Justice Wood brought down his Royal Commission findings on 16 May 1997, he used some very 1980s words to describe his findings. A 'culture of greed' existed within the New South Wales Police Force, he said.[11] This hydra-headed culture does not of course simply wear a blue uniform. It is multi-coloured and seeps, like indelible dye, throughout the social fabric.

While the Australian Securities and Investment Commission (as it is now called) is busy being the ethical rule-master to corporate Australia, its kindred regulator, the Australian Competition and Consumer Commission (ACCC), received 60,000 complaints alleging breaches of the Trade Practices Act in 1995–96. The most common complaints were for misleading and deceptive conduct

(28%); exclusive dealing (14%); misuse of market power (11%); and anti-competitive arrangements.[12]

A big win for ACCC in 1995 occurred in the Federal Court when penalties exceeding $20m were imposed on three pre-mixed concrete suppliers: Pioneer Concrete (Qld) Pty Ltd, Boral Resources (Qld) Pty Ltd and CSR Limited. The court found that a well-organised cartel had existed between these companies for the supply of pre-mixed concrete in the lucrative Brisbane, Gold Coast and Toowoomba markets between 1989 and 1994.[13] ACCC told the Federal Court that executives of the three companies agreed which company was to be successful in tendering for projects and that the other two companies would then quote at price levels designed to ensure that the nominated company secured the work.[14]

In a case that illustrates the enormous legal resources at the ready disposal of private sector giants, Pioneer Concrete (Qld) Pty Ltd was the subject of further proceedings brought by ACCC in 1991 for predatory pricing in the Warwick area between 1989 and 1991. Pioneer retaliated with a successful application to strike out important parts of ACCC's statement of claim. ACCC fought back and the original statement of claim was reinstated on appeal. Pioneer's turn, and they sought special leave to appeal to the High Court. This was refused in March 1995. The matter is now back on the Federal Court list.[15]

In another action, of a type we can expect more of as the government sector is pushed into corporate mode, the ACCC instituted court proceedings against the Commonwealth Bureau of Meteorology, claiming that the Bureau had misused its almost monopolistic control of weather-predicting services for anti-competitive purposes. ACCC alleged that the Bureau refused to supply basic meteorology data to a new competitor, the New Zealand company Met Service.[16]

In another matter, made worse by an under-tow in the wrongdoing with respect to corporate exploitation of the elderly, Mayne Nickless Limited (trading as MSS Alarm Systems) was taken to the Federal Court in February 1996 by ACCC for misleading and deceptive conduct. Based on the disclosures of a former control-room employee, the ACCC alleged that MSS had misrepresented its *Neva Alone* personal alarm. The pendant-like device was promoted as enabling the wearer to raise an alarm in a health or personal-security emergency by pressing a small button that triggered an automatic signal to the MSS control room. A monitor would then present the control room operator with a series of options, as determined by the wearer, eg 'call daughter', 'ring neighbour', 'contact doctor'. ACCC alleged that the alarm and monitoring system did not always operate effectively and that the customer data-base, including who-to-call information, was out of date. After ACCC instituted proceedings the company agreed to write to all its *Neva Alone* users advising them of ACCC's findings with respect to the quality of the alarm service. It also offered a free six-months' service or money back and agreed to appoint an independent expert to review its alarm-monitoring system.[17]

It seems that the only thing drawing to a close at the end of the century is the end of the century. Every two years the accounting firm KPMG researches the profile of corporate crime. Its study released in July 1997 found that company fraud now costs up to $20 billion a year.[18] The most common forms of fraud by management were purchases for personal use (13.5%), conflicts of interest (12%), and improper use of expense accounts (11.5%). The most common forms of employee fraud were theft of inventory and plant (17.8%), misappropriation of funds (15.6%) and petty cash fraud (12.6%).

Another corruption index is released annually by Transparency International, a non-profit organisation dedicated to curbing international business and government fraud. It ranked Australia as the eighth least corrupt nation in the world. In releasing its 1997 report in Berlin on 31 July, Transparency International chairman Peter Eigen focused his attention on the cyclopean opportunities for world-scale corruption by multinational companies. He said:

I urge the public to recognise that a large share of corruption is the explicit product of multinational corporations, headquartered in leading industrialised countries, using massive bribery and kickbacks to buy contracts in the developing world . . .[19]

If BHP is the 'Big Australian', the National Australia Bank (NAB) is the 'Big Bank'. Like BHP it too, through sheer size and power, can get away with blue murder. Take the following case. On

21 February 1998 the *Weekend Australian* carried a story with the title 'A Couple the Bank Couldn't Break'.[20] On the same page that carried this story was the regular large advertisement from the NAB promising 'home loans that look after you'. The juxtaposition between this claim and the story of gross misconduct by the bank was there for all to see.

Stories of banking misconduct bloom and die. NAB ads, on the other hand seem to go on forever. Here is an answer I think to the question as to why we have difficulty thinking about whole-of-system wrongdoing. Corporations have huge public image enhancement capacity. They can be there on the spot to neutralise wrongdoing allegations coming out of the system. So if you did not read the newspaper on the day it carried the story of NAB wrongdoing you would have missed it. But the NAB probably did not miss you. Somewhere, sometime on that day you would have seen a NAB billboard, heard a NAB radio add, or seen a NAB television advertisement. It would be different of course if stories of banking misbehaviour came to us with the regularity of their ads.[21] Then we might start to think about whole-of-system corruption. To get to that level of consciousness corporate systems would have to be depowered and their capacity to over-defend themselves with public imaging and legal resources would have to be stripped away. Further, the massive barriers to disclosure would have to be dismantled.

So what happened at the NAB? Briefly, in October 1986 Denis Maher approached a NAB branch office for a business loan. The branch manager, under pressure to write new business, apparently failed to get enough security from Maher. Rather than call Maher in and arrange extra security, the manager fraudulently altered the mortgage documents by adding two extra properties owned by Maher.

Five years later Maher's business soured and he defaulted on loan repayments. The bank quickly took possession of Maher's three properties, and declared him bankrupt. On 29 October 1991 Mrs Maher's daughter rang her at work to say sheriffs were turfing out all their belongings onto the nature strip. The bank then put the family home up for sale. In December, in a scene worthy of any Hollywood thriller, a motorcycle courier interrupted the auction of Maher's house with a Supreme Court injunction stopping the sale.

The Mahers were fighting back. They returned to their house in March 1992. In November a judge ruled that the bank's mortgage document was a forgery.

End of story? Hardly. The bank simply refused to accept the court's verdict. Two years later an Appeal Court confirmed that the mortgage was a forgery. Justice finally came four years later when the Mahers were awarded $500,000 compensation, which included an unheard of $400,000 exemplary damages against the NAB. In his decision Judge Murdoch of the Victorian County Court said:

Instead of apologising to the plaintiff [Mrs Maher] for its actions in forging the mortgage and for its subsequent actions based on the forged mortgage in evicting the plaintiff from her home ... the bank continued to harass her in the conduct of these proceeding ... Throughout its conduct of this proceeding the bank has used its very substantial financial strength to obstruct and thwart the plaintiff in her claim.[22]

The judge then criticised the bank for not getting rid of the corrupt manager. While the observation is reasonable (and usual) in the circumstances, it typifies the dominant view, mentioned previously, that wrongdoers are seen with 20–20 vision, while whole-of-system corruption comes to us as a blur. This is hardly surprising given that we have few answers to essential questions such as how consent is manufactured in the work culture to ensure a dissent-less workforce, and how officials are systematically moulded and ideologically managed.

Insofar as he absorbed and contributed to the new deregulated banking ethos of the 1980s, the manager was a child of the system. He was no rebel whose actions can be easily disowned. If he was eventually sacked or disciplined in some way, it would be the bank jettisoning inconvenient cargo. The 'bad apple' manager may go, but the 'bad barrel' organisation stays. The bank by the way announced that it intended to appeal Judge Murdoch's damages ruling![23]

Does this story reveal the new shape of the modern culture of work? If so, how do we get from there to a culture of ethics? As a measure of how important this question is I want it to remain conspicuously unanswered throughout the book.

We need to remind ourselves that we are dealing with a very dangerous situation here. The destruction of the Australian watchdog and review infrastructure, combined with a descending ethical standard, mixed with a chronic reticence on the part of the Australian public to report wrongdoing is bad news, for these conditions provide wrongdoing with a floor on which to dance.

2 | Disclosure

The Inside Story

Who are the whistleblowers, these people who, refusing to dance with wrongdoing, are feared, loathed, honoured and respected, often at the same time? At the outset we can say this – whistle-blowers are moral people of action. Like us all they locate themselves with maps of the mind. What makes them different is that they also use these maps to locate and respond to wrongdoing. This is their greatest social value, and their most sublime weakness – for they are caught up in mythology. Let me explain.

When Henry Lawson wrote in 'Freedom on the Wallaby':

> *But freedom's on the Wallaby,*
> *She'll knock the tyrants silly,*
> *She's going to light another fire*
> *and boil another billy.*
> *We'll make the tyrants feel the sting*
> *of those that they would throttle:*
> *They needn't say the fault is ours*
> *If blood should stain the wattle.*[1]

he celebrated an icon of Australian history – that ours is a land of the free. Likewise when Donald Horne wrote *The Lucky Country* we responded by sending it to the best-seller list and putting it on reading lists throughout the land. That title! We just loved it. So much so that the title became the book and few of us figured out that Horne was being ironic; that he was telling us our post-war prosperity was due more to lady luck than good management. The irony in Horne's book was simply no match for the mythology on the front cover which celebrated the desireability of living in a vast southern New Jerusalem rather than the reality of social facts like poverty and racism.

Henry Lawson's archetypal optimism that authoritarianism would not take root in Australia and Horne's book-cover celebrationism have long, strong, and intertwined traditions in Australian cultural experience. Being the idealists that they are, whistleblowers willingly tap into these patriotic traditions. These traditions act like a massive cultural womb; birthing 'heroes' who typify our deep yearnings for freedom, power and identity, and aborting anti-heroes, those who would unsettle our carefully manicured iconography.

These are the whistleblowers. For most of us these people are inscrutable contradictions with occupational death wishes. On one level we object to them and their revelations because they break cultural myths so dear to us, and pierce our comfortable ignorance with tales of their horrendous experiences. On another level, and here is the contradiction, they are as indispensable as traffic signs on an icy road. We do not want to hear what they say but we know that we must: for our own sake, our own safety, and our own national welfare.

They tell us that justice is not to be found easily in the courts, and that enlightenment has all but left our universities. They show us through their stories of poverty that egalitarianism has had its core eaten out. On discharge from hospital they tell us about the cockroaches that scurried over their beds. They reminisce about standing there unprotected at Maralinga to face experimental nuclear blasts. On release from jail they tell of the bashings and rapes.

When a whistleblower approaches we ask ourselves whether this is going to be another bad news day. While we will (sometimes reluctantly) concede that their intentions are driven by a genuine concern for the public interest, we have difficulty dealing with the fact that their messages are often so negative and disturbing. They always seem to be digging around in our socio-political garbage dumps, always coming up with something rotten or damaged to show us. In that regard they cannot match 'heroes', whose positive and gleaming accomplishments we wrap around ourselves in glory, and who allow us, just for the moment, to believe that we are a free and noble people.

Faced with the whistleblower's disclosure we often find ourselves scurrying into denial as we say to ourselves, Don't tell us about the paedophile judge or the bent copper, but tell us again how *Australia II* took the America's Cup in 1983.

The Demos Myth

Not being able to bask in the deeds of our whistleblowers as readily as we glory in the actions of our 'heroes' displays a fear that public interest disclosures have the potential to dam-bust the great barrier between myth and reality, particularly the myth that our personal behaviour and social life are relatively immune from despotic conduct. But as anybody who has ever taken action on behalf of the public interest knows, freedom can often be the myth and un-freedom the reality.

Our un-freedom is guaranteed, ironically enough, by our so-called democratic political structure. This is such a difficult and important message to convey (even to whistleblowers who muster behind the democratic flag) that it needs to be dwelt on for a while.

Immanuel Kant, the German philosopher of the Idealist School, wrote in *Perpetual Peace: A Philosophical Sketch*:

Of the three forms of sovereignty – autocracy, aristocracy, democracy – democracy, in the truest sense of the word, is necessarily a despotism, because it establishes an executive power through which all the citizens may make decisions about (and indeed against) the single individual without his consent, so that decisions are made by all the people and yet not by all the people; and this means that the general will is in contradiction with itself thus also with freedom.[2]

What I think Kant is driving at here is that of all the forms of rule, democracy, that form we think gives people real life-choice and personal autonomy, can be in fact the most despotic of all. On the surface democracy looks just fine. The people possess power. They can regularly express their wishes about the direction of the nation. They can turn ugly on a politician, or indeed a whole political party, and flick them out of office. Yes, democracy looks good and reassuring, particularly after we have switched off the news carrying some story of a bloody conflagration in some far-flung dictatorship.

What we often see in our society, however, is not what we get. Democracy's promise to build wide avenues of public participation is shadowed-out by its inner workings, comprehendible to anyone who has ever taken the system on. Democracy, or in clearer terms, democratic practice, is the rule of the 'king' through a million voices. The 'king' is shorthand for executive power. This power is visible whenever an elite rules on behalf of the people. This is the first contradiction the whistleblower learns. But there is more on the curriculum.

Being self-captivated by the myth of democracy is only half the problem. We also embrace a false identity as *citizen*. This concept is copyrighted to democracy. It implies ownership and real power of choice. It exists in no other theory of governance. We are told through the soft mantra messages of our socialisation that we are citizens in a democracy. We think this means that we are, or can be, robustly involved in the running of our body politic. We not only think of *involvement* when we think of citizenship, we also think of *rights*. We believe, for example, that we have a right to democratic representation.

The demos myth is transmitted, fresh and vigorous, through the generations and down the class structure. We must ask ourselves why we need the myth. I have partly attempted to answer this when I said it is because of our deep desire to see ourselves as free. There is something more to it.

To get to it we need to bring the raw *realpolitik* back onto our radar screen by radically re-framing ourselves from citizens to *consumers*. Rather than being free in a civic world I would argue that we are servile in an industrial one. We think that we are free to co-determine our society, when maybe all we are free to do is shop. In all other respects we are the heirs and re-generators of an economic system in which we are treated, and treat each other as anonymous, regulated, efficient producer–consumers. Here is the second whistleblower paradox. They see and report wrongdoing *as if* they lived in a working democracy. They are responded to as consumers; with all the powerlessness that concept implies.

In awakening us to our powerlessness, whistleblowers produce all sorts of crisscrossed emotions. Should we respond to them as truth-bearing ethical citizens, or spiteful, griping dobbers? I suspect that our paradoxical attitude to them derives to a certain extent from the way their attacks on unlawfulness can be so readily re-framed as the vandalisation of our central values.

Whistleblowers know from hard experience that the wrongdoing they tilt their lances at is hard-coated with the myths that build up the Australian dream-identity. Wrongdoing and Australian iconography are inseparable, like co-conspirators in a massive scam. For example, the whistleblower who exposes police on the take is attacked for transgressing the myth-code of copper mateship. The whistleblower attempting to show that a solicitor is corrupt is served a defamation writ for breaching the code of good reputation. The whistleblower attempting to draw attention to the existence of a culture of violence in a small town is castigated for tarnishing its image and chasing away the tourists. And so it goes.

Reaching for wrongdoing is a bit like catching a spider and having your hand covered in the sticky web. We impose an extra burden on the whistleblower. Not only must they embark on a dangerous act of exposure (catching the spider) they must also deal with the cultural flak (the sticky web).

These contradictions between democratic theory and practice, between ethical worker and dobber, between our need to hear the disclosure and our wish that the allegations were not so, are re-expressed every time someone dissents or discloses in the public interest. Some examples are needed to crystallise these points.

The Speakout Myth

Brian Senewiratne, a wiry medico from Sri Lanka, was senior specialist and visiting physician at what was the seriously run-down Princess Alexandria Hospital in Brisbane. In the lead-up to the 1995 Queensland State elections Senewiratne released to the media a video that showed gross overcrowding in the hospital's casualty ward as a result of years of government neglect. He was savaged by then Premier Wayne Goss for his excursion into film production.

In July 1996, in the first months of the new Borbidge government, Senewiratne circulated a memo to hospital staff in which he said, 'We are now 100 days into the new regime and nothing has changed.'[3] For this Senewiratne received a nasty rebuke from Ross Pitt, the Deputy Director-General of the Queensland Health Department, which read in part:

As a newcomer to the Health portfolio, I am astounded that you feel free to make comments to the media in the way that you do. Not only is this a breach of the most fundamental obligations of your engagement, but your allegations seem calculated to shake public confidence in the public health system ... If you are really as concerned as you say that you are, then why not resign your commission from Queensland Health?

It was reported that Senewiratne intended to tell Pitt to 'get stuffed'.[4]

Unfortunately not all dissenters and whistleblowers can be so cocky. In late 1995 staff at the National Gallery of Australia were warned by the then Director, Betty Churcher, that they would be sacked if they released information that she deemed confidential. Churcher's threat followed the release of her report to the National Gallery Council that detailed her $3.5 m request to the National Australia Bank to partly fund her controversial purchase of Arthur Streeton's *Golden Summer* in exchange for naming rights.[5] Churcher is reported to have also expressed concern that Gallery information was being provided 'so readily' to the Senate Estimates Committee.[6]

The former (and the following may explain why he is 'the former') Queensland Health Rights Commissioner, Dr Ian Siggins, hit the wall of entrenched power when, between July 1995 and June 1996, he investigated disclosure by staff and patient whistleblowers of malpractice and abuse at the Baille Henderson Psychiatric Hospital in Toowoomba. Siggins was so concerned about what his investigators uncovered in Toowoomba that he made a special report to the Queensland Parliament.[7] Health Minister Horan, on Crown Law advice, refused to have Siggins' report tabled.[8] Horan went so far as to suggest that Siggins should apologise for championing the cause of a young man at the hospital identified as P11.[9] Of P11 Siggins said:

[He has] been wrongly diagnosed ... and has not benefited from treatment (indeed, has deteriorated) ... It is unbelievable that in Queensland in 1996 this young man is now in a security forensic hospital when he has committed no other crime than to have become the subject of a Health Rights Commission investigation. I find it extraordinary that the public reports of this case have not prompted any contact by the College of Psychiatrists. The Queensland public should know that my experience in other jurisdictions in similar circumstances is the opposite of what has happened here: professional bodies, unions and health departments have properly supported their members or staff, but they have done so not at the expense of vulnerable patients, nor have they sought to shoot the messenger in such a concerted way. My sad conclusion is that patients with mental illnesses in this State are disadvantaged even more than their interstate counterparts by institutional, professional, and community attitudes and values which put the interests of providers and institutions ahead of those of the patients.[10]

Fighting words, and end-of-job words. Siggins is no longer Health Rights Commissioner.

Finally, we need to concern ourselves with the changes to the terms of employment of the Clerk of the Australian Senate. This position, along with the Clerk of the House of Representatives, unknown to most Australians, is a citadel of democracy for those who believe in its existence. In a nutshell the Clerk of the Senate has a trans-party political interest in the overall integrity of the parliamentary system. The current incumbent, Harry Evans, has guarded the citadel with great dedication and authority since 1984. His wisdom about parliamentary practice is second to none. As a result he occupies a sort of 'eminent person' position in parliaments throughout the Commonwealth.

When the present Howard government was in opposition they thought Evans was just the ant's pants. They tried not to miss any opportunities to exploit his fearless advice about the parliamentary propriety of certain government proposals. Now that they are in government he's a problem for them. Why? Because he continues to give principled advice without fear of its political inconvenience.[11]

The next thing we know Cabinet has authorised the drafting of the *Parliamentary Services Bill*, which kills off the Clerk's tenure and replaces it with ten-year non-renewable contracts. There is some suggestion that the real goal is to have the Clerk on two-year renewable contracts![12] What better way to get a lap dog, rather than watchdog, into the Clerk's position?

It would be silly and improper to suggest that the sole purpose in drafting the *Parliamentary Services Bill* was to get Evans. The Bill synchronised with the more general *Public Service Act 1997*, which ended the notion of a unified, tenured, fearless public service, and signalled the end of central public service management in favour of agency-based command centres. Be that as it may, if the government was steadfast in its belief that some responsibilities needed to be unfettered in the service of democracy then it could have immunised the Clerks of the Senate and House of Representatives from the current 'reforms'.

We should have a Hall of Remembrance, like war memorials, to honour all those public-spirited citizens 'who are no longer with us' in the sense that they have been taken out of public service as a reprisal for standing up to power. In the late 1980s the obvious site for this Hall of Remembrance would have been Brisbane, given the human rights' carnage committed during the Bjelke-Petersen rule. These days it could be anywhere! Perhaps Melbourne. Moira Rayner, the Victorian Equal Opportunity Commissioner, had her position abolished by the Kennett Government for speaking out against the government[13]. It has been reported that when former Director of Public Prosecutions, Bernard Bongiorno, considered charging Premier Kennett with contempt of court, the Premier stripped Bongiorno's position of the power to take such action[14].

Senewiratne, National Gallery staff, Siggins, Evans, Rayner and Bongiorno attempted to contradict power, legitimised through democratic rule. This legitimacy is so well grounded in our society that it remains one of the great resistances to outspokenness.

The Concord Hospital experience demonstrates another source of resistance to dissent; and that is, in the words of William Fulbright, the great tendency of power to confuse itself with virtue. On 22 August 1996, in response to public agitation by Concord Hospital staff against health cuts, Dr Diana Horvath, then CEO for the Central Sydney Area Health Service (CSAHS) wrote to Concord Hospital staff:

I wish to bring to your attention the following: A) Every employee has a duty of good faith and fidelity to his/her employer, with the consequence being that any conduct by an employee, including public criticism of the employer ... is a ground for dismissal.[15]

Here in the Horvath letter is another of the great barriers to outspokenness: the capacity of power to bring legal and *moral* sanctions to bear to ensure staff loyalty and fidelity.

Not only are dissenting individuals barricaded by power and suffer for their public-spiritedness. Whole agencies can fall victim. In July 1996 the Brisbane-based and state-funded Consumer Health Advocacy (CHA) was shut down by the Queensland Borbidge Government amidst official allegations that it was poorly managed, financially irresponsible, and a duplication of services.[16] It has been suggested that CHA was closed because it was too effective as a health lobby group and became too much of a worry to the powerful Queensland branch of the Australian Medical Association and the management elites in the Queensland Health Department.[17] The departmental report that triggered the closure of CHA stated in part: 'the preoccupation appears to be CHA exposing and decrying the abuses of the health system.'[18] One would have thought that this was a central objective of an advocacy group.

While each whistleblowing experience is unique, there is a chilling sameness about the phenomenon. So much so that whistleblowing can be represented by the following diagram:

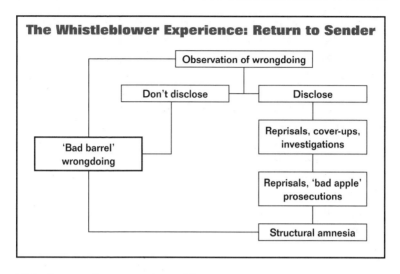

This diagram has a number of features:

1) In liberal societies icon status is ascribed to concepts like individualism and individual responsibility. Consequently it is very hard to understand let alone respond to the notion of systemic corruption, or what I call *bad-barrel wrongdoing*. Whistleblowers are usually less limited than the rest of us in this regard. Their disclosure experiences often expose previously hidden histories, contexts, interconnections, allegiances, and loyalties, as well as the lack of connections between the justice rhetoric of management and its actions against employees who disclose. Not having the experiential and ideological wherewithal to comprehend system-wide wrongdoing, we set off in search of bad apples whom we invariably find and sometimes punish.
2) When faced with wrongdoing most people do not disclose. Although we could do with a lot more research into the causes of this disturbing depth of inaction, we do have some important markers:
    - Workplace alienation means that workers are no longer sufficiently emotionally attached to their organisations to care enough to report wrongdoing.
    - The increasing popularity of contract work facilitates a new expression of workplace alienation.

- The juvenilisation of the workforce (McDonalds is the paradigm example here) means that more and more young people are visible at the service-provider point. Young people at, or just out of school, needing the money, are easily quietened by management authority. They know little of their rights, nor do they have enough experience to identify wrongdoing.
- The feminisation of the workplace[19] raises the issue of whether there is a gender bias operating in whistleblowing. Certainly a Queensland Whistleblower Study (QWS) sample had a male:female ratio of about 2:1[20] This imbalance may be nothing more than a sampling artefact. However there are enticing questions in this issue. For example, are women generally in favour of dissent strategies other than whistleblowing? Research is only now being reported that promises to shed light on questions such as these.[21]
- Media interest in the battle stories of whistleblowers scare people away from disclosure.
- Career-powered people, knowing the risks involved in disclosure, will play psychological tricks on themselves to secure their futures and allay their conscience, which is nagging them to do their public duty to disclose. A common trick is to *sanitise* the wrongdoing by making it appear less grave than it is. Another psychological device is to *trivialise* wrongdoing by seeing it as an unrepeatable aberration, or to focus on the extenuating circumstances in the wrongdoer's life (eg marriage problems which produced a gambling habit which led to stealing).
- If reporting cannot be squared with one's loyalty to colleagues or a racial group, then disclosure does not happen. Military and para-military parts of the public sector (army, police, fire brigade etc.) appear to build up stronger disclosure-resistant walls of solidarity than their civilian counterparts. Sometimes these walls follow gender divisions rather than the more common us–them divide, as female naval officers found when they disclosed sexual harassment on the HMAS *Swan* in 1993.
- A similar, but different situation arises in the Aboriginal

community. A black whistleblower disclosing on his or her own people has to cross two lines: workplace solidarity and communal solidarity. When blacks disclose they are not just disclosing wrongdoing, they are reporting their people to the white fellas[22]. A Brisbane Aborigine had to go into witness protection precisely for this reason.
- The increasing cultural diversity of the Australian workforce is another factor explaining non-disclosure. Migrants with memories of wide-scale corruption in their home countries will use this experience to measure and perhaps downplay local wrongdoing. P.P. McGuiness tells the story of having lunch with the Indian High Commissioner to Australia about ten years ago. The diplomat had just read David Hickie's account of the corruption-riddled administration of Robin Askin in New South Wales. His comment was, 'Oh, is that all?'

3) Returning to the diagram, reprisals usually start immediately after the disclosure becomes organisational knowledge. Cover-ups often start at the same time. Investigations usually start after the cover-up has been established. This is an intense time for whistleblowers as they have to service the demands of an inquiry as well as respond to reprisals.

4) After a period of time, investigations cease (but reprisals rarely stop at the same time). Because evidentiary rules are stacked against the whistleblower and they are unresourced at the critical time of evidence-collecting, investigatory conclusions and findings are often disappointing to the whistleblower, who has a strong sense of not being vindicated. Whistleblowers usually report a worrying level of incompetence and indifference in the investigative authorities. In fact one, if not the most, beneficial role whistleblowers play is what could be called the service-user-from-hell role. Whistleblowers very publicly test the effectiveness of investigatory authorities (including the courts).

5) Official intervention (if there is any) usually comes in the form of charges against some 'bad apples', pious promises of a code of ethics, and glib references to the need for 'structural change'.

Despite the limits to speaking out, and despite their consequential exposure to vilification, whistleblowers in Australia have brought public attention to bear on significant cases of wrongdoing in an alarmingly wide range of areas:

- A paedophile ring operating amongst Australian diplomats in South East Asia was exposed by a whistleblower.[23]
- It was a whistleblower who disclosed Australia's worst psychiatric atrocity.[24]
- A whistleblower triggered the Fitzgerald Inquiry into corruption in Queensland public life.[25]
- The expose of a culture of violence at the Basil Stafford Centre for the Intellectually Disabled in Brisbane was started by a whistleblower.[26]
- A whistleblower initially drew attention to gross misconduct by senior nursing staff and the former chief psychiatrist at the Hillview medical complex for disturbed adolescents in Western Australia.[27]
- It was a research whistleblower who exposed the laboratory fraud of Dr William McBride.[28]
- A whistleblower first raised the issue of the misuse of funds donated to Care Australia.[29]
- After the Seaview crash, it was a whistleblower who disclosed that the Civil Aviation Authority had failed to act on regular air safety breaches.[30]

What is Whistleblowing?

Australian whistleblowing does not have its own history. In fact I would limit its origins both here and overseas to the 1980s. Dissent, on the other hand, has a long and relatively uncomplicated history. I shall deal with both in turn, because whistleblowing and dissent are not the same thing.

It is fair to say that semantic madness has accompanied the media-fuelled rise in the level of public awareness about whistleblowing. The definition used here is the research definition developed in the Queensland Whistleblower Study:

The whistleblower is a concerned citizen, totally or predominantly motivated by notions of public interest, who initiates of her or his own free will an open disclosure about significant wrongdoing in a particular occupational role to a person or agency capable of investigating the complaint and facilitating the correction of wrongdoing, and who suffers accordingly.[31]

This definition is an exclusionary one; it takes a lot of related behaviours out. To be a whistleblower one must:

Suffer. The non-suffering whistleblower is a contradiction in terms. Here is our first opportunity to distinguish whistleblowing from related behaviours; which on this occasion is the behaviour of *reporting*. Two quick examples should help clarify this point. A few years ago a young nurse in a country town hospital in Queensland was appalled at the behaviour of the town's only doctor. An alcoholic, he would regularly do hospital rounds and surgery when he was drunk. The nurse made a public interest disclosure to her Director of Nursing. This was the beginning of the end for her in that job. Why? She saw wrongdoing, she reported it, she was doing the right thing. Why did she suffer?

What she did not understand until it was too late was that her disclosure threatened the power of the Director of Nursing. This women sat at the top of a small district health enterprise. She had known for a long about the drunken doctor, covered up his mistakes, and made excuses for him. As long as he was weak she was strong. By attempting to expose the doctor the young nurse unwittingly jeopardised the director's position, for an investigation would have discovered her cover-up of the doctor's behaviour.

Two years later, in Sydney, the story was replayed with different people and a different ending. Two doctors reported a drunk colleague to the Australian Medical Association which, on investigation, found the allegations proved and de-registered the man. The two reporting doctors were supported throughout and complimented by the AMA for their actions. The reporting doctors did not suffer because their disclosure was not a threat to the power of any party other then the de-registered doctor. These people are in my view not whistleblowers. I prefer to call them *report-makers*.

Initiate the action oneself. The disclosure process must be started by the whistleblower. This rules out second-party divulgements as a form of whistleblowing. If the young nurse in the previous example had taken her concerns to her union, and it disclosed on her behalf, that, in my view would not be an act of whistleblowing. I prefer to call it a *secondary disclosure*. While that may be so, another issue is raised here. No whistleblower law protects, as far as I know, agencies (eg unions) that make secondary disclosures. This could be seen as a deficiency in the legal schemes in so far as secondary disclosers may also fear litigation.

Act of one's own will. To qualify as a whistleblowing act, the disclosure should be a voluntary one. This stipulation excludes people forced to disclose by superiors. Involuntary admissions under oath to courts and parliamentary committees are another matter, as they are protected by tough contempt of court and parliament provisions. If our young nurse reluctantly divulged under oath facts about the doctor's professional behaviour, she would do so as a *witness*, not as a whistleblower.

Directly perceive the wrongdoing. A whistleblowing disclosure should be based on what the person directly experienced or observed. The whistleblower, in other words, works on *primary knowledge* of wrongdoing. This is why their evidence is usually of sound probative value: it is not second-hand information. In terms of our young nurse again, if she reported seeing the doctor drunk, that (all other criteria satisfied) is a whistleblowing disclosure. If on the other hand she reported that a patient saw the doctor drunk, that report does not constitute whistleblowing. It is what I would call *secondary reporting*.

Perceive wrongdoing in a work setting. I add a work-based criterion to my definition of whistleblowing. The person must report wrongdoing that they are privy to in an occupational role. For example, if our nurse sees the doctor drunk at work while she is on duty, her report is an act of whistleblowing. If she sees him drunk in the car-park of a holiday resort, her report is not whistleblowing. Some may find this criterion overly narrow. For example it precludes the unemployed from recognition as whistleblowers.

While that may be so, it does not preclude citizens from making what I call *public interest denunciations*. This is by far the most common way regulating authorities (Australian Taxation Office, Australian Consumer and Competition Commission, police, National Crime Authority etc) receive information about wrongdoing. One of the main reasons why public interest denunciations are so common is that people can usually provide the information anonymously.

Whistleblowing is coincidental to employment. If the person discloses after they have left the work setting is that an act of whistleblowing? I do not think so. Retrospective disclosures are *usually* beyond the reach of management reprisals. Hence the criterion of suffering is not present. I do not want to be too dogmatic here: a resignation, dismissal or retirement does not always give the ex-employee absolute immunity if they wish to disclose.

There are many examples of this style of disclosure. To balance the Brisbane *Courier Mail*'s rekindled love affair with ex-Lord Mayor Clem Jones on his victorious return from the 1998 Constitutional Convention, one of his old enemies, his Director of Town Planning, P. D. Day, went into print with some very strong words. Jones, Day said, had 'desecrated' the entrance to City Hall with a car park, had 'abandoned' Australia's most efficient tram system, and so on.[32] Whistleblowing? Only if Day had raised these objections during the course of his employment.

The Peter Wright case is another good example of this genre. Wright served in MI5, the British Intelligence Service, from 1955–76, at the zenith of the Cold War. In 1976 he retired to Tasmania where he wrote his memoirs, *Spycatcher*, which revealed that MI5 had involved itself in criminal activities and had been infiltrated by Soviet spies. After a dramatic series of trials and diplomatic manoeuvres Heinemann, the giant book company, was cleared to publish the book in the United Kingdom.[33] This is a lineball example, for Wright's old employer attempted to punish him as if he was still in their employ.

There is also the example of Sir Peter de la Billiere. A Gulf war hero, and at the time Britain's most decorated soldier, de la Billiere was blacklisted by the Special Air Services (SAS) and banned from attending regimental dinners, reunions, and remembrance services. His sin? On retirement he wrote *Storm Command,* in which he is alleged to have published secret SAS military secrets and to have blamed the British Defence Ministry for Royal Air Force casualties suffered in the Gulf War.[34]

Disclose openly. As far as I am concerned whistleblowing is not an anonymous act. Anonymous reporting does not need protection. Whistleblowing is open disclosure.

Act to stop the wrongdoing. The whistleblowing disclosure is one made to an official or an agency (which includes media), that has a capacity to facilitate the exposure and correction of the unearthed problem. It is not whistleblowing if the nurse, for example, only told her partner, her own doctor or her priest about the drunken doctor. I prefer to call these *disclosures in confidence.* People in these circumstances have a primary need to unburden themselves, to seek guidance and support. They may disclose in the public interest later, but at that stage it is a confidential disclosure.

Act in the public interest. This is also a very contentious criterion. I am aware of the pragmatic view that the public interest lies in the information, not in the motivation of the messenger. Let me give an example of this view. Ken Davies was a minister in the first Goss government in Queensland in the early 1990s. He subsequently failed to be preselected. He said in the heat of the conflict that if he went he would spill on the government, as he knew a few things. Clearly Davies's motivation was payback. So what? say the supporters of the view that public interest lies in the content. Davies may have had first-hand knowledge of criminal acts. Isn't his reporting of these in the public interest? Yes, of course. But he is not necessarily reporting in the public interest, he may just be out for good old-fashioned revenge.

While I argue that the whistleblower acts in the public interest, I don't wish to air-brush away private interests, nor to put whistle-blowers on an ethical pedestal. However, acting in the public interest is what whistleblowing is all about. They are, as we said at the beginning of the definition, 'concerned citizens'.

In summary so far, whistleblowing occurs when all (or most) of the criteria discussed above are present. Whistleblowing is different from:

- Reporting
- Secondary Disclosing
- Witnessing
- Secondary reporting
- Denunciating
- Disclosing in confidence
- Retrospective disclosing
- Informing.[35]

The activity that really needs to be separated from whistleblowing, however, is *informing*. Peter Ustinov once said on a visit to Sydney: 'I wouldn't be worried about a society descended from convicts, but a society descended from the guards.' To properly consider the historical context to Australian whistleblowing we must eschew Ustinov's warning and be equally concerned about the convict *and* guard traditions.

White Australia started as a convict society in 1788. There were immediate power struggles between convicts and their guards. The polarisation between those with the keys and whips and those with the ball and chains was a product of the historical stratification of homeland British society between rulers and the ruled. This served as an archetype for other power patterns that evolved in the next 200 years: freeman/assigned convict labourer; pastoralist/farm labourer; officer/soldier; employer/employee etc. The way this powerful archetype laid itself down in the national psyche greatly affected the shape and outcome of all subsequent power relationships to emerge in Australia, including and particularly the public perceptions of whistleblowing.

Within the archetypal convict/guard power relationship two roles were quickly hammered out to meet the urgent survival requisites of each group. In Australia those who act in these roles are known colloquially as 'cobbers' and 'dobbers'.[36] The cobber tradition starts with convict solidarity against the penal masters. Like all underclass societies it had to develop effective strategies to survive the brutality and oppression of its penal masters. Solidarity and loyalty became the coping strategies *par excellence*, for both groups. These strategies were used so effectively by the convicts that the guards soon found the need to develop a counterweight in what is called 'dobbing'. The Macquarie dictionary (1982) defines dobbing as a form of betrayal.[37] Interestingly, the same dictionary defines whistleblowing as a form of betrayal too.[38]

In one of the first recorded instances of dobbing in penal Australia, one Charles Cooze informed an overseer that four fellow convicts had stolen silver goods from the house of a Captain Wright in 1835.[39] Cooze, in jail for stealing mutton, was looking for a reward for his information; a remission in sentence perhaps. The tyrannical and brutal Governor of Tasmania, George Arthur, knew that dobbing was the key to unlock convict solidarity. He introduced a system of espionage 'to destabilise any unity among convicts'.[40] Those forwarding information got shortened sentences, better rations, increased clothing supplies and even positions in the penal control structure as overseers and constables.[41] If caught cooperating with the authorities, convicts were often punished or even killed by other prisoners.

Just as the oppressive relationship between convicts and guards became a model for subsequent relationships characterised by power imbalances, so too did the disciplinary protocols that developed. Dobbing is a sin for all groups. Whether it is regarded as a mortal sin whereby the offending member is killed or severely injured (for example ex-members of the IRA and prison informers), or a sin of a lesser consequence and the member is ostracised (for example public sector informers), depends on many things. One is the level of ambient violence acceptable to the group. Another is whether the group is fighting for survival at the time.

One thing to be sure is that dobbing is deeply threatening behaviour to the less powerful group and a real asset to those exercising control. Dobbing systems can be so effective that they can lead to the neutralisation, if not the demise, of subordinate groups. So sanctions are applied by the dobber's group. Dobbing systems respond by building in greater rewards and protections. Informer programs in America that offer financial inducements are an example of accelerated attempts to breach the solidarity of groups involved in activity considered threatening or illegal.[42]

We have informant programs in Australia too. Most of these are based on the voluntary exchange of information between people and regulating authorities. Some institutions such as the media and law enforcement agencies pay for information. Various statutory departments that provide public monies in the form of pensions and benefits (eg Commonwealth Department of Social Security) or administer revenue laws (eg Australian Taxation Office) rely to a great extent on usually anonymous denunciations from the public.

An example is Operation Noah, whereby the public are encouraged to dob in drug dealers and users. Local councils place large roadside signs encouraging people to report litterers anonymously. The Queensland Police, through the Crime Stoppers program, now provides for rewards up to $1000 to people who dob in drink-drivers.[43] Recently the Australian Taxation Office, concerned about lost taxation revenue through cash transactions, started to seriously consider the French scheme of giving tax credits to informants.[44]

The big worry with all these informant programs is the damage they can do to social trust and cohesion. For a start the largely clandestine nature of these programs puts them beyond the normal mechanisms of accountability. This is encouraged by official disinterest in informant identity and motivation for coming forward.

People, including innocent parties, do respond to informant programs by becoming more secretive and cautious in their interpersonal dealings. Conversely, information-gatherers, induced by monetary reward, can develop a bounty-hunter mentality, again with negative impact on the fabric of social trust. Informant damage to social cohesion is, according to the apologists for these programs, outweighed by the public benefit gained by the capacity of these programs to bring wrongdoing to light.

We have now reached the heart of the distinction between dobbing and whistleblowing. The power relations are different. Dobbing, in general terms, is the powerless reporting to the powerful on the misdeeds of the powerless. Whistleblowing, on the other hand, is the powerless disclosing the misconduct of the powerful.

Another important distinction is that dobbing is an anonymous activity that does not need to be driven by public-spiritedness. Because of this it can be quite divisive. Some years ago a woman from a small country town unsuccessfully attempted to use the Commonwealth *Freedom of Information Act* to identify an informant who had reported her to the Department of Social Security. She said that she was devastated by the report and could no longer trust anybody. She would look into the eyes of people she met in the town and wonder whether she was gazing at her informant.

On the other hand public-interested motivation and openness are extremely pertinent to the definition of whistleblowing. No whistleblower statute in Australia will offer protection to a person who does not disclose in good faith. Some jurisdictions will not protect whistleblower disclosures if they are done anonymously. Whistleblowing is quintessentially a *public* exposure of wrongdoing. While the whistleblower's public *modus operandi* releases a great deal of conflict, it appears not to have the same insidious impact on social trust as anonymous reporting.

This point, in the absence of research, is tentatively expressed. Certainly it would lack plausibility with those who conflate whistleblowing and dobbing. In that perception both forms of disclosure impact negatively on relationships, whether that be in the small town we just visited or in work relationships. A young senior constable in the NSW Police Service rushed to a motor vehicle accident in March 1997 to find his fiance dead behind the wheel of her car. The traumatised constable said, after he eventually returned to work, that the police culture was the key to him surviving his grief:

The culture has been portrayed as a bad thing but from what I have seen it's all about mateship and looking after each other... People have gone out of their way, way above and beyond the call of duty to be a friend. You can't put a value on that.[45]

The constable's experiences have confirmed for him the importance of caring workplace relationships. Here is the ethical bind many of us struggle with. The solidarity that the young constable experienced in the form of care and compassion is the same solidarity that forms around wrongdoing. Work relationships are often deemed so important that nothing should be done to damage them. Whether that damage occurs by a plea-bargaining cop ratting to investigators about other corrupt police, or by an honest officer turned whistleblower dutifully reporting on colleagues withholding drugs after a raid, makes little difference to the negative effects disclosure is popularly believed to have on work and community relationships. It will take big changes in work and community cultural life before we are released from struggling with this loyalty versus ethical conduct dilemma.

The struggle to distinguish whistleblowing from other forms of disclosure becomes a lost game in the cut-and-thrust world of politics, where the source and motivation for disclosure is of less interest than the damage such disclosures can do to one's opponents. Incumbency appears to be the central factor in determining attitudes to disclosure. Disclosers who are courted by opposition parties are often abandoned soon after those parties are returned to power.

Two examples come to mind. When Labor was defeated in Queensland in 1995 there was much talk about the existence of a Coalition Government 'hit list' of senior public servants identified as having Labor sympathies who were about to get the chop. Eventually the list materialised with 118 names on it. The ALP was getting nowhere with its investigation of who compiled the list and under what circumstances one got onto it. So it appealed to public servants 'to act as whistleblowers',[46] when all it wanted was dirt on the government. Two years before, when Labor was in power, it had turned a blind eye to the concerns of whistleblowers that the

Whistleblower Protection Bill, which it was about to write into law, did not offer real protection to whistleblowers.[47]

The second example comes from the Federal Labor Opposition, which announced on 12 June 1997 that it was setting up a new committee called the 'Federal Labor Party Waste Watch and Whistleblower Committee'.[48] People who had anything negative to report on the Howard government were encouraged to disclose to the Committee. Yet while in power the Federal ALP rejected all requests for Commonwealth whistleblower protection.

How can we sum up this analysis? Informers are usually in the service of the powerful, reporting on their own kind, often for personal gain. From the point of view of the informant's targets, the most dangerous thing about dobbers are their mouths. In what has to be the clearest (and most morbid) example of this, an intruder broke into the Brisbane home of a police informer around 10.30 am on 13 May 1997, pinned him to the floor, forced coathanger wire through his cheeks and wired his mouth shut.[49]

Unlike informers, whistleblowers are double trouble because they have a mouth *and* a social conscience, and won't easily trade ethics for expediency. I am aware that I am veering close to stereotyping the two major ways of disclosing. While it is acknowledged that both forms of reporting share attributes, there are important differences, particularly the existence in whistleblowing of a drive to protect the public interest.

Whistleblowing also needs to be distinguished from *dissenting*. Whistleblowing is ethical resistance against the usually protected existence of wrongdoing. It is carried out by people in the workplace, acting alone. Dissenters, on the other hand, often work in groups and protest against policy, rather than disclose wrongdoing. Local action against the destruction of a koala bear habitat is an action of dissent. Dissenters usually enlist different strategies, designed not so much to expose wrongdoing as to enforce a change where change is resisted. While dissenting can be a dangerous activity, its proponents are shielded to an effective extent from recrimination in rule of law countries because they act in groups, can exploit legal and constitutional guarantees of freedom of speech and association, and act in public forums.

On the other hand the whistleblower's forum is one of the most supervised and regulated sites in our society, the workplace. Workers do not have freedom of association. They cannot go where they like, nor associate with whom they wish. They certainly do not have freedom to speak out. Public servants, for instance, still sign draconian secrecy agreements on employment. Human rights, particularly the democratic guarantees, are certainly not foregone conclusions in the structure of the workplace. In this most inhospitable of rights environments, we find the toiling and reprisal-prone whistleblower.

Part 2
Whistleblowing
The Lived Experience

The previous chapters have presented whistleblowing through a wide-angle lens. With the big picture set, we can now zoom in and take a closer look at eleven case studies of whistleblowing in practice. The subjects of these chapters are a medical doctor, a veterinary pathologist, a Presbyterian minister, three academics, a television and radio producer and commentator, a union official, a fisherman, and two senior Commonwealth public servants. These people of conscience have much in common. They all reported wrongdoing, they all were traumatised by the reprisals meted out to them, they all lost something significant – be it partner, career or reputation – and none of them will ever forget what happened to them. As a group of people, however, they are widely different. That's how it should be. Whistleblowing was a defining moment *in* their lives, not the defining moment *of* their lives. Their differences show up in their choice of disclosure strategies, their reactions to reprisals, and how they have adapted to life after whistleblowing.

Let me introduce these people to you. First we have Philip Nitschke, a young doctor caught in a major cover-up at the Royal Darwin Hospital over its capacity to cope with a medical emergency if a United States nuclear warship had an accident in Darwin Harbour. Then there is David Obendorf, a dedicated veterinary pathologist from Tasmania, who was spurred into action by the nightmarish prospect that inadequate controls might lead to outbreaks of exotic animal diseases. The more he expressed his concerns, the more his organisation developed industrial deafness.

Next is a Presbyterian minister from Sydney, Reverend Peter Cameron, whose support for women and homosexuals put him on a collision course with conservative elements in the church and led to his being charged with heresy.

Behind him are three academics: Peter Jesser, Professor Kim Sawyer and Associate Professor David Rindos. Their experiences offer frightening insights into the secrecy and authoritarianism prevailing at academic institutions as the new imperatives of corporatism meet a power structure left over from the Middle Ages.

Next up, wiping his glasses for a better view, is John Millard, an articulate and intelligent ABC journalist. Millard loved the concept of the Australian Broadcasting Corporation. He loved its Australianness, its fearless editorial independence and its truth-speaking. Soon he found all these qualities being damaged by a new breed of managers determined to turn the grand old lady into a sassy young thing with plenty of commercial appeal. The ABC's traditional support of whistleblowers dried up when the blowing came from inside.

Kevin Lindeberg, who follows, still has a spring to his step, remarkable for someone who has been in whistleblower mode since 1990. Lindeberg was sacked as an official of a white-collar union after he took up the cause of a member who was being rolled by a State government department. There was more to it than that, though. Lindeberg was also asking too many questions about how the union managed its superannuation fund. One thing led to another, and critical documents were shredded on the instructions of the Queensland Cabinet. 'Shreddergate', as it has become known, is regarded as one of Australia's clearest documented accounts of an official cover-up.

Behind Lindeberg I notice the grizzled face of Mick Skrijel. He looks like a worn-out boxer. Little wonder – he's been in the ring with them all: the National Crime Authority, the South Australian and Victorian police forces, the Australian Federal Police, the Supreme Court of Victoria, the Victorian Police Ombudsman and countless politicians, bureaucrats, lawyers and official inquiries. All for what? For justice, Mick will tell you. Way back on a blue sky day in 1978, in the sea off Southend in South Australia, Mick says he saw a box of heroin bobbing in the water. He thought he was doing the right thing when he reported it to the police. His life since has been hell.

The last two members of our cast are Brendon Kelson and Michael McKernan. It seems only yesterday that these two men were in executive control of the Australian War Memorial. Little did they know that, while they were busy developing the Memorial as a dignified remembrance to fallen Australians, another war had started – a war against them and, as a federal judge finally ruled, against natural justice too. Their chapter illustrates what can happen when a culture of complaint develops without regard for the truth.[1]

Such is the line-up. You will note that they are all white males. This is parly because whistleblowing is not an across-the-demographic-board phenomenon. It is quite culturally specific; it relies on a certain faith in the existing mechanisms of redress, and this faith is not shared by all groups in our society. For example, I know of only one Aboriginal whistleblower, and that person feared so much for her life that she went into witness protection in Brisbane, never to speak out again. Similarly, many immigrants have lived under oppressive regimes and are unlikely to disclose because they have a profound distrust of the authorities. Young people, too, are deeply alienated from the adult system of rule. Confronted with the possibility of exposing wrongdoing, many kids would simply say 'why bother?' Furthermore, all these groups tend to be so far down the hierarchy in the workplace that they seldom find out what people in power are up to, and even if they come across abuses they are unlikely to disclose because their employment is insecure.

The fact that, with one exception, there are no women in the book is a matter of concern to me. The exception is Tristan Pawsey, Philip Nitschke's partner. When I started working on this project, I decided that I would not write about anyone without their consent. I figured that they had suffered enough. I approached some women whistleblowers for their stories, but they declined. Some did not know me well enough to trust me with their biographies, while others feared further ramifications. The book on female whistleblowers has still to be written, but I'm sure it will offer many insights, especially into the effects of disclosure on family and personal relationships.

3 Radioactive Whistleblowing
Philip Nitschke

There is little doubt that the experience at the Royal Darwin Hospital prepared me well for the onslaught as the euthanasia issue broke. I had watched with jaded disbelief as I was marginalised by the profession. Those few doctors who continued with their support (Tristan my partner being one) found this course harder and harder, and at some point decided that it was professionally damaging. I had become used to watching the evaporation of this support as one was systematically demonised. – Philip Nitschke.[1]

Some years before Philip Nitschke was catapulted into national prominence as a leader of the euthanasia movement, he was honing his advocacy skills and social conscience at the 300-bed Royal Darwin Hospital (RDH). The story of his experiences in that period suggests that whistleblowing in the medical world can be a health hazard.[2] It speaks also of the collateral damage to relationships when one partner becomes the target of organisational fury and the other struggles to adjust. Nitschke's partner, Tristan, will speak in these pages of that damage.

Nitschke came late to his medical career. He started out with a PhD in physics from Flinders University in Adelaide, where he learnt more than most people about how Armageddon was locked up in the atom. This insight would be used to great effect when he became a medico in Darwin.

Nitschke went to the Northern Territory in 1973, at a time of intense community conflict about Australia's mining and export of uranium. During his first stint in the Territory the report of the Ranger uranium inquiry was released and a Uranium Producers'

Forum was established to counter the peace groups, environmentalists and Aboriginal land rights activists who were calling for a ban on uranium mining. Nitschke was in the Territory as an anti-nuclear activist, but also as a white worker for the Aboriginal land rights cause. He worked with the Gurindji people at Wave Hill, which had been the site of Australia's first land rights action in June 1966.[3]

Nitschke often travelled to Katherine on station business. He recalls:

It was a difficult time, with feelings in Katherine running high about what the implications were for the pastoral industry ... So-called 'white advisers' working for the Gurindji were hated.

In Katherine Nitschke met Mike Reed, a junior Parks and Wildlife ranger in charge of Katherine Low Level, the camp where Nitschke stayed. As Nitschke describes it, his relationship with Reed was hardly love at first sight:

Reed at one stage chucked me off the camping area, claiming that I 'littered' and that my Toyota 'leaked oil'. Two years later I applied for and got a job in Central Australia as a ranger and was sent to work at Simpson's Gap Park. Within a few months, and before I was made permanent, Reed had written a letter from Katherine, urging NT Parks and Wildlife to get rid of me. Reasons given were that I had joined Parks and Wildlife to further the territorial interests of Aboriginal groups. The same letter also claimed that my qualifications ... were 'false', and that I 'littered'![4]

The letter was sent to the Northern Territory Reserves Board in 1976 soon after they employed Nitschke as a park ranger. Nitschke repeatedly tried to get a copy of this letter, but he claims the Northern Territory Reserves Board denied that they had it. It only came to light recently. It was apparently stolen from Reed's office 'for insurance' by one of his staff, who reportedly turned it over to the Australian Labor Party on his deathbed.

In the letter, Reed said that he did not wish to denigrate Nitschke unnecessarily. His motive in writing was to inform the Board that in his opinion employing Nitschke was a bad mistake. Reed referred to Nitschke as 'very radical, untrustworthy and dangerous'.[5] He claimed that the local policeman at Wave Hill had told him that Nitschke was suspected of 'illegal deals', but there was insufficient evidence to arrest him. Reed further advised that the police viewed Nitschke as an activist financed by a civil rights group at Flinders University, and he described Nitschke's personal hygiene as 'shocking' and his manner as 'obnoxious'.

What was the basis of Reed's animosity? Take your pick! Certainly the white establishment feared white civil-rights' workers. This fear was part of the multi-directional paranoia that has long characterised sections of the Territory's white population. If the invasion wasn't going to come from the north (China, Indonesia), it was going to come from the south, in the shape of standover tactics from Canberra or white activists 'stirring' up the Aborigines.

Nitschke and Reed again clashed after Nitschke set up an anti-Pine Gap group in Alice Springs.[6] Then for some years the two men's paths diverged. Reed was being groomed as a successor to Les McFarlain, the local member of the Northern Territory Assembly. He rose through the ranks to become Acting Director of Parks and Wildlife, then eventually entered the Assembly as Member for Katherine. At about the same time Nitschke went south to study medicine. He graduated from the University of Sydney in 1988 and went straight to Darwin in January 1989 as a resident medical officer (RMO) at Royal Darwin Hospital. By this stage, Reed had become Minister of Health in the Northern Territory.

For the first four years Nitschke's relations with the hospital administration were harmonious, but an activist spirit was incubating within him. On 3 March 1993 he addressed the Northern Territory Trades and Labour Council. His talk, which was critical of Medicare, was reported on ABC TV and stimulated what the Senate Committee of Privileges later described as a 'passionate letter' from Mike Reed.[7] Reed complained that Nitschke had breached the silencing provisions in the General Orders governing public servants in the Northern Territory. Nitschke was 'counselled' the next day, and the ABC apologised to Reed for having failed to make clear that Nitschke was not expressing the hospital's official view. This clash was a foretaste of more serious conflicts to come.

On Friday 26 March 1993 Darwin awoke with mixed feelings to a visitor slipping into its harbour. The nuclear-powered submarine USS *Houston*, with a crew of 133, had arrived for a six-day visit. Officials were very tense. Naval security was there to ensure that no member of the public could get on board, and water police maintained a 600-metre security zone around the vessel.

The previous morning the hospital's accident and emergency staff – including Philip Nitschke – had been told they were to spend that day and the next afternoon in training courses dealing with casualties of radiation contamination.[8] Nitschke publicly questioned the timing of the training program and suggested that it was a last-minute reaction by the hospital, which he claimed did not have a disaster plan in place, in spite of the fact that all capital cities visited by nuclear-powered ships are required to have such a plan.[9]

Because of his background in physics, Nitschke had previously been selected to attend nuclear safety training courses in Victoria. 'On return,' he wrote to me, 'I was supposedly the "radiation safety officer" at RDH. Yet I only heard of the training courses to be held that day by an announcement on the notice board.'[10] The RDH general manager, Dr David Douglas, quickly countered Nitschke's allegation that the training courses were too little too late with a media release asserting that RDH had adequately prepared key staff for nuclear emergencies.[11] The hospital administration also asked Nitschke to explain why he had gone public with his concerns rather than conveying them to the Medical Superintendent.

While medical and nursing staff were attending afternoon training sessions with the jejune title 'Management of Trauma Casualties: External Radiation Contamination',[12] thirty-six RMOs held a protest forum in support of Nitschke and his claims. Twelve other medicos who were members of the Medical Association for the Prevention of War, based in Alice Springs, declared full support for Nitschke and signed a letter to the Director of the Health Department calling on him to 'address the issue openly rather than stifling debate through disciplinary action against Dr Nitschke'.[13]

Understanding the nature of the hospital's response is crucial to understanding the wider pattern of reprisals against whistleblowers. The single event that does most to start management reprisals and lock the whistleblower into organisational conflict is the whistleblower's decision to step outside the organisation and address the public directly through the media. In the eyes of management, particularly those with something to hide or those who lord it over structures where accountability is deficient, public disclosure is a supreme act of rebellion. Managers do not use those words, of course. Instead, they rebuke the whistleblower for 'betrayal', 'ignoring the guidelines', 'disloyalty' and 'making false accusations'. While the public disclosure is an act of socially responsible dissent, unless the discloser is protected it is an also an act of career suicide. This pattern of public disclosure and management reprisal is repeated in virtually all the cases profiled in this book. It is a set-piece of the whistleblowing experience.

The initial reaction to Nitschke's statement masked a much deeper conflict about the ethical limits to Northern Territory economic growth. Only in this context can we understand why Nitschke and his colleagues were viewed as dangerous people who had to be bludgeoned into silence. The deeper story goes something like this. After the United States lost its strategic base at Subic Bay in the Philippines, it went shopping for a replacement location. In 1992 the Territory government of Marshall Perron sent a formal proposal to the US Defence Department offering Darwin harbour as a permanent base for US ships. Local politicians and business people were ecstatic when they discovered that Darwin was on the short-list. On the day the USS *Houston* left Darwin, Perron said, 'Unlike the Labor Party, the Government would be more than happy if US ships – nuclear or otherwise – chose Darwin.'[14] Nitschke and his medical colleagues were seen as spoilers who were making a noise that might go all the way to the Pentagon.

On 2 April 1993 the hospital's RMOs held a further meeting, at which about sixty doctors expressed concern about RDH's nuclear disaster contingency plan and unanimously passed three resolutions critical of hospital management. Meanwhile Nitschke, under attack from the Darwin business lobby, replied to the management directive to explain why he went to the media. He did not deny that he had talked with reporters, but explained that he had done so as a spokesperson for the Medical Association for the Prevention of War.[15]

This statement carried no weight with RDH administration, but they were forced to bide their time until they regained the ground they had lost by mishandling the early phase of the conflict and sparking resistance from the RMOs. On 15 April 1993 RDH management, the RMO Association and the Northern Territory Health Department issued a joint media release in which the hospital made the remarkable admission that it was ill-prepared for a nuclear accident from visiting US warships.[16] The hospital also acknowledged that Nitschke had made 'considerable efforts' to publicise the issue of nuclear accident unpreparedness. It further noted that Nitschke's advice to the hospital about how it should prepare itself had been ignored and that there had been little or no acknowledgement of the special expertise he brought to this issue.[17]

End of story, you think? Read on.

One of the doctors' chief complaints was the lack of warning of a visiting nuclear ship. There was no way this could be remedied, as any such warning would have been a breach of secrecy, unacceptable both to the Americans and to the sycophantic government in Canberra.[18] What chance had the whistleblower – even with the support of his colleagues – against the combined force of local economic interests and Australia's traditional appeasement of American foreign policy?

By July 1993 the Northern Territory government and RDH were back on the offensive, while Nitschke persisted with his anti-nuclear campaign. On 2 July Nitschke addressed the Northern Territory Branch of the Public Health Association. The title of his talk was 'Public Health and Private Conscience: Whistleblowing and its Impact on Health'. This, incidentally, was one of the first public statements about whistleblowing in Australia. Nitschke discussed previous examples of whistleblowing, and talked about the action at RDH over nuclear accident preparedness, as well as his fight for a needle exchange in Darwin, which was vigorously opposed by Health Minister Reed. Again his address was reported on the ABC. Reed heard the report and fumed down the phone to Pauline Wilson, the Medical Superintendent at RDH. Nitschke was again called in to explain. This time his explanation, supplemented by a strong protest letter from the Public Health Association, was accepted by Wilson.

Nitschke's opponents in hospital management, however, were determined to get rid of him. They sought advice from the highest levels of the Health Department as to whether RDH could get away with cancelling Nitschke's 1993 contract in mid-term. In view of the Medical Superintendent's acceptance of Nitschke's explanation, they were advised to back off.[19]

On 20 July Nitschke gave evidence to a Senate Industry Committee hearing in Darwin on behalf of the Medical Association for the Prevention of War. His evidence was reported on radio. Twelve hours later Mike Reed issued an attack on Nitschke. From being acknowledged as an expert in nuclear protection in April, Nitschke was now, according to Reed, clinging to 'outdated and irrelevant anti-nuclear beliefs'.[20] In his media release Reed stated that RDH was well prepared for nuclear accidents. He also suggested that Nitschke should leave RDH:

Dr Nitschke seems to have trouble coming to grips with the fact that public policy is not set by him, but by the Northern Territory Government and the Health and Community Services Department. If Dr Nitschke cannot cope with this simple fact of life, he has the option of considering going into private practice.[21]

No doubt Nitschke was grateful for this gratuitous career advice, but he was staying put. On 14 August he wrote to the Secretary of the Senate Privileges Committee, enclosing the proof copy of his evidence of 20 July. He also drew the Committee's attention to Reed's media statement and said that the release had 'certainly disadvantaged me and made my position more precarious'.[22] Although Reed's press secretary claimed that the Minister did not know that Nitschke's radio comments emanated from his Senate evidence the previous day, the Senate Privileges Committee found that Reed's statement could be regarded as constituting a threat to Nitschke.[23]

Four points can be noted in Reed's outburst. First, his evident frustration at dealing with someone who won't toe the line is a common theme in all dissenter stories. Secondly, the fact that Nitschke was personally attacked is an example of the strategy of shooting the messenger. Third, Reed sidelined Nitschke's constructive role as someone with an independent perspective, able to stimulate the deliberative process at RDH. Finally, Reed adopted a standard tactic against dissent: 'take it or leave'.

Reed's subordinates soon took up the Minister's public pronouncement that Nitschke should go. This is what I call the 'à Becket Response' after Thomas à Becket, the dissenting Archbishop of Canterbury who was assassinated by four of Henry II's knights after they heard the king uttering in anguish – and, as history has judged, rhetorically – 'Who will rid me of this turbulent priest?' When powerful people make vague and ambiguous threats, there always seem to be underlings ready to give substance to the pronouncements. These days, though, their superiors seldom feel the same guilt as Henry II, who did penance at Becket's grave.

Nitschke went into his reappointment interview on the afternoon of 21 July, only a day after his much-publicised appearance before the Senate Industry Committee. On the morning of the interview RDH General Manager Douglas met with Lyn Schmidt, the hospital's Human Resources Manager, and soon-to-retire Medical Superintendent Wilson. Douglas must have felt unsure of things. He had only become general manager seventeen days before the USS *Houston* brought controversy to Darwin. During the meeting Douglas made his concerns about Nitschke known to the other two.[24]

On 31 August Nitschke received a letter from RDH saying his contract would not be renewed at the end of 1993. This was in spite of the fact that he had five years' experience and was the most senior doctor applying to work in the unpopular accident and emergency department. The decision was quite contrary to the hospital's normal practice, as it was always looking for staff at that time of the year. Hospital authorities cited a variety of reasons for their decision, including complaints from staff and patients about Nitschke's medical competence.[25]

'This came to me as a great shock,' said Nitschke. Eleven days later an editorial in the *Northern Territory News* joined the assault on him, claiming that he had breached his conditions of employment by making public comment. The editorial continued:

Presumably Dr Nitschke was well aware of the employment conditions when he accepted the appointment, yet he chose to break the rules. Dr Nitschke was given repeated warnings but obviously he preferred to ignore them. Now, neither Dr Nitschke nor anyone else can have his cake and eat it. If he signs a bit of paper accepting certain conditions of employment he should abide by them. If he finds those conditions unacceptable, then the next course of action is quite clear. He should resign. There would be those who argue that the public good transcends those things ... But there are well-established procedures to deal with any problems internally. Dr Nitschke chose to go public instead.[26]

It is ironic that these sentiments should come from a newspaper that relies heavily on leaks from public-sector workers to source its stories.

Three days after this editorial was published, Reed again attacked Nitschke and said he should go. Reed's statement concluded:

Dr Nitschke's continued attacks on Royal Darwin Hospital are typically inaccurate and sensational, and as far as I am concerned, are totally irrelevant to the operation of Territory health services ... If Dr Nitschke doesn't like the situation, I have no doubt that RDH will be able to scrape by without him.[27]

RDH doctors rallied around Nitschke and demanded that management apologise, reinstate him and admit that it was orchestrating a vendetta against him. Some hospital patients also took up a petition in Nitschke's favour.[28]

At this stage Nitschke made contact with Jean Lennane, the Sydney psychiatrist who was President of Whistleblowers Australia. Lennane warned him that his close relationships would be endangered by the fallout from his whistleblowing. These tensions can be acute if the non-whistleblower partner is naive about the politics of disclosure or antagonistic to the partner becoming a whistleblower. Even when, as in Nitschke's case, the partner shares the whistleblower's view of the disclosure situation, this identification does not immunise the relationship from stress and strain.

Nitschke's partner was a senior paediatrician at RDH. As he puts it, Tristan Pawsey 'supported me throughout all this, and found herself ostracised as the hospital split on the issue'. Their relationship suffered, but it survived because of her sympathy and ready support:

She found herself increasingly radicalised by the experience, and at one point climbed out onto the 12th floor hospital roof at 4 am to unfurl a huge 'Free Speech?' banner, and then left the roof super-gluing keys into the lift well locks – an act of subversion and vandalism she would never have contemplated even a few months earlier.[29]

Pawsey has with great candour and sincerity shared her perspectives of being caught up in Nitschke's battle with the hospital and health authorities. Her story remains an indispensable part of the Nitschke narrative.

Up until 1993 Pawsey's and Nitschke's working life was largely in tune with the rest of the hospital, even though they were regarded by some as unusual, even eccentric. With the advent of the nuclear ship issue, Pawsey says the 'veneer of normality I felt changed'.[30]

Pawsey has always felt alienated from the ideology of mainstream medicine. She coped by 'staying out of trouble'. This strategy always niggled her conscience. She was not proud of her non-involvement, but as she explains, 'It was a matter of survival for me in what I experienced as a hostile and stressful environment.'[31] It was in this context that she met Nitschke:

... it was like the world opened up for me and for the first time in ages I felt that I had met someone who shared the same thoughts about not just medicine but in fact most aspects of life really – aspects I had kept hidden for years, and I felt less alone than ever before in my life.[32]

Pawsey admits being shocked at the swiftness that Nitschke went into campaign mode after the *USS Houston* sailed into Darwin harbour.[33] Her learning curve was sharp and before long she joined the battle. She became adept at analysing each new piece of information, and soon stood at Nitschke's side: 'I found I was very useful to Philip ... as a negotiator and go-between. I seemed to enhance Philip's credibility.'[34]

She admits that a contrary perception was alive, which saw her as misguided by the apparent Svengali powers of Nitschke. Pawsey of course did not see it that way. Nitschke helped her develop her wild side, but it was her side, not his. Coming from a protective family life with parents wanting to see the good in all, half of her was not ready for a campaign against power. Up until the *Houston* issue she had thought radically, and acted non-radically. The Houston campaign gave her something important – that valuable synchronicity between thought and deed. But it came with costs:

Our relationship suffered terribly – we used to take it out on each other instead of directing our anger where it was needed to go. This wasn't helped by the sheer volume of people traipsing through the house (media and supporters). The phone went non-stop and I felt we had very little privacy. I seem to remember that we didn't have sex for weeks on end. For weeks we were literally under siege in our flat as tension between Philip and the hospital reached its zenith.[35]

Pawsey was swept up in an imbroglio beyond her design and control. In an important sense Nitschke's central role marginalised her. To the outside eye she looked like the magician's assistant. Her needs were not being met:

Needless to say my six months' break [after her paediatric exams] in which I had planned to do all sorts of things just went up in smoke. I felt very resentful about this and felt that Philip was unable during this time to consider my feelings at all. He felt he was having to fight for his life and although I understood this, I was having my own crisis really and needed him more than ever just at the time he had the least to give me.[36]

Reciprocity, the spinal cord of healthy relationships, can snap when the whistleblower is set upon by the organisation in vendetta mode. Suddenly domestic life takes the force of the external conflict. Pawsey commented on this:

I remember one terrible night where Philip and I were really angry with each other and Philip kicked a foam esky to pieces – relatively benign really but it frightened me to see us both so out of control – not a situation I'd been in before. I think it was that moment that I realised just how dangerous it could be to take it out on each other rather than 'seeing the wood from the trees' and making a real effort to direct the frustration at those who were putting us in this position. I won't deny that a huge amount of damage was done to the relationship however during this time.[37]

Nitschke's battle with RDH kept his relationship with Pawsey hostage for the rest of 1993. By early 1994 she could take it no more:

The situation ended with me being exhausted beyond belief and seeking refuge in South Australia. I went on a houseboat holiday with my parents and I remember all I cared about was bird watching to an obsessive degree. I really could hardly talk about anything at all. My parents were very woried about me.[38]

Pawsey knew that she could not drift down the Murray forever. She took a job as a registrar in child psychiatry at the Women's and Children's Hospital in Adelaide. In retrospect, not a good move. The job was stressful and she says that she was unprepared. Even though she and Nitschke made efforts to reconcile, they were both shattered by the experiences at RDH. Reconciliation would have to wait as Pawsey went through what she calls 'a strange and long healing process.' At the beginning, she plummetted into a deep depression, and took all of 1995 off. She returned to work in Adelaide in late 1995. Her relationship with Nitschke had survived. Like the Samurai sword, it was beaten and heated to new levels of strength. About this she says:

Nietszche says that anything that doesn't kill you makes you stronger. I learned I had skills and abilities I didn't think I had. By being 'forced out into the open' I think it gave me confidence in a way to be more honest. It was a process of politicalisation too – I'm much wiser now about how the world works ... We had of course to discover some difficult truths about each other. In my case I realised that Philip could be ruthlessly exploitive and ignore my needs to an extraordinary extent – in his case that I would lose my temper with sheer frustration and I began to be really demanding in a way that I had never been before.
    Now I'd say that we are both much wiser, more loving and accept and understand each other's needs better. I think we communicate better now. Other difficult things have come and gone and we have survived them.[39]

The calamities of the 'other' in whistleblower narratives remain for the most part un-noted and un-voiced. We need a heightened inquisitiveness into the effects of disclosure on those in the whistleblower's personal orbit. Not only will this validate these 'other' experiences, it will also show that the politics of disclosure always ensure a three-cornered contest between the whistleblower, family and management. Like a high-velocity bullet, management reprisals fired at the whistleblower also hit her or his family. Sometimes a vindictive management will know full well about this pass-on effect. Other times management will be oblivious to it.

How partners and family cope with disclosure-reprisal is still poorly understood. It seems from the case studies presented here that if the unit was strong prior to the disclosure conflicts, then it will remain strong. Another strengthening factor is the similarity in worldview between the whistleblower and partner. Pawsey understood the political culture that Nitschke operated in and shared his views on critical issues like power, medical service and hospital admistration. As a community we are not yet in a position to help families and couples deal with the social effects of whistleblowing. Pawsey's account will start some fresh thinking in this area.

In returning to Nitschke we find that by September 1993 the conflict seemed beyond resolution. Nitschke continued to make media disclosures, and health officials continued to rebuke him. On 27 September Health Department Secretary Ray Norman wrote to Nitschke asking him to explain why he had publicly criticised Northern Territory Health Services on ABC Radio.[40]

Nitschke was in trouble. The next day he left Darwin for Canberra and Adelaide to seek legal advice, and to address the Senate Standing Committee on Industry, Science and Technology about his recent treatment by RDH management. The following day RDH doctors were outraged when management prevented their update on Nitschke from being circulated through the hospital mailing system.[41] Talk of a strike was in the air. On 10 October doctors unanimously agreed to close down all but accident and emergency services at the hospital for twenty-four hours on the following Thursday. The doctors were angered both by the treatment of their colleague and by the hospital's refusal to review its medical selection processes. This strike was averted when the protagonists agreed to bring in the Australian Medical Association (AMA) as mediator.

Meanwhile certain staff were making written complaints about Nitschke. One from Sister X deserves comment:

1. Dr Nitschke uses offensive language when discussing management around nursing staff and patients ...
4. Dr Nitschke lacks interest in obstetrics which is evidenced by his lack of empathy and compassion when dealing with mothers. He displays no interest in their babies' condition and progress and does not explore the mother's emotional well-being.
5. Dr Nitschke's appearance is unprofessional and his body odour is objectionable to staff and pregnant women. He presents on duty with dirty fingernails, unironed stubby shorts and malodorous sneakers. I am ashamed to introduce him as a colleague to my patients.[42]

In highly disciplined workplaces there is often an outbreak of complaints against the whistleblower when disclosures of wrongdoing are made. Under normal circumstances staff such as Sister X might not have complained or, if they had, management would have handled their complaints with some degree of suspicion. It is quite a different matter when the person who is complained against is one who has publicly questioned the probity of management or attempted to expose wrongdoing within the system. Once whistleblowers are involved in a controversial campaign, their resistance to complaints is decisively weakened. As the number of complaints increases, the principle that the whistleblower is innocent until proven guilty is further eroded. The consequence is to subvert the person's role from discloser to complained-against. Suddenly he has dirty fingernails, and it is made to sound like a hanging offence.

Sister X's complaint was forwarded through Nursing Administration to the Medical Superintendent's office, where it was filed but not forgotten. Nitschke recalls:

I was first made aware of its existence when the NT News contacted me saying 'We have in our possession a letter which we plan to publish, and which you may care to comment on.' They faxed the letter to me that night, and I felt immediately sick, and threatened them with legal action if they went ahead and published. They didn't publish, and it was never clear how the letter found its way to the media from medical administration.[43]

Nitschke also had to cope with rumours that he was gay, and that he was driven to attack Reed because he believed the minister was against homosexuals.[44]

This was the poisonous climate in which the Australian Medical Association was brought in as mediator. The AMA's attempt to break the conflict was in the form of a review with nine terms of reference, focusing on allegations of victimisation against Nitschke, the role of the General Manager, the process that led to the non-renewal of Nitschke's contract, and Nitschke's attempt to introduce new paediatric analgesic procedures into Accident and Emergency.[45] But where was the review into the ethics of the push to make Darwin a US naval base, which was the fundamental issue at stake between the 'Nitschke side' and the 'hospital side'? Facing such a massive geopolitical issue, how could the micro-processes of dispute resolution in the hospital adequately respond?

The day after the AMA review was announced, the government's Central Promotions Appeal Board brought down its own report on the non-renewal of Nitschke's contract.[46] This report was compiled without input from RDH medical officers, including Nitschke, or their association, all of whom had boycotted the proceedings. The government report found no official wrongdoing and went so far as to commend the selection procedures at RDH. The RMOs regarded the report as 'unsatisfactory and an administrative whitewash'.[47]

The AMA report appeared a few weeks later. While it at least focused on Nitschke's whistleblowing, it was influenced by common anxieties and prejudices about public interest disclosures and those who make them. The author of the report, Peter Arnold, at that time President of the NSW Branch of the AMA, stated at the beginning:

While issues of profound philosophical and political importance were originally at the heart of the matter, the resulting discord has been compounded by the unwise use of the media and the indulgence by some in inflammatory language ... There was little in fact that could not have been settled through calm rational discourse behind closed doors.[48]

Arnold did not spell out what these 'issues of profound philosophical and political importance' were. His axe was too sharp when he blamed the media alone for overemphasising the personal dimensions of social conflicts. One cannot help feeling that a deeper issue of accountability lay at the heart of Arnold's position. Could it be that when he saw 'media' he thought 'public', and concluded that most conflicts in the medical world are not of 'public' concern except in the last instance?

Arnold correctly observed that the media and the protagonists in the RDH conflict had used each other for the airing of allegations and rebuttals. The media could have been more responsible, but to treat them merely as a source of sensationalism is to ignore the fact that people in positions of power and trust have responsibility to maintain rich lines of accountability back out to the wider public.

When it came to conflict between the individual and the institution, Arnold took the institution's side, declaring that:

[It is] ... only in the ultimate that an act of whistleblowing is justified. The mere speaking out in public on an issue concerning a person's place of employment, without exhaustive efforts having been made to ventilate the issues through all available channels, both formal and informal, both direct and indirect, is mischievous and cannot be tolerated by any responsible employer. It is not sufficient that the path of grievance and of protest be strewn with boulders. It is necessary that the path be totally obstructed by an impenetrable brick wall of such height and length that it can neither be scaled nor circumvented.[49]

Arnold's view of whistleblowing as an act of last resort, and as an act indicative of organisational malaise, appears to have been influenced by a note to that effect in the *British Medical Journal* of the previous year.[50] Certainly when organisations are structurally incapable of responding to internal dissent and grievances, people will be more pressured to use external avenues. But is it right to view whistleblowing as a last resort? If we accept this position, the public will never get information that they are entitled to until the last moment – and not at all if the conflict is always resolved internally.

Arnold's inference that Nitschke and his colleagues were trigger-happy and went too quickly to the media belies the fact that they did make efforts to settle the matter internally. Whether these efforts were exhaustive enough to satisfy Arnold's criteria is another question.

Mention should also be made of Arnold's view that conflicts can be resolved with a 'calm and rational discourse behind closed doors'. This assumes that reason will invariably triumph if conflicts are resolved privately. It marginalises passion, opinions and strong views publicly expressed. It also betrays a naive understanding of power. Professional and organisational conflicts are not Oxford debates. This is an antiquated and inappropriate way to address modern disputation in an increasingly toxic organisational milieu. Often the only thing behind closed doors is the table around which the strong face off the weak.

Furthermore, it is impossible to rely on 'calm, rational discourse behind closed doors' when people in power are reluctant to accept responsibility. When Arnold asked who was responsible for not giving Nitschke a first-round offer of employment, he met a chorus of denials. 'Not I,' said the General Manager;[51] 'Not I,' said the Deputy Medical Superintendent;[52] 'Not I,' said the Medical Superintendent.[53] In the face of such behaviour, how long must whistleblowers remain 'rational' and keep their grievances quiet?

Arnold's assessment was dependent on his interpretation of these denials. Where Nitschke and his colleagues saw retribution, Arnold saw a 'misunderstanding' between the three senior hospital administrators.[54] He gravitated to the least-worst-case scenario. In fairness to Arnold, though, he did squarely focus on the most powerful person in the hospital at the time, the General Manager. He pointed out that the General Manager had 'made his attitude concerning the continued employment of Dr Nitschke quite clear' to the Medical Superintendent, the Deputy Medical Superintendent and the Manager Human Resource Services 'before and during the time of the recruitment process and on the day that Dr Nitschke was interviewed'. He added that the General Manager had known that the Deputy Medical Superintendent (DMS), who was at the hospital on provisional registration from Sri Lanka, was a more junior staff member:

[The General Manager] has acknowledged to the inquiry that the management relationship between them is such that [the DMS] would be likely to act in accordance with his wishes. The DMS has told the inquiry that she knew of the concerns of a 'senior' officer and that she was obliged to proceed in accordance with those concerns.[55]

Some of Arnold's conclusions were favourable to Nitschke. At one point Arnold congratulated him for his efforts to get the hospital on to a better pain-reduction program for children.[56]

Arnold expected, somewhat unrealistically as we now know in hindsight, that his report would produce a solution to the problem at RDH. On receipt of the draft the author of the government's report on RMO selection procedures, Bob Horne, threatened to sue for defamation, and the Deputy Medical Superintendent and the General Manager objected to its public release. In response, the draft was substantially revised, but Horne continued to threaten defamation action. As a result, Arnold and the AMA lawyers decided that the report should not be made public.[57]

While this was going on, Nitschke's application for a 1994 RMO position was reassessed. In a two to one decision, Nitschke was again not recommended. On 8 November, however, he was finally reappointed after the new Medical Superintendent, Alan Walker, pushed his application forward against opposition from senior RDH officers. This decision was accepted by the General Manager, who summed up the situation as a trade-off between the 'disruptive effects of appointing him' and the need to have 'a pair of hands'.

At this stage the situation became even more messy. The shadow health spokesperson, Maggie Hickey, tabled a leaked copy of the Arnold report in the Legislative Assembly. Mike Reed accused the AMA of breaking agreements over the release of the report,[58] and the matter of whether Nitschke was punished for his Senate Committee evidence was referred to the Senate Privileges Committee.

At the same time the *Northern Territory News*, Nitschke's media nemesis, carried a front-page story about an incident at the hospital in which Nitschke was allegedly three hours late in responding to a pager, and when questioned by a nurse was reported to have said, 'I don't give a fuck about the patients.'[59] Nitschke responded that he was under considerable pressure and the comments were not meant literally. A few days later the *Northern Territory News* ran another editorial rebuking Nitschke for his 'media antics'.[60]

At the time Nitschke was doing his Diploma of Obstetrics and Gynaecology, and was finding it impossible to work with some of the nurses. He was under enormous pressure from nurses like Sister X who, he said, waited in a predatory way to pounce on his next mistake. Nitschke readily acknowledges that his work deteriorated.

In desperation he wrote to Marilyn Beaumont, the Federal President of the Australian Nursing Federation. The reply he received was 'depressing'. Beaumont pointed out that nurses, who she claimed often found themselves in the role of whistleblowers, had a duty to rid hospitals of incompetent doctors.[61]

In the event, Nitschke did not accept the offer of reappointment. His position in some sections of the hospital was untenable. He decided instead to do postgraduate studies in gynaecology and obstetrics, encouraged by Dr Walker, his most senior supporter at RDH. Even if he had wanted to, Nitschke could not pursue these studies in RDH's Department of Obstetrics and Gynaecology, which was in a ferment of frustration and anger. This was partly to do with the long-term absence of a specialist in that department and the dissatisfaction of the midwives, who, despite strenuous efforts, would not work with Nitschke.

In facilitating Nitschke's move to another hospital for his postgraduate work, Medical Superintendent Walker wrote to a colleague:

The whole business has been something of a disaster. It has been not well managed by the hospital and I instinctively feel that I should on the basis of natural justice, try and do something for Philip Nitschke although he has been to a degree the cause of some of his own problems. I think he is a good doctor when he puts his mind to medical practice. He is a person of high intelligence and committed to unpopular causes and this is where he gets himself into a lot of trouble.[62]

Walker failed to get Nitschke a placement to complete his obstetrics diploma at Alice Springs, and Nitschke found his own position with the Lyell McEwin Health Service in Adelaide. He returned to Darwin in 1995, went into private practice and sailed straight into the eye of the euthanasia hurricane.

Nitschke stood against Kevin Andrews in the 1998 federal elections. Andrews was the Liberal Party backbencher who sponsored the controversial federal legislation which disarmed the Northern territory euthanasia act. Nitschke had been centrally involved in defending and shepherding the euthanasia bill through to enactment, and was bitterly disappointed at the actions of Andrews. After the elections Nitschke moved to Melbourne where he has set up a euthanasia advice clinic. Pawsey practises paediatric medicine from Adelaide.

Vetting the Vet

The David Obendorf Case

The real stories lie in the cover-up to protect a group of highly paid bureaucrats unethically dismantling a public instrumentality and its human cargo. – David Obendorf [1]

In April 1997 I asked Dr David Obendorf why he eventually agreed to an out-of-court settlement with his former employer, the Tasmanian Department of Primary Industry and Fisheries (DPIF).[2] This is what he said:

I'm no wimp but I was getting very tired physically and emotionally ... DPIF had been obliged to return me to work ... [but] they stopped paying me WC [workers' compensation] and offered me no job ... At the same time there was considerable pressure from HREOC [the Human Rights and Equal Opportunity Commission] and lawyers (on both sides) to accept the settlement. When my employer cut off my salary and would not give me a job, I was forced to go to DSS [Department of Social Security] for the dole ... I had terminated my lawyer of nearly two years ... [and used] the services of a ... legal advocate pro bono. She was replaced by yet another complete novice lawyer who had no feel for the case ... In addition the witnesses who had previously been so adamant and forthright 'got cold feet' at the prospect of a hearing and a subpoena ... Is that enough excuses? [3]

How can it be in that a highly qualified veterinary pathologist can find himself on a dole queue for making a public interest disclosure?

In 1992, at the start of his campaign of disclosure, Obendorf was one of about thirty staff employed at DPIF's Mt Pleasant Animal Health Laboratory (AHL) in Launceston. AHL's organisational structure was a paradox: a tight, self-assured hierarchy with a powerful decision-maker at the top lording it over faction-ridden divisions riddled with uncertainty as a result of incessant reviews. Insecurity, unaccountable power, low morale, work stress – just the setting for whistleblowing. In Obendorf's words:

Staff competed for scarce resources and favour from the Chief. Professional jealousies surfaced regularly ... People worked excessively ... with very little recognition. The Department was in constant review – 9 major reviews in 8 or 9 years. The atmosphere was turbulent, full of rumour and highly critical. Occupational stress, absenteeism, sick leave, excessive smokos and inefficiencies were the order of the day. Fractious interpersonal relationships were causing the workplace to be described by a union official for DPIF as 'toxic'. After [a] review the union [official] said he believed that it was a very sick workplace and no-one should be made to work under such psychologically stressful conditions. I used to call it a pathological (as opposed to pathology) laboratory.[4]

When public institutions experience these kinds of internal dramas, the public interest is invariably threatened. Services the public organisations are mandated to give no longer receive the attention they require. Staff become distracted by internal conflicts, standards of care plummet, and the provision of public goods deteriorates, sometimes quite rapidly. All this was true of the Animal Health Laboratory. In addition, the laboratory was being assailed from outside. It was an organisation in crisis.

AHL played a vital role in environmental testing, animal disease surveillance, quarantine monitoring, disease surveys, and research into new and emerging diseases. Obendorf's public interest disclosures only make sense in the context of the wider concern that AHL's disease-control function was being seriously curtailed through economic cutbacks, raising the spectre of new diseases entering Australia.

This has been a matter of growing concern throughout Australia in the 1990s. The destruction of papaya plantations in Northern

Queensland by a new strain of fruit fly,[5] the return of anthrax to the Shepparton–Tatura area of Victoria in the summer of 1996, the introduction of marine pests in ships' ballast water, the mysterious mass deaths of pilchards in our southern oceans,[6] the exposure of apple trees to the introduced fire blight,[7] a fear of 'mad chook' disease wiping out the Australian chicken meat industry, and the discovery of a virulent form of Newcastle's Disease on poultry farms in Western Sydney are all recent moments in Australia's long history of vulnerability to exotic pests and diseases. This historical anxiety is now being exacerbated by cutbacks to the nation's agricultural watchdogs. It was in response to rural industry's rising concern about the enforcement of controls that the federal government established a review of the Australian Quarantine Inspection Service in 1996.[8]

The point is that Obendorf was not a lone voice, although that is how he was treated. In 1995 Victorian vets had protested about the wholesale dismissal of staff from the regional veterinary laboratory at Benalla.[9] A former Department of Primary Industry official in Brisbane spoke out in 1994 about the decline of the department, which he described as a 'proud organisation with a 100-year history of high achievement in the interests of Queensland and world agriculture'.[10] In 1995 the Australian Conservation Foundation and the National Farmers Federation joined the growing list of organisations worried about the crisis in disease surveillance, while in New South Wales the Australian Veterinary Association expressed concern at the threatened closure of regional veterinary laboratories in Wagga Wagga and Armidale and called for a royal commission.[11]

The same dire concerns have been raised in Obendorf's home State. To quote a letter to the *Launceston Examiner* in 1996:

Currently we have outbreaks of hydatid disease when the State has been declared provisionally free of this; Ovine Johne's Disease has been uncontrollable since its first detection in the State in 1988; virulent footrot is reducing production in 35% of the State's sheep flock; enzootic bovine leucosis is occurring at an unknown level in the State's dairy herds; ovine brucellosis has no longer a recognised disease control program and new strains of salmonella (the peanut butter recall bacterium) capable of infecting humans continue to appear. Tasmania's primary produce exports are supported by the State's 'clean, green' image which was earned by many years of excellent work in disease surveillance and control. Over a decade the State's disease surveillance and control capability has been slowly whittled away until the clean, green image is now only a mirage.[12]

In 1992 and 1993 Obendorf made a series of reports to the Tasmanian Veterinary Board and the Tasmanian Branch of the Australian Veterinary Association on the matter of Australia's increasing vulnerability to exotic diseases as a result of the reduction in government surveillance services. These were to no avail. According to Obendorf, both organisations 'declined to investigate'.[13] Eventually Obendorf contacted Robin Gray, the Primary Industries Minister and former Tasmanian Premier. At the outset the Minister took Obendorf's reports seriously, and in March 1993 he requested a departmental investigation. Management asked for the evidence, assessed it and, according to Obendorf, advised the Minister that there was nothing to worry about.[14]

That was in April 1993. In July a number of Obendorf's work associates complained about him to Steve Balcombe, the Secretary of the Department. Obendorf says that these people were supporters of the laboratory manager with whom he had first raised his concerns about reduced disease surveillance.[15] Balcombe acknowledged that there were strong differences of opinion in the laboratory. He met Obendorf, and asked him to be more cooperative with colleagues.[16]

In this seemingly mundane request we can detect the dominant framework for interpreting and responding to conflict and disclosure. This framework reflects, preserves and even celebrates the cult of the individual. In this worldview there is only individual responsibility; no organisational malice, no systemic wrongdoing, nothing other than *individuals* doing the 'right' or 'wrong' thing. Choreographing this scene is an army of white-collar professionals – organisational psychologists, personnel officers, 'human resource' managers, equal opportunity officers, employee assistance workers and workplace counsellors – who are (often reluctantly) rushed into whistleblower–management conflicts. Blinkered by their faith in the cult of the individual, these professionals have enormous trouble seeing beyond the individual-as-victim and the individual-as-perpetrator to the political, social and economic headwaters of the conflict.

What happens instead is an exclusive focus on the players. So, in a laboratory cavitating with conflict over big issues such as its future role and how to maintain services after financial cutbacks, everything is finally boiled down to personal issues. In that distillation, David Obendorf becomes a centre of management attention, and initially (for there was more in store for him) he is told to be 'cooperative' – in other words, to be nice to people. Beyond these pious admonitions, nothing else was done when swift corrective action might have been most effective.

The matter was still festering through neglect one year after the initial complaints against Obendorf went to management. Then, in July 1994, Obendorf addressed the Wool Council of the Tasmanian Farmers and Graziers Association (TFGA) on a wool-research project he had completed the previous year. In answer to a question, he told the gathering that he could offer no commitments for future research in that area because many departmental activities, especially agricultural extension, had been put on hold. He describes the response from the farmers:

The farmers at the TFGA meeting were very surprised and aghast at the contraction in services and the stealthy changes to policy which were taking resources away from the traditional core business of DPIF. By the end of question-time some farmers wanted to know more and a few [L]iberal [Party] apologists were apparently more concerned that I had effectively 'blown the whistle on the Balcombe/Gray policy'. I suggested that they invite Balcombe to explain the new DPIF priorities to the TFGA.[17]

There ensued an extraordinary interview between Obendorf and a laboratory manager:

He was a scared, fence-sitting individual who tried to be 'all things to all people' and couldn't do it. He ... came to me to say that on the 'morrow' he would be betraying me in front of staff. He came into my room, closed the door, [and] told me of his instructions to cut me adrift, he then broke down and cried saying that he had a wife, three children under ten years and a mortgage and was frightened of the consequences if he didn't do as he was told.[18]

Shortly afterwards this man stepped down on medical advice due to stress, and it was suggested to the Secretary of DPIF that Obendorf was partly to blame for the 'division and unease' that led to the manager's demise.[19] Obendorf now became a clear target for reprisals. He was told that he was irrational and in need of personal counselling.[20] Work colleagues started to shun him. Obendorf had never experienced such virulent attacks on his integrity before. He instructed his solicitor to start defamation action against the government of Tasmania and the Secretary of DPIF,[21] and he countered that he had nothing to do with the manager's stress problems:

[The manager]'s doctors advised that he cease ... and he decided to step down as manager and take a lesser job for health reasons. I wrote to him expressing my concern for his well being. He replied with a letter saying he didn't blame me in any way for his medical condition ... He took a lesser Vet Officer job and then became very bitter and cynical about [his superiors].[22]

The stress on Obendorf was becoming unbearable. Balcombe placed him on leave with pay from July 1994.

In April 1994 Obendorf's union, the State Public Service Federation of Tasmania (SPSFT), had proposed a joint department–union review of the Animal Health Laboratory. DPIF agreed on the understanding:

that the Review group be authorised to gain an understanding of all the issues causing disputation or contributing to dissension and the high levels of stress clearly evident within the Animal Health Laboratory and the Animal Health Field Branch.[23]

DPIF went on to contradict its own requirement that 'all the issues' be canvassed when it stipulated that the review was to be limited to 'personnel issues', not conflicts over the future directions of AHL.[24]

The review met, heard from staff and reported to Balcombe, the DPIF Secretary, in early August 1994, having unearthed 'numerous serious personnel problems within the laboratory'.[25] Balcombe acknowledged that there were real problems at AHL and spoke in terms of 'rebuilding' the laboratory. Various reform measures were canvassed, without Obendorf's involvement. He was to remain on leave with pay.

Obendorf recounted what happened when he returned from his banishment in October 1994:

there was no job ... for me and no formal duty statement. [Michelle Moseley, Obendorf's immediate superior] went away and hurriedly prepared one. She told me I was to remove my belongings from the lab immediately and prepare to move to Hobart, 200 km away, to start work the next day. The [laboratory] ... staff were all at a 'conflict resolution' off campus seminar. Moseley told me I was not to interact with any staff and it was essential I was out of the building before they returned.[26]

In Hobart Obendorf was given Spartan accommodation, no computer, and told to work on two files, both of which referred to defunct rural land policies. He remained in exile until 23 December. Then, according to one report:

he was transferred back to Launceston and another office with no phone, no computer, no filing cabinet, a chair with broken casters, and a reading light with no globe.[27]

These attacks on Obendorf were too much for fifty of his colleagues, who protested to the Secretary about his mistreatment in a letter of 22 March 1995:

We wish to express concern with regard to the methods and procedures being used by DPIF administration concerning disciplinary action taken against David Obendorf and the effect this has had on him, DPIF staff and the community standing of the DPIF ... David

Obendorf's actions are not approved by all but it is believed, from what is 'known', that the treatment that he has generally received has been contrary to sound personnel management principles and practices.[28]

Not long after this the Minister had to field some difficult questions in parliament, to which he replied that, although Obendorf was a highly regarded veterinary scientist and he well understood the concerns of Obendorf's colleagues, he believed that the Secretary had handled the matter as best he could in the difficult circumstances.[29]

Seven months later, at New Year 1996, the *Bulletin* ran a strong and detailed piece that was sympathetic to Obendorf.[30] At the same time he complained to the Ombudsman about numerous administrative irregularities in the way the issue was handled by the department. In that complaint he was critical of the quality of representation and advocacy from his union, the SPSFT. This negative appraisal of union assistance hums across most whistleblowing stories.[31]

In early May 1996 the Community and Public Sector Union, representing laboratory staff at the beleaguered Animal Health Laboratory, finally got around to providing DPIF with the staff response to the August 1994 review.[32] The staff report has quite an angry tone. In the last section, which deals with Obendorf, it says:

Members believe nothing has been explained. There has been no link between David Obendorf's concerns and the Review. No poor behavioural problems have been identified. There has been no acknowledgement of policy differences as the source of the problems and the reason for David Obendorf's removal. In essence he was 'politically incorrect'.

Staff were very dissatisfied at the lack of departmental response to the review's recommendations and the apparent victimisation of people who had given information to the review, in spite of assurances that their confidentiality would be respected. The report continues:

The point about restoring stability and order to the Lab is laughable as [the victimisation of staff who spoke to the review] was the single most destabilising act of the whole exercise. The then Secretary personally rang at least four staff members to inform them that he knew all about their behaviour and to warn them against any 'further misconduct'. Staff believe, despite repeated assurances to the contrary, that there was a serious breach of confidentiality ... [All this] has led to heightened levels of cynicism and mistrust and a firm belief that this exercise was used to justify dictatorial behaviour.[33]

Obendorf has said that five people, including himself, were dealt with punitively as a result of providing information to the review. One person was transferred, two had their duties downgraded, and a fourth person was placed under close supervision, with regular audits of his performance submitted to head office.[34]

By mid-1996 Obendorf was regularly in the Tasmanian papers, alternately entering debate on a diverse range of issues to do with conservation, planning and livestock disease, or being attacked for speaking out when he was drawing worker's compensation.[35] He signed one letter to the editor 'Dr David L. Obendorf, registered veterinarian and worker's compensation recipient'.[36] Above all, he continued his great public passion: alerting all who would listen about the dangerous drop in disease surveillance. The new Minister for Primary Industries and Fisheries was not in a listening mood. In reply to a submission from Obendorf, he wrote:

I believe the tone of your letter, and your assertion that the Executive and senior management of the Animal Industries Directorate is mediocre and acquiescent, is completely without foundation and justification.

As Minister, I am in an excellent position to judge the soundness of the professional advice I am offered, and to suggest that these officers have modified their advice through fear, or for favour, is a scandalous accusation.

I trust that these comments will clarify the position and leave you in no uncertainty as to my opinion on this matter.[37]

'What's Obendorf on about?' was a question often asked by management throughout the five-year saga. In its various guises this is one of the questions most commonly asked about whistleblowers.

It's almost a gut reaction: when made aware of an actual or pending public-interest disclosure, managers are inclined to focus on the way whistleblowers express themselves rather than the worth of the disclosure. As a result, they are too ready to put the gloves on and defend the indefensible, too quick to assume that disclosure equals trouble. In these circumstances, any attempts to address the substance of organisational malaise soon give way to a campaign of management payback against the whistleblower, often implemented by management's latest weapon, the human resources department.

An answer to the question 'what's Obendorf on about?' came from Kim Evans, the new departmental secretary: 'He was regarded as a stirrer'. For 'stirrer', read 'troublemaker' and 'agitator'. But there is more to it than these well-worn dismissives. Evans again:

Not for what he was saying, because some vets agreed, but many thought the way he was doing it was undermining the credibility of the organisation.[38]

Note the use of 'many' – an indecently overused phrase that suggests, with all the subtlety of a bullroarer, that the 'stirrer' acts alone, or at best with a small cell of fellow 'troublemakers'. The inference is that there is obviously some fundamental moral or legal flaw in the whistleblower's project that deters decent people from supporting it. How many is 'many'?

Note also Evans' criticism of the way Obendorf was protesting. This assumes that there are 'right' ways to disclose and dissent, and there are 'wrong' ways to do so. In practice, however, there is no 'right' way to inform about wrongdoing. The accusation that whistleblowers are going about it the 'wrong' way is management-speak for wandering off officialdom's straight and narrow pathway, carefully constructed to monitor and then neutralise the expression of system-threatening dissent. Research evidence from the Queensland Whistleblower Study (QWS) rebuts the management-incubated stereotype that somehow whistleblowers travel free, disrespectful of the formal pathways for grievance and disclosure.

Whistleblowers by and large come not from the ideological 'outer suburbs' of our society, but from its heartland. They are good solid citizens, at least at the beginning. They sing 'Advance

Australia Fair' the loudest, they put their kids through cubs and scouts, they go to war when they are told and they make peace when they are told. They believe we live in a democracy, and point with pride to its markers: one person-one vote, the rule of law, ministerial responsibility, a free press, and the chain of command.

But by the time most whistleblowers have navigated the waters of corruption and cover-up, their faith in the system vanishes, and for some it vanishes forever. Whistleblowing is an icon-shattering experience. With new eyes whistleblowers see that courts dispense injustice, hospitals perversely make you sick, and cops are corrupt. But at the start they have faith.

This is where we pick up the Obendorf story again. In the beginning, Obendorf trusted the corrective powers of his organisation as a child trusts its mother. He cannot be accused of not playing officialdom's game in its initial phases. Let us look at this more closely. His perception was that DPIF management had breached the public's faith that they were receiving an effective disease surveillance service. With these concerns, butressed by facts and figures, Obendorf started up the DPIF chain of command, looking for reform.

In May 1992 he went to his line manager, the senior veterinary pathologist at the Mt Pleasant laboratory. Unsatisfied but undeterred, in November he then went to the manager of the laboratory. Then on to the Chief Veterinary Officer in May 1993, the departmental head in January 1994, and finally to the responsible minister.[39]

For two-and-a-half years Obendorf stuck to management's pathway of dissent and disclosure. Falsely signposted 'Justice this Way', the path was leading its traveller into trouble.

One further point needs to be made. It seems that, as far as DPIF management was concerned, Obendorf was attacking the 'credibility of the organisation'. This phrase deserves a place in the official clichés register. What does it mean? Organisations have credibility when they do what they say they do. If they say that they cure the sick and they actually do, then have a good reputation in that field. If they say that they speedily investigate complaints and take forever to do so, then they have a bad reputation. But there is another level to this phrase; to understand it, we need to think in terms of power and its Siamese partner, status.

Concerns about the 'credibility of the organisation' are usually verbalised by those at, or wishing to be at, the top of the organisation. As such the phrase is part of the discourse of power. It is code for *my* credibility, and *my* organisation. What we have here is a reassertion of management's claim to proprietorial rights over the organisations that they control. So here is a clue to why whistleblowers face so much flak. Those in power take disclosures *personally*. Often they should, because they are up to their hairlines in the wrongdoing that employees of conscience are trying to expose. But often they are blameless of the initial wrongdoing. Where they become culpable is at the point where their identity fuses with that of the organisation. Then they become dangerous to the public interest, for they have lost all objectivity. Everything, no matter how trivial, is judged as an attack on the me-organisation and is vehemently counter-attacked.

This helps to explain the massive overreaction to Obendorf. Let us try and get some perspective here. Obendorf the 'stirrer' was not involved in industrial espionage. He was not at an international court embarrassing the Tasmanian government. He was not out shooting dogs who might be hydatid carriers and dumping them on the steps of the Parliament. Nor was he organising mass rallies of farmers and vets. No, Obendorf the 'stirrer' was simply talking and writing about the effects on primary industries and wildlife of budget cuts. In the world of hard politics, he was a softie. So why was he treated so badly?

There are several answers to this question. Whistleblowers are doubly dangerous because their outspokenness is guided not by expediency but by ethics. An ethically driven employee can hold out much longer than his or her expediency driven counterpart, whether against the soft management strategy of organisational seduction or the hard strategy of threats, sackings and court action. But this is not the whole answer to Obendorf's story of oppression. There are two other elements that need to be factored in: the recent history of activism in Tasmania and Obendorf's homosexuality.

A substantial part of the Tasmanian power structure views dissent in much the same way that Obendorf sees disease. Some of the great activist battles have been fought in our island State. In July 1974, when the waters of the Serpentine rose to submerge the 'sea of diamonds' that was Lake Pedder,[40] thousands of green activists were vilified as 'stirrers' (that word again). Eleven years later, after a bitter campaign, those 'stirrers' applauded when the High Court validated the World Heritage Act, stopping once and for all the controversial proposal to dam the Franklin.

More recently, and more to the point of Obendorf's matter, there has been a successful campaign to reform Tasmania's archaic laws banning private homosexual acts. The homosexual decriminalisation campaign occurred at the same time as Obendorf was expressing his concerns about the government's reducing disease-surveillance capacity. Was there a connection? Obendorf thought so. In one meeting with staff in the Minister's office, Obendorf heard that DPIF managers had told the Minister that Obendorf was a homosexual, HIV positive, and was depressed and fatalistic after the AIDS death of his partner, University of Tasmania lecturer Dr Ewan Reid.[41]

There seems little doubt that the homosexuality card was played against Obendorf. Given the legal restraints on such discrimination, it had to be played with great stealth and duplicity. This would have infected Obendorf's workplace with distrust and uncertainty. Obendorf found himself in a common whistleblower position: he knew what was going on, but he could not prove it. Undaunted, he eventually made a complaint to the Human Rights and Equal Opportunities Commission.[42] He had witnesses ready to support his claim that an HIV phobia existed in the laboratory.[43]

The saga came to an end on 11 April 1997 when Obendorf reached an out-of-court settlement with DPIF. On that day he signed a Deed of Release resigning as a public servant and ceasing all actions against the Crown. This did not mean he had been silenced. In his last letter to his departmental boss he wrote:

I will continue to exercise my duty under Article 19 of the International Covenant on Civil and Political Rights to the freedom of opinion and expression without interference and the right to impart information and ideas through any media.[44]

In August 1997 the Commonwealth government announced a $76m shake-up of the national quarantine service in direct response to the outcry about increased vulnerability to disease.[45] In line with the recommendations of the federal review mentioned earlier, the Australian Quarantine Inspection Service would be boosted by 200 officers, new X-ray equipment introduced, and an extra 22 sniffer-dog units placed at international airports. Although peak farmer groups still had misgivings about the major quarantine threat off Cape York, it has to be said that this was a significant response to the problem. It also has to be said that people like David Obendorf have performed high public service by bringing such matters to our attention in defiance of the powers that be.

Religious Dissenter
Peter Cameron and the Heresy Trial

On the whole the status of heretic is not one that I would recommend. There is a certain image conjured up by the word which is essentially negative: not only are you suspect theologically, but it is almost as if you were unclean and should have a bell around your neck to warn people of your approach. And ancillary accusations abound such as being dishonest, or a servant of Satan. –Peter Cameron[1]

Peter Cameron was convicted of heresy by the Presbyterian Church of Australia in March 1993. At that stage he was the Principal of St Andrew's College at the University of Sydney. The charge arose out of a sermon the previous year in which Cameron had supported the ordination of women, criticised the church's hard line on homosexuality and questioned its fundamentalism.[2] This unleashed a remarkable attack on Cameron, the temper of which he thus describes:

In all walks of life of which I had experience – in the legal profession, the universities, even the underworld in Dundee – I never came across such unpleasantness, and bitterness, and anger, and sheer nastiness, as I did in the church.[3]

All this in reaction to his liberal theological ambition:

What I wanted to do was to liberate people from their slavery to the Bible and to give it a new status. I wanted to raise their own estimation of themselves and their capacity to respond to God. I wanted to open their eyes to the humanity in the Bible and the divinity in themselves.[4]

Cameron has very ably told his story in three books he wrote after the trial.[5] His experiences, however, need to be dealt with here because a heresy trial in Australia in 1993 unambiguously speaks of the rise of fundamentalism, a mortal enemy of dissent. The fundamentalism in focus here appears in our everyday experience as a loosely confederated movement of biblical literalism and patriarchy.

This powerful movement against dissent and whistleblowing needs to be constantly reappraised, for fundamentalism is to dissent as the mongoose is to the snake. There is no middle ground; no peace is possible, no mediated settlement can ever be brokered. This is no struggle between equally matched opponents. In its fight against fundamentalism, dissent usually has its back to the wall. In reflecting on Cameron's heresy trial, the social commentator Hugh McKay reflected this view:

Peter Cameron was a victim of a set of circumstances which did not favour boat-rockers and whistleblowers. He came onto the scene at a time when many people were looking for some relief from uncertainty, rather than a new set of questions to face.[6]

My re-telling of Cameron's story avoids the theological matters at issue,[7] and instead focuses on the processes of vilification that were set in train against him. It also inquires into Cameron's own contribution to his downfall. The questions that settle over the Cameron case are the same ones that appear at the end of every whistleblower story: was it all worthwhile? And did anything change? These questions stay with whistleblowers for years. The reader is invited to stay with them at least until the end of this book.

One important point to note at the outset concerns the way Cameron identified himself. He has referred to himself as a 'heretic', a cunning and courageous move.[8] By adopting the negative label that his accusers would apply to him, he assumed a huge strategic advantage. Like black Americans who from time to time referred to themselves as 'niggers' in the context of their struggle for racial emancipation, Cameron has protected himself by a pre-emptive strategy. After all, what could be worse than accepting the full force of the accusation of being a modern heretic in the Presbyterian

Church of Australia? While this is a reluctant move on Cameron's part, it also indicates that he is comfortable with his identity as a dissenter.

In dissenters' formative backgrounds there is often a subculture of familial reinforcement, powerful role-modelling and liberal conditioning that sustains outspokenness. As Cameron rightly says, 'One does not become a dissenter overnight.' Within these subcultures dissenters learn to see contradiction in all human existence and to value critical analyses honed by experience, where there are no icons above suspicion. Dissenters and whistleblowers are ethical overreachers, forever going beyond what the prevailing orthodoxy says are the central values. So Cameron the dissenter did not stop his critique at the pedestal on which the Presbyterian God sat. His questioning went through that concept, not to it.

When Cameron tells of his childhood experiences in his village church in Scotland, he displays an early leaning towards a contradiction-sensitive, dissenting personality. In *Heretic* he describes his Sunday school teacher in these terms:

In church [my teacher] wore a demure grey hat and a veneer of piety, but the vulgarity and viciousness which she displayed in the school bus were always near the surface ... As a result I have always been conscious that the church resembles a fancy-dress party: people are rarely what they seem.[9]

I could not surpass the gripping way Cameron tells of another formative experience:

We were being addressed by a visiting preacher of outstanding dreariness ... The school had lapsed into its usual stupefaction ... I was fidgeting in my corner in the back row of the chair when I happened to find in my packet a whistle, with which I had been refereeing a Rugby match that afternoon. I was at once attacked by a terrible urge to raise it to my lips and blow: to blow the whistle on all this charade, this imposture ... I can't communicate the violence of that desire to raise the whistle, the tightness of my grip on it, the tension in my arm, as the visiting preacher above went on his weary way regardless.[10]

His nerve failed him on that occasion. Years later in Australia it wouldn't.

After receiving qualifications in law and working for a time as a prosecutor, Cameron entered the ministry and was ordained into the Presbyterian Church of Scotland at the age of thirty-eight, still with his dissenting proclivities intact. He has said: 'I felt that instead of turning my back on the church, as all my instincts prompted me to do, my task was to debunk its pomposity and pharisaism from within.[11] Perhaps Cameron's atheistic parents had something to do with his less-than-complete socialisation into Presbyterianism.

Cameron and his family moved to Sydney at the beginning of 1991, when he was appointed Principal of St Andrew's College, a place not unused to the whiff of heresy in its 128-year history. In the 1930s the college had been rocked by a series of complaints against Samuel Angus, its Professor of New Testament Exegesis and Theology, who was accused of deviating from Presbyterian theology by questioning the historical basis of the divinity of Christ and the virgin birth.[12]

When Cameron took up his post, Presbyterians accounted for about 4.5 per cent of Australian Christians. Fourteen years earlier, three Australian Protestant churches had amalgamated to form the Uniting Church, but a sizeable proportion (thirty-six per cent) of Presbyterians decided not to amalgamate. These continuing Presbyterians tended to be theological conservatives, and included a much higher proportion of biblical fundamentalists than in the Scottish church. This formed the backdrop for the collision between Cameron the liberal church leader and the Sydney fundamentalist Presbyterians.[13]

The first skirmish took place within three weeks of Cameron's arrival, when he was interviewed by two members of the Sydney Presbytery, ostensibly to gather material for a church magazine. Cameron, however, felt that their other purpose was to interrogate his theological position.[14]

Seven months after Cameron's arrival, the General Assembly of Australia decided to reverse a seventeen-year-old policy of ordaining women. This was a major blow to those liberal Presbyterians left in the church after the schism. For Cameron, a strong supporter of female ordination, the church lights had just changed from green to orange. The question was: should he proceed with caution or drive straight through?

On 2 March 1992 Cameron preached a sermon called 'The Place of Women in the Church' to 300 members of a Presbyterian women's organisation. In the sermon Cameron raised objections to the slavish following of the writings of St Paul, a principal source of authority for those who reversed the policy of ordaining women and proclaimed the sinfulness of homosexuality. Cameron went on to observe that there were non-biblical reasons for the opposition to female ordination, and specifically mentioned male vanity and privilege among the elders of the church.[15]

It should perhaps be clarified that the wrongdoing that Cameron disclosed in this and similar sermons was predominantly moral in nature. He was not on about church graft or bribery, he was concerned at the moral wrong, as he saw it, of a too literal translation of the Bible, and the patriarchical exclusion of women from leadership positions in his church.

Cameron's mostly female audience greeted his sermon with enthusiasm. Many women were pleased to find a new and charismatic spokesperson for church women seeking a greater pastoral role. Cameron was able to support women's ordination in the most effective way for a Bible-centred church. He showed the congregation how the Bible could be read to a conclusion favouring women's ordination. This unresolved theological conflict was the major context for Cameron's trial, and his leadership on the women's side accounts for why he was so severely dealt with.

At that time there were only five women ministers in the Presbyterian Church.[16] One of them was present at Ashfield. She has said that she listened to his sermon with tears in her eyes because she foresaw what was going to happen to him.[17]

Indeed, this critical speech was the defining moment for Cameron. In reaching down below the Bible into the mere mortal world of patriarchy for the source of opposition to female ordination, he made some very powerful enemies. From that moment in the pulpit at Ashfield, the conflict between Cameron and the fundamentalists in the church took on a dual identity. The conflict always looked like a battle about theology. It was, to an extent. But by dragging patriarchy into the debate Cameron gave the conflict a personal dimension. He would soon be attacked by the church patriarchs for who he was, as well as what he stood for.

There was also a secondary current in the campaign against Cameron, that of church nationalism.[18] There is some evidence that elements in the Australian church felt threatened by Cameron's background and qualifications. He was from Scotland, the mother country of Presbyterianism, and had taught in one of Scotland's most prestigious theological faculties. A statement from Reverend Paul Cooper, a church spokesman at the time of the heresy trial, suggests that Cameron was targeted for his nationality as well as his views:

Though the views that Dr Cameron is spouting would be acceptable in Scotland, they are not acceptable in Australia. We are a different Church ... an independent Church. Colonialism is dead. Dr Cameron wants the Presbyterian Church to be like the Church of Scotland ... but we make our own decisions and our decision is that we don't want to be that sort of church. We stand under the authority of the Bible.[19]

Although Cameron's audience for his Ashfield sermon was predominantly women, at the front of the congregation taking notes was the Reverend Peter Hastie, minister of Ashfield Presbyterian Church, who would soon become a prime mover in Cameron's trial. Two weeks later, on 14 March, a complaint about Cameron's sermon was sent to the Clerk of the Sydney Presbytery. The complainant, a theology lecturer at the Sydney Mission Bible College, requested the Sydney Presbytery to:

ascertain what are Dr Cameron's views ... and to take what other action it thinks appropriate to fulfil its responsibility to maintain and defend the faith as understood in the Westminster Confession of Faith.[20]

Cameron's supporters would argue that the Westminster Confession of Faith is not an immutable doctrine. It can in fact be changed as a result of a 1901 theological agreement called the Basis of Union. Since then the Westminster Confession has been changed twice, and those promoting the changes were not subjected to heresy trials.[21]

The distance between Cameron and his complainants was already wide, but the institution of formal proceedings put both parties into a lose–lose situation. Cameron felt the early attacks acutely. He ended his first formal defence of his Ashfield sermon by saying to Dr Keith, the convenor of the first investigatory committee:

If you object to my views, I expect you to give a satisfactory answer to these questions. If on the other hand you do not object to my views, then I expect some sort of apology from the Presbytery for all the unpleasantness and vilification I have been subjected to as a result of this process.[22]

Two observations can be made at this point. First, according to Cameron, the reprisals started immediately. Secondly, from the outset both sides responded to what was essentially a conflict over faith with the inappropriate instruments of logic and rationality. An example of this from Cameron's side is found in his response to the conclusion of Dr Keith's committee:

Firstly, let me admit that I am slightly surprised at the Committee's conclusion, that 'Dr Cameron may not hold views which are entirely consistent with Chapter 1 of the Westminster Confession of Faith' – surprised that is, because the logical entailment of that proposition is that Dr Cameron may hold views which are entirely consistent with Chapter 1 of the Westminster Confession of Faith ... This report therefore is incompetent, illegal, and irrelevant, and I congratulate the Committee on achieving so much in the space of three sentences.[23]

Cameron's strategy (possibly learnt in his days in law) was to give the church leaders a double dose of sarcasm and logic. The more logical he became, the more his chances of failure increased, for what was being contested here were matters of faith not fact. At the end of the day legal arguments and rational discourse, a sort of *lingua franca* of the heresy proceeding, would take second place to religious belief. But what else could Cameron have done? He understood the frailty of his strategies:

Applying sarcasm and ridicule certainly made me enjoy the whole exercise more but it didn't improve my prospects. I think that having begun to hit back, the best thing I could do was what I did: go on hitting back regardless of the consequences.[24]

He also acknowledged that conflicts about fundamental issues bring out the worst in people:

The necessity to be always defending yourself, which can only be done successfully in this sort of context by attacking, makes you appear pugnacious and cantankerous; and in time you begin to think automatically in terms of confrontation.[25]

Cameron has told us, in the most eloquent fashion, what it is like to walk in the shoes of a church whistleblower. He has spoken of the isolation, the risk-taking, the challenge to his relationship to his God, and the ostracism from people he once thought of as friends. These personal reactions speak of whistleblower vulnerability and organisational supremacy.

Cameron's sense of the fearful power of church discipline was corroborated by Stuart Clements, a Presbyterian minister and Cameron supporter:

It so happens that as a young minister thirty years ago, I took part in a Commission of Assembly at the appeal of the Rev. Mr Finch against his conviction for contumacy [stubborn resistance to authority]. I went into proceedings as a commissioner and incidentally as a lawyer, thinking that it would be a matter of no great consequence compared with a conviction in a state court. I came out shaking (literally) at the appalling weight placed upon someone by a condemnation of the church.[26]

What is the nature of this 'appalling weight'? Part of the answer is that dissent transforms the authority relationship from one of accord to one of discord. In the first phase the future whistleblower is more at one with her or his organisation. Workplaces do not consciously recruit dissenters. We can go further and generally state that the relationship can be one of indoctrination, in which the worker's personal values are refashioned (some would say contorted) to conform to workplace requirements presented as 'values'. This is the period of accord. For many of us it lasts as long as we work, give or take the occasional grumble. Workplace accord provides emotional and material benefits. We experience a sense of belonging and purpose. To cap it off we are remunerated, and this gives us a comfortable, secure lifestyle. So powerful are the benefits of accord that few of us dare jeopardise them by challenging the organisation, at least not overtly.

Those who dissent have a really hard time when accord gives way to discord, because of a terrible contradiction. They have been cast out of an organisation that they previously embraced so completely that they could not tell ethically where the person finished and the organisation started. Whistleblowers in the phase of discord must deal with the terrible effects of rejection. The expelling organisation, which by definition cannot feel, closes ranks and forgets the whistleblower the moment he or she is out the gate. Whistleblowers remember the rejection forever. This was Cameron's lot.

His original surprise that church leaders would take exception to his sermon, and his shock at the speed with which they reacted, soon gave way to an appreciation of the trouble he and the church were in. A note he sent to the church after it decided not to accept the Keith Committee Report was a mixture of peace offering and dire warning:

One of the reasons why I have made a point of challenging the irregularities which have so far arisen has been to give the Presbytery a chance to rethink and to back out ... If ... they [Sydney Presbytery] ... raise some sort of libel, it seems to me that this could do untold harm to the Presbyterian Church of Australia. I must admit I don't relish the prospect myself, but I am sure that it will damage the Church far more than it will damage me ... This case threatens to become as unpleasant and as farcical as the Angus case, and all it will achieve will be to bring home to people outside just how little theological progress the Presbyterian Church of Australia has made since [the 1930s].[27]

To some the case did become as unpleasant and farcical as the Angus heresy trial. Opportunities for conciliation soon evaporated.

Each side was moving into battle. The stakes were high – the interpretative control of the Bible. Both sides saw the righteousness of their positions with clear eyes. It became a case of 'praise the ammunition and pass the Lord'. One can argue that there is never a time for rapproachment between power and dissent; that the relationship can only be transacted through conflict. That is the way Cameron's matter worked itself out as neither side seemed burdened with Luther's worry that the other side might just be right.

By now, however, it was too late for rapprochement. The next stage was a Brotherly Conference. On 23 June 1992 Cameron faced fifty members of the Sydney Presbytery. The mood on both sides was one of determination and anger. Cameron was asked whether he still stood by the sermon he preached in March. He reasserted his theological position, and also defended the claim that homosexuality and Christianity were compatible.

Cameron left the Brotherly Conference optimistic that the conflict was coming to an end. Again he had misread the charts. On 4 August the Sydney Presbytery decided to hold a Preliminary Inquiry, the next stage in its complicated procedure for the examination of allegations of heresy. Three weeks later, on 25 August, the Presbytery moved to the final stage, the Judicial Process, a heresy trial by another name.

Disagreements about the pending process occurred between the Church's most senior legal adviser, Garry Downs QC, and Cameron's prosecutor, Bruce Christian, a minister at Rose Bay and former Moderator of the church. On 17 November the Presbytery confirmed its intention to proceed to the trial.

One week later the story was out. The *Sydney Morning Herald* splashed 'Heretic? The Cleric Who Praised Women' across page one. Cameron received strong coverage in both print and electronic media, and a good deal of support from the *Sydney Morning Herald* in particular. Numerous letters of support followed, including two in different handwriting from the Archangel Michael, which Cameron found 'encouraging'.[28]

Cameron was once a public prosecutor, and knew the adversary's role well. He knew how to fight as well as how to preach. He has said that going to the media was 'the best thing I could have done',[29] but we must qualify this claim. The media are a powerful weapon for exposing clandestine activities and secret deliberations, particularly when journalists are well-informed and tenacious. This strategy can be so powerful that no government in Australia has been brave enough to protect whistleblowers who go to the media.

But, as Cameron soon discovered, the media's support can be a two-edged sword. The other edge of the media sword is felt every time the media kindergarten-ise complicated issues or gut the story of all but the sensational bits. Media exposure reflects and amplifies social conflicts, which they call 'news', and therefore entrenches adversarial positions. This is a serious problem: stereotypical images and fighting words detract from the conflict's potential to effect change.

At one level, Cameron understood this. He has said that going public 'undoubtedly hardened the hearts of the opposition and made the eventual conviction [for heresy] more or less inevitable'.[30] On the other hand, he took comfort from the public support he received.

In most cases whistleblowing is essentially a solo pursuit. Often whistleblowers have to endure long winters of despair with only their consciences for companions. One effect of this isolation is that dissenters can start to suspect that they are wrong, or even losing their minds. In this situation it was a great boost to Cameron to read the media-stimulated support letters, and hear the telephone ring with another comfort call. Reflecting on his new strength, he said: 'Now I could face the rest of the proceedings with the knowledge that most rational people, both inside and outside the church, were very much on my side.'[31] Note Cameron's continuing emphasis on the curative force of rationality.

Around this time Lindsay Moore, a prominent member of the Presbyterian Church and its former principal law agent, resigned in protest at its treatment of Cameron. Moore became Cameron's legal adviser for the trial. Moore said:

I realised that I could no longer be publicly identified with a particular religious mind-set which I found abhorrent. I felt a growing personal estrangement and cynicism, and this is not good for the soul.[32]

Moore went on to say that he was disenchanted with the religious repression in the church. Cameron's matter was only one of several issues troubling the liberal Presbyterians. He mentioned the Presbytery of Dubbo's initiation of an inquisition against the church at Coonabarabran, and a decision by the minister at Wynnum (Brisbane) to rip out a stained-glass window of the Good Shepherd against the wishes of the congregation. He also deplored the action of the General Assembly of Queensland in directing teachers at its Fairholme College to teach creation 'science'.[33] It seemed the Presbyterian Church was rocking on the precipice of yet another split.[34]

Cameron's trial was set to start on 18 March 1993, and was the subject of intense media interest. The *Sydney Morning Herald* was continuing its coverage, and *Sixty Minutes* got exclusive TV rights from Cameron under a callous agreement that there would be no story unless the verdict went against him. When Cameron arrived at the Presbyterian Theological Centre in Burwood, Sydney, he was greeted by half-a-dozen TV cameras and sundry print and radio reporters. After the media were sent out and the doors closed, the pattern of allegation and defence went on until 11.30 pm, when the elders voted by a majority of twenty-six to three to sustain the charge that Cameron had made heretical statements inconsistent with Chapter 1 of the Westminster Confession of Faith.[35] Strangely, the charge relating to his position on homosexuality was dismissed by an even bigger majority.

The church took a public-relations beating in the storm of protest and support that erupted. The next day the Council of St Andrew's College issued a statement in support of its principal.[36] For a time, the secular press and the *Presbyterian Review* were inundated with letters of support for Cameron. A writer to the *Sydney Morning Herald* (25 March 1993) compared him to Socrates, who was forced to suicide for challenging establishment views.[37] Another correspondent said:

It is appalling that the Presbyterian Church has ordered a fine man to be characterised as a heretic on the words of a man, a known misogynist [St Paul] who was not even around when Jesus Christ taught tolerance, love and kindness to one another.[38]

Another quoted Jesus Christ's words after his own trial: 'Forgive them, Father, for they know not what they do.'[39]

The question of sentence was deferred after Cameron said that he would appeal. His appeal was heard on 2 July before an Assembly of members of the church, which dismissed it by a majority of 123 to 65.[40] Cameron's prosecutor, the Reverend Peter Hastie, said:

I am genuine when I say I am saddened for Dr Cameron. The decision would have wounded him, and I took no delight in seeing him, as it were, under the pressure of the Assembly as he was.[41]

Cameron faced four possible punishments: rebuke, suspension, deposition (exclusion from the ministry) and excommunication (expulsion from the church). He thought that it was most likely to be one of the last two. To pre-empt this, he withdrew from his last appeal opportunity and resigned from the ministry on 1 August 1994.[42] His tell-all book *Heretic* was published the next day. In reflecting on his traumatic experiences, Cameron said with pride:

I have a feeling of mission accomplished. At long last I have steeled myself to raise the whistle to my lips and blow. My nerve failed me on that occasion in the school chapel thirty years ago, and I regretted it ever since.[43]

That was Cameron on a good day; that was Cameron the achiever. Soon the shine goes off this sense of achievement, as the following statement from Cameron shows:

It was said some years ago that God was dead. It might not be so absurd now to proclaim the death of the Church ... I entered the ministry as, in some sense an imposter – a double agent – hoping to change things from within. That is no longer possible for me. I have stopped preaching now because I think people come to hear me as they would the fat lady in the circus.

Cameron left Australia for good in January 1996 to return to his native Scotland.[44] He left the Presbyterian Church and was subsequently ordained into the Scottish Episcopal (Anglican) Church.

Cameron's case raises a number of issues. One important question is whether there is a place for the perpetual dissenter, or in

Steiner's words the 'discourser without end'.⁴⁵ Cameron left the church after a brief but intense engagement. Is there value to the organisation, and to the standards that it so assiduously promotes, in allowing whistleblowers to have a protected presence after they disclose? Or is their value in the short, sharp shock? The arguments appear compelling on both sides. Once the dissenter is expelled from the organisation, what happens to the torch of dissent? Is it picked up, or does the flame go out?

One thing that is clear from Cameron's case is that whistleblowers move along in currents that are stronger than they are. As one Presbyterian commentator has said:

*There was a surge of anger and disgust at the Cameron decision within the basic membership of the Church, [but] that was only from those who were involved or concerned enough to notice what was going on. Even then they had to be experienced enough to recognise it for what it was, a power struggle in which Cameron himself was only a pawn.*⁴⁶

Academic Dissenters
On Being Unfree in Free Spaces

Ever since I came to [the University of] Melbourne I have been told at intervals that I administered a hotbed of Communism, and that I ought to do something about it as a matter of urgency. A University should, of course, be a hotbed in which opinion of every sort is fermenting in the most active fashion. – Sir John Medley, Vice-Chancellor, University of Melbourne, 1950[1]

Australia is not the country it purports to be. It is . . . replete with mythology and hypocrisy. Every whistleblower eventually must come to terms with this unfortunate realisation. – Professor Kim Sawyer[2]

In July 1996 I gave a paper on the victimisation of academics to an international conference. The subject of the conference was bullying, and the venue was my university, the University of Queensland. I began by welcoming the delegates to the university that gave former Premier Joh Bjelke-Petersen an honorary degree. The university's action was symptomatic of the new climate in the academy. By honouring a man whose administration was known for its take-no-prisoners attitude to dissenters and never winced at the destruction of civil and political rights, the university had sent a signal to the community that it was at one with the Bjelke-Petersen spirit.

The cosy relationship between campus and cabinet is not new. What is new is the almost complete absence of opposition to the growth of campus authoritatianism. Forget about universities being centres of light and learning. As Professor Donald Horne has said, the word 'knowledge' was nowhere to be heard in the so-called

Dawkins and Vanstone debates on tertiary education policy.[3] Similarly, I cannot recall the last time I heard the term 'enlightenment' used on campus, and I have been an academic since 1978. Universities are now mutating into dissent-free business sites, their highly paid vice-chancellors managing directors in a vast and exploitative enterprise in which money is traded for power in the form of information.[4]

Universities have also become a major source of foreign exchange. In 1995 income from fee-paying overseas students exceeded revenue from Australian wheat exports for the first time. Overseas students accounted for about 8 per cent of the student body at the University of Queensland in 1998, yet brought in about $25 million in fees to the institution.

Where once the university was driven by the ethic of knowledge, it is now driven by the ethic of fear. Fear of not getting the administrative power, the grant, the publication, the promotion or the recognition engenders an oppressive look-right-ahead atmosphere.[5] In 1997 a commentator on higher education in Australia expressed concern that subtle forms of favouritism were emerging at universities.[6] In this climate dissenting and whistleblowing academics are virtually extinct, and those few brave or crazy souls who still manage to speak out usually pay dearly. These days academics seldom appear in the press dissenting or making a public interest disclosure. Instead, the universities' media units present a parade of powerful members of the university community crowing about hyped-up breakthroughs in areas such as medical and genetic research.

Within these oppressive and bully-prone settings, universities hide an enormous amount of wrongdoing, protect powerful perpetrators, and harass the dissenters and whistleblowers within their ranks.[7] Let me quickly offer some examples, spot-soundings in the rivers of wrongdoing that flow through academia, though their headwaters do not always lie on campus.

- Dr Beatrice Bodant-Bailey, the first female academic to win a sexual discrimination case against an Australian university, was asked to vacate her office at the Australian National University ten days after the decision was brought down in October 1995.[8]

- The Federated Clerks Union alleged in 1995 that James Cook University had offered redundancy payments to female administrative staff complaining of sexual harassment by academics.[9]
- In 1994 Steven Jones began a Masters degree in development studies at Deakin University, paying $9600 for the first two semesters. He had found out about the course through a glossy brochure at an Australian Universities Expo in Hong Kong while he was on leave from the United Nations High Commission for Refugees. Jones soon found that he had been the victim of false advertising. Study guides were obsolete; they had been prepared before the breakup of the Soviet Union. He protested internally but to no avail. So he became the first student in Australia to take a university to the Trade Practices Commission. At a meeting with the Deakin University Vice-Chancellor in July 1994, Jones was offered a negotiated settlement that included a stipulation that Jones would not discuss the matter further in public.[10]
- In 1994 the Sex Discrimination Commission found that Margaret Harvey, a former administration officer with Griffith University's Student Representative Council, had been exposed to bullying and stand-over tactics by male members of the Council's executive for fifteen months before her dismissal in February 1992.[11] She claimed that on about fifty occasions messages were written on a whiteboard denigrating her, among other things, as a 'mega-bitch' and a 'stupid old bat'. A number of the students involved were connected to the Queensland Labor Party machine; some have gone on to careers within the party.[12]
- In January 1996 the South Australian Crown Solicitor threatened legal action against both the Victoria University of Wellington (NZ) and the Australian and New Zealand Society of Criminologists unless a research paper criticising the State's crime prevention policy was withdrawn.[13]
- In November 1997 the Australian Industrial Relations Commission heard allegations that fee-paying Japanese students had been given false passing grades at the Queensland University of Technology (QUT) in order to 'keep the business'. At the same hearings it was claimed that a Vietnamese student who

had entered Australia using a QUT immigration acceptance form obtained passing grades despite never attending classes. In fact, she was arrested working in a brothel in Brisbane.[14]
- Professorships are becoming tradeable commodities. In 1997 a proposal from the School of Accountancy at Queensland University of Technology to sell adjunct professorships to Brisbane accountancy firms for $20,000 was quashed only after a media uproar.[15] In other cases, universities have sold naming rights to professorial chairs in return for sponsorship. From 1999 the giant toothpaste multinational Colgate Palmolive will provide two-thirds of the money needed to establish a chair in general practice dentistry at the University of Queensland.[16]
- In April 1997 defamation writs were issued by Lloyd Williams, chairman of the controversial Crown Casino in Melbourne. One of the writs was against Professor Miles Lewis, Associate Dean (Research) of Architecture at the University of Melbourne, for comments Lewis had made about Williams' role as a property developer. The University of Melbourne refused to indemnify Lewis against Williams' action, claiming that Lewis made his statements in a private capacity. In retaliation, staff refused to identify themselves as representing the University of Melbourne in public or media appearances.[17]

A mood of anger and despair is becoming widespread as universities settle into their new commercial mode with a mixture of missionary dogmatism and future-fear. In this mode free thought gives way to the free market; students become customers; education becomes a product; and research becomes corporate property and lawyer-guarded copyright. Investigations that offer no prospect of profit become harder to sustain. Laboratories cut corners in the race for results. Two recent cases that come to mind are the experiments with highly virulent Japanese encephalitis in an unsafe laboratory at QUT, and a breach of quarantine protocols during research into banana-attacking Panama disease at the University of Queensland.[18]

While university administrations crave deregulation in order (so they say) to play hard ball in the internationalising education and research marketplace, levels of workplace regulation are rising on campuses throughout Australia. Decision-making structures in universities, substantially unchanged since the Middle Ages, are now in deep and dramatic flux. The cumulative effect of a decade of unrelenting pressure from outside has been to open the way for a corporatising crusade by a new generation of administrators thrown up by the institutions themselves.

The issue of university autonomy was raised in an unusual context by Fay Gayle, Vice-Chancellor of the University of Western Australia, when she appeared before the Western Australian Parliamentary Standing Committee on Government Agencies in April 1996:

This inquiry raises the issue of the autonomy of the University of Western Australia and, therefore, the autonomy of all Western Australian universities. Therefore it raises the issue of academic freedom of staff. We know that academic freedom of staff is absolutely essential for them to fulfil their respective responsibilities. It is important because academics must be able to work in areas without political control or political direction.[19]

This seems like the type of thing a Vice-Chancellor would be expected to say. Except for one thing. Gayle was not defending academic freedom as the community understands it – the freedom to communicate controversial scholarship without fear of reprisal. She was appropriating the concept to argue that parliament should have no say in the way universities deal with their whistleblowers and dissenters. It would appear that academic freedom may be becoming the freedom of (senior) academics to deal with staff as they choose.

It was long accepted that universities should be able to question, to expose, and to push on the borders of new knowledge without reprisal, because this role, controversial as it inherently is, was deemed crucial to social development. With the new pact of steel between universities and business, this role is wasting away. Universities have become acutely aware of the economic consequences of supporting outspoken academics. An example of this is in Latrobe University's draft code of ethics, which makes speaking out a possible breach of the code.

Simply put, universities treat their dissenting minority badly for the same reason all corporations do. Through their outspokenness, university whistleblowers and dissenters cut across the smug contours of power and privilege that characterise the academic landscape. It seems that the higher the education, the lower the morality.

The corporatising university is no place for those who cannot see the (dollar) value of education. One of the early ones to go was Hazel Rowley, the award-winning biographer of author Christina Stead. In 1996, after twelve years as an academic, she took early retirement. Rowley explains:

The new regime is so opposed to the spirit of free inquiry and reflection, imagination and challenge, that it is no longer possible to think creatively, let alone stretch oneself to the limits of one's intellectual capacity. The word from our leaders is loud and clear: 'I don't care what you publish. Just publish.' God knows who is going to do the reading.[20]

Like many other creative academics, Rowley was spat out by the new 'free market' university regime. On her way through the exit, Rowley glanced over her shoulder and saw a community of isolated and demoralised colleagues and overworked students being rushed along on conveyor-belt curricula. 'Everything I used to respect about universities,' she said, 'has been dismantled in the last few years.' Welcome to the tertiary education worksite of the future.

The central thread that connects the three very different cases dealt with in this chapter is that they all involve academics of conscience speaking out in the public interest and being attacked, often ruthlessly and with no regard for natural justice, by the university hierarchy. The cases challenge us to ask whether universities are losing their claim to be one of the great moral enclaves in our society.

Each case presented here offers a different slant on campus oppression – that is, on academic wrongdoing and the attempts by a few to expose it. The busy campus boulevards, the gala graduation ceremonies, the teak-lined chancelry boardrooms, the landscaped gardens and lakes, the well-worn lecture theatres and the cosy little tutorial rooms all speak to us of grand medieval myth. It often takes a whistleblowing experience to reach through the mythology to the hard core of university power.

Examining Injustice: Peter Jesser and the University of Southern Queensland

In the end it is no longer a matter of who was right or who was wrong, who did what to whom or why. The treatment meted out to whistleblowers sensitises them to the reprisals and the whistleblowers act accordingly. Similarly, the organisation becomes sensitised towards the whistleblower and acts towards him or her in the same way.

Peter Jesser

In 1991 Peter Jesser was a lecturer in the Faculty of Business at the University of Southern Queensland when, in the course of his duties, he became aware of student dissatisfaction about the marking of papers in a subject taught by another lecturer in his faculty.[21] The students complained that there was evidence of arbitrary assessment, incomplete assessment of class work and errors in the recording of some students' marks. They also said that the examination questions required detailed answers, contrary to official information given beforehand, and that the failure rate was high (almost fifty per cent).

Apparently the lecturer in charge had only taught the unit once before. According to Deborah Ralston, the Acting Dean at the time:

Being under pressure to submit the exam paper by the date required, Mr X [the lecturer in charge] had set the question by relying on his memory of the unit and by a 'cut and paste' from past exam papers.

Ralston said she instructed Mr X to re-mark all papers after Jesser conveyed the students' complaints to her. She was not happy with Mr X's second attempt at assessment and asked him to mark the papers again.[22]

Meanwhile Jesser raised the matter with Professor Barnett, the Dean of the Faculty of Business, on 11 March 1991. His disclosure was forwarded to Professor Craig Littler, who handed the matter over to a colleague because he was going overseas.[23] When no response was forthcoming, Jesser took his concerns to the School of Management Board, where he claims he was verbally attacked by Ralston.[24] Jesser then went to the University Council. It in turn referred the matter to the interim Vice-Chancellor, Professor Tom Ledwidge. The Vice-Chancellor found substance in Jesser's complaint and instructed that students who failed the particular subject could ask for a supplementary examination. Professor Ledwidge commented that Jesser's action 'has resulted in an enhancement to the due academic process used within the School of Management'.[25] According to Jesser, however, while the Vice-Chancellor confirmed the complaint, deficiencies in his investigation 'left the door open to later reprisals against me'.[26] It took Jesser a further six months to get the Vice-Chancellor's decision on supplementary exams implemented.

On 19 December 1991, ten days after the interim Vice-Chancellor had handed down his findings, Jesser's wife, Rochelle, approached Professor Littler to ask if he would give her a reference for a position in the School of Management. Jesser has said that Littler told her that she should bear in mind that her husband and Professor Barnett had 'had a difference of opinion' and that this would not be forgotten.[27] Rochelle Jesser applied for the position, and appealed when she was not short-listed. Action was then taken to cancel the advertisement and readvertise the job, specifying qualifications that Rochelle Jesser did not have. She later applied for another advertised position. Again she was not short-listed and she appealed. The University Council upheld her appeal after it found that the Selection Committee had breached procedures. Again the advertisement was pulled and the position readvertised outside Rochelle Jesser's qualifications. She subsequently left USQ when it failed to renegotiate her contract.

In the meantime Peter Jesser went to see the new Vice-Chancellor to force action on the students' re-examination.[28] Three weeks later a report was written describing his performance as unsatisfactory. The circumstances of the making of this report provide a window into an organisation that has surreptitiously moved into vendetta mode.

Jesser, who held a tenurable position, was reviewed by Deborah Ralston, again acting as Dean. The normal procedure is for the reviewer (Ralston) and the reviewee (Jesser) to discuss issues relevant to academic performance. The reviewer then writes an evaluation and the reviewee writes a response, or makes statements relevant to the appraisal. The form then goes to the reviewer's immediate superior for final reportage and signature. This did not happen in Jesser's case. Ralston filled Jesser's section in herself with the comment that he had 'proved to be most unreliable and ineffective'.[29] Whatever the merits of Ralston's view, it was a breach of natural justice not to give Jesser an opportunity to respond to the critical assessment. Jesser only found out what Ralston had done through a search under Freedom of Information (FOI) a long time later. Professor Barnett apparently seized on this negative report to substantiate his view that Jesser's performance was not up to scratch.[30]

Jesser registered a grievance and was appalled at how the process bogged down:

Because I was growing concerned with the obvious delay and 'closed' manner of dealing with my grievance, on 5 January 1993 I took the precaution of requesting, under FOI, all documents which Barnett had relied upon to support his allegation of non-performance against me. At first my request was denied on the grounds that the documents did not relate to my personal affairs. I appealed and won the appeal. Then the 30 day period for the provision of the documents elapsed without the documents being supplied. I had to remind the University of its obligation to supply the documents. Finally I received the documents on 2 April 1993. The University took 88 days to meet an obligation it was required to discharge in 30 days under the Act. I later learned that Professor Goodwin had requested the same documents from Professor Barnett [and] ... he waited 100 days for his subordinate to respond to the simple request.[31]

The USQ Deputy Vice-Chancellor, Professor Goodwin, finally acknowledged that there was an 'irregularity' in the use of the review form. Goodwin found that 'Ralston used the space to comment adversely on Mr Jesser's performance'.[32] There is nothing to indicate that Ralston was admonished for this. Jesser subsequently went for promotion and was unsuccessful. Despite Jesser's protests, Professor Barnett sat on the promotion committee. In responding to Jesser's grievance, Goodwin said, 'I see little alternative than for the University to redress its neglect by granting Mr Jesser tenure immediately.'[33] Jesser was finally promoted to senior lecturer in 1994.

Jesser also claimed that the university reneged on an agreement to grant him twelve months' study leave, and that Goodwin had done so by backdating a memo.

Finally Jesser sought medical help and went on stress leave for three months in late 1994. Jesser's stress condition was recognised as work-related by the Queensland Workers' Compensation Commission. Despite this finding he was dismissed on 3 November 1995.

He sums up his case by saying:

I took justifiable and justified action on a matter of academic malpractice at the University of Southern Queensland. While some superficial corrective action was taken on that matter, it was taken reluctantly, and reprisals against both myself and my wife were swift in coming. My wife has been driven from her employment. I have been subjected to secret re-investigation of the complaint of academic malpractice. I have faced unfounded accusations of non-performance for taking action on academic malpractice. I have been obstructed in gaining promotion, and I suffer ongoing harassment and obstruction of the settlement of my grievance.[34]

Jesser claimed that his opponents fared much better. The academic who set and marked the contentious exams was given a year's study leave in 1991 to work on his doctoral thesis. The new Vice-Chancellor, Professor Leal, granted a key player several years of accelerated incremental progression, and appointed another to chair a high-powered university committee.[35]

In 1994 Jesser gave evidence to the Senate Select Committee on Unresolved Whistleblower Cases (SSCUWC), which was commissioned to inquire into persistent allegations that a group of Queensland whistleblowers had been denied justice. Jesser later alleged that USQ had intimidated him after they found out he had given evidence to the Committee. The Senate Committee was concerned at Jesser's allegation, and referred the matter to the powerful Senate Privileges Committee.[36] The university chose not to provide a detailed response to Jesser's submissions to the Privileges

Committee. USQ said that it would be a waste of time: 'there appears to be nothing to add to Peter Jesser's statement as he has, as could be expected, pre-empted the only submissions that could be made.'[37]

One of the low points in the Jesser saga was the submission that his department sent to the SSCUWC. This submission was endorsed unanimously by the Department of Human Resource Management and Employment Relations, in Jesser's absence, on 24 April 1995.[38] The department fashioned a bizarre argument to burn Jesser's bona fides. First it used an esoteric source in the disclosure literature to press the view that Jesser could not be a whistleblower because his disclosures involved a colleague of similar rank.[39] It then questioned Jesser's motivation and argued that organisations have to be protected from people like him.[40] Jesser was portrayed as someone who behaves with 'vexatious querulousness' and 'has a record of taking allegations to forums outside the University'.[41] This is another way of saying that organisations hate external scrutiny. This view was apparent in a memo from USQ's Acting Registrar to the Vice-Chancellor noting '… the undesireability of our processes being scrutinised (possibly) by the Ombudsman'.[42] The 'trip-wire' perimeter around major organisations is set off when whistleblowers move from internal to external disclosure. It is almost a universal truth of organisational conflict: those who hang out the organisation's dirty laundry will swing from the same Hills Hoist.

Once disclosure becomes public, the whistleblower is far more dangerous than when he or she is still organisationally restrained. The whistleblower is no longer interested in compromise, but a fight to the finish. All actions are subsequently conducted in an atmosphere of irreconcilable conflict, as the following extract from Professor Craig Littler's confidential submission to the SSCUWC indicates:

Let me try to illustrate Mr Jesser's state of mind. At the meeting of the Department of Human Resource Management and Employment Relations on 10 March 1995, I attempted to point out Mr Jesser's error in confusing documents. He started shaking and asserted that I was infringing his personal space and that he would 'charge me with assault'. I, like all of my colleagues, was astonished.[43]

While Jesser may have missed Littler's attempt to point out his error, Littler missed Jesser's extreme psychological aggravation at being ganged up on ('I, like all of my colleagues'). The other point is they both missed each other. At the adversarial stage, reconciliation easily gives way to retribution. Littler again:

Mr Jesser's state of mind at present is such that he regards:
1) *All attempts to disagree with him as constituting 'victimisation' or 'assault'.*
2) *All suggestions that he conform to professional norms of behaviour, like all other members of staff, as constituting 'harassment'.*
3) *All attempts to respond to his false and fraudulent allegations as constituting 'intimidation'.*[44]

Jesser may have been like this. Who wouldn't when up against a retributive system of power? But an insidious interpretation pushes itself forward: that Jesser is psychologically disturbed.

The Senate Select Committee expressed the view that many of the elements of the response by the department and USQ were typical of organisational responses to whistleblowers:

The department sought to lay some of the blame for the problems that occurred on Mr Jesser ... The department also questioned Mr Jesser's motivations and mental stability and attempted to contain dissent within the department ... [I]t is the problem raised by the complaint which needs to be objectively assessed, not the whistleblowers who raised the problem in the first instance.[45]

Jesser now works in the TAFE system in Brisbane.

Confronting the Cancer: Kim Sawyer at RMIT
The exercise of whistleblowing is really akin to removing a cancer that is growing in a public institution. The cancer depends for its existence on a number of pre-conditions, typically a high discretionary environment (both in terms of financial and managerial accountability), weakness in the host institution (that is, the weakness of members of the institution), and finally that the cancer is sufficiently embedded, that is, it exists at the very core of the institution. The whistleblower

identifies the cancer, attempts to remove it, and then is attacked by it ... The whistleblower must at all times behave honourably; the cancer can behave as it likes, it has all the power ... Unsurprisingly whistleblowing is not usually successful. – Kim Sawyer[46]

This is a deeply insightful statement about organisational malpractice. Unfortunately for Kim Sawyer he achieved this wisdom at great personal cost.

Sawyer is a tall, handsome man with integrity written all over him. He came to the Royal Melbourne Institute of Technology (RMIT) in January 1991 as its first professor of Financial Econometrics.[47] Viewing the institution with fresh eyes, he soon became aware that something was amiss with the financial management of RMIT's Department of Economics and Finance and its entrepreneurial wing, the Centre of Finance. His suspicions were aroused by practices such as the abuse of international travel guidelines, the employment of relatives, and wedding gifts to staff disguised as textbook purchases.[48]

Disquiet about management irregularities culminated on 12 October 1992 when sixteen academics (including Sawyer) signed a petition calling for a full departmental audit.[49] At the time Sawyer said he had never faced such a serious problem during his seventeen years in tertiary institutions.[50] Professor Jackson, then Dean of the Faculty of Business, asked for written complaints from Sawyer and his colleagues. On 16 December 1992 Jackson advised Sawyer that he: 'had found evidence of gross mismanagement in the Department of Economics and Finance'.[51]

Six days later Jackson presented a report by the university's lawyers and confirmed that the department was in trouble. The operating deficit was likely to exceed $50,000. The department's reserves would then be reduced below reasonable contingency standards, and there was a danger of exposure to deficits in the Centre of Finance.[52]

In February 1993 the allegations of financial impropriety were investigated by RMIT internal auditors after Sawyer furnished them with a complaint. It was later claimed on the basis of documents obtained through FOI that the findings of the audit checks were rewritten as part of a systematic cover-up.[53]

By this time there was deep division in the department. It split into two broad factions: those involved in or supporting the disclosures, and those implicated in the alleged wrongdoing or caught-up in the complex cover-ups that occurred. Trust and mutual respect, cornerstones of any effective workplace, collapsed amid volleys of allegation and rebuttal. You can only imagine the effects on staff morale and student learning.

The stakes grew steadily higher as reputations and careers were endangered. It has been claimed that most of the petitioners were subjected to systematic harassment in one form or another.[54] Desperate people began to act desperately. On a number of occasions in early 1993 Sawyer's office and the offices of four of his disclosure group were entered at night, and books and papers were interfered with. RMIT took four months to change the locks on these burgled offices.[55] At a high-level meeting in March 1993 it was suggested to Sawyer that one option was for him to resign. Like Jesser, he realised then that he would probably have to take the matter outside the university.

He approached the First Assistant Secretary of the Higher Education Division of the Department of Employment, Education and Training and made what he thought was a confidential report. Soon the matter was back on the Vice-Chancellor's desk and Sawyer felt, with justification, that his confidentiality had been dishonoured.[56] After he left RMIT Sawyer had a discussion with a very senior education policy director who told him that RMIT was 'hermetically sealed'. Sawyer took this to mean that, in the officer's view, RMIT was beyond effective external ethical surveillance.[57]

Meanwhile, Sawyer and his colleagues were being subjected to intense scrutiny. In 1993 a senior journalist with the *Age* advised Sawyer that another member of staff had hired a private detective to investigate him. On two occasions he was aware that he was being followed, a fact attested to by a colleague.[58]

On 4 June 1993 Vice-Chancellor Beanland released a press statement on the internal audit and said that the auditor had found nothing to worry about.[59] The SSCUWC, which took evidence on the matter, found plenty to worry about, and called the whole thing a cover-up.[60] Sawyer was equally concerned. He commented:

I was astounded at the statement and the findings of the audit. To protect my reputation, I submitted the documents that I had submitted to Professor Jackson in February to the Victorian Auditor-General. The Auditor-General began to investigate in July. Soon after, RMIT auditors revised their report ... [The Auditor-General] now concluded, 'The allegation ... has now been confirmed. This is of concern as it indicates that the true purpose of the expense has been concealed and expenditure inappropriately allocated in the University's accounts.' As a consequence of this, Professor [X] had to repay monies to the university, and had his authority to authorise expenditures revoked for three months in August 1993.[61]

In the meantime, in April 1993 Sawyer had participated in another public interest disclosure in conjunction with eight of his colleagues. This time the issue was alleged plagiarism by a senior member of the department. Again, according to Sawyer, a whitewash occurred.[62] Worse, he and the other complainants received letters from the Vice-Chancellor demanding the names of people who had been told about the allegations of plagiarism.[63]

Sawyer felt that the reaction to the April 1993 plagiarism complaint and Professor Beanland's press statement of 4 June 1993 'were portents of my future at RMIT'. He was becoming increasingly worried. He had yet to receive confirmation of tenure, despite the fact that his probationary period had ended in February with no adverse reports.

In July, Vice-Chancellor Beanland twice demanded that Sawyer and six of his colleagues give him the names of those who had been informed of the plagiarism allegation. On 11 August they advised Beanland that they would be taking the plagiarism issue to the University Visitor. Six days later, they received a letter (dated 9 August) in which Beanland charged them all with official misconduct for their refusal to reveal the names. The Senate Select Committee that later examined the case considered Beanland's response 'inappropriate'. 'It is not,' the committee said, 'reasonable to charge members of an academic institution with serious misconduct because they did not respond in a way the person investigating the complaint thought they should.'[64]

Sawyer's hopes were now pinned on the outcome of the review

by the University Visitor. The Official Visitor is a nineteenth-century mechanism that is still occasionally applied to deal with academic conflicts.[65] By today's appeal and review standards, it is a primitive response. The ostensible purpose is to offer an external appraisal of the matter at a sufficiently high level of authority so that both sides will feel comfortable with the final decision. A more nefarious objective has always operated: to keep conflicts out of the public eye and protect the institution's good name.

In a flurry of judicial excess, the State Governor appointed the Chief Justice of Victoria to examine the appeal of Sawyer and his three colleagues.[66] RMIT was represented by one of the largest law firms in the country, Mallesons Stephen Jaques, who managed to slip RMIT off the hook on a legal technicality. After 442 days, the Chief Justice concluded that Sawyer and his colleagues were not 'members of RMIT'. He subsequently dismissed the appeal.[67] This was a devastating result for Sawyer. In early 1994 he took Supreme Court action against RMIT for breach of contract.[68]

After the Chief Justice dismissed the appeal, Sawyer realised that he had to go. In 1994 he was invited to apply for two professorships: one at Massey University in New Zealand, the other at Griffith University in Brisbane. Massey University contacted him to say that he was shortlisted for the chair and would be flown over for an interview. The story of his conflict at RMIT, however, crossed the Tasman first. Three weeks after he was advised of the shortlisting, the consultant group managing the selection process contacted him and asked for details of his problems at RMIT. He duly sent a statement across, and a week later was told that Massey University would no longer be pursuing his application.[69]

In the second part of 1994 he was interviewed for the Griffith University job, and again he found himself the subject of suspicion. He spent a substantial portion of the interview being quizzed by the Vice-Chancellor about the RMIT issue. Even with legal action pending back in Melbourne, the Vice-Chancellor took it on himself to test the validity of Sawyer's allegations. Sawyer returned home with a bad feeling about the interview. He was right.

Eventually he reached a settlement with RMIT, the terms of which remain confidential, and moved across to the University of Melbourne. His was not the only departure. Five years on, only two of the sixteen signatories to the original petition remained in the RMIT department; the rest had left through resignation, termination of contract, transfer or legal action.[70] Sawyer is unlikely to forget his experiences at RMIT, but he has assuaged his bitterness by representing the interests of other whistleblowers.

Sawyer came forward when the Commonwealth Senate held its second whistleblower inquiry in early 1995. He became a very useful witness and earned the committee's respect and gratitude. In summing up the legal ploys used by RMIT, Sawyer said:

Most whistleblowers encounter a legal system which is antithetical to the truth. The adversarial legal system currently in place in Australia is concerned only with legal technicalities, legal game theory, legal diversions and of course their associated costs.

Sawyer went on to criticise the Chief Justice and the RMIT lawyers:

The judiciary and legal discipline in general need to be educated about the necessary and beneficial role of whistleblowers ... [T]he Chief Justice of Victoria who judged our case ... has made public and private statements which whistleblowers regard as unhelpful ... Large law firms should be subject to accountability, just as large corporates are subject to scrutiny by the Trade Practices Commission.

Sawyer also referred to the Chief Justice's decision:

Finally the judiciary should be encouraged to present rulings which accord with common sense and with the public interest. The Chief Justice of Victoria took 442 days to decide that a professor and three lecturers were not members of the University. I ask you as senators whether this accords with your view of a university ... For most Australians this would be an absurd judgement and perhaps more. Yet it carries the imprimatur of the Chief Justice of Victoria and the Governor of Victoria.[71]

Sawyer did not pull any punches about his union, either. He found the RMIT Branch of the National Tertiary Education Union unhelpful and apparently oblivious to the gross procedural anomalies at the university. He has said:

> The NTEU tried to mediate a settlement which they described as a win-win. For me and my colleagues it was a loss-loss as it failed to address the initial problems, and left us at the mercy of the university.[72]

As a result of his tenacity Sawyer was repeatedly defamed, had his intellectual property appropriated, was directed not to speak to the media, was isolated in the work-setting, had his office burgled and his mail and telephone interfered with, was investigated by a private detective, had his access to secretarial services restricted, was made to move his office away from his research staff, and, to cap it all off, was charged with serious misconduct by RMIT.[73] Yet, serious as these consequences were, he felt the worst effect of the whole episode was his loss 'of all confidence in the institution and traditions of the country':

> I [now] regard the [university] education system as corrupted, corrupted by the entrepreneurs of education, what Professor Stephen Fitzgerald recently so appropriately described as carpetbaggers and gold diggers. Corrupted also by the failure of the governing bodies of universities to accept any real accountability or public responsibility. Corrupted also by an education bureaucracy that cannot define or implement a regulatory process in a deregulated environment. And finally corrupted by a system that perceives the vice-chancellors of our universities to be above the law.[74]

The Other Side of 'Academic Freedom': David Rindos and the University of Western Australia

Those familiar with the fate of [David Rindos] know the University would steam-clean him from its pores if such purging was possible, but, as with Lady MacBeth scrubbing her blood spots, the stain has smeared the institution's psyche. – Kate Legge[75]

David Rindos, an American scholar, was appointed to a tenurable position as senior lecturer in archaeology at the University of

Western Australia (UWA) in 1989 on the strength of a cross-Pacific telephone interview.[76] He came to UWA with what has been described as a 'glittering international reputation', although this would later be disputed.[77] He had qualifications from the prestigious Cornell University and had written an acclaimed book on the origins of agriculture. Four years later Rindos was out of favour and out of a job. He had become the first academic at UWA to be denied tenure, as a result of a process that was described as being 'riddled with inequity'.[78]

The Rindos case is very bitter and messy, and it is not my intention to summarise all the matters at issue here. I am mainly interested in the workings of power when it is in cover-up and defence mode, particularly when it is exercised with little accountability.

It seems that Rindos was recruited into a department factionalised by sexual politics and unchecked professorial power. The central figure in these conflicts was Sandra Bowdler, the Foundation Professor of Archaeology at UWA. Bowdler had initially supported Rindos's application, commenting that UWA 'was very lucky to get him'.[79] Soon, however, she became one of his main opponents.

Rindos started at UWA on 13 June 1989. Almost from day one he heard disturbing stories about Bowdler. He decided to act. In December 1990 Rindos wrote a memo to Professor Oxnard, the Head of UWA's Division of Agriculture and Science, detailing serious allegations of misconduct against Bowdler.[80] He followed the issue up at a meeting with Oxnard in January 1991. Rindos, then Acting Head of the Department of Archaeology while Bowdler was on study leave, claimed that she headed a department that operated in an environment of fear and intellectual suppression.

The next month, on Bowdler's return, she sent Rindos a memo outlining aspects of his performance that she thought were 'in need of improvement'.[81] Two years into the job, this was the first time Rindos had received an unfavourable report. He was suspicious.

Between February and March 1991 Professor Bowdler wrote several memos to Rindos criticising his lack of research output, the quality of his teaching, and his behaviour towards students.[82] On 25 March, hoping to defuse the conflict between Rindos and Bowdler, Professor Oxnard had him and three postgraduate students transferred to the Department of Geography.[83]

Later, when the contents of Rindos's file came to light, it was claimed that the decision to get rid of him was taken in those early months of 1991, although it was not put into effect for more than two years.[84] According to this claim, confidential memoranda on Rindos's file only make sense if it had already been decided to deny him tenure:

The problem being discussed was how to develop a reason to deny tenure that would stand up in public. Some of these memoranda actually go so far as to worry about how his previous good performance will make firing him difficult, while others worry about the effect his heavy teaching load will have upon the administration's future plan.[85]

In June Bowdler wrote a very negative tenure report on Rindos, which he was never shown. Professor Taylor, the Head of Geography and Rindos's new boss, contradicted Bowdler's assessment. Although he could not comment on Rindos' academic achievements, Taylor described him as a colourful and eccentric person, an enthusiastic researcher and 'a pleasure to have in the Department'.[86] On the strength of Taylor's report, Professor Oxnard accepted Rindos' performance as satisfactory.[87]

Rindos' previous allegations of misconduct against Bowdler were in part informed by reports from three of his female postgraduate students. They separately complained to Professor Robert Parfitt, the Deputy Vice-Chancellor, about the treatment they were getting in the Archaeology Department. One of the complainants was a PhD student who during her undergraduate years had had an affair with Professor Bowdler, and now felt intimidated and badgered.[88] Parfitt left for an overseas posting confident that he had sorted the matter out by moving the students to a safer environment. How wrong he was.

During 1991 the Archaeology Department was reviewed by Professors Bruce, Mouldren and McBride, who reported in December. Their report contained twelve recommendations and emphasised a number of serious concerns, including deep divisions within the department and low student morale. It included an 'oblique questioning of the appropriateness of some of Professor Bowdler's actions as Head of Department'.[89] Bruce and Mouldren, the two internal members of the committee, pushed in vain for a full inquiry into what were later described as 'highly disturbing and serious allegations of misconduct' in the department.[90] They forwarded confidential memos to Vice-Chancellor Fay Gayle detailing their concerns, held private talks with senior academics at the university, and encouraged the complainants to write directly to the Vice-Chancellor.[91]

The Vice-Chancellor appears to have received these letters in early 1992. One told of a field trip to Fitzgerald National Park:

The head of department [Bowdler] and her lover [a student] had a very audible argument that began late one evening and continued until about 5 am. There was much screaming and wailing, and as we were all in our nearby tents, no one got any sleep.[92]

While heterosexual relationships between academics and students are now generally taboo on campuses,[93] it seems that same-sex relationships often enjoy a certain immunity.[94] This is not for want of trying by some concerned members of the university community.

Following consideration of the review report, Gayle stood Bowdler aside as head of department.[95] In an action subsequently described by a Western Australian Parliamentary Committee as 'premature', Rindos was relocated back into the Archaeology Department. He was now back in Bowdler's terrain, with nothing resolved.[96]

On 28 February 1992 Gayle asked Professor Clyde of the Department of Civil Engineering, who had chaired Rindos's selection committee, and Professor Hotop of the Faculty of Law to advise her on further action she could take with respect to the allegations she had confidentially received following the Archaeology Department Review Report.

Clyde and Hotop reported within a month. The university refused to make the report public. Its contents were only revealed by the *West Australian* on 9 March 1996, almost four years later. Clyde and Hotop advised Gayle that the submissions of Rindos, one of his female colleagues and seven student-complainants against Bowdler 'should be taken seriously'.[97] They further advised that Bowdler would be guilty of serious misconduct if it was proved that her 'private relationships influenced her decisions on matters of staff appointments, supervision of students and allocation of departmental resources'. Hotop and Clyde added that if the field trip incident occurred and the allegations of academic 'thuggery' were true, than Bowdler should be cautioned and told that this behaviour was unacceptable.[98]

Apparently Vice-Chancellor Gayle interviewed Bowdler on 10 April 1992 and concluded, after receiving unspecified assurances from her, that there were no grounds to pursue a charge of misconduct.[99] Gayle did not order an inquiry. She had evidently been advised that, even if the allegations against Bowdler were true, it was unlikely that Bowdler could be disciplined under the relevant staff award.[100] At the request of the National Tertiary Education Union (NTEU), records of the meeting between Bowdler and the Vice-Chancellor were removed from her file.[101]

Back to Rindos's perspective on the matter. As Kate Legge described it in the *Australian*:

[Rindos] was bothered by perceptions that the department comprised of an inbred group with a small staff that included present and former girlfriends of Bowdler and several of her former students. Rindos is no homophobe. He is proudly gay. But he took seriously concerns that academic fortunes hinged on membership of an 'inner circle'.[102]

This observation goes to one of the central issues in the Rindos affair: do senior academics wield too much power? Traditionally universities have had deep management hierarchies, in which power and favour flowed from the Vice-Chancellor's office. These are now overlaid with a recent 'reform' structure whereby, in the name of decentralisation, these deep hierarchies are repositioned at the departmental or school level. From having one all-powerful Vice-Chancellor, universities now have a Mt Olympus crowded with one-line-budget god-professors. At the same time, the professorial mean age is dropping as a new class of member is added to the academic pantheon: the boy (or girl) professor. This new management group constitutes a sort of academic *nouveau riche*, irreverently described by Associate Professor Ted Steele as 'Mickey Mouse professors'.[103] It is primarily made up of people who have soared on the updrafts of rapid tertiary-sector growth in the 1980s (not to mention a little help from nepotistic breezes!) to reach positions far beyond their experience, and often far beyond their ability. At the departmental level, professorial power is immense, and in practice virtually unreviewable. Under intense performance pressure, teaching huge classes, and burdened by the need to bring scarce research dollars in, departments easily fracture into in-groups and out-groups. This, it could be argued, was the situation at UWA.

June 1992 marked the end of the three-year probation period after which Rindos would normally have been offered tenure. But these were not normal circumstances. In May the Vice-Chancellor extended Rindos' probationary period after receiving a confidential memo from the new head of the department, Dr Partis, seeking more time to review him.[104] Partis later remarked that he found Rindos interesting, but his behaviour was 'wearing':

He came to see me regularly, and it was normally to complain about something ... I repeatedly found that the complaints had no substance or something minimal had been blown out of proportion. He cried wolf so much, I did not have too much interest.[105]

When a Parliamentary Committee asked him about his relationship with Sandra Bowdler, Partis said, 'She was and is a friend of mine.'[106]

Gayle closed the Department of Archaeology and the Centre for Prehistory in July 1992. In December Partis recommended that Rindos be denied tenure because he did not get on with Professor Bowdler and other staff.[107] Gayle, however, extended Rindos's review period a second time in December 1992. This has been interpreted as a reaction to advice from the university solicitors that Partis's reasons for denying Rindos tenure were illegal, because tenure decisions must be made on academic grounds alone.[108]

Meanwhile the counter-attack on Rindos started. Nothing serious in the beginning: memo blitzes, behind-his-back talk, opened pay slips and inconvenient workplaces. Then Rindos was accused of plagiarism and sexual misconduct with female students. These charges are among the most serious an academic can face.

Unfortunately for his tormenters, the charges were quickly dismissed. The plagiarism charge was so obviously a beat-up that it had virtually no life at all. The sex charges were interesting considering that Rindos was openly and unambiguously gay. The allegations were not that Rindos made indecent proposals to the students, but that he often made sexual comments in an unsolicited and lurid manner.[109]

Gayle's decision to extend Rindos's review period necessitated the formation of a Tenure Review Committee – the first of its kind at UWA[110] – the purpose of which, according to a Rindos supporter, was to 'develop new reasons to fire him'.[111] Although Rindos wrote reports in his own defence and there were numerous letters of collegial support, both solicited and unsolicited, the Tenure Review Committee recommended unanimously that Rindos be denied tenure. Some matters in this process require comment.

The Tenure Review Committee reached a unanimous view not to recommend tenure after little more than an hour's deliberation.[112] It has been claimed that reports favourable to Rindos were not made available to the committee.[113] A UWA Senate representative on the Tenure Review Committee voted against Rindos twice: first on the committee and then in the Senate when it confirmed the committee's recommendations.[114]

The Tenure Review Committee applied itself ostensibly to judge Rindos' performance in three areas: service to the university, teaching, and research (specifically publications). In relation to research, the committee found that Rindos' output in his three-and-a-half years at UWA was below par. A subsequent investigation by the Parliamentary Standing Committee on Government Agencies found that Rindos' publication record had been assessed by extremely rigorous standards; if the same criteria had been applied to another UWA academic who had had twenty-one publications accepted for tenure confirmation and promotion purposes, all but one of the publications would have been excluded.[115]

The Tenure Review Committee did note that Rindos' output had been satisfactory before he came to UWA, but said it was unable to judge whether the reduced output was due to 'factors that were attributable to him or beyond his control'.[116] Since this went to a central issue of Rindos' performance, the fact that the Committee put it high up on the too-hard shelf does them no credit. The obvious question – was there a causal connection between Rindos's reduced research output and the toxic environment in which he worked? – was not addressed. It also appears that the university did not tell Rindos what it expected him to do to gain tenure.[117] There seemed to be a rather cavalier view among the university hierarchy that Rindos should have known what was expected.

Vice-Chancellor Gayle later conceded that she would have reconsidered Rindos's tenure if there had been a department other than his own that was prepared to have him.[118] Here we have creeping in another clandestine standard for tenure: to research, teaching and service, now add collegial acceptance. Given the specialisation and scholastic fragmentation common in universities, this covert standard would have enormous exclusionary power. At the best of times it is difficult to transfer an academic to another department.

After Rindos responded to the adverse recommendation of the Tenure Review Committee, the Vice-Chancellor was given legal advice that set up yet another covert hurdle to granting Rindos tenure. The advice said, inter alia, that it does not necessarily follow that because a tenure applicant has high academic standing, the 'best interests of the university will be served by granting him tenure'.[119] The advice went on to say that the granting of tenure raises 'wider issues than individual merit'. Yet universities do not advise tenure applicants that they must also pass a 'best interests of the university' test. Gayle accepted this legal advice and used it to deny Rindos tenure.[120] Gayle dismissed him in June 1993, with three days notice, citing Partis' original reason: that Rindos was not able to get on with Bowdler.[121] The UWA Senate confirmed the sacking in the same month.

The Parliamentary Committee said that it was open to it to find that the Vice-Chancellor's decision was influenced by the 1991 memoranda from Bowdler criticising Rindos. These were the reports deliberately withheld from Rindos by UWA's Personnel Department. The Committee found that not to give Rindos an opportunity to rebut the report was a breach of natural justice.[122]

Like so many other justice-seeking whistleblowers, Rindos was now adrift on a windless sea of review and appeal. His first port of call was the Australian Industrial Relations Commission. With the assistance of his union, the NTEU, Rindos attempted to negotiate a settlement with the university. No agreement was reached between the parties. Rindos next approached the Western Australian Ombudsman, who said that he would not process the complaint until Rindos had gone through the Western Australian Industrial Relations Commission.[123] Rindos thought that he was getting somewhere when the Industrial Commissioner ruled that he had a strong case for unjust dismissal, but in February 1995 the university persuaded the Commission that a more 'appropriate' forum for Rindos was the antiquated University Visitor system. The cost to Rindos of mounting the appeal to the Visitor (the Western Australian Governor) was estimated at $30,000.[124] He applied to the UWA Senate for financial assistance with his appeal, but the Senate lost no time in rejecting his application. The Ombudsman began investigations into Rindos's complaint, but decided to discontinue when he discovered that a parliamentary inquiry was to be established.[125]

Meanwhile Rindos was fighting a time-consuming battle to obtain university files through the Western Australian Freedom of Information Act. After almost a year he got most of the documents he needed for his appeal to the University Visitor. Some papers, however, had mysteriously vanished. The confidential submissions that Clyde and Hotop relied on in their report had been stolen or illegally destroyed,[126] and the complainants' original submissions to the Review of the Department of Archaeology in December 1991 had also been disposed of.[127] It has also been alleged that UWA authorities set up a special file into which went all manner of scurrilous reports on Rindos. Rindos apparently never knew of its existence, and therefore never had an opportunity to access it under FOI.[128] Rindos's complete personnel file had also disappeared around March 1994. In true Inspector Gadget fashion, the university put a private detective on to the case of the missing file, but alas the trail was cold.[129]

In December 1995 West Australian Labor MLC Mark Neville, a long-time critic of UWA's handling of the affair, made a speech in the Legislative Council and tabled 329 documents related to the case. Neville referred to the Rindos affair as constituting a 'scandal without precedent in the history of education in Australia'.[130]

The influential *West Australian* newspaper had initially run the line that Rindos was an academic lightweight and the decision to deny him tenure was justified. This became difficult to sustain after the UWA Senate received testimonials about Rindos' ability from world-renowned archaeologists including Lord Renfrew from Britain and Professor Binford, the so-called 'father of modern archaeology', from America.[131] In spite of this evidence, the *West Australian* stood by its assessment of Rindos, but it was also unhappy with the university's handling of the matter:

The long running controversy has exposed serious shortcomings in the university's capacity to manage academic staff and an alarming inability to cope effectively with pressures from community and other groups beyond campus boundaries.[132]

This last point is a reference to the Vice-Chancellor's closing down the Centre for Prehistory, allegedly under pressure from the Dominion Mining Company because the centre was finding too many sacred sites around proposed mining leases.[133] In its criticism of UWA's handling of the Rindos matter, the *West Australian* added:

Since the affair erupted into a public scandal, UWA's failure to argue its case coherently and convincingly suggests a cloistered ethos out of touch with modern communication techniques and community demand for accountability by public institutions.[134]

On 21 March 1996 the powerful Western Australian Parliamentary Standing Committee on Government Agencies decided to investigate the whole Rindos matter. Rindos said:

I am overjoyed to see myself as a footnote to this story because the real story has always been what happened to the students. If the university had handled the reports in a proper manner, I wouldn't have lost my job.[135]

Not so overjoyed were a number of powerful interest groups, including, ironically enough, the National Tertiary Education Union

(NTEU), which lined up behind the university and protested about parliamentary interference in university matters.

This was not the first time that the NTEU had experienced trouble figuring out where its primary loyalties lay. The problem lies in the structure of that union. In what other union in Australia do you share membership with your boss? Rindos and Bowdler were both NTEU members. When the conflict occurred, they had no choice but to go to the same union. It appears that the union stayed with Bowdler and parted company with Rindos.[136]

The Australian Vice-Chancellors Committee, through its Vice President, Geoff Wilson, was also highly critical of parliamentary intervention. Wilson described it as an attack on university independence, and noted that it would be a costly case for the university to defend. He also remarked that there was nothing unusual about a university denying an academic tenure.[137]

The outcry about academic freedom earned a rebuke from the Chair of the Parliamentary Committee, Barry House:

The universities have for some time resisted the legitimacy of us having jurisdiction over them, but we have decided that we do ... The university has employed expensive lawyers and public relations consultants to advise on our inquiry.[138]

A few days later Gayle was before the committee. In her opening address she said that she was there under protest and claimed that the committee was setting a 'dangerous precedent'.[139] She also said that she believed that the Committee was politically motivated.[140] Gayle went on to provide the committee with an example of the UWA mindset:

I have looked at three relatively recent cases of people who refused [to accept decisions not to grant them tenure] and, as we say, took it to the wire, as did Dr Rindos. In each case, just as it was going to the Senate, one within minutes of it going to Senate, the person raced in with a resignation, aware that the possibility of gaining other employment was in their better interests.[141]

Gayle's admission is extraordinary for its candour, but no amount of candour can validate a position that valorises expediency over justice.

In a pre-emptive mood, UWA had launched its own senatorial inquiry into the Rindos matter on 26 February 1996, a month before the parliamentary committee announced its investigation.[142] Three months later, the UWA Senate modified the terms of reference of its inquiry. Now it would only investigate the adequacy of university processes currently in place to meet Rindos-type problems. It would not investigate Rindos' allegations directly.[143]

Behind the legal gobbledegook that purported to justify the narrowing of the terms of reference lies another standard organisational response to whistleblowers. By focusing on current administrative arrangements, which have usually been put in place as a face-saving reaction to the whistleblower's disclosures, management attempts to relegate the whistleblower to the dustbin of history. In moments of rare honesty, organisations may own their blemished pasts, but these moments are quickly superseded by an emphasis on the 'now'. 'Now,' we are assured, 'everything is okay. We have corrected the problems that the whistleblower discovered.' If these messages get through, and they usually do, they cut the whistleblower off from the present. Whistleblowers are demeaned as yesterday's people. As such we owe them nothing: no thanks, no compensation, no reward, only our amnesia. This is what happened to Rindos.

During May 1996 UWA–government relations became very strained. The Parliamentary Committee was tipped off by a well-placed official about the nature and location of relevant university files.[144] UWA had to face the indignity of having the Usher of the Black Rod (an officer responsible for carrying out parliamentary directions) arrive on the campus on 7 May and refuse to leave until he was supplied with the subpoenaed documents that he had come for.[145]

One of the interesting features of the Rindos case is the use made of the internet. Rindos and his supporters sent voluminous material on his case to a site at the University of Buffalo in the United States. Once UWA got news of this site it attempted to shut it down with threats of defamation.[146] University lawyers and outside solicitors (the large legal firm of Freehill Hollingdale and Page) sent threatening letters to Rindos sympathiser Dr Brian Martin at the University of Wollongong, who was also President of Whistleblowers Australia. The lawyers wrote to the editor of the widely circulated *Campus Review* and the producer of the ABC radio program *The Education Report*. Freehill Hollingdale and Page tried to argue that the mere publication of the internet address was a republication of a defamation.[147] The irony is that Rindos has gone down in internet history as the first person to sue for defamatory material transmitted on the net. In an undefended action he was awarded $40,000 from an archaeology colleague with respect to comments made on an internet mailing list.

When the university announced its inquiry, the Vice-Chancellor said that its findings would be made public.[148] She released the report on 13 January 1997, nine months after it was promised, and even then it was released with retractions. Probably following threats of legal action, comments about the role of key players were 'unreservedly withdrawn'.[149] The university's interim report immediately drew criticism. A group calling itself Archaeology Action deplored the report as a whitewash and expressed dismay that Bowdler was still in her position. It also criticised the report's avoidance of any criticism of Vice-Chancellor Gayle, who it claimed should have taken action back in 1991 after the disturbing Archaeology Department review.[150]

In early May 1997, following Western Australian elections, the government inquiry into the Rindos matter was continued by a new committee – the Legislative Council's Standing Committee on Public Administration – much to the chagrin of UWA.[151] It reported on 4 December 1997 with this conclusion:

Dr Rindos did not have adequate and fair opportunities to present his case and has not, in all circumstances, been afforded common law procedural fairness.[152]

Vice-Chancellor Gayle immediately lashed out at the report, saying it 'contains errors of fact, findings which appear to be based on evidence which is not disclosed in the report and findings which are illogical'.[153] She went on to say that UWA did not deny Rindos natural justice. Rather, the Parliamentary Committee had denied justice to the university.

The Parliamentary Committee's finding, however, came too late for David Rindos. He had died in his sleep in the early hours of 9 December 1996.[154] He was only 49. Shortly after his death his partner said to me, 'Let's be honest, the bastards killed him.'[155]

7 | Whistleblowing on Eight Cents a Day
Disclosure at the ABC

On 3 October 1996 John Millard received an award for the best television feature of 1996 from the federal Minister for Science and Technology, Peter McGauran.[1] Almost twelve months earlier, Millard had received a letter from Penny Chapman, head of ABC-TV, which concluded with the words:

I am not able to extend your employment beyond the period of your current contract which expires on 31 December 1995.[2]

What makes this case so interesting is that Millard was a whistleblower inside the ABC, a broadcasting authority with a strong and courageous tradition of assisting whistleblowers in all walks of life to expose wrongdoing.

Like many whistleblowers, Millard was an idealist caught between two powerful opposing forces: the values his organisation espoused in theory and those that governed its everyday practice. According to Millard, there are 'two ABCs':

One [is] the public's ABC – the public's perception and nostalgic belief in a trusted, ethically reliable, totally independent ABC as reflected in the honest faces of the James Dibbles, the Doogues, Olles, O'Briens, McKews and Masters. [The other is the] corporate managers' ABC – an editorially compromised and less than independent ABC motivated by self-interest, corporate empire-building, career ambition and pleasing Canberra (both sides).[3]

Officially, ABC management took a benign view of dissent within the ranks. As it said in its submission to the Senate Select Committee on ABC Management and Operations in 1995:

The ABC's most trenchant critiques [sic] are frequently within the ABC. Those who work here are often those who care most and are most vocal about this institution. This is a healthy state of affairs.[4]

The organisation's practice, however, was quite a different matter, as we can see from the following exchange during one of the Senate committee's hearings:

Senator Tierney: At the hearing in December [1994] whistleblowing protection was discussed ... What plans in this are being considered by the ABC?
Mr Lidbetter [ABC Deputy Managing Director]: ... my personal view is that it is not necessary. I know of no organisation where anybody ... can get up and give a free kick – either through a forum like this or by writing to the newspapers – to management or individuals within television, radio or whatever ...
Senator Tierney: There have been threats, have there not? It is on the Hansard record.
Mr Lidbetter: They claim that, I have yet to see them. Someone said to me ...
Senator Tierney: You were not standing in the [Senate Committee] room, but people said that people senior to them had commented 'I hope you've got a job next week' after appearing before this hearing. That would indicate the need for some ...
Mr Lidbetter: That was a joke.
Senator Tierney: Was it?
Mr Lidbetter: I have spoken to the person in radio who made that claim; he has a very good sense of humour. The person he made the joke to, it went right over his head ...
Senator Tierney: You have heard the expression said in jest and meant in deadly earnest, though, have you not? Someone is about to appear before a national inquiry and it is not something to joke about really, is it?[5]

This scenario partakes of what philosopher Hannah Arendt called the banality of evil.[6] Management strikes with great ordinariness these days. Its threats are disguised as 'jokes', its hypocrisy as pragmatism. John Millard's victimisation is a case in point.

Millard was born in Sydney in 1949. He came to the ABC in 1983 after working in rural property management. He started at ABC-Radio, working on such programs as *Morning Extra*, *Australia All Over* and the *Country Hour*. In 1985 he won the Gold and Grand Award at the International Radio Festival in New York for his documentary 'The Outback Suburb'. That year he moved to ABC-TV, where he worked on programs such as *The Investigators* and *Hot Chips*.

Millard first raised concerns about creative compromise in September 1990. His concerns were ignored.[7] Then, in 1992, while working as a reporter on *The Investigators*, he began to suspect that a story had been 'canned' because it was critical of a builder who was also a reporter on the ABC co-production *The Home Show*.[8] Millard reported his concerns to Derek Pola, then executive producer of *The Investigators*, and Stuart Scowcroft, Head of Features.[9]

By early 1993, Millard claimed to have discovered seventeen examples of improper editorial influence on stories potentially damaging to commercial interests working closely with the ABC on various co-productions. He firmly believed that this interference breached the ABC's long tradition of independence. In February and March he circulated two further memoranda to management and raised the matter at two staff meetings.[10] He claimed that ABC staff had been engaged in indirect advertising and that programs avoided making critical comments about current or future funders. He also believed that resources were being diverted from ABC programs to the co-productions.[11]

An example of the practices that aroused Millard's concern was the ABC's liaison with the Australian Tourism Industry Association (ATIA) over the 'infotainment' program *Holiday*. At the end of 1991 the ATIA urgently memoed its members saying that the ABC had asked for help in the production of *Holiday*. The memo included words to the effect that tour operators could improve their chances of being mentioned in the program if they offered free accommodation and board to the *Holiday* production crew. In response, the ABC admitted that the ATIA memo was 'misguided', but claimed no operator 'was ever asked to pay for coverage'.[12]

Millard made similar allegations about other programs in his submission to the Mansfield Inquiry into the functions of the ABC in August 1996:

The ABC's health program Everybody *was funded by the snack food, junk food and processed food industries. Everyone I have told this to both inside and outside the ABC are both astounded and appalled at such blatant editorial conflict of interests and such brash attempts at deceiving the audience – everyone that is except ABC management.*[13]

Putting himself in the shoes of a producer of a hypothetical health show, Millard said:

I am an 'independent' producer ... for a health program I am making for ABC TV. My source of funding is the snack food and junk food industries using the front name The National Good Nutrition Foundation. In making my program on the subject of kids' diets and school tuckshop food, I would indeed talk about (though not dwell on) the importance of a balanced diet, fresh fruit and exercise, but I would leave on the cutting room floor the serious health concerns about the rise in child obesity and the growing consumption of snack foods and junk foods. I would also exclude any interview grabs with the nutritionist that criticised the high fat, high salt, low fibre levels of snack and junk foods ... Is this too cynical? This has all happened ... It came as no surprise to me that it was always the Investigators that covered the vital health issues that Everybody would never touch; that covered the 'bad news' building stories that the Home Show left aside; and the many holiday and travel disaster tales that Holiday knew would upset their sponsors in the travel industry and threaten next year's funding.[14]

Millard was concerned at what he perceived to be the drift away from the ABC's first principles, and worried that he was being drawn into the duplicity:

Here I was, a reporter on The Investigators, *talking face-to-face with the trusting Australian public, exposing the unethical behaviour of all sorts of private business, from car dealers to the largest of corporations, yet I could do effectively nothing about the unethical behaviour of my own ABC bosses. I was by default a direct party to the deception of the public. I was a face that they trusted, yet what I knew they would be appalled by. But ironically it was because of my job and producing programs about whistleblowers and their inevitable fate that I knew, or at least should have known better than most, that to speak out could destroy my career completely.*[15]

Millard's comments to me about the whistleblower's 'inevitable fate' were also based on bitter experience. At a meeting on 12 March 1993, he had placed damning evidence before the Director of TV, Paddy Conroy, but Conroy apparently ignored it.[16] In June 1993 Quentin Dempster, the staff-elected director on the ABC Board, forwarded Millard's allegations to David Hill, then ABC Managing Director.[17] The following month ABC management formally refuted all of Millard's allegations.[18]

Fourteen months passed with no further developments until 18 September 1994, when Channel Nine's *Sunday* program ran a story about editorial censorship of the ABC's *The Home Show*. With nowhere to hide, management responded the same day. ABC chair Armstrong announced the setting up of an inquiry under George Palmer QC.[19] About this Millard said:

Why he [Armstrong] didn't do this when our similar but more numerous allegations were presented to the ABC Board raises questions about the Board's competence and integrity.[20]

The next day the *Sydney Morning Herald* reported that ABC management claimed to be surprised by the allegations. When he read this, Millard decided to take action:

At 6.15 am after a discussion with my wife (this was a decision that I knew could have dire family consequences) I called the ABC's AM radio program.[21]

On air, he pointed out that, far from being 'surprised' at the allegations made on *Sunday*, ABC management had known about them for about eighteen months.

Millard went to work and waited for the storm. He was fortunate enough to gain the backing of his union, the Media, Entertainment and Arts Alliance (MEAA). This is unusual. Normally unions react with inertia or befuddlement when management strikes at their whistleblower-members. The MEAA and Millard prepared a joint statement claiming that ABC management had ignored and dismissed the allegations. David Hill threatened to sue Millard and other journalists for defamation if the joint statement was published.[22] Millard commented:

Never before has a head of this important democratic institution used such bullying threats in order to suppress the facts and thus shield his reputation and that of other implicated senior managers.[23]

The union deplored Hill's action and called on him to resign or be sacked if he did not withdraw the defamation threat.[24]

Millard and his union were also unhappy with the restricted terms of reference of the Palmer inquiry established by ABC management,[25] although the terms of reference were extended to include some of Millard's specific allegations.[26] The results of the inquiry validated many of Millard's concerns. Palmer confirmed Millard's allegations of undue influence on the selection and content of stories for *Holiday* by State and federal tourist bodies who part-funded the program. Paddy Conroy accepted ultimate responsibility and resigned as head of ABC-TV in March 1995.[27] His position was taken by Penny Chapman.

Millard continued to express his concerns about editorial corruption at ABC TV, raising the issue both with the Senate Select Committee on ABC Management and Operations and an Editorial Policies Working Group established to review editorial policy after Palmer had reported.[28] The Senate Committee found that the ABC's editorial policy had been breached on several occasions and that content was compromised as a result of commercial pressure on the ABC. For example, the committee found that the distribution of 'fact sheets' relating to a telecommunications episode of the *Home Show* amounted to an advertisement for Telecom.[29]

The fact that Millard was involved in formal review processes on the issues that he had raised sets him apart from the vast majority of whistleblowers, who are usually left high and dry after they make their disclosures. Referring to Millard's *modus operandi* Phillip Coleman, the barrister appointed to investigate Millard's allegations, said:

John Millard has been very active in relation to the ABC's compliance with its editorial policies. He has pursued his concerns in relation to editorial compromise with vigour and determination. His pursuit of these matters has been at least partly responsible for the exposure of wrongdoing by ABC management. The description of him as a 'whistleblower' is not inappropriate. Mr Butler [the Chairman of the Media Entertainment and Arts Alliance House Committee at Gore Hill] who gave evidence in support of Mr Millard described him as 'almost the quintessential whistleblower – passionate, courageous and determined not to be put down in the face of corporate opposition'. Having extensively interviewed Mr Millard I do not disagree with that description.[30]

The quintessential whistleblower is also a suffering employee.[31] One thing that whistleblowers are punished for is their perceived disregard for authority, particularly the layers of authority encapsulated in their organisations' chains of command. The myth of the whistleblower as a rebel or malcontent became a source of misery for Millard. His initial response when he discovered wrongdoing was to use official channels to alert his superiors. In September 1990 he first raised his concerns with his executive producer and departmental head. 'They dismissed then ignored the matters,' he said.[32]

On 23 November 1992 Millard hand-delivered a memo on editorial compromise to head of features Stuart Scowcroft and executive producer Derek Pola. According to Millard both men grew angry about the content of the memo and demanded to see specific proof. When Millard said that he was going over their head with the evidence, Scowcroft is reported to have said, 'Your actions have been fucking disloyal to your colleagues.' Scowcroft allegedly finished the meeting with words that in anyone's language constitute a threat: 'These things, John, have a way of coming back to haunt us.'[33] Scowcroft then threw Millard out of his office because he was angry with Millard for allegedly not using the chain of command.[34] Millard's claim that he had raised some of his concerns with Scowcroft before this incident, but without satisfaction, is justified given the events of the September 1990.

On another occasion, in a conversation with Quentin Dempster, Paddy Conroy described Millard as 'mad'.[35] On questioning by Coleman, Conroy and Dempster both said that the remark was not meant seriously, but Coleman took another view:

This type of comment, particularly from such a senior manager, is potentially very damaging for Millard's reputation. I think this comment was passed to Dempster in an attempt to discredit Mr Millard and thereby dissuade Mr Dempster from taking up the editorial compromise issue.[36]

Coleman added that similar remarks had 'very probably' been made to other members of staff.

This was not the only evidence suggesting that Millard's reputation had been maligned. John Turner, Millard's last executive producer on *The Investigators*, was warned by Paddy Conroy and Derek Pola, the outgoing producer, that he should watch out for Millard.[37] Nevertheless, Turner formed a good working relationship with Millard, and made overtures on his behalf that he should fill a vacancy on the *Quantum* team.[38] After seven years on *The Investigators*, Millard was interested in leaving to work on a new program.

In his evidence to the Coleman Inquiry, Turner is clear that in early November 1993 Alison Leigh, Head of the Science Unit in the ABC's Features Department, agreed to have Millard on *Quantum* in 1994.[39] Turner passed the good news on to Millard only to receive a note a few days later from Daryl Karp, who followed Scowcroft as Head of Features:

John [Turner]
John Millard is to remain on Investigators. I have asked Alison to use Geoff Burchfield instead
    Daryl[40]

Millard only had the *Quantum* position for a day. Coleman found that Daryl Karp gave contradictory evidence about this matter when he interviewed her.[41] Millard claimed that Karp's veto of his promised position on *Quantum* was designed to frustrate his career in retaliation for his whistleblowing, leading possibly to his departure from the ABC.[42]

Millard's view here is supported by the fact that one of his seventeen allegations of editorial compromise involved Ms Karp when she was the producer of *Quantum*.[43] Karp was also involved in putting together the official ABC rebuttal of Millard's allegations.[44]

On 1 February 1994 Millard had an interview with Daryl Karp to discuss his career. In the interview Karp said to Millard, 'You are regarded as a reporter who is difficult to get on with.' Millard asked 'By whom?' and Karp said 'Across the board.'[45] Millard ran the source of this remark to ground:

When pushed further Karp admitted that her view was based on the opinion of the very EP [executive producer] against whom I had previously raised allegations of editorial compromise.

This was her sole reliable source on which she has justified her repeated slandering of my character.[46]

About all this the Coleman report said:

I conclude that Mr Millard's lack of success in his desired career move to Quantum *during the second half of 1993 was, at least partly, because of his activities in relation to the ABC's compliance with its editorial policies. If Mr Millard had not been a whistleblower then I think he would have been given the opportunity to prove himself on* Quantum *in 1994. The detriment suffered is significant because* Quantum *has continued and is an ongoing program. Assuming Mr Millard's work on that program was satisfactory, then most likely he would still be there as a reporter working in his preferred area*[47]

Each successive refusal brought Millard closer to the precipice, which was finally reached on 28 September 1995 when Penny Chapman sent him the letter referred to at the beginning of the chapter. This was a standard letter to all contract reporters on the soon-to-be-finished *Investigators*. Millard claimed that he should not have received one of these letters as he was not on *The Investigators* team any more. Coleman examined the evidence on this point and agreed.[48] Millard summed up the ABC's tactic here as one of entrapment. As he said in a letter to Chapman: '[I feel] as if you designated me to a ship that you had already planned to torpedo.'[49] Coleman thought that this view was 'not inappropriate'.[50] Coleman received evidence that *The Investigators* was under a cloud from April 1995, when Penny Chapman succeeded Paddy Conroy in the position of head of ABC TV,[51] five months before Millard received his termination letter. Coleman concluded:

All this indicates that Ms Karp wanted Mr Millard out of the Features Department for some reason. She went to some lengths to construct an 'agreement' [Millard 'agreeing' to return to The Investigators*] out of the meeting, when there was no such 'agreement'. The 'agreement', so constituted, had the effect of making Mr Millard redundant.*[52]

Coleman also implied that the attack on Millard was planned to coincide with the controversial decision to discontinue *The Investigators* and an equally controversial restructuring of the *7.30 Report*, both of which distracted attention from Millard's problem.[53]

Coleman described Penny Chapman as being 'desirous ... of having Mr Millard out of ABC TV'.[54] He found Chapman had neglected her duty in failing to respond to Millard's written concerns that Karp was victimising him. Coleman described aspects of Chapman's behaviour in this matter as 'extraordinary' and 'inappropriate'.[55]

The upshot of all of this was that, despite being vindicated by the Palmer and Coleman inquiries, Millard was out of ABC TV. Coleman's penultimate paragraph records his disappointment:

It seems to me extraordinary, considering Mr Millard's ten years of experience as a television reporter and producer; with an unblemished employment record; a manifest dedication to public broadcasting and the ABC; a successful career, having won a number of awards; and an enthusiasm and passion for his work rarely found; that ABC management decided not to renew his contract for 1996.[56]

Coleman reported in late June 1996. In August, seventy-seven Sydney-based ABC news and current-affairs journalists signed a letter calling on Brian Johns, the ABC Managing Director, to punish the three managers adversely named by Coleman. The staff noted that the Millard affair had placed the ABC in an ethical dilemma:

The ABC cannot ... expose and lecture other public and private sector organisations about their lack of accountability when we cannot demonstrate it exists within our own media organisation.

The signatories went on to warn Johns that:

ABC staff will not hesitate to take action to defend any staff member targeted by ABC management for reprisal, harassment or intimidation. Brian, trust, once destroyed, is almost impossible to regain. We cannot overlook your failure to act, to do what professionally and responsibly had to be done as a result of the inquiry that you initiated into the victimisation of John Millard in apparent good faith. Your failure to act has had the effect of poisoning the atmosphere within ABC Television and making it most unpleasant for all concerned in these difficult times.[57]

Johns was reported to have expressed full confidence in his three managers,[58] and to have formed the view that they did not act with malice.[59]

There is no doubt that by this time Millard was playing with a winning hand, thanks to an unusual combination of ingredients:

- a strong sense of public duty, which calmed his nervousness and self-doubt;
- union support (rare for whistleblowers[60]);
- neutral and (for the most part) competent external investigation; and
- strong media interest.

Being a journalist was a great plus for Millard when he went public, of course. Not only was he able to write sharp and punchy pieces for the print media,[61] he also had strong support from journalists who were prepared to do the same thing.[62]

Millard also used email to broadcast his concerns to more than 2000 ABC staff around Australia. On at least two occasions he used the internet to publicise the contents of letters that he had written to Johns.[63] Millard said:

I felt an enormous sense of freedom and democratic strength as I pressed the computer's 'send' key. I knew that ... all ABC staff would see how irresponsible the MD Johns's response had been, and more importantly, those managers still against me would feel exposed for what they were.[64]

This novel broadcast strategy produced affirming responses such as:

I just want to express sincere support for you and your fight for justice in relation to the Coleman Inquiry. You have been treated abhorrently and should know that you have many supporters ...[65]

I am shocked to read the extent of your victimisation at the hands of management. My heart goes out to you over what you've gone through in this period. For what it's worth as a colleague I'd like to personally thank you for the stand you took on co-productions, it is now apparent how brave you were to have spoken out. You have my full support.[66]

Just a short e-mail from a fellow ABC'er to show you my support. I think it's a disgrace the way ABC management have treated you. Keep the pressure on and please keep informing all staff of the latest ... Stick to your guns as you have a lot of support in the ABC.[67]

There were, however, those who objected to Millard's use of the internet. On 7 August 1996 two anonymous complaints were sent, one to the ABC Efficiency Review and Audit Manager, and the other to Millard direct. The first complaint said:

I wish to make an anonymous complaint about what I perceive to be a case of fraud inside our organisation. I attach a copy of an E-Mail I received today from John Millard. It says that it was sent to 471 addresses.

> I can see this message is not related to ABC business and represents a private matter between Mr Millard and the MD. The 471 addresses have no reason to be copied.
>
> I wish to have the cost of this message investigated. I believe it should be paid by Mr Millard himself. I know that my own manager insists that we don't use the All In One for private matters, and that the number of addresses is limited.
>
> I have copied this complaint to Mr Millard which I think is only fair.
>
> I do not wish my identity known as I do not feel my own position is necessarily safe at the moment due to the cuts and I certainly do not wish to have someone as obviously powerfully connected as Mr Millard campaigning against me as he has done against other members of staff.
>
> If this matter is not investigated and the results publicly declared I will consider doing what Mr Millard himself seems to feel is the best course of action – a discreet leak to the press.[68]

The other complaint to Millard was even more hostile in its tone:

> I am most offended at your use of the e-mail to further your case and your personal use of the ABC facilities in these times of tight fiscal restraints. Please desist from doing this as I am not interested in your situation or where you work. In fact we wish you'd stay in radio – they deserve you. WE DON'T WANT TO KNOW ANYMORE, so let's get on with it.[69]

In October 1996, three months after Coleman reported, Paul Williams, Acting Head of ABC News and Current Affairs, offered Millard a position.[70] Millard deferred a decision, and explained to Williams 'why I have genuine fears about accepting such offers'.[71] That letter makes for dramatic reading:

> The working culture in ABC management remains as hostile to my presence now as Coleman's findings showed it has been ... Neither management nor the Board have since attempted to defend or protect me and others despite the Palmer, the Senate and Coleman Inquiries supporting my allegations ... At the very time that the Managing

Director and the Chairman of the Board are saying to me ' ... you have my full support in furthering your career in the ABC', they have by their actions effectively excluded me from working in the very television quality magazine program genre that I have worked in longer than most other reporters and received more consistent national acclaim for.[72]

Two months later, on 17 December, a settlement was reached between Millard and ABC management.[73] Brian Johns, the Managing Director, said, 'We genuinely welcome John back to ABC TV and wish him well on his return.'[74] Millard was given a cash settlement to cover back-pay entitlements (but not damages), a guarantee he would be able to speak out in the future, and work in 1997 back in ABC TV on *Australian Stories*.

It would be false to conclude with 'and he lived happily ever after'. The aftershocks of whistleblowing stay in the system for a long time. Two days after the settlement, Millard received anonymous hate mail, which he believes came from or was condoned by ABC TV management. He said in response:

What is distressing for me and my family and ... other ABC staff, is that the person – or people in TV management in particular – behind this letter are in a position to threaten me and similarly threaten other staff.[75]

Co-sponsorship and the fear of losing editorial courage, the issues at the centre of Millard's story, remain a source of controversy within the ABC. One of the nineteen recommendations from the Mansfield Review urged the government to resist program sponsorship in order to maintain independence and community trust.[76] At about the same time, *Media Watch* reported on a series called *Animal Friends*:

Let's not beat around the bush. The writer/presenter of Animal Friends, *Jonica Newby, is an employee of Petcare, which is fully funded by Uncle Ben's, whose business is selling pet food. Her columns for* Women's Weekly *appeared directly opposite whole-page ads for Uncle Ben's products. If [the producers of the ABC Science Show] don't believe there was an interest requiring frank disclosure on the ABC then we wonder if they have any grasp of journalistic ethics ... The continuing silence of Dr Newby herself remains interesting, indeed. Is there something else they haven't told us?*[77]

Three months later, in November 1997, ABC staff sent the Board an open letter protesting at management plans for joint current affairs productions with commercial broadcasters. This followed a storm of protest over a $1m proposal by high-flying anchor Jana Wendt to make a series of celebrity interviews for the ABC. The open letter claimed such joint activities threatened ABC independence and integrity, and were 'both ill-conceived and self-defeating'.[78] In a separate protest, Quentin Dempster wrote to the Board saying that it was better for the ABC to have blanks in its schedule than to make deals with commercial producers.[79] Controversy over the Wendt interviews continued into August 1998, when *Media Watch* presenter Richard Ackland produced a scathing critique of the series, prompting a spate of public comment about the program's high cost, poor ratings and lack of intellectual content.[80]

Is the ABC ready for another Millard?

'Shreddergate'
The Battles of Kevin Lindeberg

Shreddergate is not really about the illegal shredding and the illegal payment, it is about my journey through the system in a quest for justice and ... its utter impotence in dealing with high level corruption at the Executive Government level ... Shreddergate reveals 'the System' in a state of anarchy. – Kevin Lindeberg [1]

It is the morning of 7 May 1993 and I am in Kevin Lindeberg's kitchen, interviewing him for the Queensland Whistleblower Study. Lindeberg's wife was forced to find a job after he was sacked; now she has left for the day, and their two eldest kids have gone to school. These interviews are often gruelling, traumatic affairs. The research team is new to the area of reprisals, and each interview has a shock for us. Lindeberg's case is no exception.

Tears are streaming down his face as he recounts the effects of the whistleblowing on his family – the innocent bystanders swept up by a tornado of power and politics. In fact, the only time Kevin Lindeberg gets really upset is when he thinks about his family. He paces the kitchen floor, protectively cradling his baby as if danger lurks. I feel like I am debriefing a soldier who has survived a mighty conflagration. At other times I feel I shouldn't be here. But he doesn't seem to mind as I resurrect the pain.

Through the mist of trauma and despair, I gain a strong sense of Lindeberg's extraordinary strength and tenacity. I am absolutely sure that if his enemies had had any inkling of this man's doggedness they would have backed off immediately. He is down, but very definitely not out. He is on the road searching for 'justice'. And he has been on that road since 1990.

We are an unlikely couple, Lindeberg and I. We have a strange division of labour. I carry all the pessimism and he carries all the hope. After hearing and analysing so many whistleblower stories, I have come to believe that there is no justice. The look this terrier of a man gives tells me he must find it.

From 1988 to early 1990 staff and their unions at the John Oxley Youth Centre (JOYC), a juvenile detention facility in Brisbane, were bombarding the State government with complaints about the administration of the centre. JOYC was starved of funds and heavily factionalised on issues such as discipline, violence, overwork and quality of services. In April 1989 a consultant's report strongly criticised JOYC's system for controlling young offenders.[2] The Centre had long been the site of violent incidents.[3]

Some of the youth workers were dissatisfied with the management style of the facility's manager, Peter Coyne. His detractors blamed Coyne for the high staff turnover at the centre – thirty resignations in two years.[4] As Coyne saw it, he was doing the best he could to maintain high standards of care. His actions were not always well received, but he did what he felt he had to do. On one occasion, for example, he reprimanded a staff member for coming to work in pyjamas.[5] The complaints against Coyne have been deliberately destroyed. We will return to this issue shortly, because Lindeberg and his supporters have always maintained that these complaints were illegally disposed of. Brisbane's *Weekend Independent* has branded this affair 'Shredder-Gate'.[6]

On 14 September 1989 the Queensland State Services Union (QSSU), acting on behalf of some youth workers, made verbal complaints[7] against Coyne to Allen Pettigrew, the Director-General of the Queensland Department of Family Services.[8] At Pettigrew's insistence, QSSU furnished written complaints on 10 October. I have seen a document that identifies seven of the complainants and summarises their concerns. One complainant remained anonymous. Coyne was accused of very serious misconduct, including child abuse (a child chained to a bed, another chained overnight to a pool fence), staff harassment and managerial incompetence.[9] Pettigrew responded by appointing retired magistrate Noel Heiner to conduct an official inquiry into Coyne and JOYC, with the staff complaints as its core terms of reference.[10]

Pettigrew's decision to investigate the allegations in this way was subsequently criticised by a number of people, including the Crown Solicitor.[11] It was three weeks before Coyne found out that these complaints included allegations of criminal conduct.

Coyne originally welcomed the inquiry, claiming he had nothing to hide, but soon developed serious misgivings about the process. On 29 November he contacted an inquiry official:

I asked for a copy of the complaints, the answer was 'no'. I asked for advice on the process of investigation of complaints and the enquiry, the answer was 'no'. I asked about the right to organise and conduct a defence, the answer was 'no'.[12]

After Labor won the Queensland election on 2 December 1989, Pettigrew, like a number of other departmental heads, was quickly replaced. His position was taken by Ruth Matchett, a social worker with limited high-level administrative experience. On 14 December Coyne wrote to Matchett, repeating his request for copies of the complaints.[13] He received only a note of acknowledgement.

Coyne was interviewed by Heiner on 11 January 1990. He felt trapped in what he believed to be a biased investigation:

I didn't know the details of the complaints against me ... or [have] transcripts of evidence. [About 30] supportive letters from staff at JOYC [had not] been tabled ... at the inquiry. No response had been made to me by the Director-General relating to the legislative base and process of the inquiry, or of the means by which I could conduct a defence ... I was not permitted to be legally represented. I was not permitted to call witnesses. I was not permitted to recall witnesses for cross-examination. I was not allowed to leave the room to obtain documents to support assertions ...[14]

Heiner asked Coyne about a number of matters, including a surprise allegation that Coyne had a sexual relationship with the JOYC Assistant Manager. Coyne and the woman concerned were alarmed by this, and they instructed solicitors to lodge complaints to Matchett about the denial of natural justice.[15]

On 18 January Coyne made a fourth unsuccessful request to

Matchett to provide him with the complaints from the youth workers.¹⁶ On the same day, the Crown Solicitor advised Matchett on a number of matters related to the Heiner Inquiry. In particular, he advised that, because the inquiry was not established under the Commissions of Inquiry Act, evidence to it did not attract privilege. This meant that Heiner and witnesses to his inquiry could be prosecuted for defamation.¹⁷ This finding worried Heiner, and the next day he wrote to Matchett saying that he was not prepared to continue with the inquiry until he had received confirmation of the legality of his appointment and his actions to date.¹⁸

Heiner was not the only one troubled by the inquiry's terms of reference. Coyne saw it as a lynching, and his solicitor was ready to seek a writ of prohibition on Heiner to prevent him from continuing his investigation.¹⁹ The two unions, the QSSU and Queensland Professional Officers Association (QPOA), were grumbling about it, with the QSSU saying 'they did not request this form of investigation'.²⁰ Senior management in the department found themselves snared in a trap of their own making. The problem was summed up by Matchett's adviser:

*If [Heiner's Report] is not released there will be allegations of a cover-up and intrigue about its content will continue into the future. If it is released but disclaimed, it will be embarrassing to everybody concerned. If it is released and potentially harmful to individuals, the Department will probably face legal action as well as a loss of senior staff at the Centre.*²¹

These were indeed desperate times for management. In an attempt to head off a crisis, it was suggested that Heiner prepare a report in three parts:

*[Part A is to be] a written document able to be released publicly ... [Part B is to be] a confidential ... report to the Director-General, [identifying] any evidence upon which police investigations or disciplinary action should be based. [Part C] should be a verbal report to the Director-General, and possibly to the Minister should she anticipate political issues as a result of the Inquiry.*²²

One wonders what the adviser had in mind when he spoke of 'political issues'.

Kevin Lindeberg, who was working at the QPOA, became involved in the affair as Coyne's union representative. On 19 January 1990 he attended a meeting at which Matchett announced that the Heiner inquiry would not proceed. But this did not solve the department's problem with Coyne's legal people, who were still pushing hard to examine and cross-examine evidence before the inquiry.[23] On 23 January 1990 Barry Thomas, a senior legal officer in the Appeals and Advisory Branch of the Crown Solicitor's office, suggested that Matchett tell Coyne's solicitor 'that the Inquiry had been terminated and that the material collected has been destroyed'.[24] The legal officer canvassed the idea of advising Coyne's solicitor that the inquiry was terminated and that the documents would be destroyed eventually, but rejected this option because it would 'only generate further problems in an already confused situation'.[25] In fact, the documents were not shredded until 23 March, two months after Thomas drafted his memorandum.

Having decided to terminate the inquiry, Matchett asked Heiner to collect all the documents and bring them to her. They were sealed in his presence and, somewhat surprisingly, sent off to the Cabinet Office for secure keeping prior to destruction.[26] At this stage Heiner was not told that his inquiry was through.

Thomas' memorandum formed the basis of a letter to Heiner on 7 February, announcing that there would be no further investigations into Coyne and JOYC. But there was a crucial difference. No mention was made of the planned destruction of the documents and tapes that Heiner had generated in the early stages of the inquiry. Rather, he was advised that the material would 'remain confidential'.[27]

Meanwhile, Coyne himself wrote to Matchett, telling her how badly he and his family had been damaged by the Heiner process:

You and your predecessor [Pettigrew] have given me no proper opportunity to defend myself against allegations. I have been humiliated by people. I and my family have been hurt and upset. I believe this was unnecessary. I have absolutely no intention of allowing anyone else to further humiliate me or further hurt my family.[28]

Coincidentally, Matchett terminated the inquiry the day after this letter was sent.

On 13 February 1990 Matchett travelled out to JOYC and told staff that on Crown law advice she had closed the Heiner inquiry.[29] On the same day Coyne was told to leave the premises, although there had been no findings against him. He was transferred against his wishes to 'special duties' at head office for six months, bearing the burden of unproven guilt.[30]

On 14 February 1990, the day after Matchett visited JOYC, Coyne's solicitor rang Matchett's office and advised that Coyne was about to start legal action to obtain the written complaints from the JOYC youth workers.[31] Two days later the issue of destroying the documents was considered by the Crown Solicitor, Ken O'Shea, in response to a query from the Goss government. O'Shea indicated that, although the documents did not attract Crown privilege, they were public records, and if their destruction went ahead the government would be eliminating evidence that might be required in a court proceeding.[32]

One week later the Cabinet Office sent the Heiner material to the State Archivist and asked her to approve the destruction of the documents as a matter of urgency. The request came from the Acting Cabinet Secretary. Why was there such high-level involvement in what was depicted as a mundane departmental matter? Premier Goss said: 'What we did was to respond to a routine departmental request to dispose of documents.'[33] So why was Cabinet involved? If there was a straightforward answer to this question, it has never been given. Official silence made a conspiracy theory just that bit more plausible.

The Secretary's letter to the Archivist did not mention that there had been a specific threat of legal action based on the documents, or that access to the documents could be legally enforced under the Queensland criminal code.[34] The Archivist sent a fax to the Acting Secretary of Cabinet the same day, saying that in her view the documents were not required for permanent retention.[35]

Meanwhile, back in the Department of Family Services, management simply didn't know what to do with Coyne. Nor did they really care, as long as he was out of JOYC, making one less issue to deal with at the troubled centre. This is how Coyne described his reassignment:

I was advised that I was seconded to 'special duties' in Head Office to undertake a task relating to a review of departmental services to young offenders. I was told I would ... co-ordinate the activities of various working parties ... When I reported for work in Head Office I quickly became aware that only one working party was in existence and I was refused a place within [it] because [it] was already too large.

About two weeks after Coyne was shifted, an anonymous caller rang Coyne's wife and told her the Heiner Inquiry had found that her husband was having an affair.[36]

On 5 March Cabinet formally decided to destroy the Heiner documents.[37] Yet two weeks later Matchett was still writing to Coyne as if the critical decision had not been made. On 23 March the Heiner documents were picked up from the Cabinet Secretariat and taken to the Family Services building, where most of them were destroyed.[38] One group of documents, however, escaped the shredder. These were precisely the materials that Coyne, his solicitor and Lindeberg wanted: copies of the statements provided to Pettigrew, the previous Director-General, by the QSSU, the statements believed to contain the defamatory material about Coyne.[39] There has never been any satisfactory official explanation of why this material was initially withheld from destruction.

What we do know now, as a result of evidence submitted to a 1997 judicial review of the Queensland Criminal Justice Commission (CJC), a government agency which investigates official misconduct, is that on 18 April 1990 the Queensland Crown Law Office advised Matchett that Coyne had a lawful right of access to the documents.[40] According to the evidence at the judicial review, Matchett then went back to the Crown Solicitor asking for advice on how to circumvent Coyne's access rights.[41] As Lindeberg has said:

By one of the most extraordinary acts in this whole affair, Crown Law then assisted her to avoid her statutory duty by drafting letters to suit her intentions that went against previous advice.[42]

On 9 May, almost six weeks after the bulk of the documents had been destroyed, Matchett wrote to the Queensland Teachers Union (which also had an interest in the preservation of the Heiner material) and told them that she was still awaiting Crown legal advice with respect to the material.[43] On 22 May Matchett finally told Coyne's solicitors and the unions that all documents submitted to the Heiner Inquiry had been destroyed.[44] Yet the official inquiry into the shredding found that at this stage the department still held copies of the complaints.[45] In its report on the case, the Senate Select Committee on Unresolved Whistleblower Cases (SSCUWC) concluded that Matchett's advice to the solicitors on 22 May was 'unacceptable ... reflecting bureaucratic ineptitude at best or deliberate deceit at worst'.[46]

The next day, on 23 May, the documents containing the original complaints were finally destroyed. The official inquiry found that this action had not been authorised by Cabinet, the Archivist or the Crown Solicitor.[47]

Coyne claims that around this time, some three months after his punitive reassignment, he was approached by a senior officer of his union, the QPOA, who offered him a good job in the department if he dropped his demands to be shown the original allegations against him.[48] Clearly the union advocate was acting as an emissary of management. The blurring of the boundaries between unions and Labor-controlled departments of state is central to the atmosphere of this case.

In August 1990, when Coyne's punitive relocation was due to end, the department struck again, extending his 'special duties' for a further six months. Coyne again:

I inquired into the nature of my duties and found that I had none ... I lived in Ipswich and travelled approximately three hours to and from my place of employment. Each day I would sit at my desk and do nothing. I found this very difficult, and very debilitating.[49]

Coyne finally cracked in December 1990:

I had been sitting at my desk with nothing to do for a couple of days and I got up and walked over to my superior as I wanted to talk to him. He has been supportive in the past. He looked up at me and at that point in time I started to weep profusely. I couldn't stop weeping. Apart from that I was in control of myself. The torture of sitting at a desk for a prolonged period with no work, on top of the events previously outlined, had taken an emotional toll on me. I demanded, in a very loud voice, that something had to be done about the way I was been treated and that I had had a 'gutful' of the way I was being treated. At no time did I swear or say or do anything which would allow disciplinary action against me. I was very conscious about this. I was very rational in my arguments, just loud and assertive, demanding and intense. My superior's boss came out and I repeated my demand for something else to be done. I then stated that if something was not done I would go public about what had happened to me.[50]

A meeting was hastily convened with QPOA and departmental officials, but all the department would offer Coyne was a social work position at the infamous Sir David Longlands Maximum Security Prison at Wacol, Brisbane. This prison was a place where there were always unfilled vacancies, because most social workers avoided it like the plague. Under extreme duress, Coyne initially said he would accept the offer provided that he kept his current salary, was given meaningful work and was not victimised. According to Coyne, he even accepted the position after a senior official told him that he could offer no such guarantees.[51] Shortly after this Coyne was told that he had been selected for involuntary redundancy.

We have gone some distance with Coyne. We need to focus now on Kevin Lindeberg, the whistleblower in this story. On 23 February 1990 Matchett had a meeting with Lindeberg, who informed her that the QPOA also wanted access to the Heiner documents. Unbeknown to Lindeberg, this was the very day that the documents had been sent to the State Archivist with a request for approval to shred them. In the first week of March, Lindeberg learned that the government had decided to shred the documents. He decided to attempt to force the government to reverse the decision. This was the beginning of the end of Lindeberg's career as a union advocate, for this diminutive Don Quixote had his lance lowered at the Cabinet door.

Lindeberg knew he had to move quickly. As events will show, however, he did not move quickly enough. He began to advocate robustly for Coyne. On 13 March he was informed that Anne Warner, the Family Services Minister, would have nothing more to do with him, and in future would deal only with Don Martindale, the QPOA General Secretary, or the Assistant General Secretary, Ross Kinder. Lindeberg passed this information on to Martindale, and on or about 15 March Martindale had a meeting with Warner. At this meeting, according to Lindeberg, Warner claimed that he had threatened her career and that of her senior departmental staff. It is difficult to see how this middle-ranking union official could have 'threatened' Warner's political career, but she insisted to Martindale that Lindeberg be taken off the case. Martindale obeyed Warner's wishes.

On 30 May 1990, seven days after the documents were destroyed, Lindeberg was called into Martindale's office and sacked for his handling of the Coyne case and for allegedly threatening the Minister's career. The following day, QPOA staff held a strike in sympathy, said to be the first such strike in the union's history. The ABC's *7.30 Report* featured the sacking in its program on 4 June. It was no mere coincidence, but a testimony to the power of responsible journalism, that Lindeberg was reinstated after a QPOA Council meeting the next day.[52]

A condition of Lindeberg's reinstatement was that he enter into arbitration with Martindale, but neither man could agree on a suitable arbitrator. Finally the QPOA President, Bill Yarrow, selected an arbitrator, but his choice was unacceptable to Lindeberg. Before the arbitration process began, according to Lindeberg, Martindale put all the charges against him in writing, and in the process added three new ones to the original four.[53]

On 2 August 1990 the arbitrator in Lindeberg's matter handed down his report. As Lindeberg saw it the arbitrator failed to sustain the charges against him yet upheld his dismissal on the grounds that there was 'an alleged irretrievable breakdown in the working relationship'.[54] Lindeberg was given half an hour to read the report, pack his belongings and leave the union premises. He refused and would not accept the dismissal until a QPOA Council vote. The Council voted 38:28 for his sacking. Lindeberg claimed that the decision was carried by proxy votes, actively canvassed by QPOA President Yarrow.[55]

It is hard to believe that Lindeberg was sacked simply for his robust advocacy of Coyne's case, but this run-of-the-mill industrial issue had political legs that was walking the misdeed all the way back to the new ALP Government.

There is another dimension to Lindeberg's sacking. Lindeberg was also alleging union misconduct. In 1989 the Ahern National Party government had established an inquiry under Marshall Cooke QC into allegations of union corruption, centred on the defrauding of QPOA's superannuation fund. QPOA, as noted, was Lindeberg's union. For various reasons the Cooke Inquiry was delayed in taking evidence, and did not get around to hearing what Lindeberg had to say about the alleged superannuation fiddle until almost twelve months after he had been dismissed.

On 13 May 1991 the Cooke Inquiry held public hearings into the circumstances surrounding Lindeberg's dismissal. He was required to fund his own legal expenses, while the QPOA allegedly spent $100,000 on legal representation for Martindale and Kinder.[56] Lindeberg spent five days in the witness box and was subjected to a gruelling cross-examination. By this time the Goss Labor government had been in power for about eighteen months. The last thing it wanted was a finding of union corruption from an inquiry set up by the National Party.

At one point in the hearing the barrister representing Martindale and Kinder asked Cooke about the likely outcome. Cooke said that he would recommend that charges of official misconduct be laid against Martindale and possibly Kinder too.[57] Public hearings finished on 27 May without Lindeberg being given an opportunity to cross-examine. Immediately after the inquiry closed, Martindale and the QPOA are reported to have threatened Cooke with a Supreme Court injunction on the basis that Cooke had denied Martindale natural justice.[58] Apparently (and somewhat surprisingly) Cooke negotiated with the union and agreed not to make a finding on whether Lindeberg's dismissal was justified.[59]

On 1 August QPOA President Yarrow received a letter from Matchett. The letter is unusual because it is all about Coyne, yet Matchett writes not to him but to his union boss. Matchett refers to a 'discussion' she had with Yarrow on 19 July. I cannot get away from the suspicion that the traditional intimacy between Labor governments and unions (restarted again in Queensland eight months previous, after thirty-two years), goes a long way to explain why Matchett negotiated Coyne's future with his union boss rather than with Coyne or his solicitors. What did these two very powerful people discuss? From the letter it is clear that Matchett was worried about what Coyne would do or say. But why was she so worried? Wasn't this a simple matter? Coyne said he was denied natural justice. Such denials occur every day in the public sector.

Matchett, through Yarrow, requested that Coyne advise her in writing of the issues that he 'does not' intend to further pursue with her, her Minister, his union, his solicitor, the Public Sector Management Commission, the Director-General, the Premier's and Cabinet Department, or the media![60] The message was clear and not subtle. Coyne's future in the department depended on him losing interest in pursuing his legal rights. Coyne got the message as if it was shouted to him. He wrote back to Matchett and said that he would not pursue any issue relating to his employment at JOYC as long as he did not experience a salary drop.[61]

Matchett wrote back. Note the menace in the final paragraph of her letter:

It would assist me to finalise matters if you would confirm that my interpretations of the intention [not to pursue JOYC matters] is correct. I will then be in a position to take up the question with you of your career path options within the Department.[62]

Coyne told Matchett that her interpretation was correct: he wouldn't be taking any further action. Coyne later said that Matchett never addressed the issue of his post-JOYC career in the Department.

With Lindeberg gone, Coyne felt disgusted by the lack of union advocacy on his behalf. He felt beaten and wanted nothing more than to get out of the public service. He angrily complained to the QPOA leadership in mid-December that he was not getting a quality advocacy service from them. This was the second time he had to resort to such tactics to get results. QPOA officials met with

Family Services management and threatened to take Coyne's case to the CJC unless they met one of two demands. The first demand, that Coyne be shown documents relating to his unsuccessful bid for the readvertised position of Manager at JOYC, was rejected. Coyne was number one as far as the selection committee was concerned, but Matchett had rejected the recommendation.[63]

The second demand – that the Department make Coyne's departure financially worthwhile – was accepted. Brian Tierney, a QPOA industrial officer, is alleged to have told Lindeberg in mid February 1991 that he attended a meeting with Anne Warner, Ruth Matchett and Jenni Eastwood (General Secretary of QPOA), at which Coyne's need for an extra $30,000 to purchase a delicatessen was discussed.[64] While on full salary Coyne was allowed special leave to work in a delicatessen 'to see whether he liked it'.[65] Tierney is alleged to have told Lindeberg that with Coyne's request in mind the high-level group, which included Warner, Matchett and Eastwood, 'just kept calculating until we nearly reached $30,000 and stopped'.[66] It was decided that Coyne was to receive $27,190 with the proviso that he never again make public comment about the shredding.[67] Warner approved the payment on 7 February. Coyne collected a departmental cheque, rather than one approved by the Governor-in-Council, to 'save time'.[68] The CJC later ruled that this payment option was illegal.[69]

Lindeberg said that Tierney asked him not to blow the whistle on the payment, and the union helped the department 'concoct' the payout.[70] Five years later a government inquiry would find that the Department's action in this regard was probably illegal.

Clearly, the payment had a number of disturbing features. First there were unusual sub-items – such as 'extra travelling time – $10,000'. Secondly, a deed of settlement laid heavy conditions on the payment. Condition No. 2, for example, required Coyne ' ... not [to] raise the issue of his removal from JOYC with the media, industrial unions or the State Industrial Commission'. Condition No. 6 said, 'The matter should not be the subject of any authorised biography or any published article.'

Both Coyne and Lindeberg were temporarily neutralised. When Lindeberg was sacked as a union official he went straight into his new job: he became a professional whistleblower. By that I mean that his principal activity became exposing a conspiracy. He believed that he had picked up a trail of wrongdoing that led right up to the door of the Queensland Cabinet. Along the way he encountered play-dead investigating authorities, specifically the Queensland Criminal Justice Commission (CJC) and the Queensland Police Service (QPS), and old boy and old girl networks that worked as mysteriously as cults.

Lindeberg tackled his new 'profession' like someone answering a powerful second calling. He didn't have all the jigsaw pieces, but he knew that once he did, they would assemble into a pattern of official corruption. Clearly Martindale had picked the wrong man to sack.

At the time of writing Lindeberg has been on this project of redemption for eight years. In that time he has made countless public interest disclosures, desperately trying to keep the investigative sentries' eyes open. The list of agencies that he approached looks like the complete directory of Queensland government services! On 14 December 1990 he disclosed the shredding matter to the CJC. In May 1991 the CJC dismissed his complaint. In commenting on this, Noel Newnham, the Queensland Police Commissioner at the time, said that the CJC had the wool pulled over its eyes by senior officials in the Department of Family Services.[71] Disappointed but undaunted, Lindeberg then went to the CJC's so-called parliamentary oversight authority, the Parliamentary Criminal Justice Committee (PCJC), which called for a CJC report. This was duly sent, and Lindeberg received a copy. In it he read a new concoction on the shredding controversy. The CJC said that the Heiner documents had been destroyed because there were no further issues between Coyne and the Department after it paid Coyne damages.[72] Coyne, contacted by Lindeberg soon after, denied that he was paid damages. Lindeberg was now at war on two fronts: trying to expose the original wrongdoing to himself and Coyne, and pressuring statutory authorities to undertake quality investigations.

The war metaphor is not used irresponsibly here. Forces are ranged to attack whistleblowers. If the stakes are high enough, these forces attempt to do more than simply warn whistleblowers off; they attempt to destroy them. The war metaphor is inaccurate in one sense: it does not convey the logistical reality that whistleblowers, forced into the mode of solo crusader through our collective fear and indifference, are usually out-gunned by the administrative and legal fire-power that large organisations can bring to bear. Perhaps it is better to say that whistleblowers are forced to run skirmish actions or guerrilla campaigns against these organisations.

Up to this point Lindeberg's case is that of the quintessential whistleblower. By that I mean his ability to sustain continual whistleblower action pivoted around a deeply felt notion that the public interest had been compromised, indeed grievously injured. Lindeberg, more than a lot of whistleblowers I know, was able from the start to conceptualise the shredding issue in *public terms*. It has never been only his fight. When you read his submissions and listen to the way he talks, you are immediately struck by this natural facility to bring all issues, no matter how minor, back to public duty and public morality.

For example, he started his submission-in-reply to the SSCUWC with a stirring extract from Mr Justice Brandeis' 1928 dissenting judgement in *Olmeast v United States*:

Decency, security and liberty alike demand that Government Officials shall be subject to the same rules of conduct that are commands to the citizens. In a Government of Laws, existence of the Government will be imperilled if it fails to observe the laws scrupulously ... If the Government becomes a law breaker, it breeds contempt for the law: it invites every man to become a law unto himself: it invites anarchy.

By this recourse to Brandeis, Lindeberg connects a few official misdeeds in Brisbane in 1990 to a global threat to democratic governance. This is a most important reframing. Note his submission in reply to the SSCUWC:

Mr Justice Brandeis in 1928 set the scene we now face in 1995. A government itself has broken the law. It has set an example of contempt for the law. Can it remain above the law? If it can then the precedent established with the shredding of the Heiner documents becomes an affront to every Australian citizen who believes that we are all equal before the law, and who faithfully allows the Executive Government power over their lives in the expectation that the law will not be wilfully broken in the Cabinet Room.

For five years I have struggled for justice ... I submit that the principles bound up in the shredding of the Heiner documents, and matters arising therefrom, transcend party political considerations and cry out for public exposure and reaffirmation. As an Australian (with the undesired appellation of whistleblower), I believe that the principles represent the very lifeblood of a nation governed by laws not by Executive Decree. It has taken and demanded five years of my life and that of my dear family to bring it to the attention of the Australian Senate and my fellow Australian citizens.

Before leaving this illustration of Lindeberg's facility to see the grand picture in the micro-shot, we must unfold the last part of his statement and note the martyrdom there. Like the saints of old, Lindeberg feels that he has been made to suffer for his beliefs. He, too, has a sense of perilously following the dictates of a higher authority. I suspect that Lindeberg's success in presenting misdeeds in a wider public context is found in his way of thinking religiously. This has saved him from the common fate of a lot of his fellow whistleblowers: the opening of a third front by way of attacks on their motivation, mental health and personal morality. Lindeberg has suffered enormously, but to my knowledge no government official or politician has ever dared open up this third front on him.

The downside of reframing one's struggle with mighty organisations into a defence of the public interest, and seeing that struggle as part of a historical campaign against wrongdoing, is that it is hard (for Lindeberg, impossible) to put the sword down. This makes it hard for people in the whistleblowers' lives who see themselves forcibly defined by the struggle.

Let's take the story back to the moment Lindeberg found what he believed was clear evidence that a statutory authority (CJC) had lied to its parliamentary supervisor, the Queensland Parliamentary Criminal Justice Committee (PCJC). One of the biggest obstacles to the justice-seeking whistleblower arises when official investigating agencies look for reasons to back out of their statutory duty. The disappearing public investigator has an enormous range of ruses to justify its failure to do right by the whistleblower. 'No resources' or 'no jurisdiction' are the big two. The backed-out public investigator leaves the whistleblower feeling very isolated. Most, understandably, cannot handle this, and soon drop their mission of disclosure.

Not Lindeberg. Faced with what he saw as a dishonest, indifferent and incompetent CJC, he went into private investigatory mode. He stayed on the case, networking media, contacting experts in relevant fields, lobbying politicians, presenting evidence to official committees, and maintaining relationships with other whistleblowers. He has had some wins in this new role. While his successes are inspirational, we should be wary of treating him as a role model. What he is doing is not for the faint-hearted.

Lindeberg referred Coyne's denial that he had been paid damages back to the PCJC. Without even analysing the denial, the committee apparently sent it on to the CJC. Lindeberg then made contact with Brisbane journalist Chris Griffith. One of the constants in whistleblower narratives is how the temperature rises every time the media become interested. On 9 August 1992 a story on the shredding was carried in the Brisbane *Sunday Mail*.

Three days later Lindeberg was called to CJC Headquarters to be interviewed by Noel Noonan, a Brisbane barrister (now a Cairns-based magistrate), who had been commissioned by the CJC to investigate the shredding. Lindeberg did not trust the CJC. A month after he went to the CJC he obtained his own barrister's opinion, which concluded that Coyne had a statutory right to the destroyed Heiner documents. Lindeberg also developed grave reservations about Noonan's capacity to conduct an impartial investigation because of his ALP links. On 7 September 1993 the *Bulletin* carried an extract of Lindeberg's evidence to the Senate Select Committee on Superannuation, in which he referred to Noonan's 'known connections to the ALP'.

Lindeberg reported that at one stage in the investigation Noonan said to him: 'What do you want me to do, charge the entire Cabinet with criminal conspiracy to pervert the course of justice?'[73] Coyne claimed that the first words Noonan said to him were: 'There will be no solace in this case for you or Mr Lindeberg. Do you realise that you are taking on the entire Cabinet?'[74] Noonan's report was released to Lindeberg on 20 January 1993. The barrister found no official misconduct.

Throughout the year Lindeberg kept up the pressure. In April he contacted Ken Davies, PCJC Chair, and told him that Noonan's report was unacceptable. In the same month he gave evidence to the Senate Select Committee on Superannuation, which was investigating the QPOA's management of its superannuation fund. In July he fed material to the Deputy Leader of the Opposition in Queensland, Kevin Lindgard, who delivered a speech on 13 July condemning the shredding. In August he made a submission to the Queensland Electoral and Administrative Review Commission, which was investigating archive legislation. In that submission he alleged that a systematic cover-up with respect to the shredding was afoot. In September the *Bulletin* published a lead story on the shredding. Lindeberg's assertion about Noonan's ALP connections were re-aired. In December Lindeberg gave evidence to the recently established Senate Select Committee on Public Interest Whistleblowing.

Lindeberg said that Noonan responded to his allegations of party-favouritism by ringing him at home on 11 September and calling him a 'pathetic bastard' three times and threatening to sue him for defamation.[75] In the midst of the call Noonan is reported to have said that the shredding was 'a political decision'.[76]

Even today, after the matter has been inquired to death, it remains maze-like. As I understand it the Coyne–Lindeberg group desperately wanted the Heiner documents. If the main players on the other side could not figure out from Coyne's *five requests* that he wanted these documents for something, this fact must have been made clear enough by Coyne's solicitor's letter on 8 February 1990 demanding the written complaints, the telephone call from his solicitor to Marchett's executive officer Trevor Walsh one week later informing him that Coyne was starting legal action for access to the complaints, and the follow-up letter of 15 February.

Yet the State Archivist (whose permission to destroy the complaints was required under the *Libraries and Archives Act* 1988 because they were public documents), was urgently faxed on 23 February 1990, seeking advice as to whether the Heiner Inquiry documents could be destroyed. She was not told that they were needed in evidence in a forthcoming legal proceeding. She approved their destruction with what Lindeberg regarded as indecent haste,[77] and after what SSCUWC called a 'cursory' examination of the material in question.[78] With a speed the general public is not accustomed to in public servants, the Archivist apparently examined 100 hours of Heiner audio-tapes, computer discs, written notes, reports, and official documents within 'a few hours'.[79] Efforts by SSCUWC to get the Archivist's version of the matter were unsuccessful as she followed the Goss Government's direction that no public servants were to co-operate with the Senate inquiry.[80]

At the time of the shredding Lindeberg claimed that Cabinet, Matchett, Crown Solicitor O'Shea and departmental officers knew that Coyne wanted the documents for a legal proceeding.[81] He claimed that the law had been broken and cited S.129 of the Queensland Criminal Code:

Any person who, knowing that any book, document, or other thing of any kind is or may be required in evidence in a judicial proceeding, wilfully destroys it or renders it illegible or indecipherable or incapable of identification, with intent thereby to prevent it from being used in evidence, is guilty of a misdemeanour and is liable to imprisonment with hard labour for three years.

Lindeberg also referred to the High Court views of Brennan J and Toohey J in *R. v Rogerson, and Ors*:

Conspiracy to pervert the course of justice may be entered into though no proceeding before the court or any competent judicial authority are pending.[82]

These judicial views fitted hand-and-glove with the facts of 'Shreddergate'. Lindeberg thought he was on a winner, and that justice was not too far away.

Official opinion was also changing in his direction. Those who sealed the fate of the Heiner documents – the Queensland Cabinet, Minister Warner, Matchett, Walsh and the Queensland Archivist – must have blanched when the CJC said in sworn evidence to the federal Senate Select Committee on Unresolved Whistleblower Cases (SSCUWC):

It is clear that Cabinet made a decision to destroy the documents knowing full well that Coyne wanted access to them.[83]

The SSCUWC was born in controversial circumstances. Its predecessor inquiry, the trail-blazing Senate Select Committee on Public Interest Whistleblowing, heard evidence from Queensland whistleblowers, including Lindeberg, that they had suffered badly at the hands of the Goss State Labor administration.[84] The Committee was sufficiently concerned about these allegations that it wrote to Premier Goss on 1 September 1994, enclosing a copy of its report and asking Goss to re-examine the Queensland whistleblower cases.[85]

Goss's reply read like a glossy Queensland travel brochure.[86] Queensland, the Premier crowed, would soon have the best whistleblower protection in Australia, 'and possibly the world'.[87] The Premier added that the CJC, the hub of the post-Fitzgerald inquiry reforms,[88] had acted correctly with Lindeberg when it found that there had been no official misconduct. Goss rejected out of hand the Senate Committee's call for a review of Lindeberg's case. He concluded by attacking the evidence given to SSCUWC:

I believe it is unfair to single out Queensland for special mention in the Committee's report on the basis of information given to the Committee by the Queensland Whistleblower Study [conducted by the author] and the Whistleblowers Action Group [established by the author].[89]

Lindeberg and his supporters were working feverishly behind the scenes to keep the momentum going. Six weeks after Goss refused to re-examine the Queensland whistleblower cases, the Senate voted to do its own review of Lindeberg and others.

On 1 December 1994 Warwick Parer, a Liberal Party senator from Queensland, successfully moved for the establishment of the Senate Select Committee on Unresolved Whistleblower Cases.[90] Parer's motion was attacked by the ALP Government:

Senator Bolkus: The government is opposed to the establishment of yet another select committee... We see it as a political stunt... to try and embarrass the Queensland Labor Government in the lead-up to the state election of next year.[91]

Parer's motion had the numbers and it was duly passed. The federal government was not going to lie down and see its star Premier defeated by a group of whistleblowers. Eight days after SSCUWC was established, its terms of reference were altered to take the investigative heat off Goss.[92] There was then a major hullabaloo over who should chair SSCUWC. On 7 December 1994 Eric Abetz, a Liberal Party senator from Tasmania, was elected to the position. Overnight calls and lobbying soon changed that. The next day Abetz was out and little-known Senator Shayne Murphy, ALP Tasmania, was in. Murphy is reported to have a reputation among his Labor colleagues as a hard man with a hot temper.[93] Abetz and Murphy appeared to hate each other, and argued continually in public throughout SSCUWC hearings.

The SSCUWC came to Brisbane on 23 February 1995 for its first hearing, and it was a dramatic event. The Goss Government had issued a direction that no public servant, other than officers of the CJC, could give evidence before the Senate Inquiry. That the Senate did not cite the Queensland Government for contempt was probably due as much to the bi-partisan composition of SSCUWC[94] as it was to advice from the Clerk of the Senate that forcing public servants to give evidence was without High Court precedent, and contrary to parliamentary procedures.[95]

The Committee was forced to meet in a ridiculously small government annexe, being refused a hearing room in the Legislative Assembly. The atmosphere in the overcrowded waiting area was one of quiet tension and great expectation. Lindeberg appeared, looking like a nervous rugby half before a scrum that had fallen into anarchy. He pushed through the compressed crowd of friend, foe and media with his own front-row forward, Ian Callinan QC. Lindeberg had come to play. This was his day in court. He has had subsequent days in subsequent 'courts', but this was his first, and he performed with drama and integrity. His speech – sorry, evidence to the Committee – was nothing less then an appeal to start a moral clean-up of the Queensland political culture.

Callinan, a burly man with the face of a boilermaker, followed. To all bar the Goss Government officials in the room, he was charisma on wheels. To those officials he was a 'Warning! shark-infested waters' sign. In his understated way he wondered whether the Goss Government had broken the law:

The real point on any view of the matter is that legal proceedings that were threatened would inevitably involve necessary recourse to the documents. The documents ought not, for that reason, to have been destroyed.

Lindeberg's brief would be one of Callinan's last advocacy jobs. Some weeks later his appointment to the High Court was announced.

The temperature in the room went up when the CJC Director, eminent QC Rob O'Regan, went as far as he could in opposing the Committee. O'Regan was of the view that the CJC had conscientiously investigated Lindeberg's complaints and had done nothing to earn his displeasure. When he tried to lay down conditions for CJC officers giving evidence Senator John Herron, SSCUWC Deputy-Chair, exploded. Herron shouted that there was only one group that would make the rules that day, and that was the Committee.[96] This exchange set the tone for the inquiry. The CJC, there under sufferance, faced-off Lindeberg and the other disgruntled whistleblowers.

SSCUWC hearings moved from Brisbane to Melbourne, back to Brisbane, and finally to Canberra. There was a sense of *deja vu* about the inquiry. It was as if SSCUWC was just another bus stop at which Lindeberg, and the other fifteen whistleblowers whose cases SSCUWC considered, scrambled off the coach ahead of their Queensland Government adversaries (which usually meant the CJC), went through the ritual of allegation and counter-allegation, then returned to the bus and on to the next inquiry. The whistleblowers were on the never-never trail to justice, and the CJC was road-sick. It was angry at the constant drain on staff resources used to defend its role in the whistleblower stories. The whistleblowers, on the other hand, figured that if the CJC had got it right the first time the trip would never have been so arduous.

No doubt SSCUWC was relieved to receive the Clerk of the Senate's advice that it only had power to inquire into subjects in respect to which the Commonwealth had power to legislate.[97] It could not, in other words, adjudicate the battle between Lindeberg and various Queensland agencies. All it could do was reflect on what the Lindeberg case said about the need for effective whistleblower legislation at the Commonwealth level.

The Committee did, however, unanimously conclude that Lindeberg made his disclosures in good faith, and commended him for bringing the shredding to the attention of authorities.[98] It was not as kind in its summation of the Criminal Justice Commission:

The CJC appears to have adopted an embattled and very defensive approach to criticism. It has responded in some cases by attacking individuals at a personal level. Whether or not these people provoked such a response by outrageous allegations of their own is immaterial. I [SSCUWC Chairman Murphy] do not believe that it brings credit upon a public institution to respond in such a vitriolic manner. Whistleblowers can have no respect for such an organisation and are deterred from seeking assistance from it ... The CJC could have done more with its powers to investigate [the Lindeberg] case more fully.[99]

Even if SSCUWC had wider powers, I doubt it would have got further given the fact that it was chaired by an ALP senator, Shayne Murphy. While Murphy became highly sympathetic to whistleblowers after listening to their evidence, and was quite critical of certain government agencies, he was immersed in a process that might have embarrassed the Goss Labor Government in Queensland. While there is no suggestion of misconduct, some questions remain. Why was Abetz, the Liberal Party senator, deposed as committee chair? Why did Murphy use his chairman's statement, tabled at the same time as the report, to make the following 'personal comments' about the Lindeberg case:

In respect to the shredding of the Heiner documents I do not believe there is any evidence of a political conspiracy on behalf of the government.[100]

You might have thought that was a judgement for the whole Committee to make.[101]

Back on the 'bus', and next stop another inquiry. Goss's two-term government had been narrowly defeated, the National–Liberal coalition was back in business and Lindeberg thought that he saw the light at the end of the justice tunnel.

The fact that Lindeberg and his supporters did not neglect the Borbidge shadow ministry in the six years it was in opposition paid off. In May 1996 Premier Borbidge announced a new inquiry into Shreddergate. It was conducted by two Brisbane barristers, Tony Morris QC and Eddie Howard. Sabotaged by 'missing' Department of Family Services files, and a refusal by Peter Beattie, the new Leader of the Opposition, to provide Cabinet documents from the previous Goss ministry, the two investigators pushed ahead to a conclusion of official misconduct.

They said that there was enough evidence to conclude that s.129 of the Queensland Criminal Code (dealing with deliberate destruction of evidence needed in a judicial proceeding) had been broken.[102] Morris and Howard also found that the evidence indicated that offences were committed under s.132 and/or s.140 of the Criminal Code. These are very serious matters – we are talking about conspiracies to defeat justice. The evidence also allowed Morris and Howard to conclude that senior officials in the Department of Family Services had abused their office. Matchett was specifically named for not obtaining archival authority for the destruction of official documents.[103] There was also evidence for laying charges of official misconduct against Matchett and other senior management under the *Queensland Criminal Justice Act*.

With respect to the $27,000 payment to Coyne, the investigators found that it was illegal;[104] that it was made principally to buy Coyne's silence;[105] that those who made the payment, including Warner and Matchett, were involved in official misconduct; and that this (except in the case Minister Warner) constituted a disciplinary breach, providing 'reasonable grounds for the termination of the officer's services'.

Premier Rob Borbidge and his ministry were delighted. Borbidge strode into the Legislative Assembly on 10 October 1996 with the Morris–Howard Report tucked firmly under his arm. 'The findings,' he said, 'represented a deeply disturbing tapestry of deceit and misinformation.'[106] Lindeberg's wife, Irene, made a rare public statement. Amidst the rejoicing at the findings she said:

There has been an enormous personal price for all this. I know because I and my family have paid it.[107]

The other side were not nearly as happy. Ex-Premier Goss claimed the report was 'rubbish,'[108] ex-Minister Warner branded the inquiry a witch-hunt[109] and Matchett accused Morris and Howard of 'fabricating outlandish allegations about my actions and motives'.[110]

The government passed the Morris–Howard Report to Royce Miller QC, the Director of Public Prosecutions, in November 1996. He reported back in March 1997.[111] Borbidge took another three months before deciding to go with the DPP's advice not to charge anyone, as too much time had elapsed.[112] Lindeberg was devastated. As far as the government was concerned he was a spent shell. They had fired him at the Goss administration, hit the targets they aimed at, and he was of no further use to them. Such is a common fate of whistleblowers.

Lindeberg dusted himself off and was back in the game. Remarkably he has sought to internationalise the matter by alerting the Paris-based International Council on Archives, which inquired into his allegations at its meeting in the Hague in June 1997.[113]

Back on the 'bus' he was headed towards the Connolly–Ryan Inquiry into the CJC. Justices Connolly and Ryan were given a brief by the Borbidge Government to examine whether the CJC had acted illegally in the way it worked. Lindeberg was on another peak of anticipation. He said to the inquiry:

It now appears that your Commission of Inquiry may be the last avenue open to have these [Shreddergate] matters aired publicly ... In that respect I am totally in the hands of honourable commissioners and Almighty God as to whether the truth of this sordid affair will be revealed in the weeks ahead ...[114]

Unfortunately for him the Supreme Court closed the inquiry down because of demonstrable bias on the part of Mr Justice Connolly.

Authorities will have to prise Lindeberg's fingers off his smoking gun; this man simply will not give up the fight for justice. Other people would have been defeated by the news that their last apparent opportunity for vindication had gone. Not Lindeberg. He waited for the results of the powerful Senate Committee of Privileges. In June 1996 the Committee received a reference from the Australian Senate to investigate whether the CJC had lied in its evidence to the Senate Select Committee on Unresolved Whistleblower Cases.[115] Lindeberg, in the background, was instrumental in drawing the Senate Committe into Shreddergate. The Committee found no evidence of CJC fabrication. Lindeberg manouvred a fresh brief to the Committee in December 1997. Again the Committee found no evidence to support his claims when it reported back to the Senate in May 1998.[116]

Still growing with each defeat, Lindeberg somehow managed to get the eleven One Nation parliamentarians, swept into office in the 1998 Queensland state elections, to adopt Shreddergate as their first *cause celebre*.[117] In July, with Liberal and National Party support, the One Nation members succeeded in forcing Premier Beattie to release the Cabinet papers on Shreddergate, twenty-two years before he was required to by law. These documents supported Lindeberg's case. On 25 August the One Nation members unsuccessfully tried to have five Labor ministers expelled from the parliament for their role in Shreddergate.[118] The House was in uproar during the debate.

An angry Premier Beattie lashed out, 'How long is this [Shreddergate] to go on?'[119] Indeed.

Up Against the NCA

The Mick Skrijel Affair

I am sure I speak for all of us when I say we are very concerned about what has happened to you and the way your life has been affected by what has happened. At the end of the day you will get justice and we would want to be part of that process. – John Bradford MHR, Chair, Joint Parliamentary Committee on the National Crime Authority[1]

In March 1997 Victorian police claimed that they were getting very close to the 'Mr Bigs' of the heroin world following the arrest of 15 suspected high-level suppliers, 174 street dealers, 221 found in possession, and 702 people charged with drug-related activities.[2] These are the reassuring stories police love to send out and we love to hear. How different matters were some years back when Mehmed (Mick) Skrijel came upon what he said was a police heroin cover-up. The Skrijel case is a long-running and highly convoluted affair that has produced an enormous amount of controversy and bitterness. It is an extraordinary, hard-to-believe saga, still ongoing at the time of writing.[3] Mick Skrijel has been in a Kafkaesque search for justice since 1978.

Skrijel is a big man with a big presence. I can see how he would hang about his allegations of wrongdoing, protecting them from the ever-present threats of ridicule and rejection. He looks tough. Anyone who gets into the ring with police must be tough. Yet I suspect that those deep crags in his face that guarantee his rugged appearance are there through erosion. Washed away is a lot of his idealism that Australia, his shelter from a berserk wartime Europe, is a land of justice. Skrijel's anger masks his deep disappointment. I heard him say at a whistleblower conference in Melbourne that he was born into Stalinism, raised under Fascism, but it was not until he came to Australia that he felt oppressed and fearful for his life and his family. I suspect that it is this disappointment that keeps his squeaky-wheeled caravan trundling over the hard official landscape. He wants to give Australia a second chance.

The trouble whistleblowers get into after they make primary disclosures of wrongdoing is compounded, and often (as in Skrijel's case) eclipsed, by the trouble that accrues to them after secondary disclosures are made. It is one thing to say to an agency such as the Australian Federal Police (AFP), 'Look at the wrongdoing over here. Please do something about it' (primary disclosure). It is entirely different to say, 'You've had my disclosure for five years now, why have you not acted? I am going to report this' (secondary disclosure). Secondary disclosures about investigative probity and competence can be more dangerous to whistleblowers than the original disclosure of wrongdoing because they bring the game right up to those who took the primary disclosures in the first place. In response, agencies often become negative, defensive, and in some cases hostile and even violent. Soon the primary disclosure becomes a mere footnote.

Mick Skrijel was born in Istanbul in 1941.[4] Before he turned two, his parents, two sisters and two brothers were killed by German forces in the family home in Novi Pazar, Yugoslavia. Skrijel survived because he had been hidden in the garden by his parents. He was found and cared for by members of the partisan resistance movement, and in 1944 he and other war orphans were sent to Russia where he stayed in orphanages for three years.

At the end of 1947 Skrijel was repatriated back to Yugoslavia, where he lived in orphanages and hostels until he was called up for military service, during which he was sent back to Russia to train with commandos. Dissatisfied with Yugoslavian life after his return, Skrijel attempted an escape into Italy with seven other soldiers. Only Skrijel and two other men got across the border without being killed. One man with severe machine-gun injuries to his stomach was carried by Skrijel and the uninjured partner the remaining distance into Italy.

Skrijel did not stay long in Italy. He hitch-hiked to France, where he was picked up for having no papers and forced into the French

Foreign Legion. He escaped after a tour to Algiers and returned to Italy. From a refugee camp in Latina he applied for migration to Australia and arrived at the Bonegilla Migrant Centre in 1961.

A recession was on and Skrijel found it tough, but with a never-say-die attitude he slowly built up a lucrative painting business. In 1966 he married a third-generation Australian woman and started a family. In 1975 he moved to Southend, South Australia, and purchased a crayfish and shark fishing licence. He did well at fishing, but the dose of good fortune doled out to him was running out.

He says that in early 1978 he was out in his boat with a deck-hand when he saw a waterproofed package being dropped from a passing ship. He then saw another fishing vessel, skippered by the deck-hand's brother, retrieve the package. Skrijel asked what it was. 'Heroin,' the deck-hand replied. The following day the deck-hand told Skrijel that he could be dealt into the drug deals or suffer the consequences.[5] Skrijel chose the latter.

He sacked the deck-hand and soon threats and intimidations started. Skrijel's wife and children were assaulted, sometimes at their homes, other times at school. The violence became so serious that Skrijel's youngest daughter took to carrying an iron bar in her school bag.[6] All of these acts were reported to the local police at Millicent who, Skrijel said, refused to act. On one occasion they claimed that they were too scared to intervene, he said.[7]

Skrijel went further and reported the violence, along with the heroin importation, to the Mount Gambier Superintendent of Police. A week later that person died. While the circumstances were apparently unrelated, it was the start of a series of coincidences that fired-up Skrijel's suspicions. Skrijel claimed that the replacement officer took another statement from him and altered it before filing it away.[8] As far as Skrijel is concerned, the officer's behaviour was an omen of things to come in his dealing with police. Skrijel reported that the violence against him and his family inexplicably stopped after he gave police this statement, only to be replaced by acts of vandalism. His mooring was cut, his dingy sunk, oil and sand were deposited in his batteries, and to top it off his boat was burned.[9] Skrijel said that not only did he lose considerable money tied up in the boat, but he also lost a year's income from fishing as his boat was destroyed at the beginning of the fishing season.

With he and his family now trapped in a pattern of recurring harassment and violence, Skrijel started to realise that he had touched a tangled web of corruption. Incredibly, the persecution of him and his family went on for years: crayfish catches were stolen, an attempt was made to rape his fourteen-year-old daughter, and Skrijel himself was bashed at a football match at Dartmoor.[10] Each time an incident occurred he demanded an investigation. Each time he collected evidence and put it before the police. Each time he was ignored or abused or both.

In the attempted rape matter for example, four local youths actually admitted their crime and police charged them. In the period leading up to the trial Skrijel says that he received at least twenty telephone threats. Two of them warned: 'If you don't stop complaining you are going to die', and 'If you come to court we will blow up your house'.[11] Inexplicably the trial judge did not make a finding in the more serious matter of attempted rape. Instead only one of the youths was convicted, and that was with the lesser offence of trespass and discharging a firearm.

Skrijel was also pressured to drop the charge of assault by two men at the Dartmoor football match. He was visited by police on 17 February 1984, and for the first time in the whole unbelievable matter Skrijel thought he was going to be killed. Soon after police pulled up outside his Digby residence, a State Electricity Commission (SEC) van arrived and Skrijel heard one of the workers say to his associate that what the police were asking them to do was illegal and that he would have no part in it.[12] The younger SEC worker, accompanied by police, went to a junction box and turned off all the power in the area. Skrijel told his family to remain in the house, and went out to confront the police. A police officer said there were reports that Skrijel had electrified his fences and they were coming onto his property to check the matter out. Skrijel asked for a search warrant and when the officer said he didn't have one, Skrijel refused entry. He claims that the officer then shoved him hard and said, 'Who's going to stop us?' Three police officers then pushed their coats back and put their hands on their guns and, according to Skrijel, 'appeared ready to use them'.[13] After a desultory inspection of the fences, the officer is alleged to have started pushing and abusing Skrijel. Within minutes the younger SEC officer, apparently concerned that police would use their guns, left shaking and went and sat in his van. The police harassment, according to Skrijel, continued for about two and a half hours. Skrijel wrote that the police left at about 1.25 am with the officer's parting shot: 'If you don't complain we won't make a report.'[14]

Skrijel complained as usual, and as usual got nowhere. His vigour and sheer irrepressibility as a complainant accounted for the numerous reprisals. He simply would not shut up, and this made the police, politicians and senior bureaucrats charged with acting on his disclosures angry and exasperated. There was something else. Uppermost in Skrijel's mind was the idea that his hostile treatment was triggered by a fear that he might have stumbled onto something big. Skrijel was the noise-maker in the Alpine valley. Would his loud behaviour eventually trigger an avalanche?

Skrijel next drew Liberal Premier David Tonkin's attention to the matter. According to Skrijel, one of the police sent to interview him was Barry Moyse, the 'Operation Noah' officer currently serving twenty-two years for drug trafficking.[15] Skrijel also made a written submission to the Costigan Royal Commission in 1984 into corruption.[16] This submission was accompanied by several thousands of pages of documents that Skrijel said corroborated his claims of police illegality, political indifference and investigative incompetence.

Soon after Skrijel's last Costigan interview, a detective on secondment to the Royal Commission breached the confidentiality conditions under which Skrijel gave evidence to the Commission. The officer interviewed the two CIB detectives adversely mentioned by Skrijel. Three days later, on 24 April 1984, Skrijel was visited by the two detectives. After some small talk one of the police officers asked Skrijel whether he knew what happened to Donald McKay, the anti-drug activist murdered by Mafia-connected Italians in Griffith, New South Wales. After Skrijel said he knew what happened to McKay, the officer is alleged by Skrijel to have said that Skrijel better look out because 'that's going to happen to you if you don't keep you mouth shut'.[17]

Commissioner Costigan was concerned enough about allegations made by Skrijel and other witnesses to recommend a royal commission into the matters detailed in Volume 7 of his report, dealing with police connections with drug dealers. The federal government rejected this recommendation and suppressed Volume 7.[18]

With the help of Senator Peter Baume, the Skrijel file was passed on to the newly formed National Crime Authority (NCA) in December 1984.[19] Baume had made contact with Skrijel in response to an article in the Hamilton *Spectator* in which Skrijel was quoted as saying:

In Canberra, I want a parliamentarian to look at my case honestly, without prejudice or fear from those involved with the drug trade. I will provide to any parliamentarian who is willing to give me a fair hearing, the evidence I have.[20]

The *Spectator* story was based on a strategy that Skrijel was using more and more: that of pamphleteering. On 16 October 1984, the day after receiving yet another ministerial fob-off, Skrijel wrote a thirteen-page document melodramatically titled 'To Live As A Slave Or Die As A Free Man'. He distributed it to all large media outlets, and to every federal and some state politicians.[21]

Something more was passed to the NCA than just Skrijel's primary disclosure of the alleged police heroin arrangement in Southend. In fact police 'appraisals' of Skrijel as a dangerous nut-case got to the NCA long before his primary disclosure, and may have formed the context within which these disclosures were considered. In response to Baume's letter to NCA Chair Justice D.G. Stewart, two detectives interviewed Skrijel for about seven hours, and compiled a report that Skrijel found bedevilled with inaccuracies and an avoidance of the substantial issues.[22]

The more Skrijel spoke out, the more he insisted that the investigators investigate. The more pamphlets he distributed, the more fronts opened up on him. The events in the first part of 1985 illustrate this clearly. In January the unsatisfactory NCA report was finished. In February his car was stolen. In the same month BP Australia advised that they were about to send Skrijel bankrupt if he didn't pay a $10,902 fuel bill, which he claimed was illegally run up on his account by the heroin traffickers at Southend. In March his wife went to court charged with assaulting a police officer in an incident related to Skrijel's disclosures. On 2 May an anonymous telephone caller said, 'Listen and shut up. If you go to Adelaide [to the NCA] and give evidence, you will be burned.' Six days later his house was burnt down.

On Skrijel's return from Adelaide he found that his house at Digby in Victoria had been burgled. Papers were strewn all over the floor and his filing cabinet had been jemmied open. Two weeks later Skrijel's wife, Loryn, was found guilty of violence to police and police property. If Skrijel's account of the contacts between the Victorian Legal Aid Commission and the police and the magistrate are to be believed, the hearing was a complete travesty of justice.[23]

To cap off a wonderful year, Skrijel himself was charged. This was how it happened. In August of that year he named NCA officers who he believed were involved in a cover-up.[24] In the following month he prepared a pamphlet naming certain detectives as corrupt, and distributed it outside NCA headquarters and the Supreme Court in Melbourne. The first pamphlet was handed personally to one of the detectives who, according to Skrijel, said, 'You're out to get my head. I'll bloody will get yours before you get mine.'[25] Soon after this incident Skrijel found himself, not the heroin dealers, facing investigation. NCA files for August and September 1985 showed that the relationship between it and Skrijel was very bad. NCA officials claimed that Skrijel had threatened to shoot police if justice was not done and that they believed that Skrijel had the 'means and the determination to carry out such threats'.[26] Skrijel has claimed that these files-notes were fabricated.[27]

Operation Southend culminated on 15 October 1985 with a raid on Skrijel's Digby property involving thirty-seven police.

Compounding the trauma of this official home invasion was Skrijel's certainty that he would soon be charged with false crimes. This was surely one of the worst times in his life in Australia. He was desperate and used the strategies of a desperate man. For eighteen days, 8–26 April 1986, he went on a hunger strike outside Parliament House in Canberra. During this time he lived out of his slogan- and sign-festooned car.[28] Politicians ignored him and the national media wrote him off as a one-story crackpot. The only beneficial result for Skrijel was the meeting with David Berthelson, a director at the National Audit Office. Berthelson became Skrijel's great advocate. He remains so to the present day. On 27 April Skrijel was admitted to hospital suffering from malnutrition and dehydration.

Skrijel was eventually charged and convicted in the County Court of Victoria at Ballarat before Mr Justice Nixon and a jury. He was sentenced in March 1987 to two years imprisonment for cultivating and possessing trafficable quantities of marijuana, and possession of explosives and a pistol.[29] At sentencing Mr Justice Nixon said to Skrijel, after reviewing five psychiatric opinions:

you were in the grip of a long standing obsession which is more accurately described in psychiatric terms as paranoid.[30]

Even if only a part of Skrijel's story is believed, who would blame him for being suspicious, non-trusting and fearful for his wellbeing?

There is always a psychiatrist somewhere ready to pathologise dissent and there is always a judge or decision-maker prepared to listen. These simple and usually scurrilous diagnoses remove our focus from system-wide wrongdoing and place it on the messenger. Psychiatric harassment is a favourite tool of management and the law, as is now well-documented in the literature.[31] If whistleblowers are not 'insane' at the start of their disclosure, the unforgiving and unrelenting system gives them every reason to be so at the end.

Skrijel was released from prison in September 1987. In May 1988 he succeeded in having the Court of Criminal Appeal of the Supreme Court of Victoria set aside all convictions on the grounds that the jury was misdirected. A *nolle prosequi* was eventually entered by the Director of Public Prosecutions on 30 June 1989.

In the same month that the Supreme Court set aside Skrijel's convictions (May 1988) the *Sunday Press* ran a story headlined 'Hell For Man Who Said "No" To The Drug Runners'.[32] Five days later Skrijel's daughter went to Tullamarine Airport to pick up her mother. Minutes after she locked the car and proceeded into the terminal, the car was engulfed in flames and destroyed.[33]

By late 1989, Skrijel and his supporters (who included the congregation of the North Belconnen Baptist Church in Canberra) were pushing for an inquiry into the NCA's dealings with Skrijel.

David Berthelson, Skrijel's indefatigable advocate, sent a number of letters to Michael Tate, then federal Justice Minister, including a thirty-seven page submission[34]. Tate referred this material to the South Australian Branch of the NCA, which undertook an 'internal investigation' into the Skrijel–Berthelson claims of NCA corruption.[35] No wrongdoing was found. Skrijel and Berthelson were very concerned that the internal inquiry did not consult Costigan's suppressed Volume 7, where many of the allegations of NCA frame-up of Skrijel were laid out, along with corroborative evidence.[36]

In addition, the NCA obtained the advice of Ian Robertson, a Victorian QC, who supported the conclusions of the NCA internal inquiry and added:

Whilst I have the greatest sympathy for the tragic plight of Skrijel and his family, I have the distinct impression upon reading the material that many of his [Skrijel's] problems are of his own making, influenced by his diagnosed mental condition.[37]

Was it pure coincidence that the phrase 'of his own making' was also used by the South Australian Commissioner of Police, David Hunt, in a press release that he issued on 23 May 1990?[38] Hunt went public to attack Senator Baume's call for an independent inquiry into Skrijel's allegations that he had been framed by the NCA and the police. Was it also a coincidence that Robertson replayed the original sentencing judge's view that Skrijel had a long-standing psychiatric condition? Skrijel-on-file was mad, self-destructive and dangerous. Skrijel-on-file was always on the next investigator's desk long before the real Skrijel appeared. What chance did he have?

This is what the Australian Law Reform Commission (ALRC) said recently about the way the NCA conducts investigations into complaints about itself:

the current ad hoc arrangements for dealing with complaints is deficient in that it lacks any formal process and any consistent external scrutiny. The system does little to generate public confidence in the accessibility and integrity of the NCA.[39]

But I'm leaping ahead here. While there was a lot of concern about the quality of NCA internal investigations into complaints against the NCA in the 1980s and 1990s (when Skrijel was fighting them), it was not until 1996 that the ALRC, helped along by a submission from Skrijel, concluded that the NCA had very poor processes in place for handling complaints against itself.

From the time of Senator Tate's decision not to take any further action on Skrijel's allegations in late 1989, it took a further three years of lobbying by Skrijel and his supporters before Duncan Kerr, the new Justice Minister, felt compelled to establish an independent inquiry. David Quick QC of the Adelaide Bar was appointed to review the matter on 20 September 1993.[40]

From the outset Quick knew that:

The allegations involve grave misconduct on the part of officers of the NCA, members of the Victorian Police Force acting under the de facto direction of the NCA and members of the Victoria and South Australia Police Forces acting independently. These allegations involve criminal conduct of a very serious nature by persons exercising police powers and they involve therefore the integrity of institutions (including the NCA) to which those persons belonged.[41]

Quick soon realised that he was the meat in the sandwich between Skrijel and the government. He says that from Skrijel he got limited cooperation, and from the government he got a set of vague guidelines. He advised the Justice Minister:

On the first occasion that I met Mr Skrijel, I discussed with him the matter of his cooperation. He advised me at the time that he had not determined whether or not he would cooperate with my investigation.[42]

Skrijel had commenced proceedings in the Victorian County Court against the NCA, alleging malicious prosecution and the abuse of police powers. He was reluctant to share his evidence with Quick because the force of it might be lost on the court.[43]

Skrijel was also mistrustful of the process that led to Quick's appointment. He had heard that Quick had previously acted for the

NCA. On questioning from Skrijel, Quick denied any connection. Skrijel was also uncomfortable with the fact that Quick practised in Adelaide, the city where most of the alleged wrongdoing occurred:

> I mentioned to him [Quick] the names of many of the people against whom I had complained and he acknowledged that he knew most of them on a first-name basis and met many at functions usually several times a year. My concerns were not resolved.[44]

Skrijel also knew that the government was only going to authorise an administrative review, with no royal commission-type powers to compel witnesses to attend and give evidence.

He was burdened by the same problem Quick had: the lack of precision in the government's brief. In his report Quick said:

> The Terms of Reference upon which I was appointed are very broad in scope. I was provided with no more particularity by those appointing me. I was directed instead to a number of documents prepared by Mr Skrijel and to a huge pile (extending to thousands of pages) of records and files maintained by the NCA.[45]

Skrijel only received legal aid when Quick's ten-month inquiry was almost finished.

Given all these problems Quick appears to have given Skrijel a fair go. Quick was critical of Robertson, the NCA counsel, for too readily accepting the view that Skrijel was paranoid, and therefore an unreliable witness. Quick recognised that even if Skrijel was paranoid, that did not necessarily corrupt his evidence. He also did not discount Skrijel's evidence on the basis of the abovementioned conviction, and said that generally his observations of facts were corroborated by other evidence.

On the matter of police planting drugs and a weapon on Skrijel, Quick said:

> the opportunity to fabricate evidence was available to NCA officers involved in the investigation, and also to members of the Victorian Police who were acting under the de facto control of the NCA.[46]

With respect to the planting of a weapon at Skrijel's property, he said:

I think it is beyond doubt that there has been some very serious misconduct whereby the weapon which was once in police possession pursuant to a forfeiture order ceased to be in police possession. If the weapon was left at Mr Skrijel's property in November 1992, and the preponderance of evidence at this stage is that it was, then it is very difficult to conceive of it being left there for any purpose than with an intention to cause him embarrassment or harm. These are very serious allegations and the events are of quite recent occurrence.[47]

The most substantial part of Skrijel's claim is that he has been seriously economically damaged if not ruined. First he was the subject of a local secondary boycott whereby essential supplies (diesel fuel, bait) were denied to him. Secondly he claims that his fishing catch was often stolen, and his reputation locally besmirched. On this harassment Skrijel (writing in the third person) has commented:

While the investigation of the [economic loss] claim would not be easy, the public interest calls for it to be pursued. A successful fisherman was hounded out of his port. He had his boat burned, gear damaged, catch stolen, and house burned. At the same time he was making allegations of criminal activity by other fishermen in the same area. If there is any truth in his allegations the consequences suffered by Mr Skrijel immediately fall into place. The truth of the allegations gives all involved the motive to engage in the activity complained of. The litany of misfortune which has befallen Mr Skrijel is such that one immediately looks for something other than a string of bad luck.[48]

Skrijel says that this harassment continued at least up until November 1995. In a statement read into the federal parliamentary record by Senator Calvert (Tasmania) on 30 November 1995 Skrijel said:

During the week that I gave my submission to the [Parliamentary National Crime Authority Committee] I was under constant surveillance. One of the vehicles used carried registration plates RBL 823.

According to Road Traffic Authority records the plates had been handed into the RTA and were still in the RTA's custody. I am not aware of anyone other than the NCA who would have the power to 'borrow' a set of plates from the RTA, use them for an illegal purpose and return them with no questions asked. On Friday 3 November (the end of the same week) between 2.30 pm and 3.25 pm my home, though fully secured, was entered and ransacked. There was no sign of forced entry and no property appears to be missing but a bullet was left beside my fax. The bullet, as the NCA would know, dispelled any doubt as to who had me under surveillance and had entered my home illegally ... My mail is being opened, sometimes ripped, before it is given to the postman and delivered with no attempt to conceal this further offence.[49]

Skrijel's investigator also had harsh words to say about the NCA:

I hoped that the NCA would behave as a fair-minded responsible prosecuting authority would behave and provide any relevant evidence whether in support or adverse to the NCA or its former officers. Regrettably, instead I received, what appears to me, to be a spirited defence of all persons associated with the NCA and of the NCA itself. The NCA response document seriously distorts what is written in my draft report [the report relied on for this chapter] and very seriously distorts, in discussion of my procedure, the process of my investigation. The NCA document contains a number of factual inaccuracies.[50]

Justice Minister Kerr rejected Quick's recommendation for a royal commission. Kerr made a public statement that cast Skrijel in a negative light and claimed that 'Mr Quick made no adverse finding against any individual or the NCA'.[51]

In recommending an inquiry with coercive powers into the Skrijel matter, Quick concluded:

In my opinion, there is substantial evidence upon which it is reasonable to base a strong suspicion that evidence was fabricated in order to incriminate Mr Skrijel on serious criminal charges involving drugs and explosives.[52]

Kerr and the Attorney-General's Department were determined to take no further action on the Quick Report. However because of adverse mention of Victorian Police, the whole box and dice was sent to the Victorian Deputy Ombudsman (Police Complaints). He reported in late 1997 with a 200-plus page report that gave no satisfaction to Skrijel.

On 11 June 1997 Skrijel appeared before the Joint Committee on the National Crime Authority, which was conducting its three-yearly review of the NCA. Skrijel came out with all guns blazing. He was offensive, accusatory, and very angry. Under normal circumstances any one of these behaviours would have guaranteed his expulsion from the parliamentary hearing. But these were not normal circumstances. All committee members had met or heard about Mick Skrijel and his infamous search for justice. This engendered an atmosphere of sympathy, which tempered the committee's resonse to his hostile performance.

Skrijel started in typical fashion by accusing the committee of accepting drug money and being a 'cheap political arm of the most corrupt police force in the world'.[53] He was, of course, referring to the NCA. He then said that the NCA had murdered witnesses.[54] Skrijel, as usual, did not have the hard evidence to corroborate this, nor the many more allegations that he made. As is the case with many whistleblowers, Skrijel, without investigative resources, was adding personal experiences with the NCA together into an insinuation of corruption. To most of the numerous investigators who have considered Skrijel's allegations over the years, he was either mad, or a poor mathematician, trying to make one and one add up to three.

Notwithstanding this, the NCA's parliamentary committee was able to realise that a guilty man could not protest his innocence for as long and as consistently as Skrijel has. The committee finished with Skrijel with this interesting exchange:

Chair: Despite what you have said about us, you are having an opportunity at the moment ... to deal directly with the Parliament of Australia. I think I speak for all of us. We really want to try and help you ...

Skrijel: I thank you too because this is the first committee that has not treated me in a hostile way, the first committee that listened to me. I apologise if I have offended any of you.

Chair: That is all right, we are used to being offended.[55]

With this review being marked by the John Elliott affair,[56] and with Skrijel providing no new evidence, the Joint Committee report did no more than affirm the conclusion that Skrijel-type cases exemplify the need for much better complaint-processing procedures at the NCA.[57]

Meanwhile Skrijel still waits for his justice. While he may have to wait a long time for that, an initiative in the wind could lead to complaint-processing reform at the NCA. On 26 July 1995 Attorney-General Michael Lavarch sent a reference to the ALRC to inquire into and report on NCA complaint-processing and whether those procedures meet public expectations with respect to accountability, effectiveness and efficiency.[58]

The ALRC circulated an issues paper in November 1995 and a draft recommendation paper in July 1996.[59] In this paper the ALRC recommended a National Integrity and Investigation Commission to investigate, manage or supervise the investigation of complaints against the NCA and the Australian Federal Police. In making such a recommendation the ALRC said:

The current ad hoc arrangement for complaints against the NCA is grossly deficient in that it lacks any publicly known or recognised process and any consistent external scrutiny. The system does little if anything to create public confidence in the accountability and integrity of the NCA. The current system is particularly inadequate for the majority of citizens who do not have the resources and time to mount expensive challenges to the exercise of NCA powers.[60]

ALRC issued a final report in late 1996.[61]

In conclusion it can be said that the Skrijel affair illustrates a number of issues common to most whistleblower cases:

- The attempt by whistleblowers to expose wrongdoing is usually met by wrongdoers countering the whistleblowers with false charges.

- In addition to false charges, whistleblowers face attacks on their morality, motivation and mental health.
- With the heat on the whistleblower the focus soon leaves the original wrongdoing, which either continues in a more clandestine manner or stops temporarily until all investigations have ceased.
- Whistleblowers face an enormous amount of corrupt, incompetent and timid investigating practices.

The case demonstrates significant flaws in the justice system, particularly that part of the system that receives and processes disclosures of criminal and official wrongdoing. To take this point further is to reflect on the whistleblower's distinctive *modus operandi*. Whistleblowers are often high-energy users of any person or agency that presents as relevant to the investigation and correction of disclosed wrongdoing.[62] They make very good guides not only into the secret mazes of wrongdoing, but also into the labyrinthine world of official investigation. Skrijel's case is particularly illuminating with respect to the latter.

There is now a stockpile of evidence, a lot of it gained recently, which shows widespread corruption and incompetence in investigative agencies, including those controlled by police.[63] Police whistleblowers have over the years made an under-rated contribution to this disturbing body of knowledge. Whistleblowers are often in good positions to make secondary public interest disclosures on the quality of investigations that follow primary public interest disclosures on wrongdoing. Skrijel did both. He bore an enormous evidentiary, moral and financial burden in trying to keep the investigators' eye on the wrongdoing rather than on him.

Finally, if Mick Skrijel made any new year resolutions for 1998, abandoning his fight was not one of them. He started the year by suing the former Justice Minister, Duncan Kerr, for defamation.[64] He's back on the road sign-posted to justice. I hope he has an extra pair of shoes.

10 The Dark Side of Whistleblowing
War at the Memorial

It is not workplace harassment for managers to manage. – Mr Justice Finn, *Kelson v. Forward (1995)*[1]

I thought that we had a pretty happy staff [at the Australian War Memorial] and on balance I think that we did, but I discounted and did not allow for the culture of complaint, the cult of the victim and the dictatorship of virtue. – Brendon Kelson[2]

I can only conclude that he [Minister Gary Johns] decided that the MPRA [Merit Protection Review Agency], like a Rottweiler, should be let off the leash. What I still don't know is why. – Michael McKernan[3]

This is a war story with a difference. The two most senior men at the Australian War Memorial, men with integrity and a great sense of public duty, men who in various ways had served Australia well, were hunted by a group of malcontents and trigger-happy investigators. This was no openly declared war. Brendan Kelson and Michael McKernan still can only guess at the identity of those in pursuit. The war only ended when the Federal Court intervened to disarm the Merit Protection Review Agency. Theirs is a story that speaks of the dark side of whistleblowing: disclosures motivated by hate and opportunism.

On 14 August 1994 Prime Minister Paul Keating visited one of the most revered sites in Australia, the Australian War Memorial (AWM) in Canberra. He was there to launch the 'Australia Remembers 1945–1995' program. An event occurred two days later that showed that the fought-for value of fair play had been forgotten in some circles .

On 16 August 1994 the Minister then responsible for the public service, Gary Johns, directed the Merit Protection Review Agency (MPRA),[4] as it was then called, to look into allegations of workplace harassment raised by still unidentified former and current AWM staff. The complaints were against the outgoing Director, Brendon Kelson, and his deputy, the Australian historian Dr Michael McKernan.[5] Johns' letter to MPRA Director Ann Forward was, given the size of the task he assigned her, suspiciously brief and to the point:

> *Recently I have had brought to my attention matters relating to staff management at the Australian War Memorial. I understand that there have been allegations made by staff at the Australian War Memorial of various types of workplace harassment over a considerable period of time.*[6]

One cannot help feeling that this letter was the public information tip of a political iceberg that had been floating towards Kelson and McKernan for some time. Another version has it that Ann Forward drafted Johns' letter to her.[7] Whichever way it happened the Minister's request was dangerously wide: ' ... I now request ... that the [MPRA] conduct an inquiry into ... workplace harassment at the Australian War Memorial.' This request, though limited somewhat by subject matter, was not limited by person, event, or time.[8] Technically the allegations could have gone back to 1917 when the Australian War Memorial started!

Johns' directive was also marked by an extraordinary amount of official aloofness in that he is alleged to have acted without consulting his colleague Con Sciacca, the Minister with portfolio responsibility for the AWM.[9] Johns told Federal Parliament that he approved the MPRA investigation on the basis of evidence from that Agency ' ... and the view of the Minister for Veteran Affairs, who was consulted on the matter on the way through'.[10] Sciacca rejected this view and claimed that he was told of the investigation after the decision to conduct it was made.[11] This led to the question being raised as to whether Johns misled parliament.[12]

Ministers scrambling for cover, investigators acting like an invading army against the shaky fortress of natural justice, and senior bureaucrats dodging their duty to uphold legal and ethical standards are threads that weave in and out of this disreputable saga.

Mr Justice Finn of the Federal Court, who stopped the hunt against Kelson and McKernan, made a strong judicial attack on the MPRA. He also raised questions about the performance of the two ministers Johns and Sciacca. One commentator has said that this was the most poignant section of Finn's judgement.[13] The judgement, at the relevant part, reads:

I cannot, and do not comment, on the extent to which these [Public Service Commissioner and officers of the Attorney-Generals Department] and other public officials (including if necessary ministers) may or should have been able to assist in the early resolution of the concerns raised by the applicants [Kelson and McKernan]. I do nonetheless invite attention to this in the hope that by so doing, proceedings brought for the reasons that these have been brought will not be found necessary in the future.[14]

Brendon Kelson could afford to be less circumspect than Mr Justice Finn about political accountability: 'How could the MPRA get it so wrong, and what responsibility does Johns take for them getting it so wrong?'[15] It appears now that even if Johns had tried to include Sciacca this would not have saved Kelson and McKernan because Sciacca appeared determined to stay right out of the matter. He said on one occasion: 'I think it would be improper of me on legal grounds to be seen to interfere in the process in any way.'[16] McKernan found this an 'astounding response' because this was an administrative inquiry, and was not in any sense yet a legal matter. 'Sciacca,' he said, 'had effectively told Kelson he was on his own.'[17]

What transpired was the first ever agency-wide inquiry into 'workplace harassment' in Australia. Now that the Federal Court has found 'procedural oppression' in the way MPRA conducted the inquiry, we can conclude that what really transpired was a successful reputational lynching of the Memorial's two most senior executives. This is the focus of this chapter: how, almost overnight, the workplace becomes very toxic, not only for whistleblowers, but for the victims of malicious reports. Kelson and McKernan hold dual identities in the Memorial saga. They were both victims of malice (and more), and the *true* whistleblowers in this black period at AWM. In this latter role they were subject to reprisals for daring to raise concerns about the absence of natural justice in MPRA's investigative procedures. Their story ends on a depressingly familiar note. No powerful culprits have been disciplined, nor even named. Worse, no enduring corrections, in systemic terms, have been made. AWM staff are as vulnerable now to bad process as Kelson and McKernan were. A more optimistic account, taken by both McKernan and Kelson, is based on the fact that Mr Justice Finn's judgement is now a part of Australian administrative law. Let us look at what happened.

Kelson met with Charlotte Blesing, the MPRA officer designated to conduct the 'inquiry', on 17 August 1994. He was in a difficult position. A career public servant with an unblemished record, he was justifiably proud of his achievements at AWM.[18] While he could not believe that there were grounds for an investigation, he trusted MPRA (initially) and did not suspect duplicity. Nor did he wish to appear to be concealing anything by not co-operating with the investigation. He now concedes that it was an error to discount the gathering storm clouds.[19]

Kelson's initial openness points to a dynamic that one often sees in cases like this. I call it 'ethical displacement'. Ethically driven people often assume that honour and ethics drive all. In the beginning Kelson thought that MPRA was an ethical enterprise and he was positive, even enthusiastic about it as an agency. After all, its official mission was merit protection, something that Kelson, as a career bureaucrat, strongly believed in. But mission statements are often a million miles from reality. Not only did Kelson initially believe the MPRA posters and brochures, he *wanted* to believe. He, an honourable man, expected to see honour in *all* the public structures that he dealt with. Twinned to this dynamic of ethical displacement was a concern that any public remonstration about the activities of MPRA would appear as a cover-up by Kelson. So in a sense he was trapped in his own ethical structure. He soon found himself in the front row, witnessing the building of gallows designed to send his and McKernan's reputations through the trapdoor.

Kelson's difficulties were compounded by MPRA duplicity. There was nothing in the letter that Blesing gave Kelson at the meeting on 17 August to indicate that the MPRA was set to fry some big fish: himself, and particularly McKernan. Blesing simply stated to Kelson that the Minister requested the investigation (probably false), that the investigation should proceed with minimal disruption to AWM (it didn't), that the investigators pledged confidentiality (broken), and that they promised to abide by the tenets of natural justice (broken).[20]

It appears that MPRA broke numerous ethical and definitional guidelines in its investigation of these two men. For a start public service guidelines emphasise that workplace harassment must not be confused with 'legitimate comment and advice – including relevant negative comment or feedback'.[21] It appears that MPRA ignored these guidelines and substituted its own catch-all definition:

harassment is any type of behaviour that can be reasonably expected to cause a person to feel threatened, uncomfortable or unable to cope with their work environment.[22]

A person scared of heights and forced to take the lift to his office could sue for harassment under this definition.

The MPRA ignored the written concerns of the Public Service Commissioner and the Office of General Counsel (Attorney-General's Department). The Public Service Commissioner said that MPRA's definition was '... very broad and goes beyond the explanatory and definitional material presented in the PSC *Guidelines*'.[23] Denis Ives, the Public Service Commissioner at the time, asked the MPRA to withdraw its 'go-it-alone' definition of workplace harassment. MPRA Director Forward refused to do so.[24] The MPRA claimed it was entitled to choose any definition that was reasonably open to it.[25] Ives incidentally became a high-ranking casualty of the war at the Memorial. When the time came, his contract was not renewed.[26]

No less an authority than the Office of General Counsel said, in a written opinion, that to the extent that MPRA was inquiring into matters other than alleged workplace harassment, its investigation was unauthorised. This opinion was later to be judicially confirmed by Mr Justice Finn. Kelson received General Counsel's advice on 5 October 1994 and personally gave it to Ann Forward two days later. It is reported that Forward refused to take notice of the opinion of General Counsel.[27] In reflecting on the process around this time, McKernan said:

Unfortunately too many senior people at the Memorial, though initially deeply hostile to the inquiry, were now diverted by the inherent absurdity of what was being proposed, and tended to adopt a complacent response. They were inclined to leave it to run into the sand all on its own. But in fact there was no room for complacency and experience would show that we should have been pushing every button available to properly construct this thing or have it closed down. At the very least we owed it to our staff to have clarification of what it was the MPRA was attempting to do. Careful thought at this stage would have indicated just how confused thinking at the MPRA was. What was under investigation? Was it workplace harassment, as the PSC had defined it, or the management of the Memorial staff and whatever that might entail? We had nothing to fear from an investigation based on the PSC's definition of workplace harassment: but what of an inquiry that roamed over any and all administrative actions and decisions of the last decade or more?

So, armed with its own designed definition of workplace harassment, the MPRA apparently went in search of crimes that matched the definition. In a four-month 'fishing expedition',[28] *all* AWM staff were invited to 'raise *any* concerns that you may have about staff management at the Australian War Memorial'[29] (emphasis added). McKernan has commented on this:

We had little to fear from current staff, constrained within a PSC definition to have regard for the appropriate rights of management. But what of disgruntled former members of staff free to indulge their unhappiness that the Memorial had moved in directions that they could not accommodate?

. . . from the earliest days of the inquiry we had evidence that

some staff, acting with some former staff, were actively recruiting witnesses for the MPRA. One of the junior members of my branch reported that he had been invited to make a submission on my managerial and personal style by people that he would not identify but who were currently members of the Memorial staff. They sought to jog his memory about the ways that I had spoken rudely to him in branch staff meetings but he rebutted the suggestion saying the only conversations he had with me were about football and that I had invariably been courteous and good humoured. They had picked the wrong target: we got on well. A former member of staff who had worked closely with me, who had given the best he could to the place, and who had created a thriving cell of activity, left to establish his own business. He went with my blessing, friendship and support. Imagine his surprise when he was asked, via telephone, to make a submission to the MPRA about me. He had left the Memorial at least six years before and had no interest in the current climate of dispute in a place he looked back on with affection. Nor did the backstabbers know that I had helped him out of a fairly deep hole at one point in his life. Again they had picked the wrong target and he told them so. But it was frustrating to know that recruitment was taking place and even worse to watch it in action. Kelson spoke to Blesing about this, but she was dismissive of any suggestion of collusion.[30]

Indeed Blesing, pressured by Kelson, said at one stage that she was unaware of the s.56 request being based on *any* specific allegations. Her view of the 'inquiry' (accepted by the Court as her view) was that it would instead be a 'trawling exercise'.[31] The nets used caught some very old fish indeed. The earliest allegation concerned matters that allegedly occurred in 1982, twelve years before the MPRA inquiry started.[32]

Kelson acknowledged that the MPRA inquiry became a 'major source of controversy, stress and division within the AWM'.[33] In addition Mr Justice Finn got very close to suggesting in his findings that the MPRA had actually harassed the Director and his Deputy.[34] When Kelson expressed his concerns about the wide ambit of the MPRA inquiry and the fact that it was using its own definition of workplace harassment, he was accused by the MPRA of attempting to frustrate the inquiry. The Federal Court rebuked the MPRA for coming to this vexatious conclusion.³⁵ When Kelson and McKernan wrote seeking a particularisation of the allegations, Ann Forward refused discovery, offering an interpretation of their request that is capable of meaning that alleged harassers are not entitled to the same level or quality of procedural fairness as their alleged victims.³⁶ This became very clear at an early meeting between Kelson and Blesing.

Even at this stage MPRA had kept its cards below the table. Blesing did say that while she didn't know what was in the Minister's mind, she knew that McKernan's name had come up in many discussions at the agency.³⁷ Only two weeks into her inquiry she told Kelson that she had heard a number of people say that McKernan must be prevented from becoming the Memorial's next Director. Blesing then apparently gave Kelson some examples of McKernan's alleged wrongdoing, all of which Kelson confidently contradicted as false and highly injurious to McKernan's reputation.

On 20 September 1994 McKernan was called to the MPRA office. 'There was no small talk,' he has said. 'I felt uncomfortable and unwelcome, as if I were a person to be wary of.'³⁸ He was handed a document, and of all things a spread-sheet that listed 396 accusations from 65 people:

*I looked up from my reading amazed to see the two investigators [Blesing and her co-worker] earnestly appraising my response. I thought that I detected in them a sense of pride in their work. I sensed that it was best to say as little as possible, and take my leave as quickly as I could. I drove the short distance back to the Memorial and told Kelson that I needed a drink.*³⁹

McKernan then showed Kelson the elaborate spread-sheet and both men struggled to make sense of it. McKernan said that it was 'a list based on rumours, lies, half-truths and some things that while true out of context took on a sinister meaning'. 'Frankly,' he said, 'we were stunned.'⁴⁰

Kelson's turn was next. He was called before the MPRA on 23 September. He left with his own spread-sheet. Rumours sprouted in the Canberra spring that a further nine senior managers would take the walk up to the MPRA officers for their charge sheets.

Many of the allegation were so small-minded and unimportant that Michael Gordon of the *Australian* raised the matter with Ann Forward. He reported that she appeared 'genuinely surprised at [their] trivial nature'. Gordon's story was accompanied by an editorial that blasted the inquiry as:

a case study in how not to conduct such an investigation ... the complaints carry the hallmark of a politically correct witchhunt.[41]

Kelson, having now abandoned any hope that the MPRA would act honourably, lobbied hard for some sanity to enter the process. He wrote to his Minister. Sciacca not only failed to respond, he blocked his Departmental Head, Dr Allan Hawke, from attending a proposed meeting with Forward at which Kelson would show Forward how the inquiry had gone off the rails.[42] In private Kelson no doubt agreed with McKernan's view that 'the inquiry was madness. It must be shut down'.[43]

Kelson, now armed with opinion from the Attorney-General's Department that the inquiry was seriously flawed, but without the support of Hawke, met with Forward on 7 October. He was accompanied by Noel Tanzer, an AWM Council Member. According to McKernan, Kelson found Forward hostile and not open to counter-argument:

She opened in a remarkably aggressive fashion and caught both Kelson and Tanzer off their guard. Forward had great certainty in the powers the MPRA Act bestowed on her and she was not a person accustomed to opposition. She explained that she had the power to investigate as the Minister had requested. She reminded Kelson that he was a subject of the inquiry and she said that the investigation would continue despite apparent efforts to frustrate it. Kelson was shocked by the force and aggression of this presentation.[44]

Relevant to Forward's mistaken view that Kelson and McKernan were attempting to frustrate the inquiry is the false allegation that Kelson took to staking out the MPRA offices and recording the names of AWM staff who went into the building.[45]

On 18 October McKernan was called again to MPRA headquarters, where he received a more formally titivated charge sheet. MPRA told him to respond in two weeks. Returning to the Memorial he shut himself away. Just him and the allegations, which he read with 'rising disbelief':

> There were no dates provided and very little at all of a specific nature... Not one of the allegations... had ever been raised with me before ... All the allegations came from those who [dealt with me] indirectly and would have only secondhand knowledge of what I had said or done. Many of the allegations referred to events of years ago [McKernan started at AWM in 1981], now encrusted with layers of legend and gossip.[46]

He finished the document feeling 'quite miserable'. A month later Sciacca announced the appointment of Peter Hawker (not McKernan) as Acting Director from 1 January 1995. McKernan was bitterly disappointed:

> Sciacca showed no interest in trying to penetrate the issues that the [MPRA] inquiry threw up. Clearly he did not want to become involved; he wanted decisions taken elsewhere, either by the MPRA report, and Johns' responses to it, or by the Federal Court. If he did nothing he could not stumble.[47]

On 20 November 1994 the *Sunday Age* published a front-page article insinuating that Kelson retired pre-emptively to avoid the MPRA 'inquiry'.[48] Four days later through his solicitors, Kelson wrote to the newspaper setting out his concerns at the libellous nature of the article. He demanded an apology, which was printed on 11 December.[49] Not satisfied with this, Kelson sued.

An MPRA report finally went to the Minister on 20 December 1994. Kelson and McKernan had been promised at the outset that if charges were recommended they would have opportunities to answer them. These opportunities never came. Kelson and McKernan sought a Federal Court injunction. Their lawyers, Crossin Barker Gosling, requested legal funding from the AWM Council.

Initially they had the support of General Peter Gration, the AWM Council Chairman, for the Memorial to carry the costs of the injunction. Early in the afternoon of 14 December Sciacca arrived at the memorial for a conference with Gration. The Minister was accompanied by two of his senior advisers. McKernan recollects:

Gration chose to go into this hastily convened meeting unaccompanied, a dangerous decision if he wished to fight resolutely for his own corner. I have no way of knowing what was discussed but I do remember that I was depressed by the length of time that the meeting took; it seemed to go on for hours. When it was over Gration told the Council Secretary that he wished to redraft his advice to Council ... Gration had inserted a new paragraph which began: 'Council should also consider factors which favour not funding a challenge.'[50]

McKernan was later told by one of Sciacca's staff that the 'factor' uppermost in the Minister's mind when he met with Gration was: 'The perception that Council was supporting senior staff against junior staff who had complained.'[51]

Incredibly the AWM Council reversed its commitment to fund the legal action within a matter of hours through a balance-tipping vote arriving by fax.[52] This was a major blow to both men. On their own now, what were they to do? McKernan recollects the difficult moment:

I tried to put the position fairly to Michalina [McKernan's wife] that evening, weighing the strength of the legal argument against the possible damage to the way we lived. Her mind was made up and I suspect that it had been from the instant that she had heard the result of the council vote. We would fight in court, she told me, regardless of the risks, because it was the right thing to do. If we ducked this now I would forever regret it, she added, and probably grow to resent her and myself for the cowards that we would have been. Since I first came to know Michalina I have admired her immensely. She is as strong and honest and good a person as I have ever met. But I never admired her more than at that moment. We celebrated the decision joyfully and I looked forward to the coming battle with relish.[53]

The next day McKernan told Kelson of his and his wife's decision:

'Good,' Kelson said, 'that was what I was hoping for. Of course I will be with you. We have been in this together from the start and we will fight together.' Nothing Brendon had ever said to me more surprised me. He would be retiring in two weeks. He could walk away from all this and never have to think of the MPRA again. As a senior public servant he would be comfortable in retirement but not lavishly so and he could ill afford large costs of the kind contemplated by our lawyers. But friendship and principle meant more to him than that. Brendon was a cautious man, disinclined for conflict or notoriety but he would stand beside me.

Brave words, but they had to face a fully resourced MPRA that briefed a senior Sydney QC. Despite this the two men were determined that the truth should break through, even if this meant somehow paying the legal expenses personally. This was not necessary. In the same month that Mr Justice Finn granted Kelson and McKernan their injunction (6 October 1995), and ordered MPRA to pay court costs,[54] the federal government funded their costs. If they had not have won they would have had a legal bill in excess of $45,000 for themselves and probably twice that to cover MPRA's bill.

The judge, in his sixty-three-page report, was scathing of the MPRA. He found that the report was 'fatally flawed' and that the two men had been denied natural justice. The judge found that MPRA had presumed to wander into unauthorised areas, misunderstood its own authority, and framed a definition of workplace harassment that was so wide it embraced perfectly reasonable and fair actions. David Solomon, a barrister and legal commentator said in the *Courier Mail*:

One of the extraordinary features of this case was that the body which was at fault, the Merit Review Protection Agency [sic], was supposed to protect the standards which it had breached in the War Memorial inquiry.[55]

Mr Justice Finn made a similar point:

An important function of the MPRA is to maintain particular values, and notably fair dealings in decisions made and actions taken in relation to Commonwealth employees. For this reason when it takes such decisions or actions itself, it quite properly can be expected to be an exemplar of those values ... [It] should be ... scrupulous in adhering to those standards. In the circumstances of this case it has fallen short of this.[56]

What was all the fuss about? Why were Kelson and McKernan handled so ruthlessly? What was behind the MPRA overkill? One view is that the attacks had covert agendas: the annihilation of any chance McKernan had to succeed Kelson as AWM Director, and the attempt by MPRA management to reposition the agency as a significant force in Canberra bureaucratic politics.

Kelson first gave hints of his intention to retire to his senior colleagues and the Chair of AWM Council in May 1994. Johns, the responsible Minister, cleared the MPRA for its 'inquiry' some weeks later. McKernan at that stage was the heir apparent. He had joined AWM in August 1981. A leading scholar and tireless promoter of Australian military history, he was supported in his bid to become the next director by retiring AWM Chair Dame Beryl Beaurepaire and former AWM Chair General Sir Thomas Daly. Beaurepaire, who believed that AWM directors should come from museum rather than military backgrounds, has said that: 'there were no significant staff problems at the Memorial. I certainly would have known about them had they existed.'[57] McKernan also had the support of current and former council members such as Sir William Keys, Harry Gordon, Professor Bryan Gandevia, and eminent figures such as Bill Hayden, Governor-General at the time. He had strong staff support too. The eleven senior managers who reported to him were strongly in favour of his promotion.[58]

The short time lapse between Kelson's expressed interest in retiring (Kelson retired in December 1994) and the announcement of the MPRA 'inquiry' is too short a period to be mere coincidence. It appears that Kelson's announcement triggered frenetic activity on the part of one some senior officer at AWM, as well as intense lobbying activity within the Armed Services and the Returned Soldiers League (RSL), which wanted a military man as director.

According to one report, conflicts had festered in the military–civilian great divide since the 1980s. In referring to a previous director, Air Vice-Marshal Jim Flemming, who was himself sacked, the report said:

In his own politicking to save his job, Flemming sought to cast himself as the saviour of the Memorial as a military shrine against, to use one of his parliamentary supporters' words, 'a small dishonest cadre of dishonest academics', who, it was said, were conspiring to turn the memorial into a peace museum.[59]

It took no time for the National President of the RSL, Major-General 'Digger' James, to call for a military replacement for Kelson.[60] It was reported that he personally conveyed this view to Minister Sciacca.[61] 'Only the Military,' James said, 'could understand the fundamental nobility of the Memorial.'[62] The RSL has tended to the view that the military are the right and proper custodians (and interpreters) of Australia's military history. This view has asserted itself throughout RSL history. In 1997, for instance, the RSL bitterly attacked the ACT government's plan to site an Australian–Japanese peace park on the shores of Lake Burley Griffin.[63]

Just over a fortnight after Finn brought in his judicial rebuke of the MPRA, an RSL commentary said:

When acrimony within an institution becomes entrenched, appointing people from within the existing ranks to top positions simply does not work ... What is needed at the Memorial is a restoring of the confidence of the staff of the institution and very importantly indeed, a restoring of the confidence of the Memorial's natural constituency, ie the serving and ex-service community ... The concept of the Memorial was that of Charles Bean, journalist and scholar, but it was to an Army Officer, Major Treloar, and to the RSL to whom Bean turned to execute his magnificent idea. We need the wisdom and courage now to turn to another Treloar.[64]

Three weeks later the RSL was back on the same theme:

When Charles Bean conceived the idea of the War Memorial at Pozieres in 1916 where 23,000 Australians died in a six-week battle, he saw it as a place that would forever perpetuate the memories of the enormity of Australian sacrifice ... The Directorship of the Memorial must be removed from the Canberra bureaucracy and from academia and placed in the hands of a proven military leader and manager.[65]

This activity was designed to destroy any possibility of a civilian successor to Kelson. It worked. Shortly before General Gower won the top position the editor of the *Canberra Times* said:

If he [McKernan] fails to get the job ... it seems that few people of talent and energy will be inspired to want to work in such a cesspool of internal and external politics from above and below. In the modern disposable public service, there's not much due process, loyalty or credit in the bank.[66]

Sciacca refused to appoint McKernan Acting Director during the course of the 'inquiry' and while the action was before the Federal Court. Sciacca went on to work against his appointment when the matter got to Cabinet. Applications for the Directorship of AWM closed, ironically, in the same week that Mr Justice Finn brought down his decision that the investigation of Kelson and McKernan was illegal. There were around fifty applications for this prestigious job that attracted a salary package of about $130,000.[67] Eventually the decision to appoint McKernan or General Gower, the military choice, as Kelson's replacement was left to Prime Minister Keating. Keating went for Gower, the next Treloar.

In reflecting on the matter soon after the Federal Court decision, Kelson, who now was in retirement, said:

Personally I have lived with this for more than thirteen months and searched my soul every day for something I might have done that could have provoked all this. My conscience is clear, but the stress for me and my family has been constant. The problem is that when people say things, some of it sticks. People that don't know you tend to look at you slightly askance.[68]

In the period leading up to his retirement, and for a time afterwards, Kelson had experiences that led him to think he was being adversely treated. Three days after the Melbourne *Sunday Age* published the article defaming him, Kelson was to attend a fundraising gathering in Melbourne for the AWM Capital Appeal. His secretary was contacted by the Chief of Protocol in Premier Kennett's office and told that Kelson's presence would not help the appeal. He felt 'terribly embarrassed and humiliated' by this.[69]

In another incident he was sounded out by a senior member of the government for a board appointment to the Sydney Symphony Orchestra. He said he was available but alerted the contact to the MPRA matter. The contact agreed that the 'time was not right', and the offer did not proceed. No new offer was ever made.[70]

During this difficult time AWM member Dame Beryl Beaurepaire took to taking Kelson around to meet potential donors 'just so that they could see he did not look like a monster'.[71] On retirement Kelson was part of a highly qualified group that tendered for the contract to restore and renovate the under-area of the Melbourne Shrine of Remembrance. He remains puzzled as to why he and his group did not even get an interview.[72]

On 3 July 1998 the decision in Kelson's defamation action against the *Sunday Age* was brought down in the ACT Supreme Court. The article was found to be libellous and Kelson awarded $75,000. Mr Justice Crispin found that:

> there was ample evidence that [Kelson] had been extremely distressed and embarrassed [by the publication]. These feelings persisted well after the publication of the article and seemed to have cast a pall over his enjoyment of his retirement. Indeed, his son Mr Adrian Kelson gave evidence that his father had been a normal, ebullient, happy and optimistic person who had enjoyed life, but as a result of the article he had withdrawn from friends and family and appeared to have been almost going through a breakdown.[73]

McKernan's fate was even worse. He was brought down on the brink of great endeavours and for all practical purposes cashiered from the public service. With the court case pending, McKernan was prevented from taking up the position of Deputy Official Secretary at Government House that was offered to him by Governor-General Bill Hayden. He now escorts tours to Australia's war sites, and writes book reviews.

Part 3
The State Control of Dissent

In the past twenty years, coinciding with a move to the right, we have been deluged with the outpourings from organisational psychology, dispute resolution studies and an emerging discipline with the Orwellian title 'human resource management'. A single theme bolts these university-based enterprises together: they are the knowledge prerogatives of management. As such we detect in their focus an interest, at times closing on obsession, in eliminating employee resistance to managerial power and masking power asymmetries in the workplace.[1]

A trickle of critical scholarship has perversely developed alongside this river of control literature. It focuses around three questions relevant to our understanding of whistleblowing. The first asks how managers, in Noam Chomsky's words, 'manufacture consent'. Note the deliberate re-contextualised use of the word 'manufacture'. Not only does the workplace produce goods and services, it also (as it must to maximise profits) 'manufactures' and secures the consent of workers. This point remains valid irrespective of whether the worker is self-employed or salaried, professional or tradesperson. The process of securing workplace consent is so precisely managed, so intimidatingly executed, yet so thoroughly misunderstood, that our very ignorance of the manufacture of consent represents another source of oppression for us.

Like the tall poppy of Australian folklore the whistleblower and public interest dissenter stand out in the workplace crowd. To some of us they stand out as heroes. To others (particularly management) they stand out as faulty goods who have somehow missed critical parts of the process of manufacturing of consent.

Equally important is the question of how employees self-discipline or auto-censor themselves when workplace wrongdoing calls for nothing less than outspokenness and direct action.

The third question concerns how employees develop strategies to circumvent and at time contest organisational power.[2] Circumvention strategies such as go-slow campaigns, absenteeism, overuse of grievance processes and the like differ from whistleblowing because they do not engage power head-on.

Whistleblowing is direct resistance to management power. This is its main strength and its main weakness. It is direct in the sense that it is unambiguous in its campaign to expose wrongdoing.

One of the effects of the enormous growth in the State since World War 11 has been the destruction of organised forms of resistance to the concentration of power in the workplace. This only serves to increase our vulnerability to the actions of the powerful, and makes the whistleblower's job even more hazardous.

Some would argue that the State is in decline, and therefore no longer a source of oppression. My own view is that the State is mutating into non-government forms. The power it has over people has not changed. What has changed are the forums in which State power is organised and exercised. In these forums, best illustrated by the examples of mega-warfare corporations and multi-national companies, power is exercised freer of public scrutiny than was the case when the State was a synonym for government. I call this the 'new servitude'.

Ranged against the State is the gathering presence of Australians of conscience who resist power by conducting micro-campaigns in their workplace. Whistleblowing is a new form of resistance to State control.

This brings us to the three chapters in the final part of the book. These chapters explore a massive three-card trick being perpetrated on the Australian people. On one hand we have been told since the end of the 1980s that the State shares the whistleblowers' concerns about rising levels of official corruption and wrongdoing. This concern is so authentic, we are told, that the State has put in place three structures to confront public wrongdoing. The first is a range of specialist authorities charged with the investigation of wrongdoing. The next is a bunch of whistleblower protection laws designed to shield disclosers from reprisals. The third is a forging of a new moral climate through the percolation of codes of ethics throughout organisations.

These look like fine cards that we have been dealt. But on closer scrutiny they resolve themselves into a miserable hand.

In chapter eleven, *The Shut-Eyed Sentry: Notes on Investigatory Incompetence and Unlawfulness,* we peer briefly into this world of official laxity, stupidity and unlawfulness. Why? Because justice stops dead in its tracks every time an opportunity to respond to a whistleblower disclosure is missed. People disclose in good faith and wait five years for a result. On other occasions straightforward complaints are transfigured into legal labyrinths. In other situations people of good conscience and intent are hunted by those who fear disclosure. On each of these occasions justice slowly bows her head, because the whistleblower enterprise has crashed. The chapter starts with a slow procession past what I call the shut-eyed sentries: people, processes, and structures, there to protect us, there to be our social justice sentries, yet asleep or oblivious to the density of wrongdoing.

In chapter twelve, *Whistleblowing Laws: The State Responds,* the statutory programs in place to protect those that disclose in the public interest in Australia are exposed for what they are, a con trick.

In the final chapter, *Codes of Ethics: Moral Bondage in the Age of Anything Goes,* the State's final 'ace', codes of ethics, are evaluated free of the hype that has surrounded their progressive endorsement in the 1990s, to the conclusion that what we have in the codes is an implicit form of moral fascism.

11 The Shut-eyed Sentries
Notes on Incompetence and Unlawfulness

First let me set the irreverent tone of this chapter by noting the logo of the New South Wales Environmental Protection Authority (EPA).

Unless I am mistaken this is a set of eyes, with one completely closed and the other indicating an advanced stage of drowsiness. The State's foremost environmental watchdog with closed and droopy eyes as its symbol! Is this some bizarre hieroglyphic, or have we reached a new level of truth in advertising? Perhaps the logo is a deep, sub-consciously expressed truth about the capacity of our protector-institutions to protect. The whistleblowers featured in Part Two would probably think so. I suggest that all protector-organisations that betray their brief should be forced to carry the closed and droopy-eyed logo; a bit like the National Heart Foundation's red tick on good food, but in reverse.

The official world of investigatory incompetence and unlawfulness is one that justice-seeking whistleblowers must enter. In October 1996 the Borbidge Government in Queensland was setting up the machinery to investigate the much hated (or much maligned, depending on your point of view) Criminal Justice Commission (CJC). Part of this required an act of parliament, the *Criminal Justice Legislation Act*, to enable the inquiry to compel CJC officers to appear and give evidence.[1] The government made an error in drafting the bill, thereby giving sweeping powers of search and seizure to the Gas Tribunal, the Podiatrists' Board and the Physiotherapists' Board.[2] John Cleese and the other writers of the Monty Python scripts would have loved this story. I can see it now. Knock on the door, 'Open up, Physiotherapists' Board here! Put your backs to the wall, we're here to do a compulsory spinal assessment!' Silly and unusual? Silly yes. Unusual? Read on.

Not only do our official sentries too often incompetently exercise their powers, they can also be very lax. In March 1997 the Victorian Government was forced into an 'embarrassing review' of community service orders after a whistleblower revealed that a convicted paedophile was sent to a Melbourne kindergarten on a working bee. The person had a history of offences against children dating back to 1983.[3]

In another matter a rapist who has attacked twenty-nine women in Western Sydney since November 1995 is still at loose because of a reported bungled police investigation. Critical evidence has been lost, a semen sample to be analysed was left in a fridge for fourteen months, and items belonging to the offender were filed as lost property instead of evidence.[4]

These last two examples are commonplace enough. The point is that they do happen (more frequently than we are led to believe) and when they do they reduce public confidence in the ability of official investigators to respond to disclosures about wrongdoing.

Added to the drop in public confidence due to slack investigators is the problem of official unlawfulness. Whistleblowers are always vulnerable to being stitched up by investigating authorities acting outside the law. Here is an example. It has been claimed that documents obtained from the abovementioned government inquiry into the CJC revealed that the CJC and the Queensland Police Service discussed revisiting old allegations about a police whistleblower in order to further discredit him.[5]

The pre-determination of issues by investigators is another major concen to whistleblowers. On 6 December 1996 a Full Bench of the Federal Court disqualified the head of an $1 million inquiry into allegations of paedophilia in the diplomatic service on the grounds of bias.[6] The removed inquiry head, Chris Hunt, was the source of a newspaper story which reported that 'sources close to the inquiry' had said that the inquiry so far had 'uncovered loose language and a possible homophobic vendetta rather than a "nest" of paedophiles'. The Federal Court, in its thirty-five-page judgement said:

> *The fact that an 'off the record' briefing [was given] to a journalist by a person in Mr Hunt's position and, secondly, the failure of Mr Hunt to make immediately a full and true disclosure when challenged about the article ... must exacerbate any reasonably held apprehension of bias.*[7]

Hunt's authority to continue with the inquiry was successfully challenged by high-profile diplomat-turned-whistleblower, Alastair Gaisford. He alleged in a Federal Court affidavit that his career started to rot on the vine after he disclosed paedophile activity among Australian diplomats in Cambodia.[8]

The breakdown of this inquiry coincided with unprecedented levels of concern in the community about the extent of paedophilia. No doubt many people were left unconvinced of the government's capacity to probe allegations of high level sexual misconduct.

It would be hard to pick a more dramatic and conclusive illustration of this problem of investigative bias than the events of the afternoon of Tuesday 5 August 1997 when Mr Justice Thomas of the Queensland Supreme Court informed a hushed court-room of his verdict that the $11 million government inquiry into the Criminal Justice Commission would be closed forthwith because of the clear and obvious bias of one of the people running it.

Mr Justice Thomas, regarded as one of Australia's leading experts on judicial behaviour and ethics, found that Peter Connolly QC, a former judge of the Queensland Supreme Court and a former Liberal Party politician, was politically biased, and that his fellow commissioner Kevin Ryan QC was tainted by his association with Connolly. The Connolly–Ryan Inquiry is the first investigation with the status of a royal commission to be stopped in Queensland's legal history. In a damning ruling Justice Thomas found that Connolly had been 'oppressive ... unfair ... [and]outrageous' in his dealings with the Criminal Justice Commission.[9] 'It was important that anyone appointed to the inquiry be seen as a commissioner, not an executioner,' Thomas said. He went onto observe that a comment by Connolly that 'now that our side of politics is back in power we can do a proper critique of the Fitzgerald experiment' was 'indicative of a continuing favourable alignment with one side of politics'.

Concern over high levels of official ineptitude and bias is matched with the growing perception that our watchdogs are chihuahuas when we need rottweilers. In February 1995 the High Court brought down a surprise decision in *Brandy's* case, that the Human Rights and Equal Opportunity Commission (HREOC) had no power to enforce its own rulings.[10] This came as a revelation to many who, up until then, had taken comfort in the existence of a powerful human rights protector in Australia. It appears that the *Brandy* decision has completely destroyed the future enforcement methodology for federal discrimination laws.[11] In a recent survey of twenty-three discrimination cases decided by HREOC only in two cases was compensation ordered by the Commission paid without the victims needing to take further legal action.[12] In the context of that very low compliance rate it was disclosed that HREOC does not, and never has monitored whether its orders are being adhered to. *Brandy* was like the first fire cracker lit in a tied bundle. The Howard Government's distrust of statutory and quasi-legal authorities powerful enough to review and set aside government decisions was brought to a head by the *Brandy* decision. Now all tribunals and commissions such as HREOC, the Refugee Review Tribunal, and the Administrative Appeals Tribunal are themselves up for review.

In my more despairing moments I see the end of external review in Australia. To be more specific, I see an end to the bold attempt (conjured under the title 'the new administrative law') to make external review accessible, informal, quick and cheap. This is a major concern given that whatever justice whistleblowers receive, they usually find it outside their organisations through some form of external review. Despite the millions of official words written on the subject, governments, departments of state and private corporations hate external scrutiny, and will go to great and secret lengths to avoid and denigrate it. If external review is finished, what next?

Travelling at a safe distance behind the tribunal plunderers is the court caravan, returning from twenty years of semi-exile as a result of the community's dimmed enthusiasm for a model of justice that was too expensive, too formal, too adversarial and too long.[13] What the future holds I think is a reassertion of the traditional model whereby courts once again become the only substantive reviewers of government and corporation decision-making.

In the Commonwealth Government's vaguely sketched plans for a return to the court model of review one policy is at least clear: *internal review*. All decision-making authorities will be expected to develop procedures within their own systems to respond to concerns, whether they be in the form of grievances or disclosures. With this primary review level in place, courts will be forums of last resort. Whether the government goes this way or not, it is clearly moving away from external review, and that will be a great shame.

Perceptive people can see the early signs of decay in the national human rights structure. In July 1997 Cabinet refused to reappoint the popular head of HREOC, former High Court judge Sir Ronald Wilson. In September Cabinet relented in the face of pressure from women's groups, and decided to upgrade the position of Sex Discrimination Commissioner, but other specialist positions remain in doubt.[14]

What is my problem with the move to internal review? As I write I am gazing over a reach of water on which ducks are swimming and preening themselves. I suspect that if I, in a moment of craziness, went down there with a bucket and some Ajax, I might not do as good a job. Large and complex organisations are not like ducks; they cannot clean themselves. They cannot, and will not, wash out their own wrongdoing, nor scrub clean their own ethical messes. It is naive in the extreme to expect complex organisations, insinuated as they are with a workplace culture that says loud and clear 'Don't do anything to discredit the organisation', to be self-cleaning. The gaze on the wrongdoing organisation must come from an external pair of eyes, not ones from behind rose-tinted glasses.

I started this part of the discussion by referring to the *Brandy* decision. The High Court decision in this case, which has led to a general weakening of external review, also appears to have provoked an attitude of disrespect for and non-compliance with the orders of the Human Right and Equal Opportunity Commission by parties subject to adverse findings. An early non-complier was the

Queensland Government. In 1995 HREOC awarded $7000 to six Palm Island elders on the basis that the Queensland Government had discriminated against them by under-paying them for twenty years.[15] The Queensland Government initially refused to comply with the restitution orders brought down by Commissioner Carter, forcing the elders to lodge an expensive Federal Court appeal on 15 November 1996[16].

Non-compliance with the orders of tribunals by cashed-up government and private sector entities is a great source of disillusionment to those who get within reach of the rare fruit of justice.

In fact, compliance control is one of the glaring omissions in the structure of the numerous official bodies that review government decision-making and inquire into official conduct and performance. Unless an individual who receives a favourable tribunal result against a government decision-maker has persistence, fortitude and money, there is nothing to stop a powerful government department ignoring the findings. Similarly, who or what is there to stop authorities ignoring the recommendations of special inquiries such as royal commissions, slowing the implementation process down or being highly discriminatory in which recommendations to implement? A case in point is the 174 recommendations from the $70 million Wood Royal Commission into police corruption in New South Wales. At the three-month mark of the release of the report barely a quarter of Wood's recommendations had been implemented.[17]

It is not just non-compliance that injures justice. Official insurgency against unfavourable court decisions is also a problem. This insurgency takes many forms, but they share a common purpose: to avoid the ruling, and in so doing avoid contempt of court. A good example is the long-running dispute between the Department of Foreign Affairs and Trade and whistleblower Alastair Gaisford. Gaisford reported alleged paedophile activity among diplomat colleagues in Cambodia where he was posted. On return from his posting he was suspended for disclosing information without authorisation and trying to damage reputations.[18] On 6 December 1996 the Federal Court found that the Department had denied Gaisford natural justice and said that his suspension could not stand. Within hours of this ruling the Department revoked the original suspension and immediately imposed another![19]

There is also official insurgency against government edicts. These cases of civil disobedience are so serious that we do not usually hear about them until much later. Take the case of the Victorian Special Branch, a Cold War fossil in the Victorian Police Force. In 1983, in response to civil libertarian objections, the Cain Government ordered the disbandment of the Special Branch and the shredding of most of the dossiers. These dossiers contained the usual conspiracy drivel found in all Special Branch filing systems throughout Australia. The Government was advised that its shredding order had been obeyed, and the Victorian Ombudsman was similarly assured. Nothing happened until early 1998 when the *Age* newspaper was sent files that the police said had been destroyed.[20] Doubts also exist as to whether government instructions to destroy Special Branch files in New South Wales and Queensland have been carried out.[21]

Sometimes official incompetence is eclipsed by the use of stand-over tactics. In a highly critical report released on 10 December 1996 the Commonwealth Ombudsman's special tax watch-dog, Peter Haggstom, forced the Australian Taxation Office (ATO) to apologise to the parents of a man wanted for tax evasion charges. The parents, it was found, had been subject to a heavy-handed approach by ATO investigators, including the quite improper threat of jailing them if they did not disclose their son's whereabouts.[22]

On the same theme, we had the spectacle recently of a young student's car being pulled over by police in a Perth suburb. Soon two other police cars were at the scene. Were police about to do a major drug bust? Were there escaped criminals in the car? No, just a few young people returning from a night out. So that it wasn't a complete waste of time, the driver was charged with ... wait for it, driving a car with insufficient water in the windscreen wiper container![23] Police later admitted that no such charge exists.

I could have bypassed this survey of our shut-eyed sentries in favour of one case that sums up all the concern. In the well known Yeldham case, a NSW transit police officer, code-named CC2, admitted before the Wood Royal Commission into police corruption that he had falsified records relating to an incident at Wynyard Station in October 1990. At that time David Yeldham, a New South Wales Supreme Court judge who had retired from the Bench ten months before, was detained by the transit police for masturbating in front of a young man in the railway toilet and offering him money.[24]

The transit police officer who finally rolled over told the Royal Commission that he lied to investigators on instruction from a fellow police officer who is alleged to have said that CC2's family 'would be visited' if he told the truth.[25] On the way to Wynyard Station to interview Yeldham, who was being detained by the Station Master, CC2 said that a colleague had stated: 'They'll cut our knees off if we lock him [Yeldham] up.'[26] CC2 then contacted an officer in the now disbanded NSW Special Branch, who allegedly told him not to take notes, to write off the complaint as one man's word [a judge] against another's [a nineteen-year-old youth] and to 'move' the incident from the toilets to the stairs.[27]

Before CC2 took the stand at the Royal Commission, no less than five Special Branch police testified under oath that they had no knowledge of the 1990 incident. That changed in the last days of the Royal Commission, when a senior Special Branch officer also rolled over and admitted that the Branch was involved in protecting Yeldham from prosecution. Yeldham gassed himself to death outside his Sydney home five hours after being interviewed by Commission investigators.

Inadequacies identified in the Australian Federal Police system of investigation would be found in most other investigative authorities, so it is worth noting them. The report found that:

- No one accepted responsibility for the integrity of the *whole* system.
- The way that the AFP's internal investigation processes were designed and implemented did not engender community trust and confidence.
- There were inexcusable delays.
- Lack of accessibility was a problem in that the complaints system was intimidating to some classes of people such as youth and indigenous Australians.[28]

The report added:

The perspective of members of the public who made submissions or who attended consultations was that the current AFP complaints system was significantly defective. The main concerns expressed were about the quality and impartiality of [internal] investigations, the ineffectiveness of the Ombudsman's role and the inaccessibility of the system. The Commission did not receive any responses from members of the public to the effect that the current system worked well or was satisfactory.[29]

The Commission did not pull any punches in locating some of the blame for AFP deficiencies in the Commonwealth Ombudsman's Office:

The Commission considered that the Ombudsman's Office could have tried to use its powers more robustly.[30]

In fact a previous Commonwealth Ombudsman, Professor Dennis Pearce, has observed that the Ombudsman's track-record in handling police complaints was the subject of significant concern and criticism.[31] He went so far as to say that the improvement in the Ombudsman's Office since a 1991 Senate review (which assessed the Office's performance as unsatisfactory) was 'marginal'.[32]

With punches like this thrown, target organisations will naturally duck for cover. The AFP has blamed the Ombudsman for delays,[33] the Ombudsman has blamed legislative restrictions,[34] and the ALRC has blamed them both.[35]

In late 1997 the Ombudsman reported on her own investigation of AFP complaint processing.[36] She found that on the whole the AFP track record with police whistleblowers was not too bad.[37] It is hoped that her review project was driven by a desire to improve essential procedures rather than simply to rebut the ALRC attack.

So far this chapter has argued that powerful forces in our culture keep wrongdoing three steps ahead of our soporific protector-institutions. In the final part of the chapter this conclusion is re-affirmed by an analysis of how the abuse of institutionalised people survives despite everything. I call it the *rhythm of strife*. This pattern is not an exclusive characteristic of the institutional abuse area. Most of the elements in the pattern are to be found in all disclosure experiences.

The challenge for our protector-agencies is to break the code on this pattern, to understand it so precisely, so intimately, that it is stopped from automatically coming into play to distract the progress of justice.

It has been reported that seven intellectually handicapped people were the victims of 'mercy killings' at the Woodstock facility in Albury between 1992 and 1994. These revelations followed a *Four Corners* program in late 1996 on an institutional care controversy in Queensland, with further stories of physical and sexual abuse at the government-run Challinor Centre at Ipswich. Some months later, in June 1997, the NSW Auditor-General released his report of an eighteen-month study of the nation's ten largest residential homes. He recommended that they should all be closed down within seven years. The report listed atrocious but familiar misconduct. For example, 3710 injuries were recorded in one of these homes in one year. Almost half the injuries were serious, such as burns, fractures and dislocations.[38] There was also widespread and unlawful use of restraint, seclusion and imprisonment.[39]

The same grim conclusions have been reached by Ronald Conway in the largest national survey into such abuse.[40] Among other things Conway found what every whistleblower knows: that 'the code of silence operating is far stronger than a will to report abuse'.[41] Conway's study also confirmed another set piece in the whistleblower experience – that official bodies are not shy to lie. He said, 'In many cases we [research team] were lied to quite deliberately by some government departments and by some non-government organisations'. He also found that 67% of those who disclosed abuse suffered a negative outcome. This is quite low figure and one cannot test it without further information about Conway's research methodology.

What does all this new research say? One of our great sources of shame, and something that future Australians will know and judge us by, is our complete failure to protect institutionalised people from grossly negligent care and atrocity. Australians continue to be harmed and die at the hands of 'carers' in warehouses for the disabled and in psychiatric asylums ('hospitals', 'homes', 'centres', are sinister euphemisms in this continuing context of violence). Why is this so? Why can't we break the rhythm of strife? A good deal of this question has been addressed in the analysis above when attention was given to such things as our cultural blind spot to *structural* wrongdoing (as opposed to *individual* wrongdoing) and the forceful socio-economic impediments to disclosure. The final analysis tries to gather these insights up by examining the pattern of inaction usually triggered by an employee of conscience.

From the deep sleep atrocities at Chelmsford Hospital in the 1970s to the Woodstock allegations, an utterly pernicious pattern keeps on revealing itself. This pattern, this rhythm of strife, is predictable, and apparently unstoppable. This pattern appears to have seven elements to it:

1) Harm and abuse continue for many years, perpetrated, or at least witnessed by staff who in other parts of their contradictory lives are exemplary citizens.
2) Finally, some person – a current or former employee, or the victim's friend or relative – braves the hostile work culture and makes a public interest disclosure. For a while the violence is transferred from the institutionalised victims to the whistleblowers who report the abuse.
3) Previously indifferent administrations, no longer able to quell the growing tide of evidence, or confronted by a build up of community rage (such as the current situation with respect to paedophilia), are forced to set up official investigations.
4) Perpetrators and their defenders, particularly the lawyers they employ and the professional associations and unions that shelter them, go into a very aggressive cover-up and counter-allegation mode. This is particularly so if the wrongdoers are economically powerful, well connected politically, or protected by powerful institutions (such as the Catholic Church with respect to the way it previously handled complaints about sexually abusive priests).
5) Most of these investigations are stacked against the complainants and victims, and work backwards to clear the organisation and the culprits within it of wrongdoing, certainly of serious wrongdoing.
6) Every so often a dedicated and unintimidated investigator brings the truth out, exposes the atrocities, and recommends sensible

and long-overdue corrective reforms to government.
7) The heat goes out of the issue at the same rate that dust gathers on the investigator's report.

End of story? Well end of story until a new atrocity emerges and the rhythm of strife starts all over again.

These elements have been present in all the known psychiatric atrocities and disabled-abuse cases in Australia in the last 30 years. Take the Chelmsford Hospital example. Under the guise of cutting-edge psychiatry, a private hospital in a leafy suburb in Sydney was transformed into a living morgue, as hundreds of people were given 'deep-sleep therapy' – maintaining patients in a narcotic-induced coma for weeks and months on end – that had been banned in the USA twenty years before. It is hard to grasp the extent of the damage done to these people's lives. Numerous investigations were met with numerous cover-ups. A Royal Commission and a High Court case never got within coo-ee of punishing the clearly identified perpetrators. The investigative process simply went into deep-sleep itself, ready to be activated at the next outrage. We did not have to wait too long for that.

The worst psychiatric atrocity in Australia since colonial times was unfolding in Townsville at Ward 10B of the General Hospital. The Carter Inquiry, established despite an enormous amount of official opposition, concluded that sixty-five Queenslanders who had been in Ward 10B 'died in circumstances that justified close investigation'. Well there was no 'close' investigation, no charges laid, and worse, some of the implicated went onto bigger and better careers. All that remains now is the sixty-five headstones.

A chilling aspect of these atrocities is that card-carrying members of professional associations such as the Royal Australian and New Zealand College of Psychiatrists, the Australian Psychological Society, the Australian Association of Occupational Therapists, the Australian Association of Social Workers, the Queensland Nurses Union and others saw or heard about evil in that ward. Some even participated in it. Yet no one came forward until the damage had been well and truly done.

The Carter Inquiry was an exemplary investigation, and the publicity of its findings produced a short period of community rage. The government of the day matched this with wild promises of reform. When Brian Burdekin came to Townsville as part of HREOC's national inquiry into mental health he received similar assurances. Carter reported in February 1991, yet a national audit done between December 1996 and January 1997 of Queensland's seventy-five mental health services found that *none* were meeting all the standards established and twenty services had not put any of the minimum standards into place. This scandalous situation mocks Carter's conclusion:

The primary lesson to be learned from the findings of this Commission of Inquiry is that what happened in Ward 10B must never be allowed to be repeated ...

Those with faith in the system thought that such a surge of institutional violence as occurred at Ward 10B could never happen again. Little did they know that the Basil Stafford atrocity was just warming up. A whistleblower-stimulated Criminal Justice Commission inquiry by New South Wales judge Mr Justice Stewart generated 6000 pages of transcript and concluded that there were residential care officers at the Basil Stafford Centre in Brisbane who were, in Stewart's view, 'a disgrace to the human race'.[42] Among other crimes a twenty-two-year-old woman with the mental age of a five-year-old was raped by her carer, became pregnant and gave birth to a baby also afflicted with microcephaly.

Once the whistleblower disclosed, all the elements of the rhythm of strife came into play: aggressive union defences of the perpetrators, obstructionist tactics by lawyers, hollow gestures of reform, and, of course, buck-passing. Never happen again? On 9 July 1997 Bradley Craig Evans, who had pleaded guilty to seven charges of abusing intellectually handicapped people in hostels on Brisbane's southside, was sentenced in the District Court to two years jail.[43] On goes the rythm of strife.

So there we have it, a State system of investigation in very poor condition. This is the system that whistleblowers and all public-spirited citizens have little choice but to trust. Yet the system is bedevilled by incompetence, indifference, unlawfulness, conservatism, narrow jurisdictions, and lack of resources.

We move now to the second area of concern for Australians who seek a role in confronting official and corporate wrongdoing: whistleblower protection legislation.

12 | Whistleblowing Laws
The State Responds

We must not make a scarecrow of the law,
Setting it up to fear the birds of prey,
And let it keep one shape, till custom make it
Their perch and not their terror.
— William Shakespeare, *Measure for Measure*

Whistleblower laws in Australia simply don't work. They don't protect whistleblowers, they don't encourage Australians to do their bit by reporting wrongdoing, and they certainly do not impact on the obese profile of wrongdoing. Four whistleblower acts are currently on the statute books: South Australia (1993), Australian Capital Territory (1994), New South Wales (1994) and Queensland (1994), and not one of them, to my knowledge, has ever been used by a whistleblower. That says something. If whistleblowers were better organised, you might think that they were mounting a national boycott.

This chapter concerns itself with the *theory* behind the flawed whistleblower statutes.[1] It is a critical analysis that seeks to demonstrate the conservatism in the drafting of the package of Acts and Bills. This suggests that those who control the law-formation checkpoints – from the often passionate and amateurish community consultations, through the intense reactive lobbying by powerful groups, on to the second and third readings and Royal Assent, and finally to implementation – do not know or do not want to know about the complex issues of whistleblowing.

I want to use the bad disclosure laws to demonstrate a socio-historical point. As a nation of crumbling communities, we are losing our capacity to think about the *national interest*. So when whistleblowers come along who not only think, but *act* in the national interest, we become scared, confused, hostile. And if we are people in power, we write awful procedures and laws for their 'protection'.

Why is this whistleblower law-formation process so utterly misconceived? One answer is that whistleblower narratives, with all the pain, disillusion and damage to personal happiness and relationships, are boiled down by politicians into hard lumps and thrown at the opposition. In the political arena whistleblowers are simply projectiles. But there is more to it. I suspect that there is also a fear of whistleblowers and dissenters. These people are often too good for their own good. They can be ethical guided missiles who show no fear or favour in choice of target. In the world of ethics they are celebrated. In the world of wrongdoing they are feared and reviled. This fear, this 'who are these damn people?' attitude infects the law-formation process to such a degree that bad and inappropriate laws are written that resemble strait-jackets rather than protective shields.

In 1993 and 1994 governments finally started to consider protecting their whistleblower citizenry against the retaliatory behaviour of employers and work colleagues. Spurred on by the corruption scandals of the 1980s, as well as high-level government reports and a stream of anecdotal evidence of whistleblower suffering, the Commonwealth government along with several State and Territory governments, put their minds to the complex issues of the reception of information about wrongdoing and the protection of those who bring disclosures forward. By 1998 fifteen whistleblower protection Bills had been drafted in Australia, but only four have proceeded to legislation.

How does one present and evaluate this total legislative effort? Will whistleblowers have confidence in the statutory shelters planned or provided? Will this legislative effort have an impact on systemic wrongdoing, or will the legislation simply be focused on 'bad-apples'? Are the Bills and statutes within this effort covertly designed primarily to protect their political and bureaucratic masters? To get a little closer to these questions each of the planned or enacted instruments are evaluated with respect to several performance criteria organised under four headings: General, Scope, Protections and Services. In each section the findings are set out in quick reference boxes to be found at the back of the book.

Current Status

The first column of Table 1 shows the current status of the legislation. The abandoned Bills give an indication of the evolution, and in some cases (Tasmania) the devolution of government thinking.

The first statute to protect whistleblowers in Australia was the *Whistleblowers (Interim Protection) and Miscellaneous Amendments Act 1990 (Qld)*. This amended the *Electoral and Administrative Review Act (Qld)* and the *Criminal Justice Act (Qld)* to provide gap protection for whistleblowers, pending the passage of a more substantive Act. The Interim Act was grossly overrated[2] and really only provided for the Criminal Justice Commission (CJC) and the now defunct Electoral and Administrative Review Commission (EARC) to seek Supreme Court injunctions against adverse personnel practices directed at fully-screened CJC and EARC whistleblowers. The CJC has only ever gone to bat for a Queensland whistleblower once in the five years the Interim Act has been in force and even then did not have an unmitigated success.[3]

In April 1991 EARC produced a draft whistleblower Bill that was subsequently rejected by the government.[4] The following April EARC's political watchdog, the Parliamentary Committee for Electoral and Administrative Review (PEARC), tabled a whistleblower report in the Legislative Assembly.[5] The draft Bill it contained was almost a photocopy of the EARC proposal, indicating that Queensland Government thinking on whistleblower policy had reached a standstill. This Bill was also abandoned.

In 1991 two abortive attempts were made to introduce whistleblower protection into New South Wales. The *Whistleblowers Protection Bill 1992 (No. 1)* was introduced into the Legislative Assembly in accordance with an agreement between the Government and the non-aligned independents. The Bill was unsatisfactory to some of the major players and it was withdrawn.[6] Five months later, the *Whistleblowers Protection Bill 1992 (No. 2)* was introduced by Premier John Fahey. After some debate it was referred to the Legislative Committee, which finally presented its report on 30 June 1993 after 'numerous problems'.[7] The Act was finally assented to on 12 December 1994.

The 'numerous problems' are still there. The NSW Branch of Whistleblowers Australia has been outspoken in its critique of the management of whistleblowers by ICAC.[8] The Wood Royal Commission into police corruption in New South Wales called for better whistleblower protection for police.[9] In the same vein, the Garnett–Freeman study of police whistleblowers registered with the NSW Police Internal Witness Support Unit found that police whistleblowers were more likely to be forced to leave the service than the officers that they exposed.[10]

The Act was reviewed in 1996.[11] This in itself was a rare moment in public administration. No other State government that has whistleblower protection law has ever expressed any official curiosity about whether its disclosure law works or not, or how the law can be reformed. One of the notable features of the 1996 review of the NSW Act was the scathing attack by the NSW Branch of Whistleblowers Australia on the Independent Commission Against Corruption. It was accused of not taking whistleblowers or their disclosures seriously.

In December 1991 the first attempt at Commonwealth protection was made when Senator Jo Vallentine (Greens, WA) tabled the *Whistleblowers Protection Bill 1991 (Cth)*. This bold Bill did not proceed for two main political reasons: whistleblowing was of no real interest to the federal government, and even if it was, it was not going to let a minority party take whatever kudos flowed from the expression of such an interest.

On 8 April 1993 the South Australian Parliament passed the first whistleblower protection statute in Australia. A well-intentioned but miserably conceived instrument, it displayed the arrogance of ignorance about the complex socio-legal issues enmeshed in the whistleblowing phenomenon. Most of the essential ingredients for a good disclosure act were missing from the South Australian legislation. There was no provision for an independent authority, whistleblowers who disclosed to the media were not protected, and the Act was silent on counselling services, compensation, entitlement to damages and the right to relocation. This was a shame as it served in part as a model for following legislation, notably the current New Zealand Act, and one of the Tasmanian formulations, the *Whistleblower Protection Bill 1997*. There has been no critical evaluation of the South Australian law to date.

The Western Australian Greens made a second attempt to get whistleblower protection legislation up at the Commonwealth level, with Christobel Chamerette tabling the *Whistleblowers Protection Bill 1993 (Cth)* on 5 October 1993. Like its predecessor, this was on the whole a high-quality Bill. On 27 October 1993 the Senate Select Committee on Public Interest Whistleblowing (SSCPIW) was established. It unanimously recommended the passage of Commonwealth whistleblower protection legislation. This is at least the tenth high-level report recommending whistleblower protection legislation at the Commonwealth level.[12]

In December 1994 the Australian Capital Territory, Queensland and New South Wales all enacted whistleblower protection laws. Still to go are the Commonwealth, Western Australia, the Northern Territory, Victoria and Tasmania.

In March 1995 a revised edition of the *Guidelines on Official Conduct of Commonwealth Public Servants* was issued by the Keating Labor Government. The amendments explained how disclosures could be made by public servants under existing federal laws. From the point of view of Commonwealth employees contemplating disclosure this document was high on promise and low on performance. These amendments were simply an easy substitute for strong protection legislation.

On 26 October 1995 Duncan Kerr, then federal Justice Minister, tabled his government's response to the reports of the Senate Select Committee on Public Interest Whistleblowing and the Senate Select Committee on Unresolved Whistleblower Cases. The Keating Government was defeated soon after that and Kerr's proposal never matured into law. This was no great loss as the proposal forecast a very inferior whistleblower statute.[13] Kerr's scheme envisaged a two-pronged strategy: internal departmental reporting and investigation, and external reporting and investigation by the Commonwealth Ombudsman and the Inspector-General of Intelligence and Security. Again essential ingredients for effective protection were missing.

Western Australia and Victoria were rocked with official corruption scandals in the 1980s and it is surprising that whistleblowing has not been on the political agenda. There is some movement in Western Australia now. A very narrow whistleblower shelter was introduced into Western Australia via an amendment to the *Official Corruption Commission Act 1988* following the WA Inc. scandal. Whistleblowing was also considered in late 1995 by the Commission on Government, which produced a report for the Joint Standing Committee on the Commission on Government in early 1996 calling for full-blown whistleblower protection legislation[14]. So far nothing has happened in that regard.

In Tasmania four bills have been formulated by the Labor Opposition, two in 1995 and two in 1997. On 29 October 1995 Opposition leader Michael Field introduced the *Public Interest Disclosure Bill 1995*. Despite some significant oversights this was the best instrument drafted anywhere in Australia. Among its attractive features was provision for a Public Interest Disclosure Agency. The Bill also recognised for the first time that the suppression of an expert opinion, report or finding was official misconduct.

The Bill was re-introduced two weeks later following discussions with the Tasmanian Branch of Whistleblowers Australia. Also known as the *Public Interest Disclosure Bill* it was almost a photocopy of Field's first Bill. Regretably it failed to attract cross-parliament support and was abandoned.

Eighteen months later the ALP Opposition again introduced a bill, the *Public Interest Disclosure Bill 1997*. The resolve to fight wrongdoing and protect Tasmanians who disclose it, so clearly evident in the 1995 bills, appeared to have evaporated; the Bill was very inadequate. Luckily it did not proceed, on a vote in which the Tasmanian Greens sided with the Liberal Government.[15] With the possibility of a State election in late 1997 the Opposition may have been influenced by the need to have an Act that would not create problems for it. On 16 April 1997 the Liberal Government circulated a second draft of its *Whistleblower Protection Bill*. The Bill, poured from the same cast as the South Australian Act, bears all its faults. Competing with this is the re-drafted bill from the Tasmanian Labor Party.

The most recent moves for statutory protection of whistleblowers have occurred at the Commonwealth level. Prime Minister John Howard's senior legal adviser has written:

The Government's Law and Justice and Public Administration recognised the need for the introduction of laws to protect whistleblowers. The Government believes tht people who act in the public interest by disclosing unlawful, wasteful and dangerous conduct should not suffer for doing so, as has occurred in the past. The Government will, in the next few months, develop its response to the Report of the Senate Select Committee on Public Interest Whistleblowing and proposals for the form of legislation.[16]

This promise was made in November 1996. Not much has happened since then. Certainly there is still no specific Commonwealth whistleblower legislation. Disclosure protection (of sorts) has been included in the 1997 *Public Service Act*.[17] Departmental procedures consistent with the thrust of this Act are now being developed throughout the Commonwealth public service in ways that accommodate the federal government's low-level interest in protected disclosure.

The clear example here is the Defence Department. A scheme has been developed whereby members of the Australian Defence Force may disclose through the chain of command or the Fraud Investigation and Recovery Directorate of the Inspector-General.[18] What may defence personnel disclose? Unlike the four whistleblower Acts currently in force, severe definitional restrictions apply as far as the Defence Department is concerned. For them a whistleblower is:

a concerned Defence employee who discloses wrongdoing, such as fraud or waste and abuse of Defence resources...[19]

What about wrongdoing of a sexual and racial nature? What of the ethical issues about armament sales, the Timor issue and the like? These appear to be outside the anorexic scope of the definition used by Defence. It is fairly obvious that for a recently corporatised Defence Department the big issues are those to do with procurement, contracting and efficiency.

I expect we will see a lot more protection of disclosure that is tethered to official agendas of government departments.

Independent Whistleblower Authority

The issue of whether or not to install a completely independent authority as the central component of disclosure protection legislation highlights how much at odds the whistleblowing community is with government on what is needed. Table 1 indicates that only four out of fifteen legislative proposals provide for an independent authority. Why is this? First there is an economic rationalist-driven reluctance to expand the State. Overlayed on this is a particular aversion to resource a new centre of power which, dedicated as it would be to investigation and protection, may eventually damage its political masters. The bringing down of Premier Nick Greiner in New South Wales after an investigation by the Independent Commission Against Corruption is a case in point here. A third reason for rejecting an independent authority comes back to our blind faith in the effectiveness of the official agencies responsible for receiving complaints about wrongdoing.

One of the principal architects of the South Australian Act expressed these reservations succinctly when he said:

> We did not want to create another bureaucracy – and we thought that we had enough authorities with investigative powers around the place to deal with issues – without having another to stumble over.[20]

Another restraint to the development of new and daring responses to the social issue of protected disclosure are the territorial jealousies of existing stake-holder departments. Invariably, whistleblower witnesses to the various pre-legislative public consultations throughout Australia have supported the need for an independent authority. Equally, agency stakeholders have either argued strongly against the proposition, or pushed for responsibility for running the Acts themselves.

A lack of understanding of the psychology of whistleblowing and the subtle forms of punishment that await those who disclose does not seem to be an impediment to bureaucratic imperialism, as shown by the Commonwealth Merit Protection Review Agency's (as it was then called) submission to the important Senate Select Committee on Public Interest Whistleblowing. The Agency sought responsibility for employment-related matters involving public service whistleblowers, including the provision of counselling and guidance and protection against discrimination or retaliatory actions. Director Ann Forward (whom we met in chapter ten) gave oral evidence, including the following telling exchange:

Ms Forward: ... we do not have a special reporting category for ... whistleblowers ...
Senator Newman [Chair]: Would that be useful, if you are going to truly know what the problem is?
Ms Forward: I would have to know what a whistleblower was before I gave you an affirmative answer to that question.
Senator Newman: You are about the only agency that seems to have a problem ... We have taken evidence now round several States as well, and I cannot think of another agency that seems to have a problem of recognising a whistleblower when they see one.
Ms Forward: I could show them some files where people really do get quite paranoid about the causes for management actions. They have to find a reason to explain the situations they are in.
Senator Newman: But to me the most extraordinary thing is for you to say that in all the years of your organisation ... you have never had any whistleblowers?
Ms Forward: We have had one or two who have claimed to be.[21]

With this mindset, it should be fairly obvious why whistleblowers rate statutory agencies very low with respect to disclosure protection and investigative competence. Research results from the Queensland Whistleblower Study show that 83 per cent of the sample of 102 thought that their immediate superiors were ineffective in dealing with their disclosures. The effectiveness rating only increased marginally as whistleblowers went up the chain of command in their public sector unit. By far the most common response to the question, 'What happened when you took the matter to your supervisor?' was, 'A superior obstructed the complaint.'[22] External agencies like the CJC and the unions were even worse, rated as ineffective in 90% of cases.[23] The Study shows that a culture of obstruction and indifference operates right out to and beyond the borders of the organisation.

Regrettably, legislators and their advisors have chosen to ignore whistleblower feedback in favour of a status quo model for managing disclosure whereby the whistleblowing phenomenon is absorbed into existing broad-agenda agencies (for example the New South Wales Independent Commission Against Corruption and the Queensland Criminal Justice Commission).

Contrary to what I have called the status quo model for the reception and investigation of public interest disclosures is the independent agency model. There are two versions of this, one weak and one strong. The weak model really only provides for a take-in and refer-out system. Whistleblowers make contact, are advised about procedures, and their disclosures are then trunked off to the investigating agency deemed most relevant. This is the model endorsed by the Senate Select Committee on Public Interest Whistleblowing, and the parliamentary review of the NSW Act.[24] The model also underpinned the Public Interest Disclosure Commissioner who figured in the Tasmanian *Public Interest Disclosure Bill 1997*.[25] Some of the weak models build-in unspecified monitoring powers over the designated agencies' handling of the disclosure.

The stronger models, as prescribed in the Commonwealth and Tasmanian (1995) Bills, and more recently the Australian Law Reform Commission Report,[26] provides for the agency to have power as well as independence. In these models disclosure-focused agencies are empowered to undertake investigations, enter premises, summon and examine witnesses, initiate and pursue actions for contempt of their proceedings, use listening devices, intercept electronic communication, and have access to taxation and other commercial records.[27] Such powers have been abused before by bodies like the CJC,[28] so there is some justifiable reluctance to endorse the strong model.

Qualification for Protection

The pathways that the whistleblower searching for justice and protection must walk are exceedingly restrictive in all the legislative schemes. I will explore a number of aspects of this. For a start protection is usually contingent upon good faith disclosures to 'appropriate' government authorities. On the surface these appear to be eminently suitable and proper conditions to be imposed in exchange for protection from what can be heavy consequences (such as action for defamation against the whistleblower). The experiences of whistleblowers indicate that officials have used sweeping discretionary powers to decide either that disclosures were in bad faith or made to inappropriate reporting agencies

Could it be that the schemes are more about State control of dissent than about the correction of wrongdoing and the protection (and indeed affirmation) of whistleblowers? The State, through these legislative instruments, has the whistleblower process sewn up. It alone defines whistleblowing, it alone lays out the pathways of disclosure, and it alone regulates the remedies available.

Exceptions to the appropriate agency stipulation do exist. As a result of an amendment moved in committee to the NSW Bill (the Hatton amendment), disclosure to a member of parliament or a journalist is protected by the *Protected Disclosures Act 1994 (NSW)*. Conditions apply. The disclosure needs previously to have been submitted to a relevant authority and that authority decided not to investigate or to complete an investigation, failed to recommend action, or simply failed to contact the whistleblower within six months of the original disclosure being made. Disclosure to a Minister of the Crown is protected by the South Australian Act, although I suggest this is quite different from disclosure to an MP. Ministers of the Crown would normally be less accessible, but potentially more effective, than their backbench colleagues. However the positive point remains that these two Acts provide, at the relevant sections, welcome flexibility for the whistleblower sent up too many cul-de-sacs.

Definitions of 'Public Interest Disclosure'

The statutory definitions of public interest disclosures include the content of the divulgence – for example, allegations about official misconduct are always regarded as public interest disclosures. However, most focus as much on the *process* of disclosure as on the nature of alleged wrongdoing. For example, in the *Whistleblowers Protection Act 1994 (Qld)*, a divulgence is deemed a public interest disclosure by virtue of:

(1) content, i.e. allegations about:
 – official misconduct
 – maladministration
 – neglect or improper management
 – damage to public health or environment, and
(2) process, i.e. disclosure to an 'appropriate entity'.

Even when the definition of protected disclosure does not prescribe correct disclosure methodology, all schemes make protection contingent on whistleblowers going through 'appropriate entities'. Why include the whistleblower's methodology in a definition of public interest disclosure? Is the public's 'interest' in the disclosure any less valid if the whistleblower does not or cannot report to an 'appropriate entity'? What if the 'appropriate entity' ignores or vilifies the whistleblowers? Does bureaucratic obstruction reduce the public merit of the disclosure?

There is an element of government paranoia in this insistence that public interest disclosure is contingent upon the whistleblower obeying official reporting directions. Dissent, that marvellous rejuvenative feature of democracy, can be too wild and threatening for modern politics and public administration. Domesticated dissent, on a leash, rolling on its back like a puppy, seems to be the undeclared goal of whistleblower legislation.

Prohibition on Reprisals

All the legislative schemes prohibit agency reprisals against whistleblowers. South Australia has established a tort of victimisation, and the Tasmanian Public Interest Disclosure Bill 1997 includes a similar provision. Others, like the Queensland Act, make reprisals indictable offences carrying a maximum penalty of three years in prison.

The Tasmanian Bill is the only drafted response that specifically refers to the need to level the playing field for the whistleblower under attack:

Powers of the Whistleblowers Protection Advocate
 13(1) To overcome the active and passive defensive measures used by the organisations in negating the claims of reprisals by the whistleblower

To provide the whistleblower with a fair contest in administrative and legislative proceedings dealing with allegations of reprisals against the whistleblower.

Public Sector Agency Penalties

Only four of the schemes get close to the enlightened third party liability provisions in some of the whistleblowing legislation in America. The *Public Interest Disclosure Act 1994 (ACT)* provides for convictions for unlawful reprisals against whistleblowers by corporate bodies, and fines of up to five times those for individuals. There were agency penalties, also five times those for individuals, in the Public Interest Disclosure Bills 1995 (Tas). The twist was that government agencies were immune from prosecution![29] Corporate penalties for the offence of unlawful reprisals were also included in the earlier Queensland Bills but were done away with in the *Whistleblowers Protection Act 1994 (Qld)* after high-level pressure from public sector management.

Collective reprisal actions (eg mobbing) and management-condoned or overlooked processes of harassment remain beyond the reach of most of the legislative schemes. Again this points to the dominance of individual action and responsibility alive in most of the legislative schemes. To singularise wrongdoers both at first instance as law-breakers, and then as reprisers, is to miss the culture of vindication ever-present in even the most benign-looking workplace. As no one acts alone in wrongdoing, no one acts alone in reprisals. This fact of work life continues to be ignored by those in the whistleblower law-formation process. Agency penalties – such as punitive and reviewable budget reductions for non-essential services in work units found jointly culpable and/or punitive and reviewable reductions to CEOs' remuneration packages – would be consistent with a social construction of wrongdoing and reprisals.

Scope of Whistleblower Protection

We now examine the breadth of whistleblower protection under the various legislative schemes. Table 2 sets out who may make protected disclosures, private sector and media protection, protection of involuntary disclosures, protection for disclosures of previous wrongdoing and, finally, the application of the instrument to politicians.

Who May Disclose

The *Protected Disclosures Act 1994 (NSW)* and the *Whistleblowers Protection Act 1994 (Qld)* restrict protected disclosures to public officials. In NSW this is unequivocal, while in Queensland there is provision for anybody to report wrongdoing related to the abuse of disabled people, 'substantial and specific' dangers to the environment and the taking of reprisals. All the other legislative schemes either allow for 'anybody' to report wrongdoing, or leave the matter unspecified.

Private Sector Protection

If one had to choose a single litmus test to demonstrate governments' determination to tackle wrongdoing and protect whistleblowers, it would have to be whether or not the protection legislation extends into the private sector. Most don't. The exceptions are the South Australian and Queensland Acts (to a very limited degree) and the 1995 Tasmanian Bills.

The Queensland Act extends into the private sector, but regrettably this extension is highly conditional. The alleged wrongdoing must be 'specific' and 'substantial' and either directed at a person with a disability or the environment, or concern the taking of reprisals against another.

However, it may only be a matter of time before private-sector coverage amendments begin to be made because the force of the argument for such an extension is very strong. The traditional interface between public and private sectors is more confused now than in the past, with the private sector offering government-type services and the public sector mimicking the private sector with respect to aligning performance with profit. Further, media attention to the exploits of marketplace buccaneers in the 1980s has left the public with a cynical view of what goes on behind the corporate door. The Senate Select Committee on Public Interest Whistleblowing favoured the protection of private sector whistleblowers:

The Committee considers that accountability and constitutional responsibility does not end with the public sector ... To align the concept of responsible government with the concept of the public sector is to give democracy so narrow a focus as to undermine its existence ...

The Committee notes that Government Business Enterprises are increasingly falling between the public and private sectors ... Scrutiny and accountability have been reduced through the hiving off of commercial activities ... The Committee recommends that [the endorsed Commonwealth Whistleblowers] legislation be given the widest coverage constitutionally possible in both the public and private sector.[30]

Media Protection

Protection for whistleblowers who expose via the media is the big no-go area for the drafters of whistleblower legislation in Australia. Only the NSW statute offers protection for media whistleblowers, and that protection is so highly conditional that its effectiveness remains to be seen.

Media exposure is often the shove governments need to get them acting in the public interest. Fanny K, a Queensland whistleblower, offers a good example of this. As a worker in the Basil Stafford Centre, a government facility for intellectually handicapped people, she claimed to have witnessed countless instances of patient abuse. She went through official channels from early 1986 to November 1990, seeking action from the authorities to stop the abuse, injury and loss of life occurring at the Centre. No notice was taken of her and she was subjected to threats and victimisation, including tampering with the brakes of her car. She finally went on the Hinch television program and the Hayden Sargent radio talkback show in Brisbane. The media pressure sparked government interest and put the CJC into a corner: a public inquiry was now the only way out.[31] The Government began damage control soon after the inquiry started and peremptorily closed the Centre.

This case also led a chastened Queensland Government to slip a provision into the new *Whistleblower Protection Act 1994 (Qld)* that was not in any previous draft, nor part of the pre-legislative consultation process. The 'Fanny K Clause' allows anybody to disclose a substantial and specific danger to the health and safety of a person with a disability. Without Fanny K's fortitude and a responsive media (in this particular case), this clause would never have been included. The Goss Government cited this and kindred provisions as offering sufficient protection to obviate the need to make contact with the media. It is interesting to note that a proposal to bar CJC whistleblowers from contacting the media was considered before the tabling of the *Whistleblower Protection Act 1994*, but abandoned as too controversial.

The argument always trundled out by government against media whistleblower protection is the risk of damage to innocent reputations by unsubstantiated media stories. While no doubt this argument has some merit it is deliberately exaggerated (usually for the purpose of cover-up), and serves to pit the public interest to be gained through disclosure against the private rights of individuals. This is a contest we should not have to have.

The main problem for government with disclosures via the media is that the whistleblower is 'off the chain'. Broken loose of the tight, cautious, prolonged, and above all semi-secret agency procedures that are mandated to be followed in the official disclosure process, an exasperated whistleblower makes media contact with stories that are usually innately newsworthy – although this is not to say that they are always followed through by the media.

The whistleblower–media relationship is virtually unresearched and seems to be different each time a whistleblower makes media contact.[32] Conflicts between sensationalism and investigative journalism, snapshot coverage and sustained reporting, and victim-focused versus system-focused stories swim below the surface, usually out of the sight of the whistleblower. Such conflicts are resolved by media management against the public interest more times than is realised. This is not to deny the crucial role media can and often plays in breaking into the citadels of secrecy and running stories and commentaries in the public interest. However the notion of a fiercely free media, exposing wrongdoing wherever it finds it, is largely a myth.

Bar some spectacular cases (such as the McBride research fraud case), wrongdoers and their protectors do not really have much to worry about from a media constantly navigating between the Scylla of profit and the Charybdis of defamation. Will the busy mainstream media consumer, forced along by the velocity of modern living, 'buy' the whistleblower's snap-shotted story, and therefore buy the newspaper or tune in to the now-you-see-it-now-you-don't electronic coverage? That question shares star-billing in the editor's mind along with the question of whether the story will lead to defamation proceedings. We can say from a vast well of anecdotes that media's defamation-twitchy and sales-centred attitude to whistleblowers certainly keeps major stories of wrongdoing, cover-up and reprisals from the public.

Protection of Involuntary Disclosures

The most common scenario for involuntary disclosure is one in which a public official is required to answer questions before Royal Commissions, Senate Select Committees or courts of law that disclose wrongdoing and thereby embarrass, if not harm, the government.

The only scheme that protects involuntary disclosures is the *Whistleblowers Protection Act 1994 (Qld)*. Drafters appear to have assumed that existing protections are sufficiently strong. While protection exists, particularly if reprisals can be seen as contempt of proceedings, it is extremely difficult for a witness to demonstrate the causal connection between what he or she said under oath and his or her current demotion (or dismissal). Protecting this class of people is important and should have been embraced throughout the legislative effort, as they are exposed to the same whistleblowing rituals. The Senate Select Committee on Public Interest Whistleblowing did not accept that these people are whistleblowers, on the grounds that their disclosures are not 'free acts of conscience'.

Disclosures of Previous Wrongdoing

Whistleblowers disclose past, present and anticipated wrongdoing. The big question is, how far back should the retrospectivity apply? Clearly the further back, the greater the forensic task. The Queensland and New South Wales statutes are the only laws that protect disclosures of wrongdoing that occurred prior to their enactments. The second Tasmanian Bill also provided for protection for disclosures of previous wrondoing if the disclosures happen within one year of the Bill's assent. The Senate Select Committee on Public Interest Whistleblowing argued for a two-fold approach: unlimited retrospectivity if disclosures were made after the commencement of legislation, and a five-year retrospectivity if disclosures were made prior to the commencement of legislation. This approach was later endorsed by the Senate Select Committee on Unresolved Whistleblower Cases.[33]

Whistleblowing on Corrupt Politicians

The only two schemes that specifically protect whistleblowing on corrupt politicians are the South Australian statute and the Tasmanian Public Interest Disclosure Bill 1997, although the abandoned Commonwealth Bills also catered for the reality of political corruption. The failure of most of the schemes to reach political corruption is the result in part of an over-focusing on the wrongdoing of non-elected officials.

Drafting whistleblower legislation schemes that make it hard to reach wrongdoing politicians serves no purpose other than the protection of political corruption.

Legal Protection for Whistleblowers

Table 3 considers specific legal safeguards and immunities, including civil and criminal indemnification, protection from contravening secrecy laws, injunctions against reprisals and absolute privilege from defamation actions.

Civil and Criminal Indemnification

Most of the legislative schemes have responded to whistleblower vulnerability by offering legal immunity against the common ways whistleblowers have been forced into silence in the past. Most offer civil and criminal indemnification to 'accredited' whistleblowers: 'accredited' because the legal protection offered has to be understood in the context of government assessment processes built into the various schemes. These processes aim not to establish whistleblower *bona fides* so much as to ensure that the whistleblower, the candidate for accreditation, matches the socio-legal thrust of the protection schemes. Preceding the question of indemnification is the issue of the state licensing of the whistleblower, in a similar way to the issue of government licences to run child-care centres or export meat – no licence, no indemnification. Having passed state accreditation, for example by disclosing to an 'appropriate agency', the whistleblower-licensee can apply for the various forms of legal protection offered in the schemes.

Protection from Contravening Secrecy Enactments

Providing legal protection against charges of contravening secrecy enactments is an important service to whistleblowers as so much of public administration is conducted in a paranoid atmosphere of semi-secrecy. Australia is, in the words of Professor Paul Finn (now of the Federal Court) 'beset with very wide, very pervasive, and very oppressive secrecy laws.'[34] The Federal Government has about 141 secrecy provision in statute form,[35] while Queensland has 160![36] Successive administrations have acquired and passed on a powerful expertise in the control of information and seem to move gradually towards the closed society more typical of dictatorships than western liberal democracies.

Whistleblowers perform the invaluable task of exposing secrecy. Through their individual struggles to achieve official correction of wrongdoing, whistleblowers peer through venetian blinds into a secret world where power transcends principles. It is entirely appropriate that they should be shielded from charges of breaching secrecy enactments but, as the table indicates, this protection is not included in all the legislative proposals.

Injunctions against Reprisals

Of the schemes in existence, only Queensland and the ACT offer injunctive relief to whistleblowers. As already mentioned, the first and only time the Queensland protection was tested in court ended in near disaster.[37] Injunctive relief for whistleblowers is important but is still an unfamiliar remedy for courts and the process is bedevilled with formality and high costs.

Absolute Privilege in Defamation

The other traditional mode of attack on whistleblowers, the defamation writ (actual or threatened), has been blocked by the granting of absolute privilege in all existing statutes apart from that in South Australia. It remains to be seen whether law reform will flow from decisions such as the 1994 *Theophanous* and *Stephens* decisions so as to make this protection largely irrelevant. They are still very fragile decisions.

Services to Whistleblowers

In Table 4, the focus is on programs that respond to whistleblower suffering and allow for whistleblower involvement in the disclosure process. I look at counselling, administrative compensation, entitlement to damages, whistleblower feedback and relocation.

Counselling

A consideration of the services available within the various schemes offers a glimpse of law-making unable to match the complexity of the subject matter of the enactments. Many whistleblowers have partners, dependent children, relatives and friends, all of whom are exposed to trauma. Yet when the issue of redress comes up, the whistleblower is considered single and childless. With the exception of the abandoned Commonwealth and Tasmanian Bills, no counselling is built into any of the schemes as a right. The Tasmanian Bills not only provided for counselling to the whistleblower and those 'concerned in or a party to the disclosures', but also offered a range of practical services not available in the other schemes, such as witness protection, re-employment assistance, document safekeeping, legal aid and full case-management.[38]

What is called 'counselling' in some of the schemes (for example, the early Queensland Bills) is nothing more than procedural advice and minor support services by staff playing the part of value-added pamphlets. Yet counselling programs are sorely needed for whistleblowers and their families. The Queensland Whistleblower Study found that 79% of the sample reported deterioration in their emotional well-being.[39] The profile of psychic pain suffered by the majority was indicative of a severe stress syndrome that has tentatively been called the whistleblower stress syndrome.[40]

Administrative Compensation

Compensation should be available not only to whistleblowers, but also their partners and children, since these people (and the relationships) suffer as the whistleblower does. There should also be affirmative action provisions to assist the whistleblower's career, which invariably stalls during the disclosure process.

The abandoned Commonwealth Bills were the only ones that provided for an administrative (as distinct from judicial or court-ordered) award of compensation through an independent whistleblower protection authority. The *Whistleblower Protection Bill 1993 (Cth)* empowered the Whistleblower Protection Agency to assess a sum to be paid to a whistleblower.[41] It was envisaged that these payments would normally be made if the whistleblower could not be reinstated. The Bill also provided for the whistleblower to recover these amounts from the employer engaged in the harassment by action in a court of competent jurisdiction.[42]

The administrative award of compensation could provide a solution to the enormous resource problems associated with whistleblowing. In the absence of collective dissent, the employee of conscience faces the fully resourced might of the organisation, alone.

Administrative compensation could allow for the following services for bona fide whistleblowers, designed to correct the individual/organisation power imbalance:

- *Defence-fund allowance* – money for costs of administering the disclosure and for self-protection. Photocopying, telephone calls, witness expenses, transport costs and typing are the sort of services required by whistleblowers.
- *Special leave* – to allow whistleblowers to take leave to administer their disclosures and protect their careers, good names and families.
- *Professional costs* – to reimburse whistleblowers for legal, medical and counselling services for themselves and family where not provided or not fully provided by legal aid and health insurance.
- *Stress leave* – the ever-tightening compensation laws with respect to access to stress leave make it important that a special provision exists for people suffering from the 'whistleblower stress syndrome'.

Entitlement to Damages

Apart from the abandoned Commonwealth Bills, only the ACT and Queensland whistleblower laws make provision for a whistleblower to sue for damages. We do not know yet the breadth of these provisions. For example, can a protected whistleblower in the ACT or Queensland claim damages for harm to her or his career, physical health, relationships, finances and emotional health, or will there be a narrow interpretation of what constitutes whistleblower damages?

Whistleblower Feedback

A few of the instruments have grappled with the issue of feedback to whistleblowers. The *Public Interest Disclosure Act 1994 (ACT)* is probably the best in this regard. It provides that a person who makes a public interest disclosure, or an authority that refers a disclosure to another proper authority, may request the authority to which the disclosure was made or referred provide a progress report. Where a request is made, a progress report must be provided to the person or authority who requested it as soon as practicable after receipt of the request. If the authority takes further action with respect to the disclosure after providing a progress report, a further report must be provided at least once in every three months while the authority is taking action and on completion of the action. The whistleblower is also entitled to know why an authority declines to act; the name of an authority a disclosure is referred to; the current status of investigation; and any findings and action taken or proposed. Similar but watered-down reporting requirements appear in the Queensland, New South Wales, and South Australian statutes, and the Tasmanian Bills.

While whistleblowers have some rights to be kept informed, the legislative effort effectively denies them any involvement in the investigative and corrective processes that, on rare occasions, follow their disclosure. The statutes authorise State structures to take over the investigation of the disclosed wrongdoing, including any complaint of victimisation. The whistleblower is denied the opportunity to provide input into the investigation other than through the giving of testimony.

Is it not possible, even highly probable, that whistleblowers have something to contribute to the form and content of the investigative process, and even more importantly, some real expertise in structuring systemic solutions to correct the wrongdoing and alleviate the possibility of its occurring again? Governments want the whistleblower only to say what they saw and cannot countenance whistleblowers who maintain an interest in the form and content of the investigation of wrongdoing.

Right to Relocation

The approach to relocation in the schemes is another example of naive law-making. The abandoned Commonwealth Bills and the whistleblower statues in the ACT and Queensland provide for relocation of whistleblowers within and between organisations as well as physical transfers. Yet we know from the research that transfers are a favourite reprisal strategy of management: in the Queensland Whistleblower Study, 31% of the sample had been punitively transferred. The strategy of transferring the 'problem' (the whistleblower) elsewhere remains the same, whether it is orchestrated by a vindictive manager or dressed up to appear as a 'service' within the legislative schemes.

Recent research into work stress carried out by Comcare has found that forced relocation and redeployment were frequently precipitating events that led to stress-related claims. Research also indicates that even when transfers are part of career advancement, and agreed to by the worker, they can produce a good deal of stress.[43]

Another problem is evident in the Queensland statute. The relocation option is contingent on the go-ahead from the chief executive officer of the unit into which the whistleblower is to be transferred. Whistleblowers rarely receive positive acknowledgment, even when their disclosures are conspicuously in the public interest.

There is a deep-seated attitude in the work culture that whistleblowers are ratbags, subversives or whingers. What CEO is going to rejoice in discovering that one of this 'suspect group' is about to come under his or her wing? CEO veto may effectively nullify the relocation option.

Sometimes relocation can lead to tragic absurdities. In 1993, Arnold L, an Aboriginal welfare worker, made a public interest disclosure about gross financial mismanagement in a welfare agency in which he worked.[44] He was sacked and finally re-employed by the Aboriginal and Torres Strait Islander Commission (ATSIC). Some months later, his new employers found out about the previous whistleblowing. His workplace soon became toxic and he went on Comcare stress leave. Now he wishes to relocate from one ATSIC office to another. His transfer application was held up because his Comcare case was still outstanding and the manager of the section into which he sought relocation said he would not consider the application until the Comcare claim was settled. Arnold L will suffer stress unless he leaves his current workplace, and he cannot leave his current workplace while he is stressed because his new manager won't consider him unless he is emotionally okay!

The Committee acknowledges that whistleblowing is a legitimate form of action within a democracy and that there have been, there are, and there will continue to be occasions on which whistleblowing is the only available avenue for the concerned ethical citizen to expose wrongdoing in the public or private sector.[45]

This declaration from the Senate Committee on Whistleblowing is an important message, as it puts whistleblowing in its right and proper context: the context of democracy. Whistleblowing is socially responsible dissent. At the very least, whistleblower legislation should honour this democratically enshrined speak-out role that gutsy Australians take on reluctantly from time to time.

13 Codes of Conduct
Moral Bondage in the Age of Anything Goes

> *I'd sooner live among people who don't cheat at cards than among people who are earnest about not cheating at cards.*
> – C.S. Lewis

Right now, in another country, Afghanistan, we are witnessing the full flourish of Islamic moral authoritarianism, as Taliban agents of the Preservation of Virtue and Elimination of Vice enforce an endless list of harsh edicts on the population.[1] Beyond the stark socio-historical differences between Afghanistan and Australia there is a comparison to be made here, for the process of ethical renewal occurring in both countries is very similar. Eras of public probity follow periods that have been successfully depicted as times of immorality. Maybe the way we Australians have came to understand the 1980s is the way the Taliban came to understand the same period in Afghanistan, when growing western influences, particularly capitalism and feminism, were seen as destroying Islam. In both countries there was a perceived sub-ethical period, followed by a period of perceived reform and correction. In this incendiary process moral authoritarianism awaits the signal to come out and play.

We have led ourselves, or allowed ourselves to be led, to the view that the 1980s was the decade of official corruption,[2] and that the 1990s, and beyond into the new millenium, is (therefore) going to be the decade of official probity.[3] Wait! There's something wrong with this picture. On a second look, through sceptical adult eyes, we still see senior bureaucrats ripping off their government-issued credit cards, politicians are still lying to us ... I could go on. I think we clench the future as a place of official integrity in much the same way we recall the Easter Bunny and the tooth fairy: we no longer believe in them, but the fantasy is comforting.

What do we do then from the 'safety' of the turn of the century? Well for a start if we are service providers we write reassuring mission statements that provide to our clients paper guarantees that we are all about best practice, which includes moral behaviour. Or we rush codes of conduct ('cut-out catechisms' according to one commentator[4]) into print. A Deakin University survey carried out in 1996 found that a quarter of the nation's top 500 companies now have codes of conduct, and almost half of these were devised since the end of the 1980s.[5]

Codes are being written for politicians[6] and public servants.[7] All manner of service providers, from hospitals to McDonalds, are hawking mission statements and conduct standards to assure clients and customers that best practice reigns above all else. The Institute of Engineers Australia, for example, has placed advertisements guaranteeing people that members of the Institute are committed to the highest professional and ethical standards.[8] Professional associations such as those of nurses, lawyers and journalists are at the same time reviewing their codes,[9] and the New South Wales government has recently increased the legislative surveillance on professional conduct.[10] Parallelling this is a mini-boom time for universities enrolling fee-paying students seeking graduate qualification in ethics.[11] Finally we have the start now of governments offering ethical guarantees on their policy making.[12]

It seems that when we are not devising these high-sounding, feel-good codes of conduct, we are enshrining 'ethical obligations' in law (eg the *Queensland Public Sector Ethics Act*), or paying enormous salaries to our official guardians of ethical conduct.[13]

So a moral clean-up campaign has started , the likes of which Australia has never experienced before. Genuine community concerns about official wrongdoing have been met by a cavalcade of remedies that appear big on form and small on substance. In the projection of reassurance to a community badly hurt by wrongdoing, you may detect a compulsion to look good rather than to act right.

If that is the case then not only will this lead to new levels of duplicity, it will inject a highly inappropriate moral authoritarianism into the important debate Australia is yet to have about a moral framework for the twenty-first century.

Clearly then I approach the new ethics movement not as a true believer, nor even as an agnostic. My lack of faith comes partly from a suspicion that the movement is seriously misrepresentational. Beyond the movement's righteousness you can feel the presence of the State. You can, in other words, feel social control. The movement, I argue, is less about developing moral codes by which people participate in corruption-free and just work relationships, and more about the further encroachment of the State. Even if this view is wrong, should the State control the agenda for the moral tune-up of the work place? One cannot, in other words, understand this ethics movement without reference to how the modern State exercises control.

In 1527 Cardinal Wolsey put his mind to solving Henry VIII's 'great scruple', the divorce from Catherine of Aragon. In August 1998, weeks after winning the Queensland election by the smallest of margins, Premier Peter Beattie engaged a professional ethicist (who by no coincidence is also a minister of religion), to investigate his family's finances for any conflicts of interest. Beattie, it was claimed, was 'outsourcing his conscience'.[14]

On one reading of the King's use of Wolsey and the Premier's use of an ethicist, the only difference is the 400 or so years that separate both matters. Throughout history our leaders have successfully used the church to sanctify their actions.

That interpretation is a bit too blase for me. Something different (and perhaps a little dangerous) is stirring in the public forum. The civic domain is becoming crowded with moral rule masters who would make Calvin blush. Carpetbaggers, too, are reaping big bucks for running ethics consultancies for the morally confused in business and public sector management.

A new moral profession is arising from the ashes of the church. Armed with their Bachelor of Applied Ethics, a swarm of do-gooders is taking us into a new era of moral bondage.

For example, in the fight against sex abuse the Catholic Church in September 1997 released a draft code of conduct. For priests, if the code is accepted, this will mean glassed-in reconciliation (confessional) rooms in every church in Australia.[15] For police, bearing a lot of community mistrust as a result of constant scandals, this could mean random integrity checks.[16] Into every copper's life now comes the probability that the ethics police will put temptation before them. How on earth will these arbitrary checks on personal integrity be conducted? Will the tests be administered without fear or favour up and down the police hierarchy? I don't think so. What ethics police officer would dare set an integrity test for their Commissioner?

Take another example of this moral overreaction. In August 1996 a Gold Coast police office was investigated and disciplined by Queensland's misconduct watchdog, the Criminal Justice Commission, and the police service's own Professional Standards Unit[17]. His crime? He overdrew his Police Services Credit Union account! The officer was found to have breached the Queensland Police Services Code of Conduct and fined $150, half the amount that he was overdrawn. Or there is the case of the sergeant charged for saying 'fuck' at work with colleagues. He was cleared, with a police tribunal determining that swearing was part of the police culture. Not satisfied, the Police Commissioner took the matter to the NSW Court of Appeal and lost there too. He then contemplated an appeal to the High Court.[18]

There are numerous examples, all serving the main point of this final chapter – that the vision of an ethical workplace, constructed from the public's manipulated experiences of official misconduct during the 1980s, both offers and masks new opportunities for State expansion.[19] Along with ethical education (preaching) and ethical codes of conduct (secularised Ten Commandments?) come new opportunities for surveillance of workers, in particular those in public settings. Hammered by economic cut-backs in the past 20 years, the public sector must now prepare itself for increased ethical regimentation, the moral equivalent of economic rationalism.

In no way does this point brush aside the record of public sector corruption in Australia. Rather it focuses our attention on structural questions. Such as: who will control the definition of ethical behaviour? Who will ensure that the definition holds across the power continuum from the base-grade clerk to the ministerial adviser, and ultimately the minister? The answer to the first question is, in simple terms, the State. The answer to the second question is no one.

Why? Partly because the new ethics movement is not a ground-level experience. It is not composed of suffering or angry people: people, for example, who have risked all to disclose in the public interest. There is no outrage, no spirit of disillusion, and no radical change agenda. Rather it is a respectable, profession-powered, distinctly un-angry interest group of nice people in ethics institutes, ethics training consortia and senior levels of the private and public sector. It is very definitely not a street-level (read 'real') phenomenon.

Not only is this ethics movement symbolised by dignitaries who history may judge as less then saintly, there are issues about the way the movers and shakers in the movement see the world. The new ethical renewal appears to have a brittle and confused conceptual base. This weak platform must bear the weight of a huge, uncompromising moral focus that yearns for ethical redemption through, of all things, the Westminster model, which for over two hundred years has formed the basis of our system of rule.[20]

Deep questions about the morality of power and the authoritarianism of the workplace are strategically avoided. This allows critics of the ethics industry to see its relationship with government as the modern articulation of the historical interface between Church and State. Indeed the bridge between this movement and government is disturbingly wide, transporting patronage in one direction (to the ethics movement) and legitimation in the other direction (to the government).

One of the most powerful forms of legitimation occurs when justifications for official power cycle through the social structure uncritiqued. A good example of this is the Westminster concept of government power mentioned above. This powerful inheritance from the United Kingdom remains the basis of our system of government. It also has a pre-eminent and unchallenged status in the current ethics debate, especially as it applies to the public sector.

Recently the Westminster system has come in for a bit of stick.[21] It has been argued that the loss of trust in the institutions of government owes much to the failure of our cherished Westminster system.[22] Seemingly oblivious to this modern view, one highly influential government report (that set the game plan for the development of the ethics industry in Australia), poses the question:

What ethical standards ought to be observed by public officials who make decisions affecting the rights and entitlements of others in a democratic, 'Westminster'-based system of responsible government and public administration?[23]

The absolutely basic conflict between democratic theory (the theory of dissent) and Westminster practice is denied in this passage. Under the Westminster system the people are supposed to be at the end of the line of accountability. But in actual fact the 'king' (prime minister, premiers, ministers) is still in a position of ultimate power. The English Revolution of 1688 has turned full circle in the reality of everyday life.

The worrying feature of the government report cited above is the automatic, critique-free acceptance of the Westminster model:

The Commission is of the opinion that there is sufficient continuing relevance, understanding and acceptance of the 'Westminster tradition' in its broadest sense, for its general principles to continue to form the basis of Codes of Conduct for Queensland public officials.[24]

More worrying is the acceptance of it as an ethical category. When a recent Time-Morgan poll showed that only 10% of people rated parliamentarians as ethical (just above real estate agents and car sellers[25]), and a recent AGB-McNair poll showed 93% of young people do not trust politicians,[26] one is drawn to the conclusion that the reaffirmation of the Westminster system of governance is based on an appalling ignorance of the widespread disaffection with it.

So here is the paradigm collision. Proponents of the Westminster model argue that governments represent the values and aspirations of the people. Many dissenters and whistleblowers would argue that governments and the people are in deep, irreversible and irreconcilable conflict.

The critical whistleblower perspective also asserts that under the Westminster system accountability pathways go the wrong way. These pathways go up to power and vested interest, not down to the people. With the Westminster system, non-elected officials are indirectly accountable to the people through ministers. That is the theory. By the time non-elected officials have reached senior executive service level, all sense of people-accountability is reframed if not gone, pushed aside by the brash new notion of minister-as-client.[27]

This is anathema to the democratic vision. On the other hand the conservative ethics industry blindly celebrates the Westminster way of doing government business, including the belief in the inherent ethicality of the chain of command. These concepts (ministerial responsibility, chain of command, etc.) are, it seems, like all sacred matter, non-negotiable and non-debatable.

That senior officials collude to bust the accountability link between themselves and their minister is constantly verified by the accumulated practical wisdom of whistleblowers who report two things. First, for a number of whistleblowers the common state of these links is brokenness not connectedness, particularly at the crucial links which separate non-elected and elected officials. Second, other whistleblowers tell us the opposite: that they have found an unbroken chain, but is a chain of collusion not accountability.

Another 'non-negotiable' for the ethics industry is the concept of 'primary obligations' of public officials:

Public officials shall uphold the laws of Queensland and Australia, and shall implement the decisions and policies of the government and shall not, without just cause, be a part to their breach, evasion or subversion.[28]

The phrase ' ... and shall implement the decisions and policies of the government' is a directive that is shouted at the public sector workforce. The phrase ' ... and shall not, without just cause, be a party to their breach' is mentioned sotto voce with a knowing wink.

After having lived through an ethical Dark Age in Queensland,[29] I find the 'primary obligation' injunction sinister and totalitarian. Respect for the law should be based on what the law does, not what we are forced to believe it should do. Put another way, respect for the law should be based on what the law does for all, not the power-connected few. The ethics movement treats respect for the law as a natural starting point, undeniable, unquestionable, and unproblematic. The whistleblower perspective centres itself around a different starting point: democracy. It would also argue, in far more cogent terms than expressed by the ethics movement, that the subversion of bad laws, regulations and practices by conscience-driven public officials is a public duty – admitted, acknowledged, and rewarded – not a marginal and dangerous dissent. On this point I can quote the late Mr Justice Murphy. In *A v. Hayden* he said:

In Australia it is no defence to the commission of a criminal act ... that it was done in obedience to the orders of a supervisor or the government. [Public Servants] have a duty to obey lawful orders, and a duty to disobey unlawful orders.[30] *(emphasis added)*

The fact that there is so little civil disobedience in the public sector indicates a shackled workforce acting in effect against their duty to the public (the duty to disobey unlawful laws and orders).

The second observation I would make is that the public sector ethics movement appears to be dangerously myopic. With modern administration daily mocking the old private/public divisions, the movement continues to focus only on public sector morality. By that I mean public life exchanges, wherever they be found: schoolyards, public housing, university research laboratories, police interrogation rooms, social security office. But what of the boardroom – secret calls over mobile phones, deals struck beyond the limits of legality? What about the private sector? With the dangerous imbalance between the ethical surveillance of public and private worksites, we stand to reconstruct a public sector that will resemble a huge Benedictine Monastery, with public sector officers the new Abbots; public sector ethics and procedures, the new Bible; and the administration of sanctions and penalties performed by a secular version of the Spanish Inquisition, monitored by Cabinet, the College of Cardinals! Meanwhile the private sector, virtually untouchable in the prevailing eco-political climate, continues to conduct a lot of its business below moral and legal standards.

So in essence we have the workplace ethics movement and the worksite dissent movement (whistleblowing) on a collision course. The former represents the new pushed-out border of state power while the latter incubates a subversive spirit that in its extreme form questions the basic philosophy and institutional arrangements of this state power.

The courageous and socially useful role of dissenting in the public interest is demonised by the work culture that sees in the whistleblower a subversive force to be reckoned with. Unlike her or his colleagues, the whistleblower has untangled ethics and expediency. Worse, they are prepared to expose wrongdoing to the world in the search for justice. That the organisation can strike back with intensity is beyond question. This strike-back capacity may actually be inadvertently encouraged by the public sector ethics movement, and whistleblowers may stand to suffer more from the assumed re-moralisation of public administration. Since the ethics movement seeks to eliminate 'evil' in the workplace, what place has the whistleblower in this new Holy City? Perhaps a place even more dangerous than before because it is going to be more difficult for their message of wrongdoing to be believed.

In Conclusion

Captured in the culture of consent, with seemingly no way out, we exploit women and men of good conscience. We weigh them down with the moral burden of reanimating democracy. This is too big a job for individuals. If we are going to once again flex the muscles of democracy, we must dismantle the *culture of consent*, or at least give it a bloody good shake-up. Over the rubble we must build a *culture of dissent*. Instead of periodically dissenting individuals we need permanently dissenting communities of interest. Until that day good Australians will continue to come forward and commit acts drenched in courage.

Appendix

Whistleblower Laws

Table 1: Whistleblower Protection – General

Name	Current Status	Independent Authority	Qualification for Protection	Disclosure Defined	Reprisals Prohibited	Sector Penalties
Commonwealth						
Whistleblowers Protection Bill 1991 (Cth)	Introduced 12/12/91, Senator Vallentine. Abandoned	Yes	Good faith disclosure to whistleblower protection authority	Yes	Yes	No
Whistleblower Protection Bill 1993 (Cth)	Introduced 25/5/93, Senator Chamarette. Abandoned	Yes	Good faith disclosure to whistleblower protection authority	Yes	Yes	No
Australian Capital Territory						
Public Interest Disclosure Act 1994 (ACT)	Enacted 7/12/94	No	Disclosure to proper authority	Yes	Yes, $10,000 fine and/or prison	Yes
Queensland						
Whistleblowers (Interim Protection) and Miscellaneous Amendments Act 1990 (Qld)	Assented to 2/11/90	No	Good faith disclosure to Criminal Justice Commission	No	No	No
Whistleblowers Protection Bills 1991, 1992 (Qld)	EARC Bill, 29/10/91. Never tabled. PEARC Bill 8/4/92. Never tabled	No	Good faith disclosure to proper authority	Yes	Yes, Max. 3 years' prison	Yes
Whistleblowers Protection Act 1994 (Qld)	Assented to 1/12/94	No	Disclosure to proper authority	Yes	Yes, Max. 2 years' prison	No

Name	Current Status	Independent Authority	Qualification for Protection	Disclosure Defined	Reprisals Prohibited	Sector Penalties
New South Wales						
Whistleblowers Protection Bill (No. 1) 1992 (NSW)	Introduced 30/6/92. Abandoned	No	Voluntary disclosure to relevant authority	No	Yes, Max. 1 year's prison	No
Whistleblowers Protection Bill (No. 2) 1992 (NSW)	Introduced by Premier Fahey, 17/11/92. Abandoned	No	Disclosure by public official to relevant authority, shows or tends to show wrongdoing	No	Yes, Max. 1 year's prison	No
Protected Disclosures Act 1994 (NSW)	Assented to 12/12/94	No	Disclosure by public official to relevant authority, shows or tends to show wrongdoing. Special disclosures possible.	Yes	Yes, Max. 1 year's prison	No
South Australia						
Whistleblowers Protection Act 1993 (SA)	Assented to 8/4/93. Operated from 20/9/93	No	Good faith disclosure to relevant authority	Yes	Yes. Tort of victimisation established	No
Tasmania						
Public Interest Disclosure Bill 1995, No. 1	Introduced by ALP Opposition Leader, Field, 29/10/95. Withdrawn	Yes	Belief on reasonable grounds that information is or may be true.	Yes	Yes	Yes

Name	Current Status	Independent Authority	Qualification for Protection	Disclosure Defined	Reprisals Prohibited	Sector Penalties
Public Interest Disclosure Bill 1995, No. 2	Introduced by ALP Opposition 4/11/95. Abandoned	Yes	Belief on reasonable grounds that information is or may be true.	Yes	Yes	Yes
Public Interest Disclosure Bill, 1997	Introduced by ALP Opposition 30/4/97. Defeated	No	None mentioned	Yes	Yes	No
Whistleblower Protection Bill, 1997	Formulated by Liberal Government, 16/4/97, version No. 2	No	Belief on reasonable grounds that information is or may be true, disclosure to appropriate person, assists in investigation	Yes	Yes	No
Public Interest Disclosure Bill, 1997	Formulated by ALP Opposition November 1997	No	None mentioned	No	Yes	No

Table 2: Whistleblower Protection – Scope

Name	Who May Disclose	Protection for Private Sector Disclosures	Media Protection	Involuntary Disclosures Protected	Protected Disclosure on Previous Wrongdoing	Application to Politicians
Commonwealth						
Whistleblowers Protection Bill 1991 (Cth)	Anybody	No	No	No	No	Yes
Whistleblower Protection Bill 1993 (Cth)	Anybody	No	No	No	No	Yes
Australian Capital Territory						
Public Interest Disclosure Act 1994 (ACT)	Anybody	No	No	No	No	No
Queensland						
Whistleblowers (Interim Protection) and Miscellaneous Amendments Act 1990 (Qld)	Anybody	No	No	No	No	No
Whistleblowers Protection Bills 1991, 1992 (Qld)	Anybody	Yes	No	No	Yes	No
Whistleblowers Protection Act 1994 (Qld)	Normally public officials. Anybody when wrongdoing to do with disabled, environment, reprisals.	No, except for disclosures regarding disabled, environment, reprisals	No	Yes	Yes	No
New South Wales						
Whistleblowers Protection Bill (No. 1) 1992 (NSW)	Only public officials	No	No	No	Yes	No

Name	Who May Disclose	Protection for Private Sector Disclosures	Media Protection	Involuntary Disclosures Protected	Protected Disclosure on Previous Wrongdoing	Application to Politicians
Whistleblowers Protection Bill (No. 2) 1992 (NSW)	Only public officials	No	No	No	Yes	No
Protected Disclosures Act 1994 (NSW)	Only public officials	No	Yes, in special circumstances	No	Yes	No
South Australia						
Whistleblowers Protection Act 1993 (SA)	Anybody	Yes	No	No	No	Yes
Tasmania						
Public Interest Disclosure Bill 1995, No. 1	Anybody	Yes	No	Yes (conditions apply)	No. 2 year retrospectivity rule on complaints	Yes
Public Interest Disclosure Bill 1995, No. 2	Anybody	Yes	No	Yes (conditions apply)	Yes, if disclosure in 1 year period after Act	Yes
Public Interest Disclosure Bill, 1997	Unspecified	No	No	No	Unspecified	No
Whistleblower Protection Bill, 1997	Unspecified	No	No	No	No	No
Public Interest Disclosure Bill, 1997	Anybody	No	No	No	No	Yes

Table 3: Legal Protections for Whistleblowers

Name	Civil and Criminal Indemnification for Whistleblowers	Protection from Contravening Secrecy Enactments	Injunctions against reprisals	Absolute privilege in defamation
Commonwealth				
Whistleblowers Protection Bill 1991 (Cth)	Yes	No	Yes	No
Whistleblower Protection Bill 1993 (Cth)	Yes	No	Yes	No
Australian Capital Territory				
Public Interest Disclosure Act 1994 (ACT)	Yes	No	Yes	Yes
Queensland				
Whistleblowers (Interim Protection) and Miscellaneous Amendments Act 1990 (Qld)	No	No	Yes	No
Whistleblowers Protection Bills 1991, 1992 (Qld)	Yes	Yes	Yes	Yes
Whistleblowers Protection Act 1994 (Qld)	Yes	Yes	Yes	Yes
New South Wales				
Whistleblowers Protection Bill (No. 1) 1992 (NSW)	Yes	Yes	No	Only for specific disclosures to Auditor-General
Whistleblowers Protection Bill (No. 2) 1992 (NSW)	Yes	Yes	No	Yes
Protected Disclosures Act 1994 (NSW)	Yes	Yes	No	Yes
South Australia				
Whistleblowers Protection Act 1993 (SA)	Yes	No	No	No

Name	Civil and Criminal Indemnification for Whistleblowers	Protection from Contravening Secrecy Enactments	Injunctions against reprisals	Absolute privilege in defamation
Tasmania				
Public Interest Disclosure Bill 1995, No. 1	Yes	No	No	No
Public Interest Disclosure Bill 1995, No. 2	Yes	Yes	No	No
Public Interest Disclosure Bill, 1997	Unspecified	No	No	No
Whistleblower Protection Bill, 1997	Yes	No	No	No
Public Interest Disclosure Bill, 1997	Yes	Unspecified	No	No

Appendix: Whistleblower Laws | 251

Table 4: Services for Whistleblowers

Name	Counselling	Compensation to Victimised Whistleblower	Entitlement to Damages	Whistleblower Feedback	Right to Relocation
Commonwealth					
Whistleblowers Protection Bill 1991 (Cth)	Yes	Yes	Yes	No	Yes
Whistleblower Protection Bill 1993 (Cth)	Yes	Yes	Yes	No	Yes
Australian Capital Territory					
Public Interest Disclosure Act 1994 (ACT)	No	No	Yes	Report on request, every 90 days report thereafter, final report	Yes
Queensland					
Whistleblowers (Interim Protection) and Miscellaneous Amendments Act 1990 (Qld)	No	No	No	No	No
Whistleblowers Protection Bills 1991, 1992 (Qld)	No (advice only)	No	Yes	On notice proper authority to report to whistleblower at least every 3 months	Yes
Whistleblower Protection Act 1994 (Qld)	No	No	Yes	'Reasonable' information about action taken and results achieved	Yes
New South Wales					
Whistleblowers Protection Bill (No. 1) 1992 (NSW)	No	No	No	No	No
Whistleblowers Protection Bill (No. 2) 1992 (NSW)	No	No	No	No	No
Protected Disclosures Act 1994 (NSW)	No	No	No	Yes, mandatory reporting to whistleblower within 6 weeks of disclosure	No

Name	Counselling	Compensation to Victimised Whistleblower	Entitlement to Damages	Whistleblower Feedback	Right to Relocation
South Australia					
Whistleblowers Protection Act 1993 (SA)	No	No	No	Notification of outcome of investigation	No
Tasmania					
Public Interest Disclosure Bill 1995, No. 1	Whistleblowers only	No	No	2 weeks for the decision to investigate, 6 months for result	No
Public Interest Disclosure Bill 1995, No. 2	Whistleblowers only	No	No	As above plus provision for progress reports	No
Public Interest Disclosure Bill, 1997	Whistleblowers and relevant others	No	No	Yes, but no time limits specified	No
Whistleblower Protection Bill, 1997	No	No	No	Feedback if practical and not contrary to law. All parties to be informed of progress of actions and outcomes.	No
Public Interest Disclosure Bill, 1997	Yes	No	No	Feedback if practical and not contrary to law. All parties to be informed of progress of actions and outcomes.	No

Notes

Preface
1 See W. De Maria, *Swinging From a Clean Rope: The Destruction of Academic whistle-blowers in The Age of Administrative Correctness*, paper presented to the Second International Bullying Conference, St. John's College, The University of Queensland, 5–6 July 1996.

Part 1: Whistleblowing – The Big Picture: Introduction
1 Textile, Clothing and Footwear Union of Australia, *The Hidden Cost of Fashion*, March 1995, p. 4.
2 Evidence of Annie Delaney, Outwork Coordinator, Textile, Clothing and Footwear Union of Australia, to Senate Economics Committee, 16 April 1996, Case Study One.

Chapter 1: Ethical Australia? – A Guided Tour
1 *Australian*, 29 December 1997. The answers, by the way, are: ARL Newcastle 22, Manly 16, and Super League Brisbane 26, Cronulla 8 for question one and Bob Woods, Michael Cobb, and Mal Colston, for question two. Cobb was convicted in October 1998.
2 Those forced to resign or sacked were: Geoff Prosser, Small Business Minister; Bob Woods, Parliamentary Secretary for Health; Jim Short, Assistant Treasurer; Brian Gibson, Parliamentary Secretary to the Treasurer; John Sharp, Transport Minister; David Jull, Administrative Services Minister; and Peter McGauran the Science Minister. ALP Senator Nick Sherry who made, under the old rules, legal claims for more than $40,000, at $320 per night, by staying at his mother's home on the outskirts of Hobart, attempted suicide when his claims become public.
3 *Courier Mail*, 5 December 1996, p. 1.
4 For background see T. Sykes, *The Bold Riders* (Allen & Unwin, St. Leonards, 1996), 2nd ed, ch. 6; P. Barry, *The Rise and Fall of Alan Bond* (Bantam, Sydney, 1990); T. Maher, *Bond* (Heineman, Sydney, 1990).
5 Bond was back in court on 22 August 1997 to learn that that the Western Australian Criminal Appeals Court had extended his four year sentence to seven years. The judges found Bond's original sentence 'so low as to be manifestly inadequate ...' See *Weekend Australian*, 23–4 August 1997, p. 2.
6 T. Sykes, op. cit., pp. 570, 572.
7 Now called the Australian Securities and Investment Commission.
8 Australian Securities Commission, *Annual Report*, 1995–96, p. 15.
9 Ibid, p. 6.

10 *Courier Mail*, 8 May 1997, p. 4. On 18 September 1997 Quinn applied to the Victorian Court of Appeal to have his appeal against the severity of his sentence struck out after the court warned that it could possibly increase his sentence. See *Australian*, 19 September 1997, p. 4.
11 *Australian*, 16 May 1997, p. 1.
12 Australian Competition and Consumer Commission, Annual Report, 1995–96, p. 11
13 Ibid.
14 Ibid, p. 12.
15 Ibid, p. 253
16 Ibid, p. 23
17 Ibid, pp. 24–5.
18 Study reported in *Australian*, 23 July 1997, p. 21.
19 *Australian*, 1 August 1997, p. 21.
20 *Weekend Australian*, 21–2 February 1998, p. 1.
21 For some of the stories of banking misconduct see Q. Dempster, *Whistleblowers*, (ABC Books, Sydney, 1997), chapter one 'The Westpac Letters', and chapter 10 'The Man who Saved the Bank'.
22 *Weekend Australian*, 21–2 February 1998, p.4.
23 Ibid.

Chapter 2: Disclosure – The Inside Story
1 H. Lawson, 'Freedom on the Wallaby' in C. Roderick, *Henry Lawson: Collected Verse* (Angus and Robertson, Sydney, 1967) pp. 400–1.
2 I. Kant *Perpetual Peace: A Philosophical Sketch* (Tr. M. Campbell-Smith, London, Sonnenschein, 1903).
3 *Sunday Mail*, 14 July 1996, p. 2.
4 *Sunday Mail*, 14 July 1996, p. 2. Senewiratne did in fact resign from a senior position at the hospital in January 1997. See *Courier Mail*, 30 January 1997, p. 6.
5 *Australian*, 14 December 1995, p. 1
6 Ibid.
7 As he was entitled to do under s.35 of the *Health Rights Commission Act*.
8 Queensland Health Rights Commission, *4th Annal Report*, op.cit, p.47.
9 *Courier Mail*, 17 December 1996, p.6.
10 Queensland Health Rights Commission, Fourth Annual Report, op. cit., p.48.
11 When the Attorney-General allegedly tried to pressure the Australian Law Reform Commission into not giving evidence before a parliamentary committee examining native title, Evans advised that the Attorney's actions were an improper interference with a parliamentary witness, and could be a criminal offence. He came out again to criticise the government's public sector reforms as constituting a politicisation of the bureaucracy. When the government, fearful of alienating Senator Mal Colston before the crucial Telstra sell-off vote, decided not to have a parliamentary inquiry into the allegations that Colston had been ripping off the parliamentary travel allowance scheme, Evans said that the government's legal opinion was 'wrong'. See *Courier Mail*, 20 October 1997, p.4.
12 Ibid.
13 *Weekend Australian*, 27–8 September 1997, (editorial)
14 Ibid.
15 Letter from Dr D. Horvath to Concord Hospital staff, 22 August 1996.
16 *Courier Mail*, 4 July 1996.
17 Ibid.
18 Ibid.
19 C. Young, *Balancing Families and Work: A Demographic Study of Women's Labour Force Participation* (Canberra, 1990).

20 W. De Maria, *Unshielding the Shadow Culture*, Queensland Whistleblower Study, Result Release One, The University of Queensland, April 1994, p. 6.
21 J. Skues & R. Kirkby, 'Women in the Workplace: Gender Differences in Occupational Stress and Coping', in P. Cotton (ed) *Psychological Health in the Workplace: Understanding and Managing Occupational Stress* (Australian Psychological Society Publication, Sydney, 1994) Ch. 17.
22 *Weekend Australian Review*, 25–6 February 1995, p.1.
23 *Courier Mail*, 6 June 1996.
24 W. Carter, *Commission of Inquiry into the Care and Treatment of Patients in the Psychiatric Unit of Townsville General Hospital* (Queensland Government Printer, Brisbane, 1991)
25 A. Fitzgerald, *Report of a Commission of Inquiry persuant to Orders in Council* (Queensland Government Printer, Brisbane, 1989).
26 D. Stewart, *Inquiry into Allegations of Official Mis-Conduct at the Basil Stafford Centre* (Criminal Justice Commission, Brisbane, 1995).
27 *Australian*, 29 September 1995.
28 W. Nicol, *McBride: Behind the Myth* (ABC Books, Sydney, 1989)
29 *Australian*, 28 February 1995.
30 *Australian*, 3 January 1994. See also Q. Dempster, *Whistleblowers* (ABC Books, Sydney, 1997).
31 The Queensland Whistleblower Study was undertaken at the University of Queensland betwen 1993–95. The first such study in Australia, it was financed through University research grant funding and managed by a small team directed by the author and assisted by final year social work students. Adds placed in newspapers and union journals, complemented by an extensive information campaign throughout the Queensland public service and professional associations attracted over 350 people. Of whom 102 respondents who had successfully passed through a 10 stage filter, were eventually brought into the study as bona-fide whistleblowers. A large data base was established through the administration of detailed questionnares to whistleblowers and their partners. Three reports were published: *Unshielding the Shadow Culture* (demographics, disclosure path anaysis, disclosure investigation evaluation); *Wounded Workers* (reprisals, financial, physical, emotional effects, value profiles, and value changes); and the 700 plus item *International Whistleblower Bibliography*. QWS was conceived and conducted as action research. Consequently a Whistleblower Action Group was established at the start of the study.
32 *Courier Mail*, (letters) 24 February 1998.
33 For an interesting account see M. Turnbull, *The Spycatcher Trial* (Mandarin, Port Melbourne, 1989)
34 See *Courier Mail*, 24 January 1997, p. 1.
35 For an elaboration of this point see W.De Maria, 'Australian Whistleblowing: The Great Betrayal', paper delivered to the Fraud, Ethics, Accountability and Risk Management in the Public Sector Conference, 17 February 1998, Sydney
36 'Cobber' is colloquial for friend or mate. While its origins are disputed it is believed to be dedived from the old British word *cob*, to form a friendship. See *Macquarie Dictionary*, 1982, p. 367.
37 Ibid, p. 535.
38 Ibid, p. 1980.
39 P. MacFie, 'Dobbers and Cobbers: Informers and Mateship Among Convicts, Officials, and Settlers on the Grass Tree Hill Road, Tasmania 1830–1850', *Tasmanian Historical Research Association Papers and Proceedings*, Vol. 35, No. 3, September 1988, p. 127.
40 Ibid, p. 122.
41 Ibid.

42 See for example E. Callanan & T. Dworkin, 'Do Good and Get Rich: Financial Incentives for Whistleblowing and the False Claims Act', *Villanova Law Review*, Vol. 37, 1992, pp. 939–48; M. Thompson, 'Cashing in on Military Fraud', *California Lawyer*, Vol. 8, October 1988, pp. 33–7.
43 *Courier Mail*, 31 January 1998, p. 2.
44 *Australian*, 2 June 1997, p. 1.
45 *Courier Mail*, 24 June 1997, p. 5.
46 *Courier Mail*, 31 August 1996. One of the people axed by the incoming government allegedly for her labor sympathies was former Family Services Department chief Jacki Byrne. Sacked within days of the new government coming to power Bryne launched an unfair dismissal action and took out a newspaper add appealing for people with information about the 'hit list' to come forward. See *Courier Mail*, 19 June 1997.
47 Queensland Whistleblower Action Group, *Mr Goss Are you Serious? Critical Analysis of the Queensland Whistleblower Protection Bill*, November 1994.
48 Senator Faulkner's Committee reported on ABC Radio News, 6.00pm 12 June 1997.
49 *Courier Mail*, 15 May 1997, p. 5.

Part 2: Whistleblowing – The Lived Experience: Introduction
1 As I write Tom Dusevic has just published his *Death in a Small Town*. It is a piece that makes you angry and sad at the same time. It tells the story of a Temora (NSW) teacher, Matthew McDermott, who was the subject of teenage girls' spitefulness. He was charged on allegations that he had touched them. A similar case to Kelson and McKernan, but with a terrible ending. Cast adrift by a nervous and over-reacting bureaucracy, McDermott hung himself.

Chapter 3: Radioactive Whistleblowing – Philip Nitschke
1 P. Nitschke to author, 10 February 1998.
2 The medical profession is only now starting to embrace this issue. See J. Lennane & W. De Maria, 'The Downside of Whistleblowing', *The Medical Journal of Australia*, No. 7, 5 October 1998, p.351.
3 See M. Griffiths, *Aboriginal Affairs: A Short History* (Kangaroo Press, Kenthurst, 1995) p. 100. The Gurindji people were given title on 11 May 1986.
4 P. Nitschke to author, 6 July 1997.
5 M.Reed to [indecipherable], 17 December 1976.
6 P. Nitschke to author, 6 July 1997.
7 Senate Committee of Privileges, 55th Report, June 1995, p. 7.
8 ABC National News, 7.00 pm, 24 March 1993.
9 Ibid. See also *Bulletin*, 29 March 1993, p. 54.
10 P. Nitschke to author, 24 December 1997.
11 RDH Media Release, 24 March 1993. See also *Northern Territory News*, 25 March 1993, p. 6.
12 RDH Safety Plan Briefing Session Notice, 24 March 1993.
13 *Northern Territory News*, 1 April 1993, p. 6.
14 *Northern Territory News*, 1 April 1993, p. 6.
15 *Sunday Territorian*, 4 April 1993.
16 Joint Media Release, 15 April 1993.
17 *Sunday Territorian*, 4 April 1993. See also *Northern Territory News*, 17 April 1993, p. 5.
18 *Sunday Territorian*, 18 April 1993.
19 Senate Committee of Privileges, op. cit., p. 11.
20 Media Release, The Hon. Mike Reed MLA, Health and Community Services Minister, 20 July 1993.

21 Ibid. See also *Northern Territory News*, 22 July 1993.
22 Senate Committee of Privileges, op. cit., p. 4.
23 Ibid, pp. 12–3, 43.
24 Ibid, p. 3.
25 Ibid, pp. 1, 3.
26 *Northern Territory News*, Editorial, 10 September 1993, p. 10.
27 *Northern Territory News*, 13 September 1993, p. 2.
28 *Northern Territory News*, 14 September 1993, p. 3.
29 P. Nitschke to author, 24 December 1997.
30 T. Pawsey to author, 22 May 1998
31 Ibid
32 Ibid, pp. 1–2.
33 Ibid, p.2.
34 Ibid.
35 Ibid, p. 3.
36 Ibid.
37 Ibid.
38 Ibid, p.4.
39 Ibid.
40 *Northern Territory News*, 28 September 1993, p. 3.
41 Ibid, 30 September 1993, p. 17.
42 Sister X Complaint. Date withheld to preserve her anonymity.
43 P. Nitschke to author, 24 December 1997.
44 Ibid.
45 Australian Medical Association, Northern Territory Branch, *Terms of Reference*, 7 October 1993.
46 Report by Chairperson, Central Promotions Appeal Board, 8 October 1993.
47 Senate Committee of Privileges, op cit. p. 18.
48 Independent AMA Review of the Dispute at the Royal Darwin Hospital, Part A, Terms of Reference 1–6 & 8, 26 October 1993, (The Arnold Report).
49 Arnold Report, op. cit.
50 R. Smith, 'Whistleblowing: A Curse on Ineffective Organisations', *British Medical Journal*, 305, 1992, pp. 1308–9.
51 Arnold Report, p. 4, point 1c.
52 Ibid, p. 5, point 1ee.
53 Ibid, p. 5, point 1ff.
54 Ibid, point 1gg.
55 Ibid, p. 6.
56 Ibid, p. 11.
57 Senate Committee of Privileges, op. cit., p. 18–20.
58 *Northern Territory News*, 8 November 1993.
59 *Northern Territory News*, 26 November 1993, p. 1.
60 *Northern Territory News*, Editorial, 1 December 1993, p. 10.
61 P. Nitschke to author, 24 December 1997.
62 Dr Alan Walker to Dr Ray Anderson, 18 January 1994.

Chapter 4: Vetting the Vet – The David Obendorf Story
1 D. Obendorf to author, 10 March 1997.
2 Author to D. Obendorf, 9 April 1997.
3 D. Obendorf to author, 15 April 1997.
4 Ibid.

5 This strain, thought to have come from New Guinea, was first detected on a Cairns farm in October 1995. A three year quarantine was started soon after, and was lifted on 23 August 1998. See *Australian*, 21 August 1998, p. 2.
6 *Sydney Morning Herald*, 1 November 1995, p. 1. Pilchard fishing was banned in South Australia in October 1998 after the discovery of a herpes-type virus. See *Weekend Australia*, 7–8 November 1998, p.9.
7 *Australian*, 20 June 1997, p. 4.
8 *Australian*, 2 April 1997, p. 15.
9 Charles El-Hage 'Tale of a Sick Cow and a Dying Lab', letter to the editor.
10 *Courier-Mail*, 30 June, 4 July 1994.
11 *Sydney Morning Herald*, 1 November 1995, p. 1.
12 S.Woinarski, letter to the editor, *Launceston Examiner*, 10 August 1996.
13 D. Obendorf to author, 21 October 1997.
14 D. Obendorf, 'Reaction/Retaliation by the Employer'.
15 D. Obendorf to author, 15 April 1997.
16 Joint SPSFT/Departmental Review of the Animal Health Laboratory Personnel Issues, 18 October 1995, pp. 13–4.
17 D. Obendorf to author, 15 April 1997.
18 Ibid.
19 Joint SPSFT/Departmental Review of the Animal Health Laboratory Personnel Issues, p. 14.
20 D. Obendorf to author, 15 April 1997.
21 R. Burton (Eugene Alexander and Associates) to Secretary, Department of Primary Industries and Fisheries, 4 November 1995.
22 D. Obendorf to author, 15 April 1997.
23 S. Balcombe (DPIF Secretary) to Greg Vines (General Secretary State Public Services Federation of Tasmania), 15 April 1994, p. 1.
24 Ibid, p.2.
25 Memorandum to All Animal Health Laboratory Staff and All Animal Health Field Branch Staff from S. Balcombe, 10 August 1994.
26 R. Burton (Eugene Alexander and Associates) to Secretary, Department of Primary Industries and Fisheries, 4 November 1995, point 28.
27 *Bulletin*, 26 December 1995–2 January 1996, p. 22.
28 Fifty DPIF signatories to S. Balcombe, 22 March 1995.
29 Tasmanian Legislative Assembly, 4 May 1995, uncorrected proofs. See also *Launceston Examiner*, 5 May 1995, p. 41.
30 *Bulletin*, 26 December 1995–2 January 1996, p. 22.
31 See W. De Maria, 'Whistleblowing and Unions: From Public Promise to Private Betrayal', paper presented to Public Sector Union Conference, Hobart, 16 May 1994.
32 K. Grey [CPSU Industrial Officer] to K. Evans, Acting Secretary, DPIF, 26 April 1996 (sent early May 1996).
33 Ibid, p.5.
34 R. Burton (Eugene Alexander and Associates) to Secretary, Department of Primary Industries and Fisheries, 4 November 1995, point 40.
35 See *Launceston Examiner*, 18 April, 6 May, 14 August, 19 August, 23 August 1996.
36 See *Launceston Examiner*, 16 September 1996; *Hobart Mercury*, 20, 27 September 1996; *Sunday Tasmanian*, 8 September 1996.
37 Bill Bonde, Minister for Primary Industry and Fisheries to D. Obendorf, 18 September 1996.
38 *Bulletin*, 26 December 1995–2 January 1996, p. 22.
39 D. Obendorf to author, 15 April 1997.

40 R. Green, *Battle for the Franklin* (Fontana, Sydney, 1981), p. 9.
41 *Sunday Tasmanian*, 14 January 1996.
42 Ibid. See also *Launceston Examiner*, 2 February 1996, p. 22.
43 D. Obendorf to author, 15 April 1997.
44 D. Obendorf to K. Evans, 13 April 1997.
45 *Courier-Mail*, 19 August 1997, p. 6.

Chapter 5: Religious Dissenter – Peter Cameron and the Heresy Trial

1 P. Cameron, *Fundamentalism and Freedom* (Doubleday, Sydney, 1995), p. 57.
2 P. Cameron, *Heretic* (Doubleday, Sydney, 1994), p. xi.
3 Ibid, p. 21.
4 Ibid, p. 25.
5 These books are: *Necessary Heresies* (UNSW Press, Kensington, 1993); *Heretic*, op. cit., and *Fundamentalism and Freedom*, op. cit. For James Murray's review of *Fundamentalism and Freedom* see *Australian*, 3 July 1995, p. 15. For Michael McGirr's review of *Necessary Heresies* see *Australian Book Review*, August 1993, pp. 6–7. For Sandra Murray's review of *Heretic* see *Canberra Times*, 24 September 1994, C11. After these books Cameron wrote an exposé of the male culture at St Andrew's College. See P. Cameron, *Finishing School for Blokes* (Allen & Unwin, Sydney, 1997). For further comment on this issue see 'Campus Battlelines: Clash of the Sexes', *Sydney Morning Herald*, 20 February 1993, p. 37.
6 H. McKay, Foreword, *Heretic*, op. cit., p. x.
7 For theological dimensions to Cameron's heresy trial see discussions in Cameron's books as well as Presbyterian Church of Australia, General Assembly, *Transcripts*, 1993. See also P. Hastie, 'The Bible and Truth in a Doubting Age', *Sydney Morning Herald*, 12 July 1993, p. 17, and various contributions to the New South Wales *Presbyterian Review*.
8 P. Cameron, *Heretic*, op. cit., p. 1.
9 Ibid, p. 1.
10 Ibid, p. 4.
11 Ibid, pp. 16–7. Pharisaism is the strict observance of religious rituals without the necessary piety and humility.
12 See S. Emilson, *A Whiff of Heresy: Samuel Angus and the Presbyterian Church in New South Wales* (UNSW Press, Kensington, 1991), pp. 3–4, and A. Dougan, *A Backward Glance at the Angus Affair* (Wentworth Books, Sydney, 1971), p. 3. See also *Canberra Times*, 21 March 1993, p. 4.
13 Schisms continue to be played out in front of this backdrop. In 1998 theological investigations were under way into three Presbyterian churches in Melbourne. Keith Bell, the Presbyterian Moderator, is on record as describing the three churches (known as the 'Fellowship') as 'evil' and 'a cancer in our midst'.
14 P. Cameron, *Heretic*, op. cit., p. 38.
15 Ibid, p. 54.
16 *Presbyterian Review*, No. 5, 1993, p. 2.
17 P. Cameron, *Heretic*, op. cit., p. 55.
18 Cameron seems to have picked up this minor theme. See *Heretic*, op. cit., pp. 59–61, 101–2, 146.
19 *Canberra Times*, 21 March 1993, p. 3.
20 Ibid, p. 57.
21 *Presbyterian Review*, No. 5, 1993, p. 2.
22 P. Cameron, *Heretic*, op. cit., p. 96.
23 Ibid, p. 67.
24 P. Cameron to author, 17 February 1997.
25 P. Cameron, *Fundamentalism and Freedom*, op. cit., p. 59.

26 *Presbyterian Review*, No. 5, 1992, p. 2.
27 P. Cameron, *Heretic*, op. cit., pp. 69–70.
28 Ibid, p. 111.
29 P. Cameron to author, 17 February 1997.
30 P. Cameron, *Heretic*, op. cit., p. 111.
31 Ibid, p. 140.
32 *Presbyterian Review*, No. 5, 1992, p. 2.
33 Ibid.
34 Ibid, No. 1, 1993.
35 P. Cameron, *Heretic*, op. cit., p. 184.
36 *Weekend Australian*, 20 March 1993, p. 6.
37 Letters to the Editor, *Sydney Morning Herald*, 25 March 1993, p. 10.
38 Ibid.
39 Ibid.
40 *Australian*, 1 July 1993, p. 3; P. Cameron, *Heretic*, op, cit. A report in the *Australian* had the vote at 141 to 107. See *Australian*, 2 July 1993, p. 4.
41 *Australian*, 17–8 July 1993, p. 18.
42 Ibid, p. 210. See also *Sydney Morning Herald*, 2 August 1994, p. 5.
43 P. Cameron, *Heretic*, op. cit.
44 *Sydney Morning Herald*, 20 January 1996, p. 11.
45 I am indebted to the Jesuit scholar Michael McGirr for this information on Steiner. See M. McGirr, 'No Churchyard Bully' *Australian Book Review*, August 1993, p. 6.
46 D. Crawford, 'Hey mister can we have our church back'? *Presbyterian Review*, No. 3, 1994, p. 3.

Chapter 6: Academic Dissenters – On Being Unfree in Free Spaces

1 *Argus* (Melbourne), 5 October 1950, quoted in Judith Armstrong, *The Christesen Romance* (Melbourne University Press, Carlton, 1996), p. 71.
2 K. Sawyer, *A Whistleblower's Tale*, no date, p. 2.
3 *Australian* 21 January 1997, p. 1.
4 In an uncontradicted report it was stated that Australia's thirty six vice-chancellors are on pay packages that range from $250,000 to $495,000. See 'State of the Uni' Special Report, *Australian*, 28 September 1998. See also *Courier Mail*, 22 August 1998, p.3.
5 For useful recent books on this subject see: L.Levine, *The Opening of the American Mind* (Beacon Press, New York, 1996); D. Damrosch, *We Scholars: Changing the Culture of the University* (Harvard University Press, Harvard, 1995); W. Readings, *The University in Ruins* (Harvard University Press, Harvard, 1996); A. Bloom, *The Closing of the Americam Mind: How Higher Education Has Failed Democracy and Impoverished the Souls of Today's Students* (Simon and Schuster, New York, 1987) and F. Crowley, *Degrees Galore: Australia's Academic Teller Machines*, published on Internet 26 September 1997. The ex-academic Frank Campbell's fiery review of Crowley's book should also be consulted. See *Australian*, 25 January 1999.
6 See Gavin Moodie, 'These are a Few of My Favourite Things', *Australian Higher Education Supplement*, 15 October 1997, p. 42.
7 Brian Martin from the University of Wollongong has done most of the work on intellectual dissent in Australia to date. See for example: B. Martin, 'Nuclear Suppression', *Science and Public Policy*, Vol. 13, No. 6, December 1986, pp. 312–20; B. Martin, C. Ann Baker, C. Manwell & C. Pugh (eds), *Intellectual Suppression: Australian Case Histories, Analyses and Responses* (Angus & Robertson, Sydney, 1986); B. Martin, 'Critics of Pesticides: Whistleblowing or Suppression of Dissent?', *Philosophy and Social Action*, Vol. 22, No. 3,

July–September 1996, pp. 33–55; B.Martin, *Suppression Stories* (Fund for Intellectual Dissent, University of Wollongong, 1997).
8 *Australian*, 11 October 1995, p. 11. See *Bailey v ANU* (1995), EOC Para 92–744.
9 *Courier-Mail*, 4 March 1995, p. 1.
10 *Bulletin*, 12 July 1994, p. 27.
11 *Courier-Mail*, 16 August 1994, p. 7; 17 August 1994, p. 18.
12 W. De Maria, 'Swinging from a Clean Rope: The Destruction of Academic Whistleblowers in the Age of Administrative Correctness', paper presented to the Second International Bullying Conference, St Johns College, University of Queensland, 5–6 July 1996, pp. 1–3.
13 *Australian*, 31 January 1996, p. 4.
14 *Courier Mail*, 27 November 1997, p. 5.
15 See *Australian Higher Education Supplement*, 3 September 1997, p. 39.
16 See *Australian Higher Education Supplement*, 22 October 1997, p. 38.
17 *Australian Higher Education Supplement*, 1 October 1997, p. 48.
18 *Australian Higher Education Supplement*, 30 July 1997.
19 Fay Gayle's evidence to Standing Committee on Government Agencies, Perth, 22 April 1996.
20 Hazel Rowley, 'Universities are Losing on Points', *Australian*, 15 December 1996, p. 13.
21 The Peter Jesser case was presented to the Senate Select Committee on Public Interest Whistleblowing (henceforth SSCPIW) and the Senate Select Committee on Unresolved Whistleblower Cases (henceforth SSCUWC). The abbreviated case documented here is derived from the evidence presented in Volume 1: Submission to SSCPIW and Volume 6: Mr Peter Jesser, Submission to SSCUWC. SSCUWC's findings on Jesser are to be found in *The Public Interest Revisited* (Senate Printing Unit, Canberra, 1995), pp. 96–103.
22 D. Ralston's statement to SSCUWC, Vol. 6, undated.
23 C. Littler to A. Hede, 3 April 1991. SSCUWC, Vol. 6.
24 SSCUWC, Vol. 6, statement by Peter Jesser, 23 January 1995, Point 10.
25 T. J. Ledwidge to P.Jesser, 9 December 1991, quoted in SSCPIW, Vol. 1, Point 13.
26 SSCUWC, Vol. 6, statement by Peter Jesser, Point 14.
27 Ibid, Point 19.
28 SSCPIW, Vol. 1, Point 22.
29 Jesser's Annual Planning and Feedback Report, 17 February 1991, in SSCUWC, Vol. 6.
30 SSCPIW op. cit., Point 62.
31 Ibid, Points 50, 51.
32 K. Goodwin to Director, Personnel, 2 December 1993, SSCUWC, Vol. 6.
33 Ibid.
34 SSCUWC, statement by Peter Jesser, Vol. 6, Point 48.
35 Ibid, point 70.
36 *The Public Interest Revisited*, op. cit., p. 100.
37 Ibid.
38 SSCUWC, Vol. 6, pp. 1–27.
39 Ibid, p. 3.
40 Ibid, pp. 4–5.
41 Ibid, p. 9.
42 G. Edmondson to Vice-Chancellor, 29 April 1992. See SSCUWC, Vol. 6.
43 Professor Craig Littler's Confidential Submission, in SSCUWC, Vol. 6, p. 4.
44 Ibid, p. 3.
45 *The Public Interest Revisited*, op. cit., pp. 102–3.
46 K. Sawyer, Submission to SSCPIW, Vol. 2, Submission 32, 1993, p. 1.
47 K. Sawyer, *A Whistleblower Tale*, p. 2.

48 *Age*, 21 June 1993, p5.
49 K. Sawyer, Submission to SSCUWC, Vol. 7, p. 2. See also *Campus Review*, 24–30 June 1993, p. 3.
50 K. Sawyer, *A Whistleblower Tale*, op. cit., p. 2.
51 Ibid.
52 K. Sawyer to author, 25 January 1998.
53 Ibid.
54 K. Sawyer, *A Whistleblower Tale*, op. cit., p. 2.
55 Ibid, p. 3.
56 Ibid, p. 4.
57 Ibid.
58 K. Sawyer to author, 9 August 1997.
59 63. Vice Chancellor's press statement, 4 June 1993. See also *Campus Review*, 24–30 June 1993, p. 3.
60 SSCUWC, op. cit., p. 124.
61 K. Sawyer, *A Whistleblower Tale*, op. cit., p. 5.
62 K. Sawyer, *A Whistleblower Tale*, op. cit., p. 5. See also K. Sawyer, Submission to SSCUWC, Vol. 7, p. 2.
63 SSCUWC, *The Public Interest Revisited*, p. 122.
64 SSCUWC, op. cit.p. 124.
65 For commentary on the Official Visitor scheme as it applies to universities (for there are official visitors to jails too). See Sader, 'The University Visitor: Visitorial Precedence and Procedure in Australia', *Tasmanian University Law Review*, Vol. 7, No. 2.
66 SSCUWC, op. cit., p. 122.
67 SSCUWC, Vol. 7, p. 3.
68 *Campus News*, February 1994.
69 K. Sawyer to author, 1 March 1998.
70 K. Sawyer, Submission to SSCUWC, Vol. 7, p. 2.
71 SSCUWC, Vol. 7, p. 3.
72 K. Sawyer to author, 4 February 1998.
73 Ibid. See also SSCUWC, op. cit., p. 123.
74 SSCUWC, Vol. 7, p. 3.
75 *Weekend Australian*, 28–9 October 1995.
76 Senate Committee Inquiry, *Report to the Senate of the University of Western Australia*, December 1996, p. 5; cf *West Australian*, 11 and 12 March 1996.
77 *Weekend Australian*, 28–9 October 1995.
78 *Australian*, Editorial, 30 October 1995. For UWA's rebuttal of this claim see *Australian* (letters) 31 November 1995.
79 Bowdler's comments are reported in Standing Committee on Public Administration (SCPA), *Fourth Report on its Inquiry into The Events Surrounding the Denial of Tenure to the Late Dr David Rindos by the University of Western Australia*, 4 December 1997, p. 8.
80 Ibid, p. 12.
81 Ibid.
82 Letter from Bowdler released to *West Australian*, 9 March 1996, p. 4.
83 SCPA Report, op. cit., p. 13.
84 'Process Used to Deny Tenure', downloaded from *Rindos/UWA* Internet Site, 10 January 1996.
85 Ibid.
86 SCPA Report, op. cit., p. 16.
87 Ibid, p. 17.
88 Ibid.

89 Ibid, p. 15.
90 *Weekend Australian*, 28–9 October 1995. See also Senate Committee Inquiry, op. cit., p. 33.
91 *Australian*, 21 May 1996, p. 27.
92 Letter quoted in ibid.
93 For a recent controversy on this subject, see Helen Garner, *The First Stone* (Picador, Sydney, 1995) and the rejoinders in Jenna Mead (ed.), *Bodyjamming* (Random House, Sydney, 1997).
94 See Associate Professor Bob Reece's letter, *Australian*, 31 November 1995.
95 SCPA Report, op. cit., p. 34.
96 Ibid, p. 20.
97 D. Clyde and S. D. Hotop to Vice-Chancellor Gayle, 31 March 1992, p. 3. See also Senate Committee of Inquiry, op. cit., p. 35.
98 Ibid, p. 36.
99 *Australian*, 21 May 1996, p. 27. There are references to Bowdler being 'disciplined' in 1992 and put under 'close scrutiny'. See *Australian*, 6 March 1996; *West Australian*, 15 March 1995, p. 10.
100 *West Australian*, 15 March 1996, p. 10; Senate Committee of Inquiry, op. cit., p. 36.
101 Senate Committee of Inquiry, op. cit., p. 12.
102 *Weekend Australian* 28–9 October 1996.
103 See Ted Steele's letter to the editor, *Weekend Australian*, 18–9 January 1997, p. 22.
104 'Process used to Deny Tenure', op. cit.
105 Dr Mike Partis's evidence to Standing Committee on Government Agencies, 31 May 1996, p. 97.
106 Ibid, p. 98.
107 Senate Committee Report, op. cit., p. 37.
108 'Process Used to Deny Tenure', op. cit., See also Partis's evidence to SCGA, 31 May 1996, p. 90.
109 *West Australian*, 9 March 1996, p. 4.
110 SCGA transcript of evidence, p.74.
111 'Process Used to Deny Tenure', op cit.
112 See evidence of Brenda Robbins to the Standing Committee on Government Agencies, 31 May 1996, p. 17. This view was officially confirmed at a subsequent meeting. The brevity of their formal deliberations was remarked on by the Standing Committee (SCPA Report, op. cit., p. 41).
113 See SCGA, *Transcript of Evidence*, 9 September 1996, pp. 4–5.
114 Ibid, pp. 17, 19.
115 Statement of Hon. Kim Chance, SCGA, 19 July 1996, p. 17.
116 Senate Committee of Inquiry, op cit. p. 38.
117 See evidence of Professor Alan Robson, ibid, 31 May 1996, p. 70, and evidence of Sally Zanetic, UWA's Director of Human Resources, 19 July 1996, pp. 3–4.
118 Vice-Chancellor Gayle's evidence to SCGA, 8 July 1996, p. 33.
119 Ibid, p. 39.
120 SCGA, op. cit., *Transcript of Evidence*, 22 April 1996, p. 4.
121 *West Australian*, 15 March 1996, p. 12.
122 SCPA Report, op, cit. p. 51. The Committee relied heavily on the High Court cases *Kioa v West* (1985) 159 *CLR* 550 and *Ainsworth v Criminal Justice Commission* (1991–1992) 175 *CLR* 564 for its analysis and conclusions here.
123 Senate Committee of Inquiry, op. cit., p. 40.
124 'The Aftermath', downloaded from the Rindos/UWA Internet Site, 10 January 1997.

125 Parliamentary Commissioner for Administrative Investigations, Western Australia, *Annual Report*, 1996, p. 71.
126 Senate Committee of Inquiry, op. cit., p. 37.
127 Ibid, p.20. It is unclear whether this earlier destruction of documents was in breach of the preservation policy of the Western Australian Public Records Office.
128 'Process Used to Deny Tenure', op. cit.
129 *Australian*, 22 May 1996.
130 *Australian*, 21 February 1996.
131 Notes on Senate Committee of Inquiry, December 1996, point 3.
132 *West Australian*, 15 March 1996, p. 12.
133 Ibid, 15 March 1996, p. 10.
134 Ibid, 15 March 1996, p. 12.
135 Ibid. See also Western Australian Legislative Council, *Hansard*, 14 December 1995, pp. 13192, 13203.
136 SCGA, *Transcript of Evidence*, 22 April 1996, p. 3. The question of whether the NTEU had withdrawn its support to Rindos was raised by the Hon. Tom Stephens at the parliamentary inquiry. Rindos appeared to hedge around the question, which suggests that he may have been dumped by the union. See *Transcript of Evidence*, 22 April 1996, p. 24.
137 *West Australian*, 18 April 1996, p. 34.
138 Ibid.
139 SCGA, op. cit., *Transcript of Evidence*, 22 April 1996, p. 1.
140 *West Australian*, 24 April 1996, p. 7.
141 Ibid, p. 2.
142 *Australian*, 6 March 1996. The UWA Senate Inquiry tabled an 'interim report' on 13 January 1997, nine months after it was promised. See *West Australian*, 2 March 1996, p. 34.
143 The Senate Committee of Inquiry, op. cit., p. 2.
144 *West Australian*, 11 May 1996, p. 44. See also *West Australian*, 8 May 1996, p. 3.
145 *Australian*, 15 May 1996.
146 *Campus Review*, 15–21 May 1996.
147 *West Australian*, 7 June 1996, p. 35.
148 *West Australian*, 2 March 1996, p. 34.
149 Document headed 'The Review Committee wishes to amend their report and include the following…', no date. See also *Sunday Times*, 9 March 1997, p. 33.'.
150 Pro-forma letter from Archaeology Action Group to UWA Senators, no date. See also University response from Registrar to Archaeology Action Group, 26 March 1997.
151 *Australian*, 7 May 1997, p. 37. The 1996 Committee held more than 20 meetings, took evidence from 17 witnesses and written submissions from 60 others.
152 SCPA Report, op. cit., p. 57.
153 *Australian Higher Education Supplement*, 10 December 1997, p. 29.
154 *Australian Higher Education Supplement*, 11 December 1996, p. 25.
155 David Goddard to author, 2 January 1997.

Chapter 7: Whistleblowing on Eight Cents a Day – Disclosure at the ABC

1 *Sydney Morning Herald*, 4 October 1996. Millard's other awards include the Michael Daly Science and Technology Award (1993), Peter Grieve National Award for Medical Journalism (1991), the Sir Donald Anderson National Award for Aviation Journalism (1986), and the New South Wales Free Speech Committee's Dean Wells Award (1996).
2 Penny Chapman to John Millard, 28 September 1995.
3 J. Millard to author, 17 September 1997.
4 ABC Supplementary Submission to Senate Select Committee on ABC Management and Operations, 11 January 1995.

5 Senate Select Committee on ABC Management and Operations, *Hansard*, 3 February 1995, pp. 803–4.
6 H. Arendt, *Eichman in Jerusalem: A Report on the Banality of Evil* (Penguin, New York, 1994).
7 J. Millard, *The Maltreatment of a Diseased ABC and of Those Who Exposed the Symptoms*, 27 October 1995, p. 1.
8 Co-production is not an easy term to understand. In referring to shows such as the *Homeshow* an acting director of television has said:
By way of information, *Everybody, Holiday* and the *Homeshow* are not co-productions. The ABC pays a licence fee, for which (sic) this acquires transmission rights. We [ABC TV] activate the editorial control by insisting that an ABC executive producer is assigned to the project. [co-production is] any project which involves the ABC and another party where the ABC contribution is more than straight cash … [where ABC] contribution is purely cash then ABC TV regards this as a purchase not as a co-production. K. Williams [Acting Director of Television] to Quentin Dempster [ABC Staff Elected Director] 8 July 1993, pp. 4, 7.
9 *Report of ABC Inquiry into Allegations Concerning the Employment of John Millard by Phillip Coleman, Barrister at Law, 27 June 1996*. (Henceforth called the Coleman Report), pp. 14–5.
10 Ibid.
11 Ibid, p. 23.
12 Millard's allegations are in J. Millard, 'ABC Co-Production Compromise', 3 March 1993, p. 4. This 12-page document was appended to Quentin Dempster's letter to David Hill, 8 June 1993. For the ABC management's rebuttal, see K. Williams to Q. Dempster, op cit, p. 15.
13 J. Millard, 'Outsourcing the ABC's Independence', Submission to Mansfield Inquiry, 30 August 1996, p. 6. Bob Mansfield, a successful and high-profile businessman, was appointed by the Howard Government in 1996 to review the functions of the ABC.
14 Ibid, pp. 5–6.
15 J. Millard to author, 17 September 1997.
16 J. Millard, 'The Maltreatment of a Diseased ABC', op. cit., p. 1.
17 Coleman Report, op. cit., p. 16. Hill was the only relevant ABC person to refuse to cooperate with Coleman's inquiry. See ibid p. 11. Coleman uses an incorrect christian name with respect to Hill.
18 K. Williams to Q. Dempster, op cit, 16 pp.
19 ABC Media Release, 18 September 1994.
20 J. Millard, 'The Maltreatment of a Diseased ABC, op. cit., p. 3.
21 J. Millard to author, 17 September 1997.
22 ABC Media Release, 27 September 1994.
23 J. Millard, *The Maltreatment of a Diseased ABC*, op. cit., p. 4.
24 Federal Industrial Committee, Media Entertainment and Arts Alliance, *Recommendation to ABC Members*, 28 September 1994.
25 K. Williams to Q. Dempster, op. cit.
26 J. Millard, *The Maltreatment of a Diseased ABC*, p. 17.
27 Ibid, p. 18.
28 Millard notes that at the Senate Inquiry the Deputy Managing Director of the ABC, Peter Lidbetter responded to a question on disclosure protection by saying, 'My personal view is it [whistleblower protection] is not necessary [at the ABC], See J. Millard, *The Maltreatment of a Diseased ABC*', op. cit., p. 5.
29 Senate Select Committee on ABC Operations and Management, op. cit., p. 35.
30 Coleman Report, op. cit., pp. 18–9.

31 For a suffering-centred definition of whistleblowing see W. De Maria, *Unshielding the Shadow Culture*, Queensland Whistleblower Study, The University of Queensland, Result Release One, April 1994, p. 3.
32 J. Millard, *The Maltreatment of a Diseased ABC*, op.cit, p.1.
33 J. Millard, Submission to ABC Palmer Inquiry, 27 September 1994, p.20.
34 Coleman Report, op. cit., p. 38. Scowcroft does not deny this action. See Coleman Report, transcript of evidence, p.622.
35 Ibid, p. 42.
36 Ibid.
37 Ibid, p. 63.
38 Ibid, p. 66
39 Ibid, p. 67.
40 Ibid.
41 Ibid.
42 Ibid, p. 68.
43 Ibid.
44 Ibid.
45 Ibid, p. 61.
46 J. Millard, 'The Maltreatment of a Diseased ABC' op. cit., p. 3.
47 Coleman Report, op. cit., pp. 74–5.
48 Ibid, p. 85.
49 Ibid, p. 89.
50 Ibid, p. 92.
51 Ibid, p. 90.
52 Ibid, p. 90.
53 Ibid, p. 93.
54 Ibid, p. 96.
55 Ibid.
56 Ibid, p. 109.
57 Concerned Staff to Brian Johns, August 1996, p. 2.
58 Ibid, p. 1.
59 *Australian*, 18 December 1996, p. 5.
60 W. DeMaria, *Whistleblowing and Unions: From Public Promise to Private Betrayal*, paper presented to Public Sector Union Conference, Hobart, 16 May 1994.
61 See for example: 'Outsourcing of ABC Programs Encourages a 'Blind-Eye Culture', *Sydney Morning Herald*, 21 February 1997, p.21 (Opinion); 'Editorial Iintegrity Isn't As Easy as ABC', *Australian*, 19 July 1996, p.11.
62 See for example the stories by Errol Simper in the *Australian*, Brian Toohey in the *Sun Herald*, and Peter Wilmoth in the *Sunday Age*.
63 Millard's handwritten notes to author on top of copy of his letters to Brian Johns, 6 August, 4 September 1996.
64 J. Millard to author, 17 September 1997.
65 This e-mail to Millard designated e-mail 1.
66 This e-mail to Millard designated e-mail 2.
67 This e-mail to Millard designated e-mail 3.
68 ABC Staffer to Manager Efficiency Review & Audit, 7 August 1996.
69 Anonymous letter to J. Millard, 7 August 1996.
70 P. Williams to J. Millard, 1 October 1996.
71 J. Millard to P. Williams, 15 October 1996.
72 Ibid.
73 *Australian*, 18 December 1996, p. 5.

74 Johns' statement quoted in J. Millard to J. Hutchinson, 14 December 1996.
75 J. Millard to J. Hutchinson, 14 December 1996.
76 *Courier Mail*, 25 Jnuary 1997.
77 David Salter, executive producer of Media Watch, *Australian*, 6 August 1997, p. 2 (letters). Millard unsuccessfully applied for the position of *Media Watch* presenter when Stuart Littlemore resigned.
78 *Australian*, 13 November 1997, p. 1.
79 Ibid.
80 See *Australian*, 4 March 1998, p12 (letters); 18 August 1998, p.3;

Chapter 8: 'Shreddergate' – The Battles of Kevin Lindeberg

1 K. Lindeberg to author, 5 February 1998.
2 Queensland Cabinet Office Submission, 31 July 1995, Document 11, Senate Select Committee on Unresolved Whistleblower Cases (henceforth SSCUWC).
3 One typical situation occurred on 15 May1998 when juveniles rioted, injured staff and took a hostage. The drama ended with the arrival of the dog squad. See *Courier Mail*, 16 May 1998, p.8.
4 CJC submission to SSCUWC, 15 August 1995, p. 2.
5 SSCUWC, *The Public Interest Revisited*, October 1995, Senate Printing Unit, Canberra, p. 64.
6 *Weekend Independent*, 12–25 July 1996, p. 1.
7 SSUWC, Attachment 3, Volume 3, *Shredding of the Heiner Documents*, Kevin Lindeberg's submission to SSCUWC is however a document that purports to summarise the complaints and identifies the complainants.
8 This is the most familiar title of a department that seems to change its name every three years after a state election! For reference to the complaints that went to Pettigrew see SSCUWC, Attachment 1, p. 9.
9 Coyne's submission to SSCUWC, Attachment 3. Nine years after the allegations were made they were re-exposed in a series of front cover stories in the *Courier Mail*. Coyne, as far as I know, has never denied that he ordered the chaining up of children. He claimed that the children were uncontrollable and restraint was the only option available to him. See *Courier Mail*, 30 May 1998, p.1.
10 SSCUWC, Vol. 3, Attachment 2.
11 Attorney-General's statement, 21 February 1995. Pettigrew set the Heiner Inquiry up with the authority of his Minister, the National Party's Beryce Nelson. In 1996 she claimed she gave Pettigrew the go-ahead on the advice of Ken O'Shea the Crown Solicitor. O'Shea has denied that he or his officers gave such advice. See *Courier Mail*, 29 August 1996, p. 4.
12 Coyne's submission to SSCUWC, Vol. 3, p. 3.
13 Ibid, p. 5.
14 Ibid, p. 6.
15 Ibid.
16 SSCUWC, Vol. 3, Attachment 4.
17 The Crown Solicitor's advice and discussion of it is to be found in *Report to the Honourable the Premier of Queensland and the Queensland Cabinet of an Investigation into Allegations by MrKevin Lindeberg and Allegations by MrGordon Harris and Mr John Reynolds*, by A. Morris QC and E. Howard, Barrister, no date, presented September 1996. Henceforth referred to as the Morris-Howard Report.
18 Ibid, p. 43.
19 Ibid, p. 45.
20 Ibid.
21 Ibid, p. 44.

22 Ibid.
23 SSCUWC, Vol. 3, Attachment 14.
24 Morris–Howard Report, Op. cit., p. 48.
25 Ibid, p. 49.
26 Attorney-General's statement, 21 February 1995, p. 16.
27 Morris–Howard Report, op. cit., p. 52.
28 Ibid, p. 53.
29 SSCUWC, Vol. 23, pp. 11–2.
30 Ibid, Attachment 15.
31 Ibid, p.5.
32 Ibid, p.11.
33 *Gold Coast Weekend Bulletin*, 12–3 October 1997, p. 6.
34 SSCUWC, *The Public Interest Revisited*, op. cit., p. 54. Tait only referred to 'questions' being raised during the Heiner Inquiry about the 'possibility' of legal action.
35 Ibid, p. 12.
36 Morris–Howard Report, op. cit., p. 62.
37 SSCUWC, op. cit., p. 12.
38 Ibid. See also Howard-Morris Report, op. cit., p. 65.
39 Ibid, p. 66.
40 Exhibit 1, Submission 0394, Connolly-Ryan Judicial Review into the Effectiveness of the Criminal Justice Commission.
41 Ibid, exhibit 5.
42 K. Lindeberg to author, 5 February 1998.
43 Coyne's submission to SSCUWC, Vol. 3, p. 14.
44 SSCUWC, op. cit., p. 12.
45 Morris-Howard Report, op. cit., p. 75.
46 Ibid, pp. 60–1.
47 Morris-Howard Report, pp. 75–6.
48 Coyne's submission to SSCUWC, Vol. 3, p. 13.
49 Ibid, pp. 11–2.
50 Ibid, p. 15.
51 Ibid.
52 Morris–Howard Report, op. cit., p. 76.
53 K. Lindeberg, submission to SSCUWC, op. cit., Vol. 3, p. 68.
54 Ibid, p. 69.
55 Ibid, p. 70.
56 K. Lindeberg, submission to SSCUWC. op. cit., p. 73.
57 D. O'Neil's submission to SSCUWC op. cit., p. 10.
58 Ibid.
59 K. Lindeberg, submission to SSCUWC, op. cit., p. 38.
60 The letter is in SSCUWC, op. cit., Attachment 19.
61 Ibid, Attachment 19a.
62 Ibid, Attachment 20.
63 SSCUWC, *The Public Interest Revisted*, op. cit., pp. 54–5.
64 Ibid.
65 Ibid, p. 71.
66 Ibid, p. 72.
67 Ibid.
68 Ibid.
69 CJC submission to SSCUWC, February 1995, pp. 33–4.
70 K. Lindeberg's submission to the SSCUWC, op, cit, p. 72.

71 Newnham's comments are reported in *Weekend Independent*, May 1997, p. 8. It summarises Newnham's evidence to the Connolly–Ryan Inquiry into the CJC. See also *Gold Coast Bulletin*, 20 May 1997, p. 9.
72 SSCUWC, op. cit., Vol. 3, p. 25.
73 K. Lindeberg, submission-in-reply, SSCUWC, op. cit., p. 8.
74 Ibid.
75 K. Lindeberg, submission to SSCUWC, op. cit., p. 29.
76 Ibid.
77 Ibid, p. 5.
78 SSCUWC, *The Public Interest Revisited*, op. cit., p. 59.
79 Ibid.
80 Ibid.
81 Ibid.
82 R. v Rogerson and Ors, *ALJR*, Vol. 66, 1992, p. 503.
83 Evidence of Michael Barnes, CJC's Chief Complaints Officer, to SSCUWC, 29 May 1995, *Transcript of Evidence*, p. 655.
84 Senate Select Committee on Public Interest Whistleblowing, *Official Hansard Report*, Brisbane, 8 March 1994. This committee was established by resolution of Senate on 2 September 1993, after Senator Jocelyn Newman had raised for public debate the experiences of some people known to her, after they made public interest disclosures. Newman became the chair of the committee. The other members were: Senator Calvert (Liberal Party Tasmania), Senator Denman (ALP Tasmania), Senator Chamarette (Greens Western Australia), and Senator Murphy (ALP Tasmania).
85 Senator J. Newman to Premier Goss, 1 September 1994.
86 Premier Goss to Senator Newman, 10 October 1994.
87 Ibid, p. 3.
88 The Report of the Fitzgeral Commission of Inquiry into official misconduct in Queensland was presented in 1989. In response the Goss Government enacted the *Criminal Justice Act 1989*, thus setting up the Criminal Justice Commission.
89 Premier Goss to Senator Newman, op. cit.
90 Senate *Hansard*, 1 December 1994, p. 3628.
91 Ibid, p. 3630.
92 Under the amended terms of reference SSCUWC's inquiry was not restricted to the Queensland whistleblower cases, but was to include any 'unresolved' matter referred to, and considered by the former Senate Committee on Public Interest Whistleblowing. See *The Public Interest Revisited*, op. cit., p. 22
93 For these comments see the *Australian* (editorial), 17 December 1998, p.14.
94 SSCUWC was established by resolution of Senate on 1 December 1994. The membership was: Senator Shayne Murphy (ALP Tasmania), Senator John Herron (Liberal Party Queensland), Senator Eric Abetz (Liberal Party Tasmania), Senator Christabel Chamarette, Greens Western Australia), Senator Kay Denman (ALP Tasmania), Senator Sandy Macdonald (National party New South Wales), Senator John Woodley (Australian Democrats Queensland).
95 SSCUWC, *The Public Interest Revisted*, October 1995, p. 3.
96 Sometime later, explaining why he did not make himself available for re-appointment as CJC Director, O'Regan said that to do so would 'constitute cruel and unusual punishment'. Behind the half joke was O'Regan's frustration at being in charge of the biggest no-win agency in Queensland, and from his point of view, the most scrutinised. His appointment in December 1998 to chair the Australian Cricket Board's inquiry into the Indian betting scandal will have him observing some hot deliveries rather than being expected to hook them.
97 Clerk of the Senate to Senator S. Murphy, 6 December 1994.

98 SSCUWC, *The Public Interest Revisited*, op. cit., p. 63.
99 Statement by Senator Shayne Murphy, 26 October 1995.
100 Ibid, p. 3.
101 This view of Murphy supervising damage control for the Labor Party is apparently no longer tenable. In mid-December 1998 there was speculation that Murphy was disillusioned with the party and was thinking of becoming an independent. See *Australian*, 16 December 1998, p.4; *Australian*, (editorial) 17 December 1998, p. 14.
102 Morris-Howard Report, op. cit., p. 131.
103 Ibid, p. 141.
104 Ibid.
105 Ibid, p. 205.
106 *Australian*, 11 October 1996, p. 5.
107 *Gold Coast Weekend Bulletin*, 12–3 October 1996, p. 6.
108 Ibid.
109 *Courier Mail*, 12 June 1997, p. 10.
110 *Courier Mail*, 12 October 1996.
111 *Gold Coast Bulletin*, 20 May 1997, p. 9.
112 *Courier Mail*, 12 June 1997, p. 10.
113 Speech by Senator John Woodley, *Hansard*, 26 May 1997.
114 K. Lindeberg, Statement to Connolly-Ryan Judicial Review into the Effectiveness of the Criminal Justice Commission, 16 June 1997.
115 Parliament of Australia, The Senate Committee of Privileges, *Possible False or Misleading Evidence before the Senate Select Committee on Unresolved Whistleblower Cases*, 63rd Report, December 1996, p.1.
116 See *Courier Mail*, 30 May 1998, p.10.
117 There are now ten One nation members in the Queensland Parliament. Charles Rappolt, the member for Mulgrave, resigned on 4 November 1998, citing intimidation by the Murdoch press. He attempted suicide three days later.
118 *Courier Mail*, 26 August 1998, p.1.
119 Ibid.

Chapter 9: Up Against the NCA – The Mick Skrijel Affair

1 Bradford's comments came after Skrijel finished giving evidence to the Committee. See Joint Parliamentary Committee on the National Crime Authority (henceforth JPCNCA) *Third Evaluation of the NCA*, Official Hansard Report, Melbourne, 4 June 1997, NCA 734–5.
2 *Australian*, 4 April 1997, p. 7.
3 A useful summary to the beginning of 1997 has been done by Max Wallace in the *Alternative Law Journal*, February 1997. An extract is published in *The Whistle* (Newsletter of Whistleblowers Australia), May 1997, pp. 6–9.
4 Biographical information from *Mehmed Skrijel on the Scales of Justice*, Submission to JPCNCA, 5 November 1990. This document was originally lodged with the Victorian Court of Criminal Appeal for *Queen v Skrijel*, 18 April 1988.
5 Ibid, p. 3. See also D. Quick, *Report to Attorney-General and Minister for Justice with Respect to Dealings of the National Crime Authority with Mr Mehmed Skrijel and his Family*, 4 April 1994, pp. 1, 3, 5. The Quick Report is a primary source for the Skrijel case presented in this chapter. I have used the draft report which contains Skrijel's responses. Access to the final report was denied to the author by the NCA.
6 *Mehmed Skrijel on the Scales of Justice*, op. cit., p. 3.
7 Ibid.
8 M. Skrijel, *Crime, Justice and Mr Kerr*, Pamphlet, 1996.
9 *Mehmed Skrijel on the Scales of Justice*, op. cit., pp. 5–6.

10 Ibid, pp. 35–9.
11 Ibid, p. 22.
12 Ibid, pp. 48–9.
13 Ibid, p. 49.
14 Ibid, p. 50.
15 M. Skrijel, *Crime, Justice and Mr Kerr*, op. cit., See also *Australian*, 24 August 1988.
16 D. Berthelson and M. Skrijel, *Submission to the Joint Committee on the National Crime Authority*, 28 September 1990, p. 1.
17 *Mehmed Skrijel on the Scales of Justice*, op. cit., p. 55.
18 Ibid, p. 57.
19 D. Berthelson and M. Skrijel, *Submission to the Joint Committee on the National Crime Authority*, op. cit.
20 Hamilton *Spectator*, 15 November 1984. See also *Mehmed Skrijel on the Scales of Justice*, op. cit., p. 66.
21 Ibid, p. 65.
22 Ibid, pp. 67–73.
23 Ibid, p. 76, 83.
24 Ibid, pp. 89–96.
25 Incident cited in D. Berthelson to Mr Leckie, Acting Chairman NCA, 3 April 1990. Letter in Submission No. 19 to Joint Parliamentary Committee on the NCA.
26 D. Quick, op. cit., p. 6.
27 Ibid.
28 *Sunday Press*, 29 May 1988.
29 D. Quick, op. cit., p. 8.
30 D. Berthelson and M. Skrijel, op. cit., Enclosure 4, p. 34.
31 See for example J. Lennane, 'What Happens to Whistleblowers and Why', paper presented to the Criminal Justice Commission seminar, *Whistleblowers: Concerned Citizens or Disloyal Mates*, Brisbane, 23 November 1993; J. Lennane, 'Whistleblowing: A Health Issue', *British Medical Journal*, No. 307, 11 September 1993, pp. 667–70; W. De Maria & C. Jan, *Wounded Workers*, Queensland Whistleblower Study, Result Release Two, The University of Queensland, August 1994. One of the findings of the Commonwealth Ombudsman's report into the Australian Federal Police (*Professional Reporting and Internal Witness Protection in the Australian Federal Police: A Review of Practices and Procedures*, November 1997) was that psychiatrists were used inappropriately to deal AFP whistleblowers. See Finding on p. ii.
32 *Sunday Press*, 28 May 1988.
33 D. Berthelson and M. Skrijel, op. cit., Enclosure 4, p. 36.
34 Momentum for this really started in late 1988. See particularly D. Berthelson to Senator M. Tate, 6 September 1988. This letter was sent eventually to the Joint Committee on the National Crime Authority.
35 Senator M. Tate to Senator B. Teague, 28 December 1989.
36 See Enclosure 18 (plus commentary) of the Skrijel–Berthelson submission to the Joint Committee on the National Crime Authority, 4 October 1990.
37 Ibid.
38 D. Berthelson and M. Skrijel, op. cit., p. 9.
39 Australian Law Reform Commission, *Integrity: But Not By Trust Alone. AFP and NCA Disciplinary Systems*, (AGPS, Canberra, 1996) Report No. 82, p. 107.
40 *Sunday Age*, 12 September 1993, News 5.
41 Quick Report, op. cit., Point 1.2.3.
42 Ibid, p. 16.
43 Ibid, p. 16.
44 Ibid, p. 22.

45 Ibid, p. 11.
46 Ibid, p. 61.
47 Ibid, p. 67.
48 Ibid, p. 86.
49 Commonwealth of Australia, *Hansard*, 30 November 1995.
50 D. Quick, op. cit., p. 54.
51 D. Kerr, *Ministerial Statement*, House of Representatives, Canberra, 26 October 1995.
52 D. Quick, op. cit., p. 185.
53 M. Skrijel to JPCNCA, 17 April 1997.
54 JPCNCA, *Third Evaluation of NCA*, Transcript of evidence, op. cit., NCA 719.
55 Ibid, p.735.
56 John Elliott is a high profile businessman who, through a series of mergers, formed the powerful Elders IXL Group, and later the Fosters Brewing Group. From 1987 to 1990 he was president of the Liberal Party of Australia. In 1990 a NCA investigation of his business practices started. He spent millions of dollars defending himself. For Elliott's no-holds-barred view of the NCA see his evidence to JPCNCA, transcript of evidence, Thursday 12 June 1997, Melbourne.
57 JPCNCA, *Third Evaluation Report*, op. cit., ch. 6.
58 Australian Law Reform Commission, *Issues Paper 16*, November 1995, p.147.
59 Australian Law Reform Commission, Draft Recommendation Paper, *Complaints Against the AFP and NCA, July 1996*.
60 Ibid, pp. 21–2.
61 Australian Law Reform Commission, *Integrity But Not By Trust Alone:: AFP and NCA Complaints and Discipliniary Systems*, AGPS, Canberra, 1996, Report No. 82.
62 W. De Maria, *Unshielding the Shadow Culture*, Queensland Whistleblower Study, Result Release One, The University of Queensland, April 1994, pp. 21–34.
63 See for example Australian Law Reform Commission, *Complaints Against Police* (AGPS, Canberra, 1975); Australian Law Reform Commission, *Complaints Against Police, Supplementary Report* (AGPS, Canberra, 1978); P. Arantz, *A Collusion of Power* (Dunedoo, 1993); Australian Law Reform Commission, *Under the Spotlight: Complaints Against the NCA and AFP*, Issues Paper 16, November 1995; Australian Law Reform Commission, *Complaints Against the NCA and AFP*, Draft Recommendations Paper, July 1996; Australian Law Reform Commission, Report No. 82, *Integrity But Not By Trust Alone. AFP and NCA Complaints and Disciplinary Systems*, AGPS, Canberra, 1996. Commonwealth Ombudsman, *Own Motion Investigation into Improper Accessing of Information by Members of the Australian Federal Police*, 20 September 1995; Royal Commission into the New South Wales Police Force, *Interim Report*, February 1996; Parliament of Western Australia, Select Committee on the Western Australian Police Service, *Interim Report*, Terms of Reference 3, June 1996; Independent Commission Against Corruption, *Investigations into the Relationships Between Police and Criminals–First Report*, February 1994; New South Wales Ombudsman, *Police Internal Investigations. Poor Quality Investigations into Complaints of Police Mis-Conduct*, January 1995; Criminal Justice Commission, *Submission to the Police Services Review Committee*, July 1996; Commonwealth Ombudsman, Submission to the Attorney-General's Department, Response to the Australian Law Reform Commission Report No. 82, 'Integrity: But Not By trust Alone', March 1997; Commonwealth Ombudsman, *Professional Reporting and Internal Witness Protection in the Australian Federal Police: A Review of Practices and Procedures*, November 1997. See also W. De Maria, 'Hero, or just a dobber'? *Age*, 21 April 1997, p. 11; W. De Maria, 'Whistleblowers Left With No More Than a Squeak', *Age*, 5 January 1998, News Extra, p. 9.
64 Personal communication from M. Skrijel to W. De Maria, 23 January 1998.

Chapter 10: The Dark Side of Whistleblowing – War at the Memorial

1 *Kelson v Forward in her capacity as Director of the Merit Protection and Review Agency*, No. ACT AG 86 of 1994. Finn, J. Canberra, 6 October 1995, henceforth Finn decision. See also 'War at the Memorial', *Australian*, 11 October 1995, p. 27.
2 B. Kelson to author, 10 May 1997. Kelson was Assistant Secretary, The Department of Prime Minister and Cabinet 1973–77. From there he became the General Manager of the Australian National Gallery until 1982 when he was appointed Assistant Director of AWM. He served in that capacity for eight years and became the Memorial's Director in 1990. After nearly five years in that position he retired. He is now a museum consultant and photographer.
3 *Australian*, 11 October 1995, p. 27. McKernan was born and educated in Melbourne. He entered the Society of Jesus (Jesuits) in 1963 and took vows in February 1965. He left the Jesuits in 1970 (for reflections on this period see G. Windsor, *Heaven Where the Bachelors Sit*, (Queensland University Press, Brisbane, 1996). McKernan has a first class honours degree in history as well as the 1971 University Medal from the Australian National University. He has written a number of highly acclaimed histories. From 1975–81 he was on academic staff at the University of New South Wales.
4 Johns acted pursuant to s.56 of the Merit Protection (Australian Government Employees) Act 1984.
5 Gary Johns, Assistant Minister for Industrial Relations and Minister assisting the Prime Minister for Public Service Matters to Ann Forward, MPRA, 16 August 1994. See also Finn decision, op. cit., p. 6.
6 Ibid.
7 *Courier Mail*, 14 October 1995, p. 31.
8 Finn decision, op. cit., p. 6.
9 M. McKernan, *Summary*, March 1996, p. 1.
10 *Australian*, 11 October 1995, p. 27; *Courier Mail*, 14 October 1995, p. 31, House Commonwealth of Australia, House of Representatives, *Hansard*, 28 September 1995.
11 Ibid.
12 The question was raised by the then Shadow Minister for public administration John Moore.
13 Ibid.
14 Finn decision, op. cit., pp. 60–1.
15 *Australian*, 11 October 1995, p. 27.
16 M. McKernan, *Fatally Flawed*, Chapter 4, 1996, p. 5 (unpub. ms.).
17 Ibid, p. 6.
18 Among other notable achievements Kelson conceived and designed the Tomb of the Unknown Soldier. See *Australian*, 11 October 1995, p. 27.
19 B. Kelson to author, 10 May 1997.
20 C. Blesing to B. Kelson, 17 August 1994. See also M. McKernan, *Fatally Flawed*, op. cit., ch. 4, p. 1.
21 Public Service Commission, *Guidelines on Official conduct of Commonwealth Public Servants*, 7 March 1995, Point 1.3.
22 MPRA argued in the Federal Court that this was not the first time that this definition had been used. See Finn decision, op. cit., p. 31. They cited the use of the definition by Carmel Niland, the former President of the NSW Anti-Discrimination Board in her, *Report of the Independent Inquiry into Matters Relating to the Resignation of the former Minister for Police and Minister for Emergency Services, Terence Griffiths MP*. This case became something of a *cause celebre* for high-placed feminists.
23 Public Service Commissioner to B. Kelson, 11 November 1994.
24 M. McKernan, *Summary*, op. cit., p. 2.

25 Finn decision, op. cit., p. 31.
26 J. Waterford, 'War at the Memorial', *Eureka Street*, Vol. 5, No. 9, November 1995, p. 18.
27 M. McKernan, *Summary*, op. cit., p. 2.
28 *Courier Mail*, 14 October 1995, p. 31.
29 AWM–MPRA Staff Memo, 18 August 1994. Trawling for evidence is more common than people think. For example three years before MPRA threw its nets into the Australian War Memorial, the Queensland Criminal Justice Commission (CJC) investigated a complaint that a Brisbane TAFE teacher was improperly inducing students to buy hydroponic systems from his wife's company. Sworn evidence to the Connolly–Ryan Inquiry into the CJC showed that the CJC sent out questionnaires to 700 students and clients of the hydroponic business, asking for details of commercial transactions. Potential customers of the business were warned off by the CJC pending the outcome of the investigation. The end result, according to the evidence was a failed marriage between the TAFE teacher and his wife, a bankrupt business with losses of $3.5 million, and a suicide attempt. No one was committed for trial as a result of the CJC inquiry. See *Australian*, 13 June 1997, p. 4.
30 M. McKernan, *Fatally Flawed*, ch. 4, p. 8.
31 Finn decision, op. cit., p. 10.
32 M. McKernan, *Summary*, op. cit., p. 1.
33 Finn decision, op. cit., p. 20.
34 Ibid.
35 Ibid, p. 43.
36 Ibid, p. 25.
37 M. McKernan, *Fatally Flawed*, op. cit., ch. 4, p. 9.
38 Ibid, p. 10.
39 Ibid.
40 Ibid, p. 11.
41 *Australian*, 11 October 1995, editorial.
42 M. McKernan, *Fatally Flawed*, op. cit., ch. 4, p. 12.
43 Ibid.
44 Ibid, p. 15.
45 *Australian*, 11 October 1995, p. 27.
46 M. McKernan, *Fatally Flawed*, op. cit., ch. 5, p. 2.
47 Ibid, ch. 6, pp. 1–2.
48 *Sunday Age*, 20 November 1994, pp. 1, 4. See also *Canberra Times*, 5 December 1994.
49 *Sunday Age*, 11 December 1995, p.3.
50 M. McKernan, *Fatally Flawed*, op.cit, ch. 6, p. 3.
51 Ibid.
52 M. McKernan, *Summary*, op. cit., p. 3. See also Kelson to author, 17 April 1997. General Peter Gration was Chief of the General Staff 1984–87. His last military posting was Chief of Defence Force, which he left in 1993. For the next two years he was Chairman of the strife-ridden Civil Aviation Authority. He became Chairman of Transfield Defence Systems in 1994.
53 M. McKernan, *Fatally Flawed*, op. cit., ch. 6, p. 5.
54 *Australian*, 11 October 1995, p. 27.
55 *Courier Mail*, October 1995.
56 Finn decision, op. cit., p. 51.
57 Beryl Beaurepaire to Brendon Kelson, 27 August 1994.
58 M. McKernan to author, 12 March 1997.
59 J. Waterford, op. cit., p. 18. Flemming had a distinguished RAAF career. He flew in the first RAAF sortie of the Korean War. He was also the first RAAF officer to fly at twice the speed of sound. He became AWM Director in 1982. After five years in that position he went

to the private sector, as Managing Director of Mirage Enterprises. He was dismissed by the Governor-General on the advice of the government and became involved with Amway.
60 *Canberra Times*, 5 December 1994.
61 Ibid.
62 Ibid.
63 *Australian* (editorial) 2 April 1997.
64 *House Magazine*, 25 October 1995, p. 23.
65 Ibid, 12 November 1995, p. 44.
66 J. Waterford, op. cit., p. 21.
67 *Courier Mail*, 14 October 1995, p. 31.
68 B.Kelson to author, 17 April 1997 (phone call).
69 Ibid.
70 Ibid.
71 *Brendon Kelson v David Syme & Co. Pty Ltd*, [1998] SCACT 60 (3 July 1998) p. 23.
72 Ibid.
73 Ibid, point 73.

Part 3: The State Control of Dissent: Introduction
1 See for example D. Collinson, 'Strategies of Resistance. Power, Knowledge and Subjectivity in the Workplace', in J. Jermier, D. Knights & W. Nord (eds) *Resistance and Power in Organisations* (RKP, London, 1994), p. 26.
2 Work in this area includes the Jermier, Knight and Nord book mentioned above. They note the additional works of S. Clegg, *Frameworks of Power* (Sage, London, 1989); C. Grey, 'A Helping Hand: Self Discipline and Management Control', paper delivered at the 11th Annual Labour Process Conference, Blackpool, March 1993; G. Sewell & B. Wilkinson, 'Someone to Watch Over Me: Surveillance, Discipline and the Just-In-Time Labour Process', *Sociology*, Vol. 26, No. 2, 1992, pp. 271–89.

Chapter 11: The Shut-eyed Sentries – Notes on Incompetence and Unlawfulness
1 The relationship between the government and the CJC being then at an all-time low. See *Australian*, 23 December 1996, p. 5.
2 *Courier Mail*, 12 October 1996, p. 6. The *Criminal Justice Legislation Act* amended the *Commissions of Inquiry Act 1950* and the *Criminal Justice Act 1989*.
3 *Australian*, 14 March 1997, p. 2.
4 *Australian*, 5 March 1997, p. 3.
5 *Courier Mail*, 11 September 1997, p. 1.
6 *Weekend Australian*, 7–8 December 1996, p. 1. The inquiry was established in response to persistent allegations of child sex by diplomats and the subsequent cover-up of those acts by senior officers in the Department of Foreign Affairs and Trade, Austrade and Ausaid. See also *Age*, 7 December 1996.
7 Gaisford, A.J. v Hunt, C.T. anor, Federal Court of Australia, 6 December 1996, (Beaumont, O'Lachlan and Lenhane J.J.) decision 1072/96, unreported.
8 *Age*, 7 December 1996.
9 *Australian*, 6 August 1997, p. 1.
10 Brandy v Human Rights and Equal Opportunities Commission, *Commonwealth Law Reports*, Vol 183, p. 245. See also S. Ratnapaia, 'Brandy's Case' *University of Queensland Law Journal*, Vol. 18, No. 2, 1995 p. 233; E. Henderson, 'Brandy' *Sydney Law Review*, Vol. 17, No. 4, December 1995, pp. 581–90; *Australian* 8 September 1995, p. 15; *Weekend Australian*, 2–3 March 1996, p. 40. Brandy, an aboriginal Australian, was found to have racially abused a white colleague, John Bell. Both men were employed at the time by the Aboriginal and Torres Strait

Islander Commission (ATSIC). An ATSIC investigation substantiated Bell's claim and ordered Brandy to apologise, pay $2,500 damages for pain, humiliation, distress and loss of personal dignity suffered by Bell. ATSIC determined to take disciplinary action against Brandy, and to also apologise to Bell and to pay him $10,000. Brandy appealed and won on the basis of the High Court determining that a critical part of the HREOC Act was unconstitutional and as such HREOC rulings are legally unenforceable because it is only a tribunal and therefore without judicial power. Bell has recently claimed that the inability of HREOC to enforce its own decisions has destroyed his life. See *Australian*, 17 September 1997, p. 4. He has never received the apologies nor the money. In the wake of the High Court case Bell accepted a redundancy package. He has been on the dole ever since.

11 See Bernard Lane's views 'Rights Fighter', *Australian*, 8 September 1995, p. 15.
12 *Australian*, 15 September 1997, p. 1.
13 Readers are advised to consult the writings of author and jouralist, Evan Whitton, who is a major critic of the adversarial model.
14 *Weekend Australian*, 20–1 September 1997, p. 9.
15 Bligh & Ors v State of Queensland *Equal Opportunity Commission Reports*, 1996, 92/848.
16 *Courier Mail*, 16 November 1996. There was talk of the court challenge being abandoned because of lack of funds. See *Courier Mail*, 19 December 1996, p. 4. Compensation was finally paid in 1998.
17 *Weekend Australian*, 9–10 August 1997, p. 11.
18 *Age*, 7 December 1996.
19 Ibid.
20 *Australian*, 28 January 1998, p. 6.
21 *Australian*, editorial, 28 January 1998.
22 *Australian*, 11 December 1996, p. 3.
23 *Australian*, 28 January 1998, p. 3.
24 *Australian*, 4 December 1996, p. 3.
25 Ibid.
26 Ibid.
27 Ibid.
28 Australian Law Reform Commission, *Integrity: But not by Trust Alone. AFP and NCA Complaints and Discipliniary Systems*, Report No. 82 (AGPS, Canberra, 1996).
29 Ibid, pp. 74–9.
30 Ibid, p. 81.
31 Ibid, p. 79. I believe that the Ombudsman was equally robust in denying this charge.
32 D. Pearce, 'The Commonwealth Ombudsman: The Right Office in the Wrong Place', Speech given at Public Law Conference, 31 August 1996.
33 Australian Law Reform Commission, Report No. 82, op cit. p. 85.
34 Ibid, p. 77.
35 Ibid, p. 80.
36 Commonwealth Ombudsman, *Professional Reporting and Internal Witness Protection in the Australian Federal Police: A Review of Practices and Procedures*, November 1997.
37 Ibid, p. ii.
38 *Australian*, 27 June 1997.
39 Ibid.
40 Dr Ronald Conway from the University of Newcastle conducted the study on behalf of the Australian Society for the Study of Intellectual Disability and the National Council on Intellectual Disability. See the *Age*, 28 September 1996.
41 R. Conway, 'Abuse and Adults with Intellectual Disability Living in Residential Services', conference paper delivered in Hobart 27 September 1996.

42 Criminal Justice Commission, *Report of an Inquiry Conducteed by the Honourable DG Stewart into Allegations of Misconduct at the Basil Stafford Centre* (Brisbane, 1995).
43 *Courier Mail*, 10 July 1997, p. 9.

Chapter 12: Whistleblowing Laws – The State Responds

1 Much of this chapter is taken or drawn from W. De Maria, 'Whistleblowing', *Alternative Law Journal*, Vol. 20, No. 6, December 1995, pp. 270–81.
2 For example, letter from Wayne Goss to Senator Jocelyn Newman, Chair of the Senate Select Committee on Public Interest Whistleblowing, 10 October 1994.
3 Yolanda Brookes, Shire Clerk of the Whitsunday Shire Council, made disclosures to the CJC in the course of its investigation of corruption complaints against some Shire Councillors, It was alleged that steps were then taken to terminate her appointment. The CJC applied to the Supreme Court for an injunction restraining the Council from dismissing Ms Brookes. An interim injunction was granted but a substantive injunction refused because the judge found an inconsistency between the Queensland Act (which prohibited reprisals) and the Qld Government Officers Award (Cth) invalidating that section of the Qld Act. On appeal Judges Fitzgerald, Pincus and McPherson found no inconsistency (decision of 28 July 1994, 27 and 31 of 1994). A final 2–1 determination on 8 March 1995 stayed the sacking permanently. Ms Brookes had been on stress leave for five months.
4 EARC, *Report on Protection of Whistleblowers*, Qld Govt Printer, Brisbane, 1991, Appendix A.
5 PEARC, *Whistleblowers Protection*, Qld Govt Printer, Brisbane, 1992.
6 The structure of the Bill was criticised heavily at a seminar sponsored by the Royal Institute of public Administration (NSW Branch) held on 1 September 1992. See paper presented by Margaret Allars, 'Whistleblowing: Where Public Interest Pars Company with Government Interest'. See also John Goldring, 'Blowing the *Whistle*', *Alternative Law Journal*, Vol. 17, No. 6, 1992, p. 299.
7 Parliament of NSW, *Report of the Legislative Committee on the Whistleblowers Protection Bill (No. 2) 1992*, June 1993, p. 1.
8 See for example Whistleblowers Australia (NSW Branch) submission to Committee on the Office of the Ombudsman and the Police Integrity Commission, Review of the Protected Disclosures Act 1994. The Committee published its report in September 1996.
9 Royal Commission into the New South Wales Police Service, *Interim Report*, February 1996; *Final Reports*, Vols 1–3, May 1997.
10 See P.Freeman and B. Garnett, *Internal Witness Research Project*, NSW Police Service, December 1996. See also *Australian*, 2 July 1997, p. 5. See also C. Smith, 'Development and Management of the Internal Witness Support Program in the NSW Police Service, Royal Institute of Public Administration, *Investigation Techniques Conference*, 25–6 June 1996.
11 NSW Legislative Assembly, Joint Parliamentary Committee on the Office of the Ombudsman and the Police Intgrity Commission, *Review of the NSW Protected Disclosures Act*, 1996. See also Independent Commission Against Corruption (ICAC), *Monitoring the Impact of the Protected Disclosures Act 1994, Phase 1: Survey of NSW Public Sector Agencies and Local Councils*, Interim Report, April 1996; ICAC, *Monitoring the Impact of the Protected Disclosures Act 1994, Phase 2: Interviews with NSW Public Sector Agencies and Local Councils*, Interim Report Summary, June 1996.
12 Recent Commonwealth reports recommending public interest disclosure protection include: Review of Commonwealth Criminal Law, *Final Report*, December 1991, Parliamentary paper 371 of 91; Senate Standing Committee on Finance and Public Administration, *Review of the Office of the Commonwealth Ombudsman*, December 1991, Parliamentary Paper 519 of 1992; Senate Standing Committee on Finance and Public Administration, *Report on the Management and Operations of the Department of Foreign*

Affairs and Trade, December 1992, Parliamentary Paper 525 of 1992; House of Representatives Standing Committee on Banking, Finance and Pubic Administration, *Focussing on Fraud*, Report of the Inquiry into Fraud on the Commonwealth, November 1993, Parliamentary Paper 235 of 1993; Senate Select Committee on Public Interest Whistleblowing, *In the Public Interest*, August 1994, Parliamentary Paper 148/1994; Senate Select Committee on Unresolved Whistleblower Cases, *The Public Interest Revisited*, October 1995, Parliamentary Paper No. 344/1995; House of Representatives, *Report of the Senate Select Committee on Public Interest Whistleblowing: Government Response*, 26 October 1995; Australian Law Reform Commission, *Integrity, But Not By Trust Alone*, Report No. 82, November 1996; Commonwealth Ombudsman, *Annual Report*, 1996–97; Joint Committee on Public Accounts, *An Advisory Report on the Public Service Bill 1997 and the Public Employment (Consequential and Transitional) Amendment Bill 1997*, Report No. 353, September 1997; Commonwealth Ombudsman, *Professional Reporting and Internal Witness Protection in the Australian Federal Police: A Review of Practices and Procedures*, November 1997

13 For a critique of the Kerr Proposal see W. De Maria, 'Fridges That Don't Freeze ... Planes That Don't Fly ... Laws That Don't work. Design Failure in Australia's Whistleblower Legislation', paper presented to Second National Whistleblower Conference, Melbourne, 28–30 June 1996.

14 Western Australia Commission on Government Report, 1996.

15 Tasmanian Legislative Assembly, *Hansard* 30 April 1997.

16 Catherine Murphy to Alwyn Johnson, 7 November 1996.

17 See Public Service and Merit Protection Commission, *The Public Service Act 1997: Accountability in a Devolved Management Framework*, Canberra, 16 May 1997.

18 See Department of Defence, *Circular memorandum*, No. 48/97, 24 July 1997.

19 Ibid, p. 2.

20 M. Goode, 'A Guide to tthe South Australian Whistleblower Protection Act 1993', Australian Institute of Administrative Law, *Newsletter*, No. 13, 1993, p. 14.

21 Senate Select Committee on Public Interest Whistleblowing, Public Hearings, Canberra, 25 March 1994, pp. 1232, 1258–9.

22 For the obstructive strategies used by management see W. De Maria, *Unshielding the Shadow Culture*, Queensland Whistleblower Study, Result Release One, The University of Queensland, April 1994, pp. 23–4. See W. De Maria & C. Jan, 'Behold the Shut-eyed Sentry – Whistleblower Perspectives on Government Failure to Correct Wrongdoing' in *Crime, Law and Social Change*, Vol. 24, No. 2, 1996, pp. 151–66.

23 W. De Maria, *Unshielding the Shadow Culture*, op. cit., pp. 25, 33.

24 NSW Committee on the Office of the Ombudsman and the Police Integrity Commission, *Review of the Protected Disclosures Act 1994*, September 1996, p. 142.

25 Public Interest Disclosure Bill 1997 (Tas), Part 2.

26 Whistleblowers Protection Bill 1991 (Cth), clause 10; Whistleblowers Protection Bill 1993 (Cth), Clause 9; Public Interest Disclosure Bill 1995 (Tas), Clause 6a; Austalian Law Reform Commission, *Integrity: But Not By Trust Alone. AFP and NCA Complaints and Discipliniary Procedures*, (AGPS, Canberra, 1996), ch. 6.

27 These are ALRC'S envisaged powers for its proposed National Integrity and Investigations Commission. The Commonwealth (1991, 1993) and Tasmanian (1995) Bills include similar powers. See ALRC, op. cit., p. 142.

28 This was the tenor of evidence before the Connolly–Ryan Inquiry into the CJC. See Ch. 11.

29 Public Interest Disclosure Bill 1995 (Tas) Clause 15 (1)(b)(ii).

30 Senate Select Committee on Public Interest Whistleblowing, op. cit.

31 Hon. D.G. Stewart, *Report of an Inquiry into Allegations of Official Misconduct at the Basil Stafford Centre*, Qld CJC, March 1995.

32 W. De Maria, *Unshielding the Shadow Culture*, op. cit., pp. 35–8; B. Grundy, 'Who Sets the New Agenda: The Turkey or the Chooks?', in S. Prasser, R. Wear & J. Nethercote (eds), *Corruption and Reform: The Fitzgerald Vision*, (University of Queensland Press, Brisbane, 1990), Section 4(f). It is uncertain whether such disclosures are protected under s.4.5 of the NZ Bill.
33 SSCUWC, op. cit., p. 25.
34 P. Finn, Evidence to the Senate Select Committee on Public Interest Whistleblowing, Canberra, 29.11.93, p. 61. Finn goes on to say that at the Commonwealth level the combined effect of the *Public Service Act* and the *Crimes Act* virtually makes it a criminal offence for public sector workers to tell us who occupies the room next to them.
35 Figure based on information prepared in October 1992 for the House of Representatives Standing committee on Legal and Constitutional Affairs inquiry into the protection of confidential information held by the Commonwealth.
36 Qld Law Reform Commission, *The Freedom of Information Act 1992 Review of Secrecy Provision Exemption*, Report No. 46, March 1994, Appendices C & E.
37 See Brookes case, referred to above.
38 Clauses 12(1)(a, b), *Public Interest Disclosure Bill 1997 (Tas)*.
39 W.De Maria and C.Jan, *Wounded Workers*, op.cit. p.45.
40 Ibid.
41 See clause 30 (1–5). The similar provisions in the Whistleblowers Protection Bill 1991 (Cth) are clauses 17 (2)(e) and 17 (3–5).
42 Ibid, clauses 30 (3, 5)
43 See J. Toohey, 'Managing the Stress Phenomenon at Work', paper presented to national Occupational Stress Conference, *Stress and Well-Being at Work*, Gold Coast, 16–7 June 1994, p. 16; A. Munton and N. Forster, 'Job Relocation: Stress and the Role of the Family', 4 (1), *Work and Stress*, 75–81; J. Brett, 'Job Transfer and Well-Being', (1982) 67, *Journal of Applied Psychology*, 450–63. There are numerous other articles on relocation stress.
44 For a discussion of the plight of Aboriginal whistleblowers, see R. Neill and D. Fagan, 'Whistling Up A Storm', *Weekend Australian Review*, 25 February 1995, pp. 1–2.
45 *In the Public Interest*, op. cit., p. xiii.

Chapter 13: Codes of Conduct – Moral Bondage in the Age of Anything Goes
1 See C. Amanpour, 'Tyranny of the Taliban', *Time*, 13 October 1997, p.50.
2 H. Armstrong, 'The Tricontinental Affair', in M. Considine & B. Costar (eds) *Trials in Power: Cain, Kirner and Victoria 1982–1992* (MUP, Melbourne, 1992). See also C. Kenny, *State of Denial* (Wakefield, Adelaide, 1993); A. Peachment, *Westminster Inc: A Survey of Three States* (Federation press, Sydney, 1995).
3 P. Finn, *Official Information*, Integrity in Government Project, Interim Project One, Australian National University, 1991; Electoral and Administrative review Commission, *Report on the Review of the Codes of Conduct for Public Officials*, Brisbane, 1992; K. McKonkey, G. Huon, & M. Frank, *Practical Ethics in the Police Service*, National Police Research Unit, Ethics and Policing, Study No. 3; Queensland Criminal Justice Commission, *Ethical Conduct and Discipline in the Queensland Police Service: The Views of Recruits, First Year Constables and Experienced Officers*, Brisbane, 1996.
4 M. Simmons, 'Born Again Business', *Weekend Australian Review*, 28–9 December 1996, p. 1.
5 Deakin University survey carried out by Greg Woods and reported in ibid.
6 NSW Legislative Council, Standing Committeee on parliamentary Privileges and Ethics, *Draft Code of Ethics*; J. Warhurst, 'Politicians and Redemption. The Catholic Church has proposed a Code of Ethics for Politicians', *Australian*, 6–7 January 1996.
7 *Queensland Public Sector Ethics Act 1994*.

8 *Weekend Australian*, 31 August 1996.
9 M. Benjamin & J. Curtis, *Ethics in Nursing*, (OUP, Sydney, 1992); A. Bates.'Law and Professional Ethics', *Law Letter* (Hobart), No. 70, September, 1994; R. Darvall-Stevens, 'Police Codes of Ethics in Australia', *Criminology Australia*, Vol. 6, No. 2, November, 1994; G. Turner, 'Journalistic Ethics in Australia', *Australian Journalism Review*, Vol. 16, No. 1, January–June 1994. M. Johnstone, 'The Scandalous Neglect of Mental Health Care Ethics', *Contemporary Nurse*, Vol. 4, No. 4, December, 1995.
10 *NSW Professional Standards Act (1994)*.
11 Charles Sturt University *Graduate Certificate in Professional and Applied Ethics*, Brochure, 1996.
12 On 11 December 1996 the *Charter of Budget Honesty Bill* was introduced into the House of Representatives. The Bill aims to ensure that governments are held accountable for their fiscal policirs. At the time of writing the Bill was before the Joint Committee of Public Accounts.
13 For example the West Australian Commissioner for Public Sector Standards was paid a salary in 1997 of $196, 851 to safeguard the integrity of the public sector, and to develop codes of conduct. Details taken from job description published in *Weekend Australian*, 18–9 January 1997.
14 Peter Wear's article in the *Courier Mail*, 12 August 1998.
15 *Australian*, 25 September 1997, p. 1.
16 This was a recommendation in the 21 page interim report from the Wood Royal Commission, issued in November 1996. See *Australian*, 13 November 1996, p. 1.
17 *Courier Mail*, 13 August 1996.
18 *Australian*, October 1996.
19 For a consideration how government-controlled mediation services are part of the expending state see W. De Maria, 'Social Work and Mediation: Hemlock in the Flavour of the Month, *Australian Social Work*, Vol. 45, No. 1, 1992, pp. 17–28.
20 K. Denhardt, *The Ethics of Public Service: Resolving Moral Dilemmas in Public Organisations* (Greenwood, New York), p. 1.
21 See for example the paper presented to the Australasian Political Studies Association Annual Conference in 1998 by Dr Ken Coghill, a former speaker of the Victorian Legislative Assembly. An article based on this paper was published in the *Australian*, 10 November 1998, p.13.
22 Ibid.
23 Electoral and Administrative Review Commission (EARC), *Report on the Review of Codes of Conduct for Public Officials* (Queensland Government Printer, Brisbane, 1992). p. vi.
24 EARC, op. cit., p. 20.
25 Time-Morgan Poll, April 1994.
26 AGP-McNair Poll, April 1994.
27 R. Alaba, 'An Obituary to the Career Service', paper presented to Annual Conference of royal Institute of Public Administration (Qld Branch), Brisbane, 14 November 1994. A recent study conducted by the Public Sector Research Unit at Curtin University found that SES members in Western Australia gave little regard to ethical codes when deciding on courses of action.
28 EARC, op. cit., p. ix.
29 ... and refusing to believe that this period finished in December 1989 when the Labor party took control.
30 A. v. Hayden, *ALJR*, Vol. 59, No. 2, 1985. pp. 6–36.

Selected Readings

This is an updated and edited version of a much larger bibliography on whistleblowing. The full version is available from the author.

Adler, J.N. and Daniels, M., 'Managing the Whistleblowing Employee', *The Labor Lawyer*, Vol. 8, Winter 1992, pp. 19–70

Alcorn, G., 'Whistleblowers: Doctor Fallout', *Time Australia*, 29 November 1993, pp. 54–55

Allars, M., 'Whistleblowing: Where Public Interest Parts Company with Government Interest', paper presented to Royal Institute of Public Administration Australia (NSW Division) seminar, 'Blowing the Whistle', Sydney, 1 September 1992

Anderson, P., 'Controlling and Managing the Risk of Whistleblower Reprisal', 'National Occupational Stress Conference', Brisbane, 1996

Aron, M.W., 'Whistleblowers, Insubordination, and Employee Rights of Free Speech', *Labor Law Journal*, Vol. 43, April 1992, pp. 211–20

Atkins, C.A., 'The Whistleblower Exception to the At-will Employment Doctrine: An Economic Analysis of Environmental Policy Enforcement', *Denver University Law Review*, Vol. 70, 1993, pp. 537–55

Australian Law Reform Commission, *Integrity, but Not By Trust Alone*, Report No. 82, November 1996

Australian Press Council, 'Submission to the New South Wales Parliament Legislation Committee on the Whistleblowers Protection Bill 1992 (No. 2)', *Australian Press Council News*, Vol. 5, No. 2, May 1993, p. 21

Baran, A., 'Federal Employment: The Civil Service Reform Act of 1978: Removing Incompetents and Protecting Whistle Blowers', *Wayne Law Review*, Vol. 26, 1979, pp. 97–118

Barnett, T.R., Cochran, D.S., Taylor, G.S., 'The Relationship between Internal Dissent Policies and Employee Whistleblowing: An Exploratory Study', paper presented to 50th annual meeting of the Academy of Management, San Francisco, 1990

Barnett, T.R., Cochran, D.S., Taylor, G.S., 'The Internal Disclosure Policies of Private-Sector Employers: An Initial Look at their Relationship to Employee Whistleblowing', *Journal of Business Ethics*, Vol. 12, No. 2, February 1993, pp. 127–136

Bedau, H., *Civil Disobedience: Theory and Practice*, (Pegasus, New York, 1969)

Bok, S., *Secrets: On the Ethics of Concealment and Revelation*, (Pantheon Books, New York, 1982)

Bok, S., 'Blowing the Whistle', in J. Fleishman (ed.), *Public Duties: The Moral Obligations of Government Officials*, (Harvard University Press, Cambridge, 1981), pp. 204–220

Bok, S., 'Whistleblowing and Professional Responsibility', *New York University Education Quarterly*, Vol. 10, Summer 1980, pp. 2–10

Bowman, J.S., Elliston, F.A., and Lockhart, P., *Professional Dissent: An Annotated Bibliography and Research Guide*, (Garland, New York, 1983)

Bowman, J.S., *Managerial Ethics: Whistleblowing in Organizations: An Annotated Bibliography and Resource Guide*, (Garland, New York, 1982)

Bowman, J.S., 'Whistle Blowing in the Public Sector: An Overview of the Issues', in Richter, W.W., Burke, F., and Doig, J.W. (eds.), *Combating Corruption/Encouraging Ethics: A Sourcebook for Public Service Ethics*, American Society for Public Administration, Washington DC., 1990

Brabeck, M., 'Ethical Characteristics of Whistle-blowers', *Journal of Research in Personality*, Vol. 18, No. 1, 1984, pp. 41–53

Bullock, J.R., 'The Pebble in the Shoe: Making the Case for the Government Employee', *Tennessee Law Review*, Vol. 60, Winter 1993, pp. 365–92

Caiden, G.E., Truelson, J.A., 'An Update on Strengthening the Protection of Whistleblowers', *Australian Journal of Public Administration*, Vol. 53, No. 4, December 1994, pp. 575–583

Callahan, E.S. and Collins, J.W., 'Employee Attitudes Toward Whistleblowing: Management and Public Policy Implications', *Journal of Business Ethics*, Vol. 11, No. 12, December 1992, pp. 939–948

Callahan, E.S. and Dworkin, T.M., 'Do Good and Get Rich: Financial Incentives for Whistleblowing and the False Claims Act', *Villanova Law Review*, Vol. 37, 1992, pp. 273–336

Clark, D., 'The Implementation of Whistleblower Protection Legislation: Problems and Prospects in the South Australian Case', paper presented to Criminal Justice Commission/Royal Institute of Public Administration (Queensland Division) seminar, 'Whistleblowers: Concerned Citizens or Disloyal Mates?', Brisbane, 23 November 1993

Clark, D., 'Whistleblowing: Theory and Practice', *Australian Institute of Administrative Law Newsletter*, No. 4, 1993, pp. 22–32

Clift, E., 'Women Whistleblowers: What They Say, The Price They Pay', *On the Issues*, Vol. 25, Winter 1992, pp. 18–21

Commonwealth of Australia, *In the Public Interest*, Report of the Senate Select Committee on Public Interest Whistleblowing, (Senate Printing Unit, Canberra, 1994)

Commonwealth of Australia, *The Public Interest Revisted*, Report of the Senate Select Committee on Unresolved Whistleblower Cases, (Senate Printing Unit, Canberra, 1995)

Coulter, J., 'Intellectual Suppression', paper presented to Tasmanian Council of Social Service Symposium, 'Information, Freedom, Democracy', Hobart, 21 November 1992

Cripps, Y., *Employees' Disclosures and the Public Interest: An Analysis of Prohibitions and Protections*, (University of Cambridge, 1982)

Cripps, Y., 'Disclosure in the Public Interest: The Predicament of the Public Sector Employee', *Public Law*, 1983, pp. 600–633

Cripps, Y., 'Protection from Adverse Treatment by Employers: A Review of the Position of Employees Who Disclose in the Belief that Disclosure is in the Public Interest', *Law Quarterly Review*, No. 101, October 1985, pp. 506–539

Cripps, Y., *The Legal Implications of Disclosure in the Public Interest: An Analysis of Prohibitions and Protections with Particular Reference to Employers and Employees*, (ESC Publishing, Oxford, 1986)

Dandekar, N., 'Contrasting Consequences: Bringing Charges of Sexual Harassment Compared with Other Cases of Whistleblowing', *Journal of Business Ethics*, Vol. 9, 1990, pp. 151–158

De Maria, W., 'Queensland Whistleblowing: Sterilising the Lone Crusader', *Australian Journal of Social Issues*, Vol. 27, No. 4, November 1992, pp. 248–261

De Maria, W., 'The Queensland Whistleblower: A Harassed Hero?', paper presented to United Scientists for Environmental Responsibility and Protection meeting, Brisbane, 16 March 1993

De Maria, W., 'Beyond the Harassed Hero: From Dissenting Individuals to Dissenting Cultures', paper presented to Whistleblowers Australia Conference, Canberra, 28 March 1993

De Maria, W., Whistleblower Bibliography, University of Queensland, 1993 (ongoing)

De Maria, W. and Keyes, T., 'Blaming the Circuit Breaker: Early Messages from the Queensland Whistleblower Study', paper presented to research seminar, Department of Social Work and Social Policy, University of Queensland, Brisbane, 4 June 1993

De Maria, W., 'Whistleblowing in the Queensland Public Service', paper presented to symposium, 'Social Responsibility in Science', Ecopolitics VII Conference, Griffith University, July 1993

De Maria, W., 'The Welfare Whistleblower: In Praise of Difficult People', paper presented to the 23rd National Conference of the Australian Association of Social Workers, Newcastle NSW, September 1993

De Maria, W., 'The Queensland Whistleblower: Chipping Away at the Ethical Enamel', paper presented to First National Conference, Australian Association for Applied and Professional Ethics, Adelaide, 23–24 April 1994

De Maria, W., 'Whistleblowing and Unions: From Public Promise to Private Betrayal', paper presented to Public Sector Union Conference, Hobart 16 May 1994

De Maria, W., 'Unshielding the Shadow Culture', Queensland Whistleblower Study, The University of Queensland, Result Release One, April 1994

De Maria, W., 'The Community Sector Whistleblower: Dismantling the Lone Crusader', paper presented to Third Human Services Conference, Tasmania Council of Social Service, 17 May 1994

De Maria, W., and Jan, C., 'Wounded Workers', Queensland Whistleblower Study, The University of Queensland, Result Release Two, August 1994

De Maria, W., 'Queensland Whistleblowers: Fugitives from Injustice', paper presented to Annual Conference of the Royal Institute of Public Administration (Queensland Branch), Brisbane, 14 October 1994

De Maria, W., 'Public Disclosure Laws in Australia and New Zealand: Who Are They Really Protecting?', *Alternative Law Journal*, Vol. 20, No. 6, 1995, pp. 270–281

De Maria, W., 'Quarantining Dissent: The Queensland Public Sector Ethics Movement', *Australian Journal of Public Administration*, December 1995

De Maria, W., 'The Stormbird Calls: Whistleblower Warnings in the Age of Corruption', paper presented to conference 'Whistleblowers: Protecting the Nation's Conscience', Melbourne University, 17 November 1995

De Maria, W., 'The Welfare Whistleblower: In Praise of Difficult People', *Australian Journal of Social Work*, Vol. 49, No. 3, 1996, pp. 15–24

De Maria, W. and Jan, C., 'Behold the Shut-Eyed Sentry: Whistleblower Perspectives on Government Failure to Correct Wrongdoing', *Crime, Law and Social Change*, Vol. 24, No. 22, 1996, pp. 151–166

De Maria, W., 'Swinging from a Clean Rope: The Destruction of Academic Whistleblowers in the Age of Administrative Correctiveness', paper presented to the Second International Bullying Conference, The University of Queensland, 5–6 July 1996

De Maria, W., 'Casualties of Conscience: Whistleblowing in Australia', paper presented to the Fifth International Conference of Public Sector Ethics, Hilton Hotel, Brisbane, 5–9 August, 1996

De Maria, W., 'Whistleblowing in the Commonwealth Public Sector', paper presented to 'Ethics in a Changing Environment', Commonwealth Directions Development Committee, Carlton Crest Hotel, Brisbane, 6 August 1996

De Maria, W., 'Fridges That Don't Freeze, Planes That Don't Fly, Laws That Don't Work: Design Failure in Whistleblower Protection', paper presented to Second National Whistleblowers Conference, 'From Whistleblowing to a Culture of Dissent', Melbourne, 29–30 June 1996

De Maria, W. and Jan, C., 'Eating Its Own: The Whistleblowers Organization in Vendetta Mode', *Australian Journal of Social Issues*, Vol. 32, No. 1, 1997, pp. 37–60

De Maria, W., 'The British Whistleblower Protection Bill: A Shield too Small?', *Crime, Law and Social Change*, Vol. 27, 1997, pp. 139–163

De Maria, W., 'Whistleblowers left with no more than a squeak', Melbourne *Age*, 31 January 1998

De Maria, W., 'Whistleblowing: The Great Betrayal', paper presented to 'Managing the Critical Issues of Fraud, Ethics, Accountability and Risk Management in the Public Sector', Sydney, 16–17 February 1998

De Maria, W. and Lennane, J., 'The Downside of Whistleblowing', *The Medical Journal of Australia*, Vol. 169, No. 7, 5 October 1998

De Maria, W., 'Information: The Vital Artery', *Courier-Mail*, 20 March 1999

De Maria, W., 'Revealing State Secrets', *Courier-Mail*, 12 April 1999

Dempster, Q., *Whistleblowers*, (ABC Books, Sydney, 1997)

Devine, T.M. and Aplin, D.G., 'Abuse of Authority: The Office of the Special Counsel and Whistleblower Protection', *Antioch Law Journal*, Vol. 4, Summer 1986, pp. 5–71

Devine, T.M. and Aplin, D.G., 'Whistleblower Protection: The Gap Between the Law and Reality', *Howard Law Journal*, Vol. 31, 1988, pp. 223–39

Devine, T., 'A Whistleblowers Checklist', *Chemical Engineering*, Vol. 98, No. 11, November 1991, pp. 207–281

Dewry, G., 'The Ponting Case: Leaking in the Public Interest', *Public Law*, 1985, pp. 203–212

'Dos and Don'ts for Whistleblowers: Planning for Trouble', *Technology Review 82*, May 1980

Dozier, J.B., 'Is Whistle-Blowing Helping Behaviour?: A Laboratory Study of Team Members' Reporting of an Unethical Team Leader', Dissertation, Ohio State University, Columbus OH, 1988

Dozier, J.B. and Miceli, M.P., 'Whistle-blowing as Prosocial Behaviour: A Review of Potential Predictors', Working paper 84–8, College of Administrative Science, Ohio State University, Columbus OH, 1984

Dozier, J.B. and Miceli, M.P., 'Potential Predictors of Whistle-Blowing: A Prosocial Behaviour Perspective', *Academy of Management Review*, Vol. 10, No. 4, 1985, pp. 823–836

Dworkin, T. and Callahan, E., 'Internal Whistleblowing: Protecting the Interests of the Employee, the Organization, and Society', *American Business Law Journal*, Vol. 29, No. 2, Summer 1991, pp. 267–308

Dworkin, T. and Callahan, E., 'Employee Disclosures to the Media: When is a 'Source' a 'Sourcerer'?', *Hastings Communications and Entertainment Law Journal*, Vol. 15, Winter 1993, pp. 357–97

Dworkin, T.M. and Near, J.P., 'Whistleblowing Statutes: Are They Working?', *American Business Law Journal*, Vol. 25, Summer 1987, pp. 241–64

Egler, T. and Edwards, E.L., 'Retaliating Against the Whistleblower', *Risk Management*, Vol. 39, No. 8, August 1992, pp. 24–32

Electoral and Administrative Review Commission (Qld), Issues Paper No. 10: 'Protection of Whistleblowers', Brisbane, December 1990

Electoral and Administrative Review Commission (Qld), *Report on Protection of Whistleblowers*, Brisbane, 29 October 1991

Electoral and Administrative Review Commission (Qld), *Report on Review of Codes of Conduct for Public Officials*, Brisbane, May 1992

Elliston, F.A., 'Anonymous Whistleblowing: An Ethical Analysis', *Business and Professional Ethics Journal*, Winter 1982, pp. 39–58

Elliston, F.A., 'Civil Disobedience and Whistleblowing: A Comparative Appraisal of Two Forms of Dissent', *Journal of Business Ethics*, Vol. 1, 1982, pp. 23–28

Elliston, F.A., 'Anonymity and Whistleblowing', *Journal of Business Ethics*, Vol. 1, 1982, pp. 167–177

Elliston, F.A. (ed.), *Conflicting Loyalties in the Workplace*, (University of Notre Dame Press, Notre Dame, 1985)

Elliston, F., Keenan, J., Lockhart, P. and Van Schaick, J., *Whistleblowing: Managing Dissent in the Workplace*, (Praeger, New York, 1985)

Elliston, F. Keenan, J., Lockhart, P. and Van Schaick, J., *Whistleblowing Research: Methodological and Moral Issues*, (Praeger, New York, 1985)

Feerick, J.D., 'Toward a Model Whistleblowing Law', *Fordham Urban Law Journal*, Vol. 19, Spring 1992, pp. 585–97

Finn, P., 'Confidentiality and the Public Interest', *Australian Law Journal*, Vol. 58, 1984, p. 497

Finn, P., 'The "Public Interest" and "Whistleblowing"', in Finn, P., *Official Information: Integrity in Government Project*, Interim Report 1, The Australian National University, Canberra, 1991, Part B, Section 4, pp. 218–250

Finn, P., 'Secrecy, Dissent and Whistleblowing', in Finn, P., *Official Information: Integrity in Government Project*, Interim Report 1, Australian National University, Canberra, 1991, Part A, Section 2, pp. 45–84

Finn, P., 'Whistleblowing', *Canberra Bulletin of Public Administration*, Vol. 66, October 1991, pp. 169–171

Fisher, 'The Whistleblower Protection Act 1989: A False Hope for Whistleblowers', *Rutgers Law Review*, Vol. 43, Winter 1991, p. 355–416

Fong, F.D., 'Whistleblower Protection and the Office of the Special Counsel: The Development of Reprisal Law in the 1980s', *American University Law Review*, Vol. 40, No. 3, Spring 1991, pp. 1015–1063

Fox, R., 'Protecting the Whistleblower', *Adelaide Law Review*, Vol. 15, 1993, pp. 137–163

Garrison, A., 'The Mysterious Case of Karen Silkwood', *The Ecologist*, November/December, Vol. 9, No. 8, 9

General Accounting Office (US), *Whistleblower Complainants Rarely Qualify for Office of the Special Counsel*, (U.S. Government Printing Office, Washington DC, 1985)

General Accounting Office (US), *Whistleblower Protection: Survey of Federal Employees on Misconduct and Protection from Reprisal*, (GAO/GGD-92–120FS, July 1992)

Glazer, M., 'Ten Whistleblowers and How They Fared', *Hastings Centre Report*, 13, 1983, pp. 33–41

Glazer, M.P. and Glazer, P.M., 'Pathways to Resistance: An Ethical Odyssey in Government and Industry', in Lewis, M. and Miller, J.L. (eds.), *Research in Social Problems and Public Policy*, (JAI Press, Greenwich, 1987), Vol. 4, pp. 193–219

Glazer, M.P. and Glazer, P.M., *The Whistleblowers: Exposing Corruption in Government and Industry*, (Basic Books Inc., New York, 1989)

Goldring, J., 'Blowing the Whistle', paper presented to Royal Institute of Public Administration Australia (NSW Division) seminar 'Blowing the Whistle', Sydney, 1 September 1992

Goldring, J., 'Blowing the Whistle', *Alternative Law Journal*, Vol. 7, No. 5, December 1992, pp. 298–300

Goode, M.R., 'A Guide to the South Australian Whistleblowers Protection Act 1993', Australian Institute of Administrative Law Newsletter, Vol. 13, 1993, pp. 13–22

Government Accountability Office, *Whistleblower Protection: Survey of Federal Employees on Misconduct and Protection for Reprisal*, 14 July1992

Government Accountability Office, *Whistleblower Protection: Agencies Implementation of the Whistleblower Statutes Has Been Mixed*, 5 March 1993

Graham, J.W., 'Principled Organizational Dissent', unpublished doctoral dissertation, Department of Organization Behaviour, Northwestern University, Evanston IL, August 1983

Graham, J.W., 'Principled Organizational Dissent: A Theoretical Essay', in L.L. Cummings and B.M. Staw (eds.), *Research in Organizational Behaviour*, Vol. 8, (JAI Press, Greenwich, 1986), pp. 1–52

Grodin, M.L., and Keith, A.B., 'Nuclear Whistleblowers', *Federal Bar News and Journal*, Vol. 41, February 1994, pp. 98–105

Hansen, I., 'Freedom of Expression, Whistleblowing and the Canadian Charters', *Canadian Parliamentary Review*, Vol. 13, Spring 1990, pp. 30–32

Harders, J., 'Whistleblowing: Counting the Cost', *Canberra Bulletin of Public Administration*, Vol. 66, October 1991, pp. 29–37

Hawkins, G., review of *A Collusion of Powers* by Philip Arantz, *Weekend Australian*, 24–25 July 1993, *Weekend Review*, p. 6

Hoffman, W., 'The Ford Pinto', in W. Hoffman and J. Moore (eds.), *Business Ethics: Readings and Cases in Corporate Morality*, (McGraw-Hill, New York, 1984), pp. 249–260

Hughes, H.R., et. al., 'Counselling the Whistleblower', *The Practical Lawyer*, Vol. 38, June 1992, pp. 37–62

Hunt, G. (ed), *Whistleblowing and the NHS*, (Edward Arnold, London, 1995)

Independent Commission Against Corruption, *Monitoring the Impact of the Protected Disclosures Act 1994: Phase One, Survey of NSW Public Sector Agencies. Phase Two, Interviews with NSW Public Sector Agencies and Local Councils*, April, June 1996

Jan, C., 'Thoughts on Whistleblowers', University of Queensland, Brisbane, September 1993, unpub. ms

Jan, C., 'Whistleblowing: The Moral of the Story', speech to Queensland Justices Association Inc. Annual General Meeting, Brisbane, 17 December 1993

Johnson, R.A., 'Bureaucratic Whistleblowing and Policy Change', *Western Political Quarterly*, Vol. 43, 1990, pp. 849–874

Jos, P.H., 'The Nature and Limits of the Whistleblower's Contribution to Administrative Responsibility', *American Review of Public Administration*, Vol. 21, 2, June 1991, pp. 105–118

Jos, P.H., Tompkins, M.E. and Hays, S.W., 'In Praise of Difficult People: A Portrait of the Committed Whistleblower', *Public Administration Review*, Vol. 9, No. 6, November/December 1989, pp. 552–561

Keenan, J. and Krueger, C., 'Whistleblowing and the Professional', *Management Accounting*, Vol. 74, No. 2, August 1992, pp. 21–24

Keyes, T., 'Queensland Whistleblowing: Democratic Dissent in Public Employment', paper presented to Criminal Justice Commission Seminar, 'Whistleblowers: Concerned Citizens or Disloyal Mates?', Brisbane, 23 November 1993, pp. 4–23

Laframboise, H.L., 'Vile Wretches and Public Heroes: The Ethics of Whistleblowing in Government', (a) *Canadian Public Administration*, Vol. 4, No. 1, Spring 1991, pp. 73–77; (b) in K. Kernaghan (ed.), 'Do Unto Others: Proceedings of a Conference on Ethics in Government and Business', Institute of Public Administration of Canada

Legislation Committee on the Whistleblowers Protection Bill (No.2) 1992 (NSW) (D. Page MLA, Chair), 'Report', NSW Parliament, Sydney, June 1993

Lennane, K.J., 'What Happens to Whistleblowers and Why', paper presented to Criminal Justice Commission seminar, 'Whistleblowers: Concerned Citizens or Disloyal Mates?', Brisbane, 23 November 1993

Lennane, K.J., 'Whistleblowing: A Health Issue', *British Medical Journal*, No. 307, 11 September 1993, pp. 667–670

Lewis, D., 'Whistleblowers and Job Security', *Modern Law Review*, Vol. 58, 1995, pp. 208–221

Lewis, D., 'Employment Protection for Whistleblowers: On What Principles Should Australian Legislation be Based?', *Australian Journal of Labour Law*, Vol. 9, 1996, pp. 135–152

Leymann, H., 'Mobbing and Psychological Terror at Workplaces', *Violence and Victims*, Vol. 5, No. 2, 1990, pp. 119–126

Martin, B., Baker, C.M.A., Manwell, C. and Pugh, C. (eds.), *Intellectual Suppression: Australian Case Histories, Analysis and Response*, (Angus and Robertson, North Ryde, 1986)

Martin, B., *Suppression Stories*, (Fund for Intellectual Dissent, Wollongong, 1997)

Martin, B., *The Whistleblower's Handbook: How to be an Effective Resister*, (Envirobooks, Sydney, 1999)

W.W., Burke, F., and Doig, J.W. (eds.), *Combating Corruption/Encouraging Ethics: A Sourcebook for Public Service Ethics*, (American Society for Public Administration, Washington, 1990)

McKiernan, M.J., 'Protection for Private Employee Whistleblowers in Texas?', *Texas Bar Journal*, Vol. 54, July 1991, pp. 667–8

McMillan, J., 'Principled Organizational Dissent: Whistleblowing in Response to Corruption', paper delivered to Fourth International Anti-Corruption Conference, Sydney, 1988

McMillan, J., 'Legal Protection of Whistleblowers', in Prasser, S., Wear R. and Nethercote, J. (eds.), *Corruption and Reform: The Fitzgerald Vision*, (University of Queensland Press, Brisbane, 1990), pp. 203–211

McMillan, J., 'The Whistleblower Versus the Organisation – Who Should be Protected?', in Campbell, T. and Sadurski, W., (eds), *Freedom of Communication in Australia: a Study in Applied Philosophy*, (Dartmouth Press, 1994)

McMillan, J., 'Whistleblowing' in N. Preston (ed.) *Educating for Public Sector Ethics*, (Federation Press, Sydney, 1994)

Mellor, B., 'Whistleblowers', *Time Australia*, 21 October 1991, p. 46

Mellor, W., 'Integrity and Ruined Lives', *Time Australia*, 21 October 1991, pp. 46–51

Miceli, M.P., Dozier, J.B. and Near, J.P., 'Blowing the Whistle on Data-Fudging: A Controlled Field Experiment', *Journal of Applied Social Psychology*, Vol. 21, 1991, pp. 301–325

Miceli, M.P. and Near, J.P., *Blowing the Whistle: Organizational and Legal Implications for Companies and Employees*, (Lexington Books, New York, 1992)

Miceli, M.P, Near, J.P. and Schwenk, C.R., 'Who Blows the Whistle and Why?', *Industrial Labor Relations Review*, Vol. 45, No. 1, October 1991, p. 113–130

Minahan, D., 'The Whistleblower Protection Act: Death of a Statute', *Federal Merit Systems Reporter*, Vol. 93, No. 3D, 26 April 1993, p. V-3-5

Mitchell, G., *Truth ... And Consequences: Seven Who Would Not Be Silenced*, (December Books, New York, 1981)

Nader, R., Petkas, P.J. and Blackwell, K. (eds.), *Whistleblowing: The Report on the Conference on Professional Responsibility*, (Grossman, New York, 1972)

Near, J.P. and Jensen, T.C., 'The Whistleblowing Process, Retaliation and Perceived Effectiveness', *Work and Occupations*, Vol. 10, No. 1, February 1983, pp. 3–28

Near, J.P. and Miceli, M.P., 'Organizational Dissidence: The Case of Whistle-blowing', *Journal of Business Ethics*, Vol. 4, 1985, pp. 1–16

Near, J.P. and Miceli, M.P., 'Retaliation Against Whistle-blowers: Predictors and Effects', *Journal of Applied Psychology*, Vol. 71 (1), 1986, pp. 137–145

Near, J.P. and Miceli, M.P., 'Whistleblowers in Organizations: Dissidents or Reformers?' in Barry, M.S. and Cummings, L.L. (eds.), *Research in Organizational Behaviour*, (JAI Press, Greenwich, 1987, Vol. 9, pp. 321–368

Nevill, H., 'Calling the Tune on Whistleblowers', *Canberra Times*, 21 August 1986, p. 6

New South Wales Parliament, *Review of the Protected Disclosures Act*, Report of the Committee on the Office of the Ombudsman and the Police Integrity Commission, September 1996

Nichols, L., '"Whistleblower" or "Renegade": Definitional Contests in an Official Inquiry', *Symbolic Interaction*, Vol. 14, No. 4, Winter 1991, pp. 395–414

Nicol, W., *McBride: Behind they Myth*, (ABC Books, Sydney, 1989)

Paige Whitaker, L., *Whistleblower Protections for Federal Employees*, Congressional Research Service Report for Congress, 10 January 1990

Parliamentary Committee for Electoral and Administrative Review (Qld), *Report on Whistleblowers Protection*, (Government Printer, Brisbane, 8 April 1992)

Parliamentary Committee for Electoral and Administrative Review (Qld), *Report on Codes of Conduct for Public Officials*, (Government Printer, Brisbane, 21 May 1993)

Peters, C. and Branch, T. (eds.), *Blowing the Whistle: Dissent in the Public Interest*, (Praeger, New York, 1972)

Petersen, J. and Farrell, D., *Whistleblowing: Ethical and Legal Issues in Expressing Dissent*, (Dubuque, I.A., 1986, Kendall Hunt)

Pinnock, J., 'Whistleblowers Protection Bill 1992: The Ombudsman's Perspective', paper presented to Royal Institute of Public Administration Australia (NSW Division) Seminar, 'Blowing the Whistle', Sydney, 1 September 1992

Ponting, C., *The Right to Know: The Inside Story of the Belgrano Affair*, (London, Sphere, 1985)
Ponting, C., 'Why I Blew the Whistle', *The Observer*, 17 February 1985, p. 11
Ponting, C., 'Ponting Inquiry is Dropped', *The Times*, 23 April 1985, p. 3
Prasser, S., Wear, R. and Nethercote, J., (eds) *Corruption and Reform: The Fitzgerald Vision*, (University of Queensland Press, Brisbane, 1990)
Preston, N., 'Can Virtue be Regulated? An Examination of the EARC Proposals for a Code of Conduct for Public Officials in Queensland', *Australian Journal of Public Administration*, Vol. 51, No. 4, December 1992, pp. 410–415
Price, P.A., 'An Overview of the Whistleblower Protection Act', *Federal Circuit Bar Journal*, Vol. 2, Spring 1992, pp. 69–97
Public Concern At Work, 'The Advice Service: First Report', Lincoln's Inn House, 42 Kingsway London, January 1994
Public Service and Merit Protection Commission, *Public Interest Whistleblowing*, (PSMPC, Canberra, 1998)
Pyper, R., 'Sarah Tisdall, Ian Willmore, and the Civil Servant's Right to Leak', *Political Quarterly*, Vol. 6, 1985, pp. 72–81
Ridley, F.F., 'Political Neutrality in the British Civil Service: Sir Thomas More and Mr Clive Ponting v. Sir Robert Armstrong and the Vicar of Bray', in Williams, B., Stevenson, J., Ridley, F.F., Couzens, K., Grey, A. and Jay, P., *Politics, Ethics and Public Service*, (Royal Institute of Public Administration, London, 1985)
Rose, N., 'Whistleblowing – Time for a Change?', *New Law Journal*, Vol. 145, No. 6680, 27 January 1995, pp. 113–115
Sahlin, C., 'Protection for Whom? Proposals of the Draft Whistleblower Protection Bill', paper to Royal Institute of Public Administration Australia (NSW Division) Seminar 'Blowing the Whistle', Sydney, 1 September 1992
Singer, A.W., 'The Whistleblower: Patriot or Bounty Hunter?', *Across the Board*, Vol. 29 (11), November 1992, pp. 16–22
Smith, B. 'How Not to Protect Whistleblowers', *Freedom of Information Review*, No. 47, October 1993, pp. 54–57
Smith, K.M. and Oseth, J.M., 'The Whistleblowing Era: A Management Perspective', *Employee Relations Law Journal*, Vol. 19, Autumn 1993, pp. 179–92
Smith, R., 'Whistleblowing: A Curse on Ineffective Organisations', *British Medical Journal*, 305, 28 November 1992, pp. 1308–1309
Squire, M., 'The Mikado Revisited via the Whistleblowers Protection Bill 1992', paper presented to Royal Institute of Public Administration Australia (NSW Division) Seminar, 'Blowing the Whistle', Sydney, 1 September 1992
Starke, J.G., 'The Protection of Public Service Whistleblowers: Part 1', *Australian Law Journal*, Vol. 65, No. 4, April 1991, pp. 205–219
Starke, J.G., 'The Protection of Public Service Whistleblowers: Part 2', *Australian Law Journal*, Vol. 65, No. 5, May 1991, pp. 252–265
Stewart, J., Devine, T. and Rasor, D., 'Courage Without Martyrdom: A Survival Guide for Whistleblowers', Government Accountability Project and Project on Government Procurement, Washington DC, October 1989
Sumner, C.J., 'The Whistleblowers Protection Bill [SA]: Its Genesis and Rationale', *Australian Institute of Administrative Law Newsletter*, Vol. 14, 1993, pp. 9–13
Tasmanian Council of Social Service, Submission to Senate Select Committee on Public Interest Whistleblowing, November 1993

Toohey, J., 'Occupational Violence: A Problem Becoming an Issue', *Journal of Occupational Health and Safety*, February 1992, pp. 3–4

Tremblay, P.R., 'Ratting', *The American Journal of Trial Advocacy*, Vol. 17, Summer 1993, pp. 49–100

Trevino, L.K. and Victor, B., 'Peer Reporting of Unethical Behaviour: A Social Context Perspective', *Academy of Management Journal*, Vol. 5, No. 1, 1992, pp. 38–64

Truelson, J.A., 'Blowing the Whistle on Systemic Corruption', PhD. dissertation, School of Public Administration, University of Southern California, Los Angeles, 1986

Truelson, J.A., 'Blowing the Whistle on Systematic Corruption: On Maximizing Reform and Minimizing Retaliation', *Corruption and Reform*, Vol. 2, No. 1, 1987, pp. 55–74

Tucker, D., 'Whistleblowing Without Tears: The Exposure of Brisbane's King George Square Car Park Fraud', paper presented to the Australasian Political Studies Association Annual Conference, Melbourne, September/October 1993

Vickers, L., *Protecting Whistleblowers at Work*, (Institute of Employment Rights, May 1995)

Vincent, M., 'Welcome disclosure', *Alternative Law Journal*, Vol. 20, No. 2, April 1995, pp. 74–78

Weinstein, D., *Bureaucratic Opposition*, (Pergamon, New York, 1979)

Weinstock, M., 'Blowing in the Wind', *Occupational Hazards*, Vol. 54, No. 8, August 1992, pp. 37–39

Weisband, E., *Resignation in Protest: Political and Ethical Choices Between Loyalty to Team and Loyalty to Conscience in American Public Life*, (Grossman Publishers, New York, 1975)

Weiseman, M., 'The American Experience with Ethics and Whistleblowing', paper to Royal Australian Institute of Public Administration (Queensland Division) seminar, 'Do Unto Others: Ethics in the Public Sector', Brisbane, 5–7 September 1990

Welford, R.J., 'Whistleblowing in the Private Sector', paper to Australian Securities Commission Corporate Lawyers Forum, Brisbane, 10 February 1993

Westin, A. (ed.), *Whistle Blowing! Loyalty and Dissent in the Corporation*, (McGraw-Hill, New York, 1981)

Westman, D.P., *Whistleblowing: The Law of Retaliatory Discharge*, (BNA Books, Washington DC, 1991)

Winfield, M., *Minding Your Own Business: Regulation and Whistleblowing in British Companies, Social Audit*, (London, 1990)

PROFESSIONS
Auditing

Abrams, A.L., 'Whistleblowers', *Business and Economic Review*, Vol. 39, No. 2, January–March 1993, pp. 28–30

Arnold, D.F. and Ponemon, L.A., 'Internal Auditors' Perceptions of Whistle-Blowing and the Influence of Moral Reasoning: An Experiment', *Auditing: A Journal of Practice and Theory*, Vol. 10, No. 2, Fall 1991, pp. 1–15

Barlas, S., 'Whistleblower Bill Likely to Move Quickly', *Internal Auditor*, Vol. 50, No. 1, February 1993, pp. 10–11

Benson, G., 'Codes of Ethics, Whistleblowing and Managerial Auditing', *Managerial Auditing Journal*, 1992, pp. 37–40

Courtemanche, G., 'The Ethics of Whistle Blowing', *Internal Auditor*, February 1988, pp. 36–41

Flesher, D., and Buttross, T., 'Whistleblowing Hotlines', *Internal Auditor*, Vol. 49, No. 4, August 1992, pp. 54–58

Garrett, A.D., 'Auditor Whistle Blowing: The Financial Fraud Detection and Disclosure Act', *Seton Hall Legislative Journal*, Vol. 17, 1993, pp. 91–136

Near, J.P. and Miceli, M.P., *The Internal Auditor's Ultimate Responsibility: The Reporting of Sensitive Issues*, (Institute of Internal Auditors Research Foundation, Altamonte Springs FL, 1988)

Tidrick, D., 'Ethics and Whistleblowing in the Workplace', *Internal Auditing*, Vol. 7, No. 3, Winter 1992, pp. 3–10

Vinten, G., *Whistleblowing Auditors: A Contradiction in Terms?*, (Chartered Association of Certified Accountants, 1992)

Vinten, G., 'The Whistleblowing Internal Auditor', *Internal Auditing*, Vol. 8, No. 2, Fall 1992, pp. 26–33

Williams, J. and Davidow, B., 'Cancelling out Corruption: A Group of Australian Internal Auditors is Waging War Against Fraud and Corruption', *Internal Auditor*, Vol. 50, June 1993, pp. 33–37

Conservation

Association of Forest Service Employees for Environmental Ethics and Government Accountability Project, Protecting Integrity and Ethics Report (Proceedings of a Conference for Government Employees of Environmental, Wildlife and Natural Resources Agencies), Association of Forest Service Employees for Environmental Ethics, Eugene OR, 1992

Blumenfeld, K., 'Dilemmas of Disclosure: Ethical Issues in Environmental Auditing', *Business and Professional Ethics Journal*, Vol. 8, No. 3, 1989, pp. 5–28

Engineering

Baker, M., 'Employer Response to Professional Complaints and Alarms: Can Corporate Scientists and Engineers Speak Out?', paper presented to the annual meeting of the Institute for Chemists, Atlantic City NJ, May 1983

Carew, W.E., 'Views on Professional Practice and Ethics', *Journal of Professional Issues in Engineering*, Vol. 110, No. 2, 1984, pp. 70–73

Carlson, P., 'A. Ernest Fitzgerald: His Commitment to Cutting Costs Has Made Him No. 1 on the Pentagon's Hate List', *People*, 9 December 1985, pp. 77–81

Chalk, R. and Von Hippel, F., 'Due Process for Dissenting Whistle-blowers: Dealing with Technical Dissent in the Organization', *Technology Review*, Vol. 81, June/July 1989, pp. 48–55

Dandekar, N., Whistleblowing and Other Ethical Issues for Women Engineers, *New England Society of Women Engineers*, (Boston University, Boston, 1986)

Hughson, R.V. and Kohn, P.M., 'Ethics', *Chemical Engineering*, Vol. 87, No. 19, 22 September 1980, pp. 132–147

Knowles, J., 'Engineers Have Ethics – So What? Why Engineers Won't Blow the Whistle and What to do About It', paper presented to Australia and New Zealand Association for the Advancement of Science Congress, 16 September 1992

Koehn, E., 'Practitioner Involvement with Engineering Ethics and Professionalism', *Journal of Professional Issues in Engineering Education and Practice*, Vol. 118, 1, pp. 49–55

Ladenson, R.F., 'The Social Responsibilities of Engineers and Scientists: A Philosophical Approach', Occasional Papers No. 1, Center for the Study of Ethics in the Professions, April 1979

Martin, Mike W., 'Whistleblowing: Professionalism, Personal Life, and Shared Responsibility for Safety in Engineering', *Business and Professional Ethics Journal*, Vol. 11, 1992, pp. 21–40

Matley, J., Greene, R. and McCauley, C., 'Health, Safety and Environment: CE Readers Say What's Right', *Chemical Engineering*, Vol. 94, No. 13, 28 September 1987, pp. 108–120

Neary, V., *The Trials of a Whistleblower: Interim Report on Victimisation and Harassment for Blowing the Whistle*, (Turramurra, NSW, 1992)

Neary, V., *Second Report on Victimisation and Harassment*, (Turramurra, NSW, 1993)

Olson, J., 'Engineering Attitudes Toward Professionalism, Employment and Social Responsibility', *Professional Engineer*, Vol. 42, No. 8, pp. 30–32

Perrucci, R., Anderson, R.M., Schendel, D.E., Trachtman, L.E., 'Whistleblowing: Professionals' Resistance to Organizational Authority', *Social Problems*, Vol. 28, 1980/81, pp. 149–163

Pletta, D.H., 'Professional Support for Safety-Conscious Whistleblowers', *Journal of Professional Issues in Engineering*, Vol. 112, No. 2, 1986, pp. 141–149

Sawyier, F.H., 'What Should Professional Societies do About Ethics?', *Journal of Professional Issues in Engineering*, Vol. 110, No. 2, 1984, pp. 88–99

Vandivier, K., 'The Aircraft Brake Scandal', *Harper's*, April 1972, pp. 45–52

Environment

Garrison, A., 'The Mysterious Case of Karen Silkwood', *The Ecologist*, November/December, Vol. 9, No. 8, 9

Grodin, M.L., and Keith, A.B., 'Nuclear Whistleblowers', *Federal Bar News and Journal*, Vol. 41, February 1994, pp. 98–105

Matley, J., Greene, R. and McCauley, C., 'Health, Safety and Environment', *Chemical Engineering*, Vol. 94, No. 13, 28 September 1987, pp. 108–120

Weinstock, M., 'Blowing in the Wind', *Occupational Hazards*, Vol. 54, No. 8, August 1992, pp. 37–39

Health and Safety

Alcorn, G., 'Whistleblowers: Doctor Fallout', *Time Australia*, 29 November 1993, pp. 54–55

Beardshaw, V., *Conscientious Objectors at Work: Mental Health Workers – A Case Study*, (Social Audit, London, 1981)

Borrow, S., *Enemies of the People? Whistleblowing in the New South Wales Health Industry*, (Faculty of Law, University of Wollongong, 1996)

British Medical Association, *Whistleblowing: The View from the BMA*, (Health Policy and Economic Research Unit, BMA Books, London, 1996)

Curtin, L., *Ethical Issues in Nursing and Nursing Education*, (National League for Nursing, New York, 1980)

De Maria, W. and J. Lennane, 'The Downside of Whistleblowing', *Australian Medical Association Journal*, Vol. 169, 5 October 1998, p. 351

Fidell, E.R., 'Federal Protection of Private Sector Health and Safety Whistleblowers', *Administrative Law Journal*, Vol. 2, 1988, p. 84

Fiesta, J., 'Whistleblowers: Heroes or Stool Pigeons? – Part I', *Nursing Management*, Vol. 21, No. 6, June 1990, pp. 16–17

Fiesta, J., 'Whistleblowers: Retaliation or Protection? – Part II', *Nursing Management*, Vol. 21, No. 7, 1990, p. 38

Fry, S.T., 'Whistle Blowing by Nurses: A Matter of Ethics', *Nursing Outlook*, Vol. 37, No. 1, p. 56

Lennane, J., '"Whistleblowing": A Health Issue', *British Medical Journal*, Vol. 307, 11 September 1993, pp. 667–670

Matley, J., Greene, R. and McCauley, C., 'Health, Safety and Environment', *Chemical Engineering*, Vol. 94, No. 13, 28 September 1987, pp. 108–120

Misbrener, J.M., 'An Action Plan for Chemical Safety', *Occupational Hazards*, Vol. 52, No. 7, July 1990, p. 35

Smith, R., 'Whistleblowing: A Curse on Ineffective Organisations', *British Medical Journal*, Vol. 305, No. 28 November 1992, pp. 1308–1309

Tattam, A., 'Whistle Blowing: You Can Survive It!', *Australian Nursing Journal*, Vol. 1, No. 4, October 1993, pp. 17–19

Journalism

Australian Press Council, 'Submission to the New South Wales Parliament Legislation Committee on the Whistleblowers Protection Bill 1992 (No. 2)', *Australian Press Council News*, Vol. 5, 2, May 1993, p. 21

Dworkin, T. and Callahan, E., 'Employee Disclosures to the Media: When is a "Source" a "Sourcerer"?', *Hastings Communications and Entertainment Law Journal*, Vol. 15, Winter 1993, pp. 357–97

Editorial, 'Science, Journalism and Whistleblowing', *Science*, Vol. 240, No. 4852, 29 April 1988, p. 585

Fried, L.I., 'PandG's Search for Leaks Toughens Reporters' Jobs', *Folio: The Magazine for Magazine Management*, Vol. 20, No. 10, 1 October 1991, p. 37

Koshland, D.E., 'Science, Journalism and Whistleblowing', *Science*, Vol. 240, No. 4852, 1988, p. 585

Law and Police

Arantz, P., *A Collusion of Powers*, (Dunedoo NSW, 1993)

Commonwealth Ombudsman, *Professional Reporting and Internal Witness Protection in the Australian Federal Police*, (November 1997)

Greenwald, J., 'A Matter of Honor', *Time Magazine*, 21 June 1993, pp. 49–50

Hawkins, G., Review of *A Collusion of Powers* by Philip Arantz., *Weekend Australian*, 24–25 July 1993, *Weekend Review*, p. 6

Maas, P., *Serpico*, (Viking Press, New York, 1973)

Rosecrance, J., 'Whistleblowing in Probation Departments', *Journal of Criminal Justice*, Vol. 16, 1988, pp. 99–109

Management

Barnett, T.R., 'Will Your Employees Blow the Whistle?', *HR Magazine*, Vol. 7, No. 7, July 1992, pp. 76–78

Barnett, T., 'Why Your Company Should Have a Whistleblowing Policy', *SAM Advanced Management Journal*, Vol. 57, No. 4, Autumn 1992, pp. 27–42

Barnett, T., 'A Preliminary Investigation of the Relationship Between Selected Organizational Characteristics and External Whistleblowing by Employees', *Journal of Business Ethics*, Vol. 11, No. 12, December 1992, pp. 949–959

Barnett, T.R. and Cochran, D.S., 'Making Room for the Whistleblower', *HR Magazine*, 36 (4), January 1991, pp. 58–61

Barnett, T., Cochran, D.S., Taylor, G.S., 'The Internal Disclosure Policies of Private-Sector Employers: An Initial Look at their Relationship to Employee Whistleblowing', *Journal of Business Ethics*, Vol. 12, No. 2, February 1993, pp. 127–136

Duska, R., 'Whistleblowing and Employee Loyalty', in Desjardins, J.R. and McCall, J.J., *Contemporary Issues in Business Ethics*, (Wadsworth Publishing Company, Belmont CA, 1985), pp. 295–300

Egler, T. and Edwards, E.L., 'Retaliating Against the Whistleblower', *Risk Management*, Vol. 39, 8, August 1992, pp. 24–32

Ewing, D., 'The Employee's Right to Speak Out: The Management Perspective', *Civil Liberties Review*, September–October, 1978, pp. 10–15

Keenan, J. and Krueger, C., 'Whistleblowing and the Professional', *Management Accounting*, Vol. 74, No. 2, August 1992, pp. 21–24

Vinten, G., 'Whistle Blowing: Corporate Help or Hindrance?', *Management Decision*, Vol. 30, No. 1, 1992, pp. 44–48

'Whistleblowers: Saint or Snitch', *Credit Union Executive*, Vol. 32, No. 1, January/February 1992, pp. 30–34

Winfield, M., *Minding Your Own Business: Regulation and Whistleblowing in British Companies*, (Social Audit, London, 1990)

Military

Thompson, M., 'Cashing in on Military Fraud. Stealth Law. Whistleblowers and Their Lawyers are Manoeuvring to Cash in on Military Fraud', *California Lawyer*, Vol. 8, October 1988, pp. 33–37

Nursing

Anderson, S. 'Patient Advocacy and Whistleblowing in Nursing: Help for Helpers', *Nursing Forum*, Vol. 25, 1990, pp. 5–13

Anon, 'Blowing the Whistle on Incompetence: One Nurse's Story', *Nursing*, 1989, pp. 47–50

Curtin, L., *Ethical Issues in Nursing and Nursing Education*, (National League for Nursing, New York, 1980)

Fry, S.T., 'Whistleblowing by Nurses: A Matter of Ethics,' *Nursing Outlook*, Vol. 37, No. 1, January/February 1989, p. 56

Hammond, P., 'Whistle While You Work,' *Nursing Times*, Vol. 89, No. 28, July 19, 1993, p. 22

O'Connor, T., 'A Professional Struggle,' *Nursing New Zealand*, Vol. 86, No. 7, August 1993, pp. 22–24

Parker, N., 'Out of Sympathy with the Whistleblower', *British Medical Journal*, Vol. 304, 1992, pp. 1253–4

Parks, R., 'Give Voice to Your Thousand Silent Screams, *Australian Nursing Journal*, Vol. 1, No. 2, August 1993, pp. 3–4

Queensland Nurses' Union of Employees, Submission to the Department of Health Concerning the Review of Queensland Mental Health Law, (unpub.), December 1992

Slane, B., 'Privacy Act Permits Some Whistleblowing', *New Zealand Family Physician*, Vol. 24, 1997, pp. 29–30

Tattam, A., 'Blowing the Whistle', *Nursing Times*, Vol. 85, No. 23, 7 June 1989, p. 20

Public Administration

Baran, A., 'Federal Employment: The Civil Service Reform Act of 1978: Removing Incompetents and Protecting Whistle Blowers', *Wayne LawReview*, Vol. 26, 1979, pp. 97–118

Campbell, E., 'Appearance of Public Servants as Witnesses before Parliamentary Committees', in J.R. Nethercote (ed.), *Parliament and Bureaucracy*, (Hale and Iremonger, Sydney, 1982), pp. 179–226

Harvey, F., 'Detecting and Investigating Fraud in the Public Sector', paper presented to Public Sector Accounting and Auditing Conference, Sydney, September 1990

Kernaghan, K., 'The Conscience of the Bureaucrat: Accomplice or Constraint?', *Canadian Public Administration*, Vol. 27, Winter 1984, p. 590

Kernaghan, K. (ed.), *Do Unto Others: Proceedings of a Conference on Ethics in Government and Business*, (Institute of Public Administration of Canada, Toronto, 1991)

Kernaghan, K., 'Whistleblowing in Canadian Governments', *Optimum*, Vol. 22, No. (1), 1991/92, pp. 34–43

Kernaghan, K. and Langford, J., *The Responsible Public Servant*, (Institute of Public Administration of Canada, Toronto, and Institute for Research on Public Policy, Halifax NS, 1990)

Jay, P., *Politics, Ethics and Public Service*, (Royal Institute of Public Administration, London, 1985)

Research

Lowe, I., 'A Doctor With a Beef against Growth Hormones', *New Scientist*, 2 October 1993, p. 62

Maslen, G., 'What Happens to Whistleblowers Who Help Expose Academic Fraud?', Melbourne *Age*, 10 August 1992

Moodie, G., 'Fraud in Australian Science: Towards Guidelines on Academic Fraud', *Search*, Vol. 20, No. 2, March–April 1989, pp. 35–37

Science

Baker, M., 'Employer Response to Professional Complaints and Alarms: Can Corporate Scientists and Engineers Speak Out?', paper presented to the annual meeting of the Institute for Chemists, Atlantic City NJ, May 1983

Caton, H., 'Truth Management in the Sciences', *Search*, Vol. 19, No. 5/6, September/November 1988, pp. 242–244

Chalk, R. and Von Hippel, F., 'Due Process for Dissenting Whistle-blowers: Dealing with Technical Dissent in the organization', *Technology Review*, Vol. 81, June/July 1989, pp. 48–55

Culliton, B.J., 'Credit for Whistle-Blower Vanishes', *Science*, Vol. 244, 12 May 1989, p. 643

Culliton, B.J., 'The Dingell Probe Finally Goes Public', Science, Vol. 244, 12 May 1989, pp. 643–646

Hollis, B.W., 'I Turned in My Mentor', *The Scientist*, Vol. 1, No. 14, December 1987, pp. 1–13

'Jottings: Blowing the Whistle', *Bioethics News*, Vol. 12, No. 1, October 1992, Ethics Committee Supplement, p. 1

Kohn and Carpenter, 'Nuclear Whistleblower Protection and the Scope of Protected Activity under Section 210 of the Energy Reorganization Act', *Antioch Law Journal*, Vol. 4, 1986, p. 73

Koshland, D.E., 'Science, Journalism and Whistleblowing', *Science*, Vol. 240, No. 4852, 1988, p. 585

Ladenson, R.F., 'The Social Responsibilities of Engineers and Scientists: A Philosophical Approach', Occasional Papers No. 1, Center for the Study of Ethics in the Professions, April 1979

Leibel, W., 'When Scientists are Wrong: Admitting Inadvertent Error in Research', *Journal of Business Ethics*, Vol. 10, 1991, pp. 601–604

Steene, M., 'AIMS Worker Seeks Censored Information', Townsville *Daily Bulletin*, 26 August 1992, p. 10

Stokes, T., 'The Briggs Enquiry', *Search*, Vol. 20, No. 2, March–April 1989, pp. 38–40

Index

A

ABC, *see* Australian Broadcasting Corporation (ABC)
Abetz, Senator, Eric, 154, 156
Aborigines
 communal solidarity, 22
ACCC (Australian Competition and Consumer Commission), 6–8, 27
Ackland, Richard, 133
Administrative Appeals Tribunal, 199
AFP, *see* police and police forces, Australian Federal (AFP)
AHL, *see* Animal Health Laboratory (AHL)
ALP, 154
 and whistleblowing, 33–4
 Queensland, 90
ALRC, *see* Australian Law Reform Commission (ALRC)
Andrews, Kevin, 59
Angus, Samuel, 77, 82
Animal Friends, 132
Animal Health Laboratory (AHL), 61–72
Archaeology Action, 117
Archivist, State (Qld), 139, 141–2, 151–2
Arnold, Peter, 54–7
Arthur, Governor George, 30
ASC (Australian Securities Commission), 6
Ashfield Presbyterian Church, 79
Askin, Robin, 23
Attorney-General's Department, 173, 180, 184
Auditor-General, NSW, 205
Auditor-General, Victoria, 102
Australian and New Zealand Society of Criminologists, 90
Australian Association of Occupational Therapists, 208
Australian Association of Social Workers, 208
Australian Broadcasting Corporation (ABC), 38, 45, 133
 and Dr Nitschke, 42, 52
 and John Millard, 119–32
 Editorial Policies Working Group, 124
 radio, 117
Australian Coachline, 6
Australian Competition and Consumer Commission (ACCC), 6–8, 27
Australian Conservation Foundation, 62
Australian Industrial Relations Commission, 90
Australian Labor Party, 154
 and whistleblowing, 33–4
 Queensland, 90
Australian Law Reform Commission (ALRC), 168–9, 174, 204–5
 Report, 219
Australian Medical Association, 25, 53–4
 Queensland, 20, 25
Australian National University, 89
Australian Nursing Federation, 58
Australian Psychological Society, 208
Australian Quarantine Inspection Service, 62, 73
Australian Securities and Investment Commission, 6
Australian Securities Commission (ASC), 6
Australian Stories, 132

Australian Taxation Office, 27, 31, 202
Australian Tourism Industry Association (ATIA), 121–2
Australian Universities Expo, 90
Australian Veterinary Association, 62–3
Australian Vice-Chancellors Committee, 115
Australian War Memorial (AWM), 39
 and Merit Protection Review Agency, 176–91
 Capital Appeal, 191
Australian, The, 109, 184

B

'Bad-barrell' wrongdoing, 21
Baille Henderson Psychiatric Hospital, 17
Balcombe, Steve, 63–6
Barnett, Professor, 94–7
Basil Stafford Centre for the Intellectually Disabled, 24, 224
Baume, Senator Peter, 165, 168
Bean, Charles, 189
Beanland, Vice-Chancellor, 101–2
Beattie, Peter, 157, 159, 236
Beaumont, Marilyn, 58
Beaurepaire, Dame Beryl, 188, 191
Berthelson, David, 166, 168
BHP, 8
Binford, Professor, 114
Bjelke-Petersen, Sir Joh, 19, 88
Blesing, Charlotte, 179–80, 182–3
Bodant-Bailey, Dr Beatrice, 89
Bolkus, Senator, 153
Bond, Alan, 5–6
Bongiorno, Bernard, 19
Boral Resources (Qld) Pty Ltd, 7
Borbidge, Rob, 20, 157–8
Bowdler, Professor Sandra
 and Dr Partis, 110
 and Associate Professor Rindos, 106–18
Brandeis, Mr Justice, 148
Brandy decision, 199, 201
British Medical Journal, 55
Brotherly Conference, 83
Bruce, Professor, 83, 107–8
Bulletin, the, 67, 150–1
Burchfield, Geoff, 126
Burdekin, Brian, 208
Bureau of Meteorology, 7
Butler, Mr, 125

C

CAA, *see* Civil Aviation Authority
Callinan, Ian, QC, 154–5
Calvert, Senator, 171
Cameron, Reverend Peter, 37
 accomplishment, 86
 and Presbyterian Church of Australia, 74–87
 background, 76–7, 79
 support, 78–9, 81, 83–5
Campus Review, 117
Canberra Times, 190
Care Australia, 24
Carter Inquiry, 207–8
Carter, Commissioner, 201
Carter, Garry Allan, 6
Catholic Church, 207, 236
Central Promotions Appeal Board, 54
Central Sydney Area Health Service (CSAHS), 20
CHA, *see* Consumer Health Advocacy (CHA)
Chamerette, Senator Christobel, 214
Chapman, Penny, 119, 124, 127–8
Chelmsford Hospital, 206–7
Christian, Brian, 83
Churcher, Betty, 17
Civil Aviation Authority, 24
CJC, *see* Criminal Justice Commission (CJC)
Clements, Stuart, 81
Clerk of the House of Representatives, 18–19
Clerk of the Senate, 18–19, 154–5
Clyde, Professor, 108–9, 113
codes of conduct, 235, 237
Coleman, Phillip, 125–9, 131
Coleman Inquiry, 126
Coles Myer, 6
College of Psychiatrists, 18, 208
Commission on Government, 215
Commissions of Inquiry Act, 137
Commonwealth Bureau of Meteorology, 7
Community and Public Sector Union, 67
company fraud, 8
Concord Hospital, 19–20
conflicts of interest, 8, 236
Connolly, Mr Justice, 158, 199
Connolly, Peter, QC, 198
Connolly–Ryan Inquiry, 158, 199

Conroy, Paddy, 123–4, 126, 128
Consumer Health Advocacy (CHA), 20
Conway, Ronald, 205
Cooke Inquiry, 144–6
Cooke, Marshall, QC, 144
Coonabarabran, 85
Cooper, Reverend Paul, 79
Cooze, Charles, 30
corporate crime, 8
Costigan Royal Commission, 164
counselling, 65, 213, 218, 229–30
Courier Mail, 27, 187
Coyne, Peter, 135–40, 145, 151, 157
   and JOYC inquiry, 135–9
   subsequent treatment, 140–7, 150–3
   and Kevin Lindeberg, 147, 150–1, 153
   and Queensland Professional Officers Association, 144–6
Coyne, Mrs, 140
Crime Stoppers program, 31
Criminal Justice Act (Qld), 157, 212
Criminal Justice Commission (CJC), 140, 146–7, 152–3, 155, 196–7, 208, 212, 219, 224
   and Basil Stafford Centre, 224
   and Kevin Lindeberg, 149–56, 159
   and Senate Committee of Privileges, 159
   Connolly–Ryan Inquiry, 158
   whistleblowers' views on, 218–19
Criminal Justice Legislation Act, 196
Crispin, Mr Justice, 191
Crossin Barker Gosling, 185
Crown Casino, 91
Crown Solicitor, 90, 136–40, 152
CSR Limited, 7

D
Daly, General Sir Thomas, 188
Davies, Ken, 28, 151
Dawkins, John, 89
de la Billiere, Sir Peter, 28
Deakin University, 90, 235
defamation, 16, 57, 65, 91, 117, 124, 137, 151, 175, 191, 220, 225–8
Democracy, 1, 14–15
Demos Myth, 14–15
Dempster, Quentin, 123, 126, 133
Department of Family Services, 135, 139, 147, 157
Department of Primary Industry (Queensland), 62

Department of Primary Industry and Fisheries, Tasmania (DPIF), 60–72
Department of Social Security, 31–2, 60
Dominion Mining Company, 114
Douglas, Dr David, 43, 47
Downs, Garry, QC, 83
DPIF (Department of Primary Industry and Fisheries), Tasmania, 60–72
DSS, *see* Department of Social Security
Dubbo, 85

E
EARC (Electoral and Administrative Review Commission), 151, 212
Eastwood, Jenni, 146
Education Report, 117
Eigen, Peter, 8
Electoral and Administrative Review Act (Qld), 212
Electoral and Administrative Review Commission (EARC), 151, 212
Elliott, John, 174
Environmental Protection Authority (EPA), 196
Equal Opportunity Commissioner, Victoria, 19
Equity Group Ltd, 6
Euthanasia Act, 59
Evans, Bradley Craig, 209
Evans, Harry, 18–19
Evans, Kim, 69

F
Fahey, John, 212
Fairholme College, 85
Federal Court, 7, 176, 178, 182, 185, 190, 198, 201–2, 228
   and ACCC, 7
Federated Clerks Union, 90
feminisation, 22
Field, Michael, 215
Finch, Reverend Mr, 81
Finn, Mr Justice, 176, 178–9, 181–2, 187, 189, 190, 228
Fitzgerald Inquiry, 24
Fitzgerald, Professor Stephen, 24, 105
Flemming, Air Vice-Marshal Jim, 189
Forward, Ann, 176–7, 180–1, 183–4, 218
Four Corners, 205
Freedom of Information, 32, 96
Freedom of Information Act, 32, 113

Freehill Hollingdale and Page, 117
Fulbright, William, 19

G

Gaisford, Alistair, 198, 202
Gandevia, Professor Bryan, 188
Garnett–Freeman study, 213
Gayle, Fay, 92, 108–12, 115, 117–18
Gold Coast, 7
Goldberg, Abe, 5
Goodwin, Professor, 96–7
Gordon, Harry, 188
Gordon, Michael, 184
Goss, Wayne, 16, 139, 153–4, 158
Gower, General, 190
Gration, General Peter, 185–6
Gray, Robin, 63–4
Greens, 213–14
　Tasmania, 215
Greiner, Nick, 217
Griffith University, 103
　Student Representative Council, 90
Griffith, Chris, 150
Guidelines on Official Conduct of Commonwealth Public Servants, 214
Gurindji people, 41

H

Haggstom, Peter, 202
Harvey, Margaret, 90
Hastie, Reverend Peter, 79, 86
Hawke, Dr Allan, 184
Hawker, Peter, 185
Hayden, Bill, 188, 191
Health and Community Services, Department of (NT), 46
Health Department
　Northern Territory, 43, 45–6, 52
　Queensland, 17, 20
Health Rights Commissioner, 18
Heiner, Noel, 135–8
Heretic, 76, 86
Herron, Senator John, 155
Hickey, Maggie, 57
Hickie, David, 23
High Court, 72, 155, 199–201
　appeals to, 7
Hill, David, 123–4
Hillview medical complex, 24
HMAS *Swan*, 22
Hobart, 66

Holiday, 121–2, 124
Home Show, 122, 124
Hong Kong, 90
Horan, Mike, MP, 17
Horne, Bob, 57
Horne, Donald, 12–13, 88
Horvath, Dr Diana, 19–20
Hot Chips, 121
Hotop, Professor, 108–9, 113
House, Barry, 115
Howard, Eddie, 157–8
Howard, John, 216
Human Rights and Equal Opportunity Commission (HREOC), 60, 72, 199–201, 208
Hunt, Chris, 198
Hunt, Commissioner David, 168

I

Independent Commission Against Corruption (ICAC), 213, 217, 219
Inspector-General of Intelligence and Security, 214
Institute of Engineers Australia, 235
institutional care, failures in, 205–9
Internal Witness Support Unit, 213
International Council on Archives, 158
Ives, Denis, 180

J

Jackson, Professor, 100, 102
James Cook University, 90
James, Major-General 'Digger', 189
Jesser, Peter, 38, 94–7, 99, 101
　and University of Southern Queensland, 94–9
Jesser, Rochelle, 95
John Oxley Youth Centre (JOYC)
　and Peter Coyne, 135–41, 145
Johns, Brian, 129–30, 132
Johns, Gary, 176–8, 185, 188
Joint Committee on the National Crime Authority, 173
Joint Standing Committee on the Commission on Government, 215
Jones, Clem, 27
Jones, Steven, 90
JOYC, *see* John Oxley Youth Centre (JOYC)
juvenilisation, 22

Index | 301

K

Kant, Immanuel, 14
Karnet Prison Farm, 5
Karp, Daryl, 126–8
Katherine, 41–2
Keating, Paul, 176, 190, 214
Keith Committee Report, 80, 82
Keith, Dr, 80
Kelson, Adrian, 191
Kelson, Brendon, 39, 176, 190–1
   and MPRA, 176–91
Kennett, Jeff, 6, 191
   and Director of Public Prosecutions, 19
Kerr, Duncan, 169, 172–3, 175, 214
Keys, Sir William, 188
Kinder, Ross, 143–4
KPMG, 8

L

Latrobe University, 92
Launceston, 61, 66
Launceston Examiner, 62
Lavarch, Michael, 174
Lawson, Henry, 12–13
Leal, Professor, 97
Ledwidge, Professor Tom, 95
Legal Aid Commission, Victorian, 166
Legge, Kate, 106, 109
legislation
   Commissions of Inquiry Act, 137
   Criminal Justice Act (Qld), 157, 212
   Criminal Justice Legislation Act, 196
   Electoral and Administrative Review Act (Qld), 212
   Euthanasia Act, 59
   Freedom of Information Act, 32, 113
   Official Corruption Commission Act 1988, 215
   Parliamentary Services Bill, 19
   Protected Disclosures Act 1994 (NSW), 220, 223
   Public Interest Disclosure Act 1994 (ACT), 222, 231
   Public Interest Disclosure Bill 1995, 215
   Public Interest Disclosure Bill 1997, 215, 219, 221, 227
   Public Sector Ethics Act (Queensland), 235
   Public Service Act, 19, 216
   Trade Practices Act, 6
   Whistleblower Protection Act 1994 (Qld), 224, 225
   Whistleblower Protection Bill, 33, 214–15, 230
   Whistleblowers (Interim Protection) and Miscellaneous Amendments Act 1990 (Qld), 212
   Whistleblowers Protection Act 1994 (Qld), 220, 222–3, 226
   Whistleblowers Protection Bill
      1991 (Cth), 213
      1992 (No. 1), 212
      1992 (No. 2), 212
      1993 (Cth), 214
   World Heritage Act, 72
Leigh, Alison, 126
Lennane, Jean, 48
Lewis, Professor Miles, 91
Libraries and Archives Act, 151
Lidbetter, Mr, 120
Lindeberg, Irene, 134, 157
Lindeberg, Kevin, 38
   and 'Shreddergate', 134–59,
   and CJC, 149–59
   and Cooke Inquiry, 144–6
   and Peter Coyne, 147, 150–1, 153
   and QPOA, 142–7, 151
   support, 135, 157
Lindgard, Kevin, 151
Littler, Professor Craig, 94–5, 98–9
Lyell McEwin Health Service, 59

M

McBride, Dr William, 24, 225
McBride, Professor, 107
McDonalds, 22, 235
McFarlain, Les, 42
McGauran, Peter, 119
McGuiness, P. P., 23
Maher, Denis, 9, 10
McKay, Donald, 164
McKay, Hugh, 75
McKernan, Dr Michael, 39,
   and MPRA, 176–91
McKernan, Michalina, 186
Mallesons Stephen Jaques, 103
Mansfield Inquiry, 122
Mansfield Review, 132
Maralinga, 13
Martin, Dr Brian, 117
Martindale, Don, 143–4, 147
Massey University, 103
Matchett, Ruth, 136–42, 144–6, 152, 157–8
Mayne Nickless Limited, 7

Media, Entertainment and Arts Alliance
  (MEAA), 124
  ABC house committee, 125
Media Watch, 132–3
Medical Association for the Prevention of
  War, 43–4, 46
Mengler, Carl, 197
Merit Protection Review Agency (MPRA),
  176, 217
  and Australian War Memorial, 176–91
  brief, 177
Millard, John, 38
  and ABC, 119–33
  background, 121
  support, 130–1
Miller, Royce, QC, 158
Mistral fans, 3
Moore, Lindsay, 84
Morris, Tony, QC, 157–8
Moseley, Michelle, 66
Mouldren, Professor, 107–8
Moyse, Barry, 164
MPRA (Merit Protection Review Agency),
  176, 217
  and Australian War Memorial, 176–91
  brief, 177
MSS Alarm Systems, 7
Mt Pleasant, 61, 70
Murdoch, Judge, 10
Murphy, Mr Justice, 241
Murphy, Senator Shayne, 154, 156

N

National Australia Bank (NAB), 8–10, 17
National Crime Authority (NCA),
  27, 38, 160, 168–9, 172–4
  and Australian Law Reform
    Commission, 168–9, 174
  and Mick Skrijel, 165–75
National Farmers Federation, 62
National Gallery, 17, 19
National Tertiary Education Union,
  105, 109, 113, 115
NCA (National Crime Authority),
  27, 38, 160, 168–9, 172–4
  and Australian Law Reform
    Commission, 168–9, 174
  and Mick Skrijel, 165–75
Neville, Mark, MLC, 114
Newby, Dr Jonica, 132–3
Newman, Senator, 218
Newnham, Noel, 147

Nitschke, Dr Philip, 37, 41–2, 45–8, 52,
  54, 57–9
  and Mike Reed, 41–2, 45–9, 54
  and nuclear campaign, 43–52, 54
  and Royal Darwin Hospital, 40, 43–59
  and Tristan Pawsey, 39–40, 48–52
  background, 40, 42–3, 59
  support for, 48
Noonan, Noel, 150–1
Norman, Ray, 52
North Belconnen Baptist Church, 168
Northern Territory *News*, 47, 53, 57–8

O

O'Regan, Rob, QC, 155
O'Shea, Ken, 139, 152
Obendorf, David, 37
  and Department of Primary Industry
    and Fisheries, Tasmania, 60–73
  and union, 67
  defamation actions, 65
  support, 66–8, 71
Office of General Counsel, 180
*Official Corruption Commission
  Act 1988*, 215
Ombudsman, 38
  and David Obendorf, 67
  and universities, 98
  Commonwealth, 202, 204, 214
  Victoria, 202
    police complaints, 173
  Western Australian, 113
One Nation, 159
Operation Noah, 31, 164
Oxnard, Professor, 106–7

P

P11 case, 17
paedophiles and paedophile rings,
  5, 24, 197–8, 202
Palm Island, 201
Palmer, George, QC, 123–4, 128, 131
Parer, Warwick, Senator, 153–4
Parfitt, Professor Robert, 107
Parks and Wildlife (NT), 41–2
Parliamentary committees
  Electoral and Administrative Review
    (PEARC), 212
  Criminal Justice Committee (PCJC),
    147, 149–51
  National Crime Authority Committee,
    171

Standing Government Agencies, 92, 111, 114
Parliamentary Services Bill, 19
Partis, Dr, 110, 112
Pawsey, Tristan, 39–40, 48–52, 59
Pearce, Professor Dennis, 204
Perron, Marshall, 44
Petcare, 132
Pettigrew, Allen, 135–6, 140
Pine Gap, 42
Pioneer Concrete (Qld) Pty Ltd, 7
Pitt, Ross, 17
Pola, Derek, 121, 125–6
police and police forces, 197
    Australian Federal Police (AFP), 38, 161, 174, 203–5
    corruption, 33, 175, 201, 213
    culture, 32
    Northern Territory
        and Philip Nitschke, 42
        water, 43
    NSW, 6, 32, 237
        bungled investigations, 197
        corruption, 201, 213
        Special Branch, 202
        transit, 203
    Queensland, 147
        Crime Stoppers, 31
        informers, 34
        Professional Standards Unit, 237
        Special Branch, 202
    South Australian, 38, 168
        and NCA, 169
        Millicent, 162
        Mount Gambier, 162
    Victoria, 38, 160, 166, 170
        and drug dealers, 165
        and NCA, 169–70, 173
        complaints, 173
        Dartmoor, 163
        Ombudsman, 38
        Special Branch, 202
    Western Australia, 202–3
    whistleblowers, 213
Port Douglas, 5
Presbyterian Church of Australia
    and ordination of women, 77–80
    and Reverend Peter Cameron, 74–87
    General Assembly of Queensland, 85
Protected Disclosures Act 1994 (NSW), 220, 223
Public Health Association (NT branch), 45
Public Interest Disclosure Act 1994 (ACT), 222, 231
Public Interest Disclosure Bill 1995, 215
Public Interest Disclosure Bill 1997, 215, 219, 221, 227
Public Interest Disclosure Commissioner, 219
Public Sector Ethics Act (Queensland), 235
Public Sector Management Commission, 145
Public Service Act, 19, 216
Public Service Commissioner, 178, 180

Q

QPOA, *see* Queensland Professional Officers Association (QPOA)
QPS, *see* police and police forces, Queensland
QSSU, *see* Queensland State Services Union (QSSU)
Quantum, 126–7
Queensland Health Rights Commissioner, 17
Queensland Nurses Union, 208
Queensland Police Service, 197
Queensland Professional Officers Association (QPOA), 137–51
    alleged corruption, 144
    and Kevin Lindeberg, 138
Queensland State Services Union (QSSU), 135, 137, 140
Queensland Teachers Union, 141
Queensland University of Technology (QUT), 90–1
Queensland Whistleblower Study (QWS), 22, 24–5, 69 134, 153, 218–19, 229, 232
Queensland Workers' Compensation Commission, 97
Quick Report, 172–3
Quick, David, QC, 169, 171–2
Quinn, Brian, 6

R

Ralston, Deborah, 94–7
Rayner, Moira, 19
RD, *see* Royal Darwin Hospital
Reed, Mike, 41–42, 45–9, 54, 57
Refugee Review Tribunal, 199
Reid, Dr Ewan, 72

relocation, 141, 213, 229, 232
Renfrew, Lord, 114
Returned Soldiers League (RSL), 188–9
Rindos, Associate Professor David, 38,
   and University of Western Australia,
      105–18
   background, 106
   support, 111, 117
RMIT (Royal Melbourne Institute of
   Technology)
   and Professor Kim Sawyer, 99–105
RMO Association, 45
Road Traffic Authority, 172
Robertson, Ian, QC, 168, 170
Rowley, Hazel, 93
Royal Darwin Hospital (RD),
   37, 40, 42–59
Royal Melbourne Institute of Technology
   (RMIT)
   and Professor Kim Sawyer, 99–105
RSL, *see* Returned Soldiers League (RSL)
Ryan, Kevin, QC, 199

S

Sargent, Hayden, 224
Sawyer, Professor Kim, 38, 88
   and RMIT, 99–105
Schmidt, Lyn, 47
Sciacca, Con, 177–8, 184–6, 190
Science Show, 132
Scowcroft, Stuart, 121, 125–6
Seaview crash, 24
Senate committees
   Estimates, 17
   Industry, 46–7
   Privileges, 42, 46, 57, 159
   Whistleblowing, 233
   Select
      ABC Management and Operations,
         120, 124
      Public Interest Whistleblowing
         (SSCPIW), 151, 153, 214, 216,
         218–19, 223, 226
      Superannuation, 150–51
      Unresolved Whistleblower Cases
         (SSCUWC), 97–9, 102, 141,
         148, 152–6, 159, 214, 226
   Standing
      Industry, Science and Technology, 52
      Public Administration, 117
Senewiratne, Brian, 16–17, 19
7.30 Report, 128, 143

Sex Discrimination Commission, 90
Sex Discrimination Commissioner, 200
'Shreddergate', 134–159
Siggins, Dr Ian, 17–19
Simpson's Gap, 41
Sir David Longlands Maximum Security
   Prison, 142
Sixty Minutes, 85
Skase, Christopher, 6
Skrijel, Loryn, 165–6
Skrijel, Mehmed (Mick), 38, 160–1, 163–4,
   167–9, 171
   and Costigan Royal Commission, 164
   and NCA, 165–75
   and police, 162–7
   and Quick Inquiry, 169–71
   background, 161–2
   support, 166–8
Solomon, David, 187
Special Air Services (SAS), 28
Spectator, 165
Spycatcher, 27
SSCPIW *see* Senate Select Committee on
   Public Interest Whistleblowing
   (SSCPIW)
St Andrew's College, 74, 77, 85
State Electricity Commission (SEC), 163
State Public Service Federation of
   Tasmania (SPSFT), 65, 67
Stead, Christina, 93
Steele, Associate Professor Ted, 110
Stewart, Justice D. G., 165, 208
Subic Bay, 44
Sunday, 76, 123
Sunday Age, 185, 190–1
Sunday Mail, 150
Sunday Press, 167
Sydney Mission Bible College, 79
Sydney Morning Herald, 83, 85, 123
Sydney Presbytery, 77, 79, 82, 83
Sykes, Trevor, 5

T

Tanzer, Noel, 184
Tasmanian Farmers and Graziers
   Association (TFGA), 64
Tasmanian Greens, 216
Tasmanian Veterinary Board, 63
Tate, Senator Michael, 168–9
Taylor, Professor, 107
TFGA (Tasmanian Farmers and Graziers
   Association), 64

The Home Show, 121, 123
The Investigators, 121–2, 126, 128
The Lucky Country, 12
Thomas, Barry, 47, 138
Thomas, Mr Justice, 198–9
Tierney, Brian, 120, 146
Tonkin, David, 164
Toowoomba, 7, 17
Townsville, 207–8
Trade Practices Act, 6
Trade Practices Commission, 90, 104
Trades and Labour Council (NT), 42
Transparency International, 8
Treloar, Major, 189
Turner, John, 126

U

unions and union officials, 26, 37–8, 61, 144
   and ABC, 124
   and AHL, 65
   and David Obendorf, 67
   and DPIF, 61, 65
   criticism of, 67
   MEAA, 124
   NTEU, 105, 113, 115
   QPOA, 137–47, 151
   QSSU, 137
   whistleblowers' views on, 218
University of Melbourne, 88, 91, 104
University of Queensland, 88–9, 91
University of Southern Queensland,
   and Peter Jesser, 94–9
University of Western Australia, 92, 114
   and Associate Professor David Rindos, 105–18,
   Tenure Review Committee, 111–12
University of Wollongong, 117
Uranium Producers' Forum, 40
USS *Houston*, 43, 44, 47, 49
Ustinov, Peter, 29

V

Vallentine, Senator Jo, 213
Vanstone, Amanda, 89
Victoria University, Wellington, 90

W

WA Inc. scandal, 215
Wacol, 142

Walker, Alan, 57–8
Walsh, Trevor, 151–2
Warner, Anne, 143, 146, 152, 157–8
Wave Hill, 41–2
Weekend Australian, 9
Weekend Independent, 135
Wendt, Jana, 133
West Australian, 109, 114
Western Australian Industrial Relations Commission, 113
Westminster Confession of Faith, 79, 80, 85
Westminster system, 238–40
Whistleblower Protection Agency, 230
Whistleblower Protection Bill, 33, 214–15, 230
Whistleblowers (Interim Protection) and Miscellaneous Amendments Act 1990 (Qld), 212
Whistleblowers Action Group, 153
Whistleblowers Australia, 48, 117
   NSW branch, 213
   Tasmania, 215
Whistleblowers Protection Act 1994 (Qld), 220, 222–6
Whistleblowers Protection Advocate, 221
Whistleblowers Protection Bill
   1991 (Cth), 213
   1992 (No. 1), 212
   1992 (No. 2), 212
   1993 (Cth), 214
Williams, Lloyd, 91
Williams, Paul, 131
Wilson, Geoff, 45, 115
Wilson, Pauline, 45, 47
Wilson, Sir Ronald, 200
witness protection, 23, 39, 229
Women's Weekly, 132
Wood Royal Commission, 6, 201, 203, 213
Wood, Mr Justice, 6
Woodstock, 205–6
World Heritage Act, 72
Wright, Peter, 27
Wynnum, 85

Y

Yarrow, Bill, 143–5
Yeldham, David, 203

Wakefield Press has been publishing good Australian books for over fifty years. For a catalogue of current and forthcoming titles, or to add your name to our mailing list, send your name and address to

Wakefield Press, Box 2266, Kent Town, South Australia 5071.

TELEPHONE (08) 8362 8800 FAX (08) 8362 7592
WEB www.wakefieldpress.com.au

Wakefield Press thanks Wirra Wirra Vineyards and Arts South Australia for their continued support.